Rick Steves

SNAPSHOT

Sevilla, Granada & Andalucía

CONTENTS

INTRODUCTION

This Snapshot guide, excerpted from my guidebook *Rick Steves Spain*, introduces you to southern Spain's two top cities—Sevilla and Granada—and the surrounding Spanish heartland. When Americans think of Spain, they often picture this region, with its massive cathedrals, Moorish palaces, vibrant folk life, white-washed villages, bright sunshine, and captivating rat-a-tat-tat of flamenco.

Sevilla is the soulful cultural heart of southern Spain, with an atmospheric old quarter and riveting flamenco shows. Granada, formerly the Moorish capital, is home to the magnificent Alhambra palace. Córdoba features Spain's top surviving Moorish mosque, the Mezquita. Make time to delve into Andalucía's sleepy, whitewashed hill towns: Arcos de la Frontera, Ronda, and Grazalema. Spain's south coast, the Costa del Sol, is a palm-tree jungle of beach resorts and concrete, but has some appealing destinations—Nerja, Tarifa, and Gibraltar—beyond the traffic jams. And since it's so easy, consider an eye-opening side-trip to another continent by hopping the ferry to Tangier, the newly revitalized gateway to Morocco (and to Africa).

To help you have the best trip possible, I've included the following topics in this book:

• **Planning Your Time,** with advice on how to make the most of your limited time

• **Orientation,** including tourist information offices (abbreviated as TI), tips on public transportation, local tour options, and helpful hints

• **Sights** with ratings:

   ▲▲▲—Don't miss

   ▲▲—Try hard to see

   ▲—Worthwhile if you can make it

No rating—Worth knowing about

• **Sleeping** and **Eating,** with good-value recommendations in every price range

• **Connections,** with tips on trains, buses, and driving

Practicalities, near the end of this book, has information on money, staying connected, lodging, restaurants, transportation, and more, plus Spanish survival phrases.

To travel smartly, read this little book in its entirety before you go. It's my hope that this guide will make your trip more meaningful and rewarding. Traveling like a temporary local, you'll get the absolute most out of every mile, minute, and dollar.

Buen viaje!

Rick Steves

SEVILLA

Flamboyant Sevilla (seh-VEE-yah) thrums with flamenco music, sizzles in the summer heat, and pulses with the passion of Don Juan and Carmen. It's a place where bullfighting is still politically correct and little girls still dream of growing up to become flamenco dancers. While Granada has the great Alhambra and Córdoba has the remarkable Mezquita, Sevilla has a soul. (Soul—or *duende*—is fundamental to flamenco.) It's a wonderful-to-be-alive-in kind of place.

The gateway to the New World in the 16th century, Sevilla boomed when Spain did. The explorers Amerigo Vespucci and Ferdinand Magellan sailed from its great river harbor, discovering new trade routes and abundant sources of gold, silver, cocoa, and tobacco. In the 17th century, Sevilla was Spain's largest and wealthiest city. Local artists Diego Velázquez, Bartolomé Murillo, and Francisco de Zurbarán made it a cultural center. Sevilla's Golden Age—and its New World riches—ended when the harbor silted up and the Spanish empire crumbled.

In the 19th century, Sevilla was a big stop on the Romantic Grand Tour of Europe. To build on this tourism and promote trade among Spanish-speaking nations, Sevilla planned a grand exposition in 1929. Bad year. The expo crashed along with the stock market. In 1992, Sevilla got a second chance at a world's fair. This expo was a success, leaving the city with impressive infrastructure: a new airport, a train station, sleek bridges, and the super AVE bullet train (making Sevilla a 2.5-hour side-trip from Madrid). In 2007, the main boulevards—once thundering with noisy traffic and mercilessly cutting the city in two—were pedestrianized, dramatically enhancing Sevilla's already substantial charm.

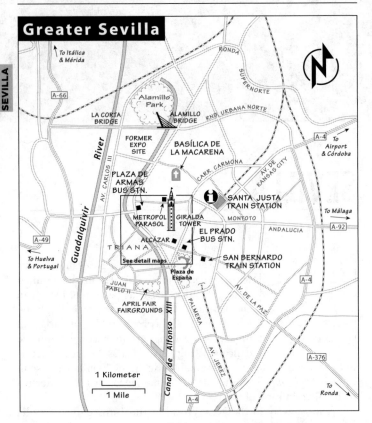

Today, Spain's fourth-largest city (pop. 700,000) is Andalucía's leading destination, buzzing with festivals, color, guitars, castanets, and street life, and enveloped in the fragrances of orange trees, jacaranda, and myrtle. James Michener wrote, "Sevilla doesn't *have* ambience, it *is* ambience." Sevilla also has its share of impressive sights. It's home to the world's largest Gothic cathedral. The Alcázar is a fantastic royal palace and garden ornamented with Mudejar (Islamic) flair. But the real magic is the city itself, with its tangled former Jewish Quarter, riveting flamenco shows, thriving bars, and teeming evening paseo.

PLANNING YOUR TIME

On a three-week trip, spend two nights and one day here. On even the shortest Spanish trip, I'd zip here on the slick AVE train for a day trip from Madrid. With more time, if ever there was a Spanish city to linger in, it's Sevilla.

The major sights are few and simple for a city of this size. The cathedral and the Alcázar can be seen in about three hours, and a wander through the Barrio Santa Cruz district takes about an hour. Tour groups clog the Alcázar and cathedral in the morning; go late in the day to avoid the crowds, or at least reserve a time slot on the Alcázar website to minimize the ticket lines.

You could spend a second day touring Sevilla's other sights. Stroll along the bank of the Guadalquivir River and cross Isabel II Bridge to explore the Triana neighborhood and to savor views of the cathedral and Torre del Oro. An evening in Sevilla is essential for the paseo and a flamenco show. Stay out late to appreciate Sevilla on a warm night—one of its major charms. Or consider a bullfight if one is taking place during your visit.

Córdoba is a convenient and worthwhile side-trip from Sevilla, or a handy stopover if you're taking the AVE to or from Madrid or Granada.

Orientation to Sevilla

For the tourist, this big city is small. The bull's-eye on your map should be the cathedral and its Giralda bell tower, which can be

seen from all over town. Nearby are Sevilla's other major sights, the Alcázar (palace and gardens) and the lively Barrio Santa Cruz district. The central north-south pedestrian boulevard, Avenida de la Constitución, stretches north a few blocks to Plaza Nueva, gateway to the shopping district. A few blocks west of the cathedral are the bullring and the Guadalquivir River, while Plaza de España is a few blocks south. The

colorful Triana neighborhood, on the west bank of the Guadalquivir River, has a thriving market and plenty of tapas bars, but no major tourist sights. With most sights within walking distance, taxis or buses are only needed to get to the Basílica de la Macarena and the Plaza de Armas bus station.

TOURIST INFORMATION

Sevilla has tourist offices at the **airport** (Mon-Fri 9:00-19:30, Sat-Sun 9:30-15:00, tel. 954-782-035), at **Santa Justa train station**

SEVILLA

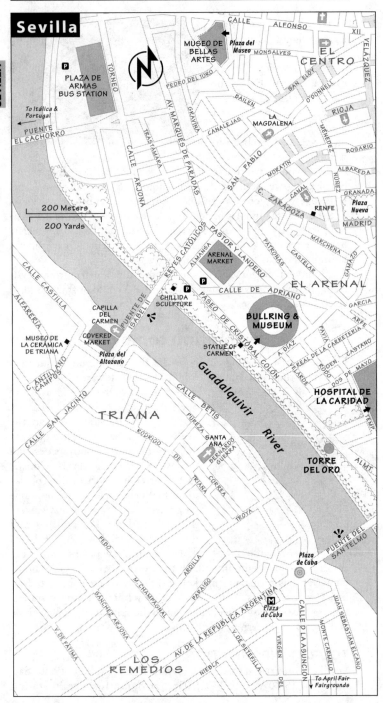

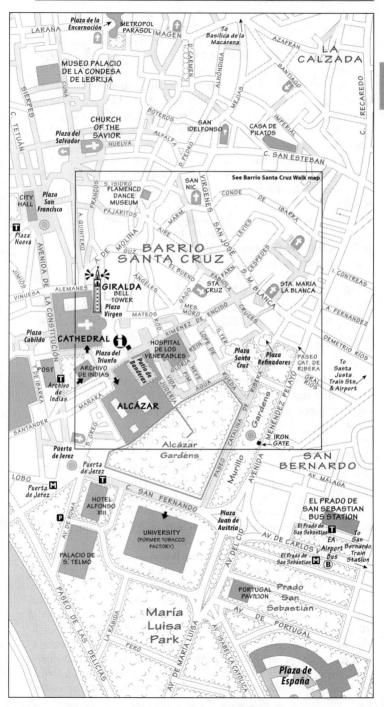

(just inside the right-hand doors of the main entrance, same hours as airport TI, tel. 954-782-003), and near the cathedral on **Plaza del Triunfo** (Mon-Fri 9:00-19:30, Sat-Sun 9:30-19:30, tel. 954-210-005).

At any TI, ask for the English-language magazine *The Tourist* (also available at www.thetouristsevilla.com) and a current listing of sights with opening times. The free monthly events guide—*El Giraldillo,* written in Spanish basic enough to be understood by travelers—covers cultural events throughout Andalucía, with a focus on Sevilla. At the TI, ask for information you might need for elsewhere in the region (for example, if heading south, pick up the free *Route of the White Towns* brochure and a Jerez map). Helpful websites are www.turismosevilla.org and www.andalucia.org.

Steer clear of the "visitors centers" on Avenida de la Constitución (near the Archivo General de Indias) and at Santa Justa train station (overlooking tracks 6-7), which masquerade as TIs but are private enterprises.

ARRIVAL IN SEVILLA

By Train: Most trains arrive at modern Santa Justa station, with banks, ATMs, and a TI. Baggage storage is below track 1 (follow signs to *consigna,* security checkpoint open 6:00-24:00). The easy-to-miss TI sits by the sliding doors at the main entrance, to the left before you exit. The plush little AVE Sala Club, designed for business travelers, welcomes those with a first-class AVE ticket and reservation (across the main hall from track 1). The town center is marked by the ornate Giralda bell tower, peeking above the apartment flats (visible from the front of the station—with your back to the tracks, it's at 1 o'clock). To get into the center, it's a flat and boring 25-minute walk or about an €8 taxi ride. By city bus, it's a short ride on #C1 or #21 to the El Prado de San Sebastián bus station (find bus stop 100 yards in front of the train station, €1.40, pay driver), then a 10-minute walk or short tram ride (see next section).

By Bus: Sevilla's two major bus stations—El Prado de San Sebastián and Plaza de Armas—both have information offices, basic eateries, and baggage storage.

The **El Prado de San Sebastián bus station,** often called just "El Prado," covers most of Andalucía (daily 8:00-20:00, information tel. 954-417-111, generally no English spoken; baggage lockers/*consigna* at the far end of station, same hours). From the bus station to downtown (and Barrio Santa Cruz hotels), it's about a 10-minute walk: Exit the station straight ahead. When you reach the busy avenue (Menéndez Pelayo) turn right to find a crosswalk and cross the avenue. Enter the Murillo Gardens through the iron gate, emerging on the other side in the heart of Barrio Santa Cruz. Sevilla's tram connects the El Prado station with the city center (and many of my recommended hotels): Turn left as you exit the bus station and walk to Avenida de Carlos V (€1.40, buy ticket at machine before boarding; ride it two stops to Archivo General de Indias to reach the cathedral area, or three stops to Plaza Nueva).

The **Plaza de Armas bus station** (near the river, opposite the Expo '92 site) serves long-distance destinations such as Madrid, Barcelona, Lagos, and Lisbon. Ticket counters line one wall, an information kiosk is in the center, and at the end of the hall are pay luggage lockers (purchase tokens from info kiosk). Taxis to downtown cost around €7. Or, to take the bus, exit onto the main road (Calle Arjona) to find bus #C4 into the center (stop is to the left, in front of the taxi stand; €1.40, pay driver, get off at Puerta de Jerez).

By Car: To drive into Sevilla, follow *Centro Ciudad* (city center) signs and stay along the river. For short-term parking on the street, the riverside Paseo de Cristóbal Colón has two-hour meters and hardworking thieves. Ignore the bogus traffic wardens who direct you to an illegal spot, take a tip, and disappear later when your car gets towed. For long-term parking, hotels charge as much as a normal garage. For simplicity, I'd park at a garage (€18-22/day) on one of the drivable major avenues and catch a taxi to my hotel. Try the Cristóbal Colón garage by the Puente de Isabel II (near the bullring), or the one at Avenida Roma/Puerta de Jerez (cash only). For hotels in the Barrio Santa Cruz area, the handiest parking is the Cano y Cueto garage near the corner of Calle Santa María la Blanca and Avenida de Menéndez Pelayo (about €22/day, open daily 24 hours, at edge of big park, underground).

By Plane: Sevilla's San Pablo Airport sits about six miles east of downtown (airport code: SVQ, tel. 954-449-000, www. aena.es). The Especial Aeropuerto (EA) bus connects the airport with both train stations, both bus stations, and several stops in the town center (2-3/hour from 4:30 to 24:00, about 40 minutes, €4, buy ticket from driver). The two most convenient stops downtown are south of the Murillo gardens on Avenida de Carlos V, near El Prado de San Sebastián bus station (close to my recommended Barrio Santa Cruz hotels); and on the Paseo de Cristóbal Colón, near the Torre del Oro. Look for the small *EA* sign at bus stops. If you're going from downtown Sevilla *to* the airport, the bus stop is on the side of the street closest to Plaza de España. To taxi into town, go to one of the airport's taxi stands to ensure a fixed rate (€22 by day, €25 at night and on weekends, extra for luggage, confirm price with the driver before your journey).

GETTING AROUND SEVILLA

Most visitors have a full and fun experience in Sevilla without ever riding public transportation. The city center is compact, and most of the major sights are within easy walking distance (the Basílica de la Macarena is a notable exception). However, on a hot day, air-conditioned buses can be a blessing.

By Taxi: Sevilla has plenty of taxis. You can hail one showing a green light anywhere, or find a cluster of them parked by major intersections and sights (weekdays: €1.35 drop rate, €1/kilometer, €3.60 minimum; Sat-Sun, holidays, and after hours, 21:00-7:00: €1.60 drop rate, €1.15/kilometer, €4.50 minimum; calling for a cab adds about €3). A quick daytime ride in town will generally fall within the €3.60 minimum. Although I'm quick to take advantage of taxis, because of one-way streets and traffic congestion it's often just as fast to hoof it between central points.

By Bus, Tram, and Metro: A single trip on any form of city transit costs €1.40. A Tarjeta Turistica card is good for one (€5) or three (€10) days of unlimited rides (€1.50 deposit, buy at TUSSAM kiosks, airport, or Santa Justa station). For half-price trips, you can buy a Tarjeta Multiviaje card that's rechargeable and shareable (€7 for 10 trips, €1.50 deposit; buy at kiosks or at the TUSSAM transit office near the bus stop on Avenida de Carlos V, next to El Prado de San Sebastián bus station, daily 8:00-20:00; scan it on the card reader as you board; for transit details, see www.tussam.es).

The various #C **buses,** which are handiest for tourists, make circular routes through town (note that all of them except the #C6 eventually wind up at Basílica de La Macarena). For all buses, buy your ticket from the driver or from machines at bus stops. The #C3 stops at Murillo Gardens, Triana, then La Macarena. The #C4 goes the opposite direction, but without entering Triana. And the spunky little #C5 is a minibus that winds through the old center of town, including Plaza del Salvador, Plaza de San Francisco, the bullring, Plaza Nueva, the Museo de Bellas Artes, La Campana, and La Macarena, providing a relaxing joyride that also connects some farther-flung sights.

A **tram** *(tranvía)* makes just a few stops in the heart of the city, but can save you a bit of walking. Buy your ticket at the machine on the platform before you board (runs about every 7 minutes Sun-Thu until 23:00, Fri-Sat until 1:45 in the morning). It makes five city-center stops (from south to north): San Bernardo (at the San Bernardo train station), Prado San Sebastián (next to El Prado de San Sebastián bus station), Puerta Jerez (south end of Avenida de la Constitución), Archivo General de Indias (next to the cathedral), and Plaza Nueva (beginning of shopping streets).

Sevilla also has an underground **metro,** but most tourists won't need to use it. It's de-signed to connect the suburbs with the center and only has one line. There are stops downtown at the San Bernardo train station, El Prado de San Sebastián bus station, and Puerta Jerez.

HELPFUL HINTS

Festivals: Sevilla's peak season is April and May, and it has two one-week spring festival periods when the city is packed: Holy Week and April Fair.

While **Holy Week** (Semana Santa) is big all over Spain, it's biggest in Sevilla. It's held the week between Palm Sunday and Easter Sunday (for 2018, starts March 25 and culminates on Easter Sunday, April 1). Locals start preparing for the big event up to a year in advance. What would normally be a five-minute walk can take an hour if a procession crosses your path, and many restaurants do not offer meat options during this time. But any hassles become totally worthwhile as you listen to the *saetas* (spontaneous devotional songs) and let the spirit of the festival take over.

Then, after taking two weeks off to catch its communal breath, Sevilla holds its **April Fair** (April 15-22 in 2018). This is a celebration of all things Andalusian, with plenty of eating, drinking, singing, and merrymaking (though most of the revelry takes place in private parties at a large fairground).

Book rooms well in advance for these festival times. Prices can go sky-high and many hotels have four-night minimums. Food quality at touristy restaurants can plummet.

Rosemary Scam: In the city center, and especially near the cathedral, you may encounter women thrusting sprigs of rosemary into the hands of passersby, grunting, *"Toma! Es un regalo!"* ("Take it! It's a gift!"). The twig is free...and then they grab your hand and read your fortune for a tip. Coins are "bad luck," so the minimum payment they'll accept is €5. While they can be very aggressive, you don't need to take their demands seriously—don't make eye contact, don't accept a sprig, and say firmly but politely, *"No, gracias."*

Wi-Fi: Sevilla is fairly Wi-Fi friendly. You'll find free Wi-Fi at the Museo de Bellas Artes, and in Plaza de la Encarnación, among other public spaces.

Post Office: The main post office is at Avenida de la Constitución 32, across from the Archivo General de Indias (Mon-Fri 8:30-20:30, Sat 9:30-13:00, closed Sun).

Laundry: **Lavandería Tintorería Roma** offers quick and economical drop-off service (Mon-Fri 10:00-14:00 & 17:30-20:30, Sat 10:00-14:00, closed Sun, a few blocks west of the cathedral at Calle Arfe 22, tel. 954-210-535). Near the recommended Barrio Santa Cruz hotels, **La Segunda Vera Tintorería** has

Holy Week (Semana Santa)

Holy Week—the week between Palm Sunday and Easter—is a major holiday throughout the Christian world, but nowhere is it celebrated with as much fervor as in Andalucía, especially Sevilla. Holy Week is all about the events of the Passion of Jesus Christ: his entry into Jerusalem, his betrayal by Judas and arrest, his crucifixion, and his resurrection. In Sevilla, on each day throughout the week, 60 neighborhood groups (brotherhoods, called *hermandades* or *cofradías*) parade from their neighborhood churches to the cathedral with floats depicting some aspect of the Passion story.

As the week approaches, anticipation grows: Visitors pour into town, grandstands are erected along parade routes, and TV stations anxiously monitor the weather report. (The floats are so delicate that rain can force the processions to be called off—a crushing disappointment.)

By midafternoon of any day during Holy Week, thousands line the streets. The parade begins. First comes a line of "penitents" carrying a big cross, candles, and incense. The *penitentes* perform their penance publicly but anonymously, their identities obscured by pointy, hooded robes. (The penitents' traditional hooded garb has been worn for centuries—long before such hoods became associated with racism in the American South.) Some processions are silent, but others are accompanied by beating drums, brass bands, or wailing singers.

A hush falls over the crowd as the floats *(los pasos)* approach. First comes a Passion float, showing Christ in some stage of the drama—being whipped, appearing before Pilate, or carrying the

two self-service machines and drop-off service (Mon-Fri 9:30-14:00 & 17:30-20:30, Sat 10:00-13:30, closed Sun, about a block from the eastern edge of Barrio Santa Cruz at Avenida de Menéndez Pelayo 11, tel. 954-536-376).

Supermarket: Spar Express has all the basics, plus a takeaway counter for sandwiches, salads, and smoothies (Mon-Sat 9:00-23:00, Sun from 10:30, Calle Zaragoza 31, tel. 954-221-194). Also look for **Carrefour Express** stores around town for prepared foods and picnic supplies (daily 10:00-23:00).

Bike Rental: Sevilla is an extremely biker-friendly city, with designated bike lanes and a public bike-sharing program (€14 one-week subscription, first 30 minutes of each ride free, €1-2 for each subsequent hour, www.sevici.es). Ask the TI about this and other bicycle-rental options.

cross to his execution. More penitents follow—with hundreds or even thousands of participants, a procession can stretch out over a half-mile. All this sets the stage for the finale—typically a float of the Virgin Mary, who represents the hope of resurrection.

The elaborate floats feature carved wooden religious sculptures, most embellished with gold leaf and silverwork. They can be adorned with fresh flowers, rows of candles, and even jewelry on loan from the congregation. Each float is carried by 30 to 50 men *(los costaleros)*, who labor unseen—although you might catch a glimpse of their shuffling feet. The bearers wear turban-like headbands to protect their heads and necks from the crushing weight (the floats can weigh as much as three tons). Two "shifts" of float carriers rotate every 20 minutes. As a sign of their faith, some men carry the float until they collapse.

As the procession nears the cathedral, many pass through the square called La Campana, south along Calle Sierpes, and through Plaza de San Francisco. (Some parades follow a parallel route a block or two east.) Grandstands and folding chairs are filled by VIPs and Sevilla's prominent families. Thousands of candles drip wax along the well-trod parade routes, forming a waxy buildup that causes shoes and car tires to squeal for days to come.

Being in Sevilla for Holy Week is both a blessing and a curse. It's a remarkable spectacle, but it's extremely crowded. Parade routes can block your sightseeing for hours. Check printed schedules if you want to avoid them. If you do find a procession blocking your way, look for a crossing point marked by a red-painted fence, or ask a guard. Even if all you care about on Easter is a chocolate-bearing bunny, the intense devotion of the Andalusian people during their Holy Week traditions is an inspiration to behold.

Tours in Sevilla

ON FOOT
Sevilla Walking Tours

Concepción Delgado, an enthusiastic teacher who's a joy to listen to, takes small groups on English-only walks. Using me as her guinea pig, Concepción designed a fine two-hour **Cultural Show & Tell** walk. In this introduction to her hometown, she shares important insights the average visitor misses. I think it's worthwhile even if

you're only in town for one day (€15/person, Mon-Sat at 10:30, check website for schedule in Dec-Feb and Aug, meet at statue in Plaza Nueva).

For those wanting to really understand the city's two most important sights, the company offers in-depth visits to the **cathedral** and the **Alcázar,** each lasting about 1.25 hours (€10 each plus entrance fees, €3 discount if you also take the Show & Tell tour; meet at 13:00 at statue in Plaza del Triunfo; cathedral tours—Mon, Wed, and Fri; Alcázar tours—Tue, Thu, and Sat).

Other tours include one for fans of the TV series *Game of Thrones* (visits to key locations; only available as add-on to Alcázar tour), and the **Only Culture** tour (social life and popular traditions).

Although you can just show up for Concepción's tours, it's smart to confirm departure times and reserve a spot (4-person minimum, none on Sun or holidays, tel. 902-158-226, mobile 616-501-100, www.sevillawalkingtours.com, info@sevillawalkingtours.com). Because she's a busy mom, Concepción sometimes sends her equally excellent colleagues Alfonso and Mercedes to lead these tours.

All Sevilla Guided Tours

This group of three licensed guides (Susana, Jorge, and Elena) offers good, family-friendly private tours and day trips (€130/3 hours, €160/half-day, mobile 606-217-194; monument tours leave Mon-Sat at 11:15 from Plaza del Triunfo—€22, www.allsevillaguides.com, info@allsevillaguides.com).

Really Discover Seville

Englishman David and Sevillian Luis have teamed up to show off their city with several creatively conceived, good-value walks and bike rides—all run with small groups and a personal touch. Their **Seville Bike Tour** takes riders on a 2.5-hour journey around the city, stopping at—but not entering—all the major sights (€25, 2-10 people per group, includes bike, daily at 10:00, meet near the cathedral by the tall white monument in Plaza del Triunfo). Each morning they also lead a two-hour **Seville Walking Tour** (€20, 2-10 per group, daily at 10:00), then give you the option to tack on a lunchtime tapas tour (€35 more). Call or email to confirm before showing up (tel. 955-113-912, www.reallydiscover.com, davidcox@reallydiscover.com).

BUS, BOAT, AND BUGGY TOURS
Hop-On, Hop-Off Bus Tours

Two competing city bus tours leave from the curb near the riverside Torre del Oro. You'll see the parked buses and salespeople handing out fliers. Each tour does about an hour-long swing through the

Sevilla at a Glance

▲▲▲**Flamenco** Flamboyant, riveting music-and-dance performances, offered at clubs throughout town. **Hours:** Shows start as early as 19:00. See page 58.

▲▲**Sevilla Cathedral** The world's largest Gothic church, with Columbus' tomb, treasury, and climbable bell tower. **Hours:** Mon 11:00-16:30, Tue-Sat 11:00-18:00, Sun 14:30-19:00. See page 21.

▲▲**Royal Alcázar** Palace built by the Moors in the 10th century, revamped in the 14th century, and still serving as royal digs. **Hours:** Daily 9:30-19:00, Oct-March until 17:00. See page 29.

▲▲**Hospital de la Caridad** Former charity hospital (funded by likely inspiration for Don Juan) with gorgeously decorated chapel. **Hours:** Daily 10:30-19:30. See page 40.

▲▲**Basílica de la Macarena** Church and museum with much-venerated Weeping Virgin statue and two significant Holy Week floats. **Hours:** Church daily 9:00-13:30 & 17:00-20:30, museum closes 30 minutes earlier. See page 48.

▲▲**Triana** Energetic, colorful neighborhood on the west bank of the river. See page 51.

▲▲**Bullfight Museum** Guided tour of the bullring and its museum. **Hours:** Daily 9:30-21:00, Nov-March until 19:00, closes at 15:00 on fight days. See page 54.

▲▲**Evening Paseo** Locals strolling in various zones around the city. **Hours:** Spring through fall; best paseo scene 18:00-20:00, until very late in summer. See page 61.

▲**Museo Palacio de la Condesa de Lebrija** 18th-century aristocratic mansion. **Hours:** July-Aug Mon-Fri 10:00-15:00, Sat until 14:00, closed Sun; Sept-June Mon-Fri 10:30-19:30, Sat 10:00-14:00 & 16:00-18:00, Sun 10:00-14:00. See page 44.

▲**Flamenco Dance Museum** High-tech museum on the history and art of flamenco. **Hours:** Daily 10:00-19:00. See page 45.

▲**Museo de Bellas Artes** Andalucía's top paintings, including works by Murillo and Zurbarán. **Hours:** Mid-June-mid-Sept Tue-Sun 9:00-15:00; mid-Sept-mid-June Tue-Sat 9:00-20:00, Sun until 15:00; closed Mon. See page 45.

▲**Bullfights** Some of Spain's best bullfighting, held at Sevilla's arena. **Hours:** Fights generally at 18:30 on most Sundays in May and June, on Easter and Corpus Christi, and daily through the April Fair and in late September. See page 54.

city with recorded narration. The tours, which allow hopping on and off at four stops, are heavy on Expo '29 and Expo '92 neighborhoods—both zones of little interest nowadays. While the narration does its best, Sevilla is most interesting in places buses can't go (€16, green bus slightly cheaper online, daily 10:00-22:00, off-season until 18:00, green bus: http://sevilla.busturistico.com, red bus: www.city-sightseeing.com).

Horse-and-Buggy Tours

A carriage ride is a classic, popular way to survey the city and a relaxing way to enjoy María Luisa Park (€45 for a 45-minute clip-clop, much more during Holy Week and the April Fair, find a likable English-speaking driver for better narration). Look for rigs at Plaza de América, Plaza del Triunfo, the Torre del Oro, the Alfonso XIII Hotel, and Plaza de España.

Boat Cruises

Boring one-hour panoramic tours leave every 30 minutes from the dock behind the Torre de Oro. The low-energy recorded narration is hard to follow, but there's little to see anyway (overpriced at €16, April-Oct 11:00-22:00, last boat at 19:00 off-season, tel. 954-561-692, www.crucerosensevilla.com).

Barrio Santa Cruz Walk

Of Sevilla's once-thriving Jewish Quarter, only the tangled street plan and a wistful Old World ambience survive. This classy maze of lanes (too tight for most cars), small plazas, tile-covered patios, and whitewashed houses with wrought-iron latticework draped in flowers is a great refuge from the summer heat and bustle of Sevilla. The streets are narrow—some with buildings so close they're called "kissing lanes." A happy result of the narrowness is shade: Locals claim the Barrio Santa Cruz is three degrees cooler than the rest of the city.

Orange trees abound—because they never lose their leaves, they provide constant shade. But forget about eating the oranges. They're bitter and used only to make vitamins, perfume, cat food, and that marmalade you can't avoid in British B&Bs. But when they blossom (for three weeks in spring, usually in March), the aroma is heavenly.

The barrio is made for wandering. Getting lost is easy, and I recommend doing just that. But to get started, here's a self-guided plaza-to-plaza walk that loops you through the *corazón* (heart) of the neighborhood and back out again.

Barrio Santa Cruz Walk

100 Meters
100 Yards

❶ Plaza de la Virgen de los Reyes
❷ Nun Goodies
❸ Plaza del Triunfo
❹ Patio de Banderas
❺ Calle Agua
❻ Plaza de Santa Cruz
❼ Casa de Murillo
❽ Monasterio de San José del Carmen
❾ Plaza de los Venerables, Hospital de los Venerables & Centro Velázquez
❿ Plaza de Doña Elvira
⓫ Plaza de la Alianza

Tour groups often trample the barrio's charm in the morning. I find that early evening (around 18:00) is the ideal time to explore the quarter.

❶ **Plaza de la Virgen de los Reyes:** Start in the square in front of the cathedral, at the fountain in the middle that dates from Expo '29. This square is dedicated to the Virgin of the Kings—see her tile on the white wall, diagonally across from the cathedral. She is one of several different versions of Mary you'll see in Sevilla, each appealing to a different type of worshipper. This particular one is big here because the Castilian king reportedly carried her image with him when he retook the town from

the Moors in 1248. To the left of Mary's tiled plaque is a statue of newly sainted Pope John Paul II, who performed Mass here before a half-million faithful Sevillians during a 1982 visit. The reddish Baroque building on one side of the square is the Archbishop's Palace.

Notice the columns and chains that ring the cathedral, as if put there to establish a border between the secular and Catholic worlds. Indeed, that's exactly the purpose they served for centuries, when Sevillians running from the law merely had to cross these chains—like crossing the county line. (People in trouble didn't escape justice; they just had a bit of a choice as to who would administer it.) Many of these columns are far older than the cathedral, having originally been made for Roman and Visigothic buildings, and later recycled by medieval Catholics.

From this peaceful square, look up the street leading away from the cathedral and notice the characteristic (government-protected) 19th-century architecture. The ironwork, typical of Andalucía, is the pride of Sevilla. Equally ubiquitous is the traditional whitewash-and-goldenrod color scheme.

Another symbol you'll see throughout Sevilla is the city insignia: "NO8DO," the letters "NODO" with a figure-eight-like shape at their center. *Nodo* means "knot" in Spanish, and this symbol evokes the strong ties between the citizens of Sevilla and King Alfonso X (during a succession dispute in the 13th century, the Sevillians remained loyal to their king).

• *Keeping the cathedral on your right, walk toward the next square.*

❷ **Nun Goodies:** The white building on your left was an Augustinian convent. Step inside the door at #3 to meet (but not see) a cloistered nun behind a fancy *torno* (a lazy Susan the nuns spin to sell their goods while staying hidden). The sisters raise money by producing local goodies, such as tasty communion wafer *tabletas* or the leftover bits called *recortes* (€1—eating them is like having sin-free cookies) and lovely rosaries (€4). Consider buying something here just as a donation. The sisters, who speak only Spanish, have a sense of humor (Mon-Sat 9:00-13:00 & 16:45-18:15, Sun 10:00-13:00).

• *Then step into...*

Barrio Santa Cruz Walk 17

❸ **Plaza del Triunfo:** The "Plaza of Triumph" is named for the 1755 earthquake that destroyed Lisbon but only rattled Sevilla, leaving most of this city intact. A statue thanking the Virgin for protecting the city is at the far end of the square, under a stone canopy and surrounded by a wrought-iron fence. That Virgin faces another one (closer to you), atop a tall pillar honoring Sevillian artists, including the painter Murillo.

• *Before leaving the square, consider stopping at the TI for a map or advice. Then pass through the arched opening in the Alcázar's crenellated wall. You'll emerge into a courtyard called the...*

❹ **Patio de Banderas:** The Banderas Courtyard (as in "flags," not Antonio) was once a military parade ground for the royal guard.

The barracks surrounding the square once housed the king's bodyguards. A Moorish palace also stood here; archaeologists excavated what remains of it, then covered the site of the dig for protection. The far-left corner of this square is a favorite spot for snapping a postcard view of the Giralda bell tower (do a 180-degree turn).

• *Exit the courtyard at the far-left corner, through the Judería arch. Go down the long, narrow passage. Emerging into the light, you'll be walking alongside the Alcázar wall. Take the first left at the corner lamppost, then go right, through a small square and follow the narrow alleyway called...*

❺ **Calle Agua:** As you walk along the street, look to the left, peeking through iron gates for occasional glimpses of the flower-smothered patios of exclusive private residences. If its blue security gate is open, the patio at #2 is a delight—ringed with columns, filled with flowers, and colored with glazed tiles. The tiles are not merely decorative—they keep buildings cooler in the summer heat (if the gate is closed, the next door is often open; or just look up to get a hint of the garden's flowery bounty). Emerging at the end of the street, turn around and look back at the openings of two old pipes built into the wall. These 12th-century Moorish pipes once carried water to the Alcázar  (and today give the street its name). You're standing at an entrance into the pleasant Murillo Gardens (through the iron gate), formerly the fruit-and-vegetable gardens for the Alcázar.

SEVILLA

Sevilla's Jews

In the summer of 1391, smoldering anti-Jewish sentiment flared up in Sevilla. On June 6, Christian mobs ransacked the city's Jewish Quarter (*Judería*). Around 4,000 Jews were killed, and 5,000 Jewish families were driven from their homes. Synagogues were stripped and transformed into churches. The former Judería eventually became the neighborhood of the Holy Cross—Barrio Santa Cruz. Sevilla's uprising spread through Spain (and Europe), the first of many nasty pogroms during the next century.

Before the pogrom, Jews had lived in Sevilla for centuries as the city's respected merchants, doctors, and bankers. They flourished under the Muslim Moors. After Sevilla was "liberated" by King Ferdinand III (1248), Jews were given protection by Castile's kings and allowed a measure of self-government, though they were confined to the Jewish neighborhood. But by the 14th century, Jews were increasingly accused of everything from poisoning wells to ritually sacrificing Christian babies. Mobs killed suspected Jews, and some of Sevilla's most respected Jewish citizens had their fortunes confiscated.

After 1391, Jews faced a choice: Be persecuted (even killed), relocate, or convert to Christianity. The newly Christianized—called *conversos* (converted) or *marranos* (swine)—were always under suspicion of practicing their old faith in private, and thereby undermining true Christianity. Longtime Christians were threatened by this new social class of converted Jews, who now had equal status, fanning the mistrust.

To root out the perceived problem of underground Judaism, the "Catholic Monarchs," Ferdinand and Isabel, established the Inquisition in Spain (1478). Under the direction of Grand Inquisitor Tomás de Torquemada, these religious courts arrested and interrogated *conversos* suspected of practicing Judaism. Using long solitary confinement and torture, they extracted confessions.

On February 6, 1481, Sevilla hosted Spain's first *auto-da-fé* ("act of faith"), a public confession and punishment for heresy. Six accused *conversos* were paraded barefoot into the cathedral, made to publicly confess their sins, then burned at the stake. Over the next three decades, thousands of *conversos* were tried and killed in Spain.

In 1492, the same year the last Moors were driven from Spain, Ferdinand and Isabel decreed that all remaining Jews convert or be expelled (to Portugal and ultimately to Holland or North Africa). Spain emerged as a nation unified under the banner of Christianity.

• *Don't enter the gardens now, but instead cross the square diagonally to the left, and continue 20 yards down a lane to the...*

❻ **Plaza de Santa Cruz:** Arguably the heart of the barrio, this pleasant square, graced by orange trees and draping vines, was once the site of a synagogue (there used to be four in the barrio; now there are none), which Christians destroyed. They replaced the synagogue with a church, which the French (under Napoleon) later demolished. It's a bit of history that locals remember when they see the oversized blue, white, and red French flag marking the French consulate, now overlooking this peaceful square. A fine 16th-century iron cross marks the center of the square and the site of the church the French destroyed. The Sevillian painter Murillo, who was buried in that church, lies somewhere below you.

Opposite the French consulate at #9, you can peek into a lovely courtyard that's proudly been left open so visitors can enjoy it. The square is also home to the recommended Los Gallos flamenco bar, which puts on nightly performances.

• *Go north on Calle Santa Teresa. At #8 (find the plaque on the left, near the big wooden doors) is...*

❼ **Casa de Murillo:** One of Sevilla's famous painters, Bartolomé Esteban Murillo (1617-1682), lived here, soaking in the ambience of street life and reproducing it in his paintings of cute beggar children.

• *Directly across from Casa de Murillo is the...*

❽ **Monasterio de San José del Carmen:** This is where St. Teresa stayed when she visited from her hometown of Ávila. The

convent keeps artifacts of the mystic nun, such as her spiritual manuscripts. The church is closed to the public for visits, but the devout can sneak a peek at its Baroque charm by going to early morning Mass (Mon-Fri 8:45, Sun 9:00, none on Sat).

Continue north on Calle Santa Teresa, then take the first left on Calle Lope de Rueda (just before Las Teresas café), then left again, then right on **Calle Reinoso.** This street—so narrow that the buildings almost touch—is one of the barrio's "kissing lanes." A popular explanation suggests the buildings were built so close together to provide maximum shade. But the history is more complex than that: this labyrinthine street plan goes back to Moorish times, when this area was a tangled market. Later, this was the Jewish ghetto, where all the city's Jews were forced to live in a very small area.

• *Just to the left, the street spills onto...*

❾ Plaza de los Venerables: This square is another candidate for "heart of the barrio." The streets branching off it ooze

local ambience. When the Jews were expelled from Spain in 1492, this area became deserted and run-down. But in 1929, for its world's fair, Sevilla turned the plaza into a showcase of Andalusian style, adding the railings, tile work, orange trees, and other too-cute, Epcot-like adornments. A different generation of tourists enjoys the place today, likely unaware that what they're seeing in Barrio Santa Cruz is far from "authentic" (or, at least, not as old as they imagine).

The large, harmonious Baroque-style Hospital de los Venerables (1675), once a retirement home for old priests (the "venerables"), is now a cultural foundation worth visiting for its ornate church and the excellent Centro Velázquez, with its small but fine collection of paintings.

• *Continue west on Calle de Gloria, past an interesting tile map of the Jewish Quarter (on the right). You'll soon come upon...*

❿ Plaza de Doña Elvira: This small square—with orange trees, tile benches, and a stone fountain— sums up our barrio walk. Shops sell work by local artisans, such as ceramics, embroidery, and fans.

• *Cross the plaza and head north along Calle Rodrigo Caro; keep going until you enter the large...*

⓫ Plaza de la Alianza: Ever consider a career change? Gain inspiration at the site that once housed the painting studio of John Fulton (1932-1998; find the small plaque above the double *hotel* signs), an American who pursued two dreams. Though born in Philadelphia, Fulton got hooked on bullfighting. He trained in the bullrings of Mexico, then in 1956 he moved to Sevilla, the world capital of the sport. His career as matador was not top-notch, and the Spaniards were slow to warm to the Yankee, but his courage and persistence earned their grudging respect. After he put down the cape, he picked up a brush, making colorful paintings in his Sevilla studio.

• *From Plaza de la Alianza, you can return to the cathedral by turning left (west) on Calle Joaquín Romero Murube (along the wall). Or, if you're ready for a bite, head northeast on Calle Rodrigo Caro, which intersects with Calle Mateos Gago, a street lined with tapas bars.*

Sights in Sevilla

▲▲SEVILLA CATHEDRAL

Sevilla's cathedral (Catedral de Sevilla) is the third-largest church in Europe (after St. Peter's at the Vatican in Rome and

St. Paul's in London) and the largest Gothic church anywhere. When they ripped down a mosque of brick on this site in 1401, the Reconquista Christians announced their intention to build a cathedral so huge that "anyone who sees it will take us for madmen." They built for about a hundred years. Even today, the descendants of those madmen proudly display an enlarged photocopy of their *Guinness Book of Records* letter certifying, "Santa María de la Sede in Sevilla is the cathedral with the largest area: 126.18 meters x 82.60 meters x 30.48 meters high" (find the letter at the end of the following self-guided tour).

Cost and Hours: €9 combo-ticket also includes Giralda bell tower and entry to the Church of the Savior; Mon 11:00-16:30, Tue-Sat 11:00-18:00, Sun 14:30-19:00; closes one hour earlier in winter, last entry to cathedral one hour before closing; WC and drinking fountain just inside entrance and in courtyard near exit, tel. 954-214-971, www.catedraldesevilla.es.

Crowd-Beating Tip: Though there's usually not much of a line to buy tickets, you can avoid the queue altogether by buy-

ing your combo-ticket at the Church of the Savior, a few blocks north. See that church first, then come to the cathedral and walk around the line to the turnstile.

Tours: My self-guided tour covers the basics. The €3 audioguide explains each side chapel for anyone interested in old paintings and dry details. For €10, you can enjoy Concepción Delgado's tour instead (see "Tours in Sevilla," earlier).

◑ Self-Guided Tour

Enter the cathedral at the south end (closest to the Alcázar, with a full-size replica of the Giralda's weathervane statue in the patio).

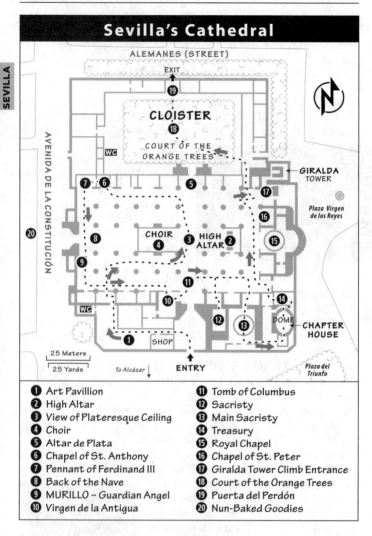

Sevilla's Cathedral

ALEMANES (STREET)

EXIT ⓳

CLOISTER ⓲

COURT OF THE ORANGE TREES

WC

AVENIDA DE LA CONSTITUCIÓN

GIRALDA TOWER

Plaza Virgen de los Reyes

❼ ❻ ❺ ⓱ ⓰

❽ CHOIR ❸ HIGH ❷ ⓯
    ❹ ALTAR

❾ ⓴

⓫ ⓮

⓾ DOME

WC ⓬ ⓭ CHAPTER HOUSE

SHOP

25 Meters
25 Yards

To Alcázar ↓   ENTRY   Plaza del Triunfo

❶ Art Pavillion	⓫ Tomb of Columbus
❷ High Altar	⓬ Sacristy
❸ View of Plateresque Ceiling	⓭ Main Sacristy
❹ Choir	⓮ Treasury
❺ Altar de Plata	⓯ Royal Chapel
❻ Chapel of St. Anthony	⓰ Chapel of St. Peter
❼ Pennant of Ferdinand III	⓱ Giralda Tower Climb Entrance
❽ Back of the Nave	⓲ Court of the Orange Trees
❾ MURILLO – Guardian Angel	⓳ Puerta del Perdón
❿ Virgen de la Antigua	⓴ Nun-Baked Goodies

• Pick up a church map from the rack in this room before you pass through the...

❶ **Art Pavilion:** Just past the turnstile, you step into a room of paintings that once hung in the church, including works by Sevilla's two 17th-century masters—Bartolomé Murillo (*St. Ferdinand*, depicting the king who freed Sevilla from the Moors) and Francisco de Zurbarán (*St. John the Baptist in the Desert*). Find a painting showing two of Sevilla's patron saints—Santa Justa and Santa Rufina, killed in ancient Roman times for their Christian faith. Potters by trade, these two are easy to identify by their palm branches (symbolic of their martyrdom) and their pots (at their feet or in their hands), and the bell tower symbolizing the town they protect. As you tour the cathedral, keep track of how many depictions of this dynamic and saintly duo you spot. They're everywhere.

• *Enter the actual church (you'll pass a WC on the way). In the center of the church, sit down in front of the...*

❷ **High Altar:** Look through the wrought-iron Renaissance grille at what's called the largest altarpiece *(retablo mayor)* ever

made—65 feet tall, with 44 scenes from the life of Jesus and Mary carved from walnut and chestnut, blanketed by a staggering amount of gold leaf. The work took three generations to complete (1481-1564). The story is told left to right, bottom to top. Find Baby Jesus in the manger, in the middle of the bottom row, then follow his story through the miracles, the Passion, and the Pentecost. Look way up to the tippy-top, where a Crucifixion adorns the dizzying summit. Now crane your neck skyward to admire the ❸ **Plateresque tracery** on the ceiling.

• *Turn around and check out the...*

❹ **Choir:** Facing the high altar, the choir features an organ of more than 7,000 pipes (played Mon-Fri at the 10:00 Mass, Sun at the 10:00 & 13:00 Mass, not in July-Aug, free entry for worshippers). A choir area like this one—enclosed within the cathedral for more intimate services—is common in Spain and England, but rare in churches elsewhere. The big, spinnable book holder in the middle of the room held giant hymnals—large enough for all to chant from in a pre-Xerox age when there weren't enough books for everyone.

• *Now turn 90 degrees to the right to take in the enormous...*

❺ **Altar de Plata:** Rising up in what would be the transept, the gleaming silver altarpiece adorned with statues resembles an oversized monstrance (the vessel used during communion), with the statue of the Virgin installed among the gleaming silver. Sevilla's celebration of La Macarena's "jubilee" year culminated here (in 2014, to mark the 50th year of her canonical coronation).

• *Go left, up the side aisle and head to the last chapel on the right.*

❻ **Chapel of St. Anthony** (Capilla de San Antonio): This chapel is used for baptisms. The Renaissance baptismal font has

Bartolomé Murillo (1617-1682)

The son of a barber of Seville, Bartolomé Murillo (mur-EE-oh) got his start selling paintings meant for export to the frontier churches of the Americas. In his 20s, he became famous after he painted a series of saints for Sevilla's Franciscan monastery. By about 1650, Murillo's sugary, simple, and accessible religious style was spreading through Spain and beyond.

Murillo painted street kids with cute smiles and grimy faces, and radiant young Marías with Ivory-soap complexions and rapturous poses (Immaculate Conceptions). His paintings view the world through a soft-focus lens, wrapping everything in warm colors and soft light, with a touch (too much, for some) of sentimentality.

Murillo became a rich, popular family man, and the toast of Sevilla's high society. In 1664, his wife died, leaving him heartbroken, but his last 20 years were his most prolific. At age 65, Murillo died after falling off a scaffold while painting. His tomb is lost somewhere under the bricks of Plaza de Santa Cruz.

delightful carved angels dancing along its base. In Murillo's painting, *Vision of St. Anthony* (1656), the saint kneels in wonder as Baby Jesus comes down surrounded by a choir of angels. Anthony, one of Iberia's most popular saints, is the patron saint of lost things—so people come here to pray for his help in finding jobs, car keys, and life partners. Above the *Vision* is *The Baptism of Christ*, also by Murillo. You don't need to be an art historian to know that the stained glass dates from 1685. And by now you must know who the women are...

Exiting the rear of the chapel, look for a glass case that displays the ❼ **pennant of Ferdinand III,** which was raised here over the minaret of the mosque on November 23, 1248, as Christian forces finally expelled the Moors from Sevilla. For centuries, it was paraded through the city on special days.

Continuing on, stand at the ❽ **back of the nave** (behind the choir) and appreciate the ornate immensity of the church. Can you see the angels trumpeting on their Cuban mahogany? Any birds? Before you is the gravestone of Ferdinand Columbus, Christopher's second son. Having given the cathedral his collection of 6,000 precious books, he was rewarded with this prime burial spot.

Turn around. To the left, behind an iron grille, is a niche with ❾ **Murillo's** *Guardian Angel* pointing to the light and showing an astonished child the way.

• *Now turn around, passing a massive candlestick holder to the right of the choir that dates from 1560, and march down the side aisle to find the...*

🔟 **Virgen de la Antigua:** Within this chapel is a gilded fresco of the Virgin delicately holding a rose and the Christ Child, who's holding a bird. It's the oldest art here, even older than the cathedral itself: It was painted onto a horseshoe-shaped prayer niche of the mosque that formerly stood on this site. After Sevilla was reconquered in 1248, the mosque served as a church for about 120 years—until it was torn down to make room for this huge cathedral. The Catholic builders, who were captivated by the fresco's beauty and well aware of the Virgen de la Antigua's status as protector of sailors (important in this port city), decided to save the fresco. Gaze up to find flags of all the New World countries where the Virgen de la Antigua is revered.

• *Exit the Virgen de la Antigua chapel by the side door to find the...*

⓫ **Tomb of Columbus:** In front of the cathedral's entrance for pilgrims are four kings who carry the tomb of Christopher Colum-

bus. His pallbearers represent the regions of Castile, Aragon, León, and Navarre (identify them by their team shirts). Notice how the cross held by Señor León has a pike end, which is piercing an orb. Look closer: It's a pomegranate, the symbol of Granada—the last Moorish-ruled city to succumb to the Reconquista (in 1492).

Columbus didn't just travel a lot while alive—he even kept it up posthumously. He was buried first in northwestern Spain (in Valladolid, where he died), then moved to a monastery here in Sevilla, then to what's now the Dominican Republic (as he'd requested), then to Cuba. Finally—when Cuba gained independence from Spain in 1902—his remains sailed home again to Sevilla. After all that, it's fair to wonder whether the remains in the box before you are actually his. Sevillians like to think so. (Columbus died in 1506. Five hundred years later, to help celebrate the anniversary of his death, DNA samples did indeed give Sevillians some evidence to substantiate their claim.)

On the left is a 1584 mural of St. Christopher, patron saint of travelers. The clock above has been ticking since 1788.

• *Facing Columbus, duck into the first chapel on your left to find the...*

⓬ **Sacristy:** This space is where the priests get ready each morning before Mass. The Goya painting above the altar features another portrayal of Justa and Rufina with their trademark bell tower, pots, and palm leaves. This beautiful work by Goya is remarkable because it was painted specifically for this space, and the two girls look like fashionable women of the artist's time—certainly not like third-century martyrs.

• *Two chapels down is the entrance to the...*

❸ Main Sacristy: Marvel at the ornate, 16th-century dome of the main room, a grand souvenir from Sevilla's Golden Age. The intricate masonry, called Plateresque, resembles lacy silverwork (*plata* means "silver"). God is way up in the cupola. The three layers of figures below him show the heavenly host; relatives in purgatory—hands folded in prayer—looking to heaven in hope of help; and the wretched in hell, including a topless sinner engulfed in flames and teased cruelly by pitchfork-wielding monsters.

Dominating the room is a nearly 1,000-pound, silver-plated monstrance (vessel for displaying the communion wafer). This is the monstrance used to parade the holy host through town during Corpus Christi festivities.

• *The next door down leads you through a pair of rooms to one with a unique oval dome. It's in the 16th-century chapter house (sala capitular), where monthly meetings take place with the bishop (he gets the throne, while the others share the bench). The paintings here are by Murillo: a fine* Immaculate Conception *(1668, high above the bishop's throne) and portraits of saints important to Sevillians.*

Then, enter the...

❹ Treasury: This wood-paneled Room of Ornaments shows off gold and silver reliquaries, which hold hundreds of holy body

parts, as well as Spain's most valuable crown. This jeweled piece (the Corona de la Virgen de los Reyes, by Manuel de la Torres) sparkles with thousands of tiny precious stones, and the world's largest pearl—used as the torso of an angel. This amazing treasure was paid for by locals who donated their wealth to royally crown their Madonna.

• *Leave the treasury and cross through the church, passing the closed-to-tourists* **❺ Royal Chapel,** *the burial place of several kings of Castile (open for worship only—access from outside), then the also-closed* **❻ Chapel of St. Peter,** *which is filled with paintings showing scenes from the life of St. Peter.*

In the far corner—past the glass case displaying the Guinness Book certificate declaring that this is indeed the world's largest church by area—is the entry to the Giralda bell tower. It's time for some exercise.

Immaculate Conception

Throughout Sevilla—and all of Spain—you'll see paintings titled *The Immaculate Conception,* all looking quite similar (see example on page 24). Young, lovely, and beaming radiantly, these virgins look pure and untainted...you might even say "immaculate." According to Catholic doctrine, Mary, the future mother of Jesus, entered the world free from the original sin that other mortals share. When she died, her purity allowed her to be taken up directly to heaven (in the Assumption).

The doctrine of Immaculate Conception can be confusing, even to Catholics. It does not mean that the Virgin Mary herself was born of a virgin. Rather, Mary's mother and father conceived her in the natural way. But at the moment Mary's soul animated her flesh, God granted her a special exemption from original sin. The doctrine of Immaculate Conception had been popular since medieval times, though it was not codified until 1854. It was Sevilla's own Bartolomé Murillo (1617-1682) who painted the model of this goddess-like Mary, copied by so many lesser artists. In Counter-Reformation times (when Murillo lived), paintings of a fresh-faced, ecstatic Mary made abstract doctrines like the Immaculate Conception and the Assumption tangible and accessible to Catholics across Europe.

Most images of the Immaculate Conception show Mary wearing a radiant crown and with a crescent moon at her feet; she often steps on the heads of cherubs. Paintings by Murillo frequently portray Mary in a blue robe with long, wavy hair—young and innocent.

⓱ Giralda Bell Tower Climb: Your church admission includes entry to the bell tower, a former minaret. Notice the beautiful Moorish simplicity as you climb to its top, 330 feet up (35 ramps plus 17 steps), for a grand city view. The graded ramp was designed to accommodate a donkey-riding muezzin, who clip-clopped up five times a day to give the Muslim call to prayer back when a mosque stood here. It's less steep the farther up you go, but if you get tired along the way, stop at balconies for expansive views over the entire city.

• *Back on the ground, head outside. As you cross the threshold, look up. Why is a wooden crocodile hanging here? It's a replica of a taxidermied specimen, the original of which is said to have been a gift to King Alfonso X from the sultan of Egypt in 1260 (when the croc died, the king had him stuffed and hung here). You're now in the...*

⓲ Court of the Orange Trees: Today's cloister was once the mosque's patio for ablutions. Twelfth-century Muslims stopped at the fountain in the middle to wash their hands, face, and feet before praying. The ankle-breaking lanes between the bricks were once irrigation streams—a reminder that the Moors introduced irrigation

to Iberia. The mosque was made of bricks; the church is built of stone. The only large-scale remnants of the mosque today are the Court of the Orange Trees, the Giralda bell tower, and the site itself.

• *You'll exit the cathedral through the Court of the Orange Trees (WCs are at the far end of the courtyard, downstairs). As you leave, look back from the outside and notice the arch over the...*

⑲ Puerta del Perdón: As with much of the Moorish-looking art in town, this doorway is actually Christian—the two coats of arms are a giveaway. The relief above the door shows the Bible story of Jesus ridding the temple of the merchants...a reminder to contemporary merchants that there will be no retail activity in the church. The plaque on the right honors Miguel de Cervantes, the great 16th-century writer. It's one of many plaques scattered throughout town showing places mentioned in his books. (In this case, the topic was pickpockets.) The huge green doors predate the church. They are bits of the pre-1248 mosque—wood covered with bronze. Study the fine workmanship.

Giralda Bell Tower Exterior: Step across the street from the exit gate and look at the bell tower. Formerly a Moorish minaret from which Muslims were called to prayer, it became the cathedral's bell tower after the Reconquista. A 4,500-pound bronze statue symbolizing the Triumph of Faith (specifically, the Christian faith over the Muslim one) caps the tower and serves as a weather vane (in Spanish, *girar* means "to rotate"; *la giralda* refers to the female figure that turns with the wind). In 1356, the original top of the tower fell. You're looking at a 16th-century Christian-built top with a ribbon of letters proclaiming, "The strongest tower is the name of God" (you can see *Fortísima*—"strongest"—from this vantage point).

Now circle around for a close look at the corner of the tower at ground level. Needing more strength than their bricks could provide for the lowest section of the tower, the Moors used Roman-cut stones. You can actually read the Latin that was chiseled onto one of the stones 2,000 years ago. The tower offers a brief recap of the city's history: It sits on a Roman foundation and has a long Moorish section, which is capped by the current Christian age.

Today, by law, no building in the center may be higher than the statue atop the tower. (But the skyscraper just across the river, Torre Sevilla, is by far the tallest erection in the greater city—and that offends locals in this conservative town. The fact that it was financed by one of Spain's major banks, which many Spaniards blame for the economic crisis, hasn't helped its popularity.)

• Your cathedral tour is finished. If you've worked up an appetite, get out your map and make your way a few blocks for some...

❷⓿ **Nun-Baked Goodies:** Stop by the El Torno Pastelería de Conventos, a co-op where various orders of cloistered nuns send their handicrafts (such as baptismal dresses for babies) and baked goods to be sold. You won't actually see *el torno* (a lazy Susan), since this shop is staffed by laypeople, but this humble little hole-in-the-wall shop is worth a peek, and definitely serves the best cookies, bar nun. It's located through the passageway at 24 Avenida de la Constitución, directly across from the cathedral's main front door: Go through the passageway marked *Plaza del Cabildo* into the quiet courtyard (Mon-Fri 10:00-13:30 & 17:00-19:30, Sat-Sun 10:30-14:00, closed Aug, Plaza del Cabildo 2, tel. 954-219-190).

▲▲ROYAL ALCÁZAR

Originally a 10th-century palace built for the governors of the local Moorish state, this building still functions as a royal palace—the

oldest in Europe that's still in use. The core of the palace features an extensive 14th-century rebuild, done by Muslim workmen for the Christian king, Pedro I (1334-1369). Pedro was nicknamed either "the Cruel" or "the Just," depending on which end of his sword you were on. Pedro's palace embraces both cultural traditions.

Today, visitors can enjoy several sections of the Alcázar (Real Alcázar). Spectacularly decorated halls and courtyards have distinctive Islamic-style flourishes. Exhibits call up the era of Columbus and Spain's New World dominance. The lush, sprawling gardens invite exploration.

Cost and Hours: €9.50, free Mon one hour before closing; daily 9:30-19:00, Oct-March until 17:00; tel. 954-502-324, www.alcazarsevilla.org.

Crowd-Beating Tips: To skip the ticket-buying line, reserve a time slot ahead online. Mornings are the busiest with tour groups

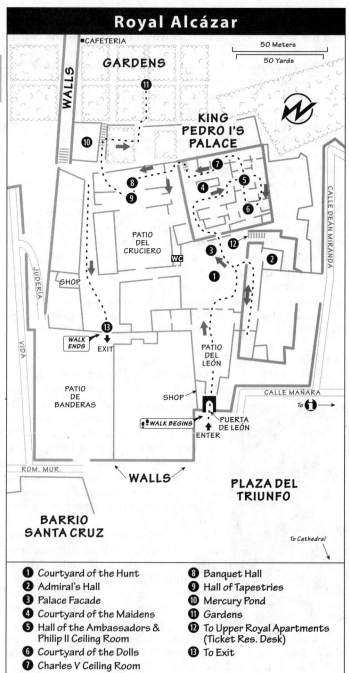

Royal Alcázar

CAFETERIA

GARDENS

WALLS

50 Meters

50 Yards

KING
PEDRO I'S
PALACE

CALLE DEÁN MIRANDA

PATIO
DEL
CRUCIERO

WC

SHOP

JUDERIA

VIDA

WALK
ENDS

EXIT

PATIO
DE
BANDERAS

SHOP

PATIO
DEL
LEÓN

CALLE MAÑARA

To

WALK BEGINS

PUERTA
DE LEÓN

ENTER

WALLS

ROM. MUR.

PLAZA DEL
TRIUNFO

BARRIO
SANTA CRUZ

To Cathedral

1 Courtyard of the Hunt
2 Admiral's Hall
3 Palace Facade
4 Courtyard of the Maidens
5 Hall of the Ambassadors &
Philip II Ceiling Room
6 Courtyard of the Dolls
7 Charles V Ceiling Room

8 Banquet Hall
9 Hall of Tapestries
10 Mercury Pond
11 Gardens
12 To Upper Royal Apartments
(Ticket Res. Desk)
13 To Exit

SEVILLA

(especially on Tuesdays). It's less crowded late in the day—but note that the Royal Apartments can only be visited before 13:30. Avoid the free admission time on Monday as lines are often so long that your time inside is cut short.

Tours: The fast-moving, €5 audioguide gives you an hour of information as you wander. My self-guided tour hits the highlights, or you could consider Concepción Delgado's Alcázar tour.

The **Upper Royal Apartments** can be visited only with a separate tour (€4.50, includes separate audioguide, must check bags in provided lockers). For some, it's worth the extra time and cost just to escape the mobs in the rest of the palace. If you're interested, once inside the main courtyard go directly to the upstairs desk and reserve a spot. Groups of 15 leave every half-hour from 10:00 to 13:30, listening to the 30-minute audio tour while escorted by a security guard. If all the time slots are full the day you visit, have the guard at the exit stamp your ticket when you leave—you can reenter through the exit the following day and try your luck again.

❍ Self-Guided Tour

This royal palace is decorated with a mix of Islamic and Christian elements—a style called Mudejar. It offers a thought-provoking

glimpse of a graceful Al-Andalus world that might have survived its Castilian conquerors...but didn't. The floor plan is intentionally confusing, to make experiencing the place more exciting and surprising. While Granada's Alhambra was built by Moors for Moorish rulers, what you see here is essentially a Christian ruler's palace, built in the Moorish style by Moorish artisans.

• *Buy your ticket and enter through the turnstiles. Pass through the garden-like Lion Patio (Patio del León), with the rough stone wall of the older Moorish fortress on your left (c. 913), and through the arch into a courtyard called the...*

❶ Courtyard of the Hunt (Patio de la Montería): Get oriented. The palace's main entrance is directly ahead, through the elaborately decorated facade. WCs are in the far-left corner. In the far-right corner is the staircase and tick-

et booth for the Upper Royal Apartments—if you're interested, reserve an entry time now.

The palace complex was built over many centuries, with rooms and decorations from the various rulers who've lived here. Moorish rulers first built the original 10th-century palace and gardens. Then, after Sevilla was Christianized in 1248, King Pedro I built the most famous part of the complex. During Spain's Golden Age, it was home to Ferdinand and Isabel and, later, their grandson Charles V; they all left their mark. Successive monarchs added still more luxury. And today's king and queen still use the palace's upper floor as one of their royal residences.

• *Before entering the heart of the palace, start in the wing to the right of the courtyard. Skip the large reception room for now and go directly to the...*

❷ **Admiral's Hall** (Salón del Almirante): When Queen Isabel debriefed Columbus in Barcelona after his New World discoveries, she realized what he'd found could be big business. She created this wing in 1503 to administer Spain's New World ventures. In these halls, Columbus recounted his travels, Ferdinand Magellan planned his around-the-world cruise, and Amerigo Vespucci tried to come up with a catchy moniker for that newly discovered continent.

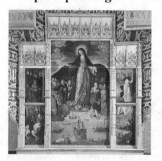

In the pink-and-red Audience Chamber (once a chapel), the **altarpiece painting** is *St. Mary of the Navigators* (*Santa María de los Navegantes,* Alejo Fernández, 1530s). The Virgin—the patron saint of sailors and a favorite of Columbus—keeps watch over the puny ships beneath her. Her cape seems to protect everyone under it—even the Native Americans in the dark background (the first time "Indians" were painted in Europe).

Standing beside the Virgin (on the right, dressed in gold, almost joining his hands together in prayer) is none other than Christopher Columbus. He stands on a cloud, because he's now in heaven (this was painted a few decades after his death). Notice that Columbus is blond. Columbus' son said of his dad: "In his youth his hair was blond, but when he reached 30, it all turned white." Many historians believe this to be the earliest known portrait of Columbus. If so, it's also likely to be the most accurate. The man on the left side of the painting, with the gold cape, is King Ferdinand.

Left of the painting is a **model** of Columbus' *Santa María,* his flagship and the only of his three ships not to survive the 1492 voyage. Columbus complained that the *Santa María*—a big cargo

ship, different from the sleek *Niña* and *Pinta* caravels—was too slow. On Christmas Day it ran aground off present-day Haiti and tore a hole in its hull. The ship was dismantled to build the first permanent structure in America, a fort for 39 colonists. (After Columbus left, the natives burned the fort and killed the colonists.) Opposite the altarpiece (in the center of the back wall) is the family **coat of arms** of Columbus' descendants, who now live in Spain and Puerto Rico. Using Columbus' Spanish name, it reads: "To Castile and to León, Colón gave a new world."

Return to the still-used reception room, filled with big canvases. The **biggest painting** (and most melodramatic) shows a key turning point in Sevilla's history: King Ferdinand III humbly kneels before the bishop, giving thanks to God for helping him liberate the city from the Muslims (in 1248). Ferdinand promptly turned the Alcázar of the Moors into the royal palace of Christian kings.

Pop into the room beyond the grand piano for a look at some ornate **fans** (mostly foreign and well-described in English). A long painting (designed to be gradually rolled across a screen and viewed like a primitive movie) shows 17th-century Sevilla during Holy Week. Follow the procession, which is much like today's, with traditional floats carried by teams of men and followed by a retinue of penitents.

• *Return to the Courtyard of the Hunt. Face the impressive entrance to the...*

❸ **Palace Facade:** This is the entrance to **King Pedro I's Palace** (Palacio del Rey Pedro I), the Alcázar's 14th-century nucleus. The facade's elaborate blend of Islamic tracery and Gothic Christian elements introduces us to the Mudejar style seen throughout Pedro's part of the palace.

• *Enter the palace. Go left through the vestibule (impressive, yes, but we'll see better), and emerge into the big court-yard with a long pool in the center. This is the...*

❹ **Courtyard of the Maidens** (Patio de las Doncellas): You've reached the center of King Pedro's palace. It's an open-air courtyard, surrounded by rooms. In the center is a long, rectangular reflecting pool. Like the Moors who preceded him, Pedro built his palace around water.

King Pedro cruelly abandoned his wife and moved into the Alcázar with his mistress, then hired Muslim workers from Granada to re-create the romance of that city's Alhambra in Sevilla's stark Alcázar. The designers created a microclimate engineered for coolness: water, sunken gardens, pottery, thick walls, and darkness. This palace is considered Spain's best example of the Mudejar style. Stucco panels with elaborate designs, colorful ceramic tiles, coffered wooden ceilings, and lobed arches atop slender columns create a refined, pleasing environment. The elegant proportions and symmetry of this courtyard are a photographer's delight.

• *You'll explore the rooms branching off the courtyard in the next few stops. Through the door at the end of the long reflecting pool is the palace's most important room, called the...*

❺ **Hall of the Ambassadors** (Salón de Embajadores): Here, in his throne room, Pedro received guests and caroused in luxury. The

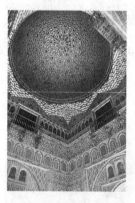

room is a cube topped with a half-dome, like many important Islamic buildings. In Islam, the cube represents the earth, and the dome is the starry heavens. In Pedro's world, the symbolism proclaimed that he controlled heaven and earth. Islamic horseshoe arches stand atop recycled columns with golden capitals.

The stucco on the walls is molded with interlacing plants, geometrical shapes, and Arabic writing. Here, in a Christian palace, the walls are inscribed with unapologetically Muslim sayings: "None but Allah conquers" and "Happiness and prosperity are benefits of Allah, who nourishes all creatures." The artisans added propaganda phrases, such as "Dedicated to the magnificent Sultan Pedro—thanks to God!"

The Mudejar style also includes Christian motifs. Find the row of kings, high up at the base of the dome, chronicling all of Castile's rulers from the 600s to the 1600s. Throughout the palace (as in the center of the dome above you), you'll see coats of arms—including the castle of Castile and the lion of León. There are also natural objects (such as shells and birds), which you wouldn't normally find in Islamic decor, as it traditionally avoids realistic images of nature.

Notice how it gets cooler as you go deeper into the palace. Straight ahead from the Hall of the Ambassadors, in the **Philip II Ceiling Room** (Salón del Techo de Felipe II), look above the arches to find peacocks, falcons, and other birds amid interlacing vines. Imagine day-to-day life in the palace—with VIP guests tripping on the tiny steps.

• *Make your way to the second courtyard, nearby (with your back to the Hall of the Ambassadors, circle right). This smaller courtyard is the...*

❻ **Courtyard of the Dolls** (Patio de las Muñecas): This delicate courtyard was reserved for the king's private family life. Origi-

nally, the center of the courtyard had a pool, cooling the residents and reflecting decorative patterns that were once brightly painted on the walls. The columns—recycled from ancient Roman and Visigothic buildings—are of alternating white, black, and pink marble. The courtyard's name comes from the tiny doll faces found at the base of one of the arches. Circle the room and try to find them. (Hint: While just a couple of inches tall, they're eight feet up.)

Pedro's original courtyard was a single story; the upper floors and skylight were added centuries later by Isabel's grandson, Charles V, in the 16th century. See the different styles: Mudejar below (lobed arches and elaborate tracery) and Renaissance above (round arches and less decoration).

• *The long adjoining room with the gilded ceiling, the **Prince's Room** (Cuarto del Príncipe), was Queen Isabel's bedroom, where she gave birth to a son, Prince Juan.*

Return to the Hall of the Ambassadors, continue straight through, then turn left to find the...

❼ **Charles V Ceiling Room** (Salón del Techo del Carlos V): Emperor Charles V, who ruled Spain at its peak of New World wealth, expanded the palace. The reason? His marriage to his beloved Isabel—which took place in this room—that joined vast realms of Spain and Portugal. Devoutly Christian, Charles celebrated his wedding night with a midnight Mass, and later ordered the Mudejar ceiling in this room to be replaced with the less Islamic (but no less impressive) Renaissance one you see today.

• *We've seen the core of King Pedro's palace, with the additions by his successors. Return to the Courtyard of the Maidens, then turn right. In the corner, find the small staircase. Go up to rooms decorated with bright ceramic tiles and Gothic vaulting. Pass through the chapel (with its ma-jestic mahogany altar on your right) and into a big, long room, the...*

❽ Banquet Hall (Salón Gótico): This airy banquet hall is where Charles and Isabel held their wedding reception. Tiles of yellow, blue, green, and orange line the room, some decorated with whimsical human figures with vase-like bodies. The windows open onto views of the gardens.

❾ Hall of Tapestries (Salón Tapices): Next door, the walls are hung with 18th-century Spanish copies of 16th-century Bel-

gian tapestries showing the conquests, trade, and indus-triousness of Charles' prosper-ous reign. (The highlights are described in Spanish along the top, and in Latin along the bot-tom.) The map tapestry of the Mediterranean world has south pointing up. Find Genova, Italy on the bottom; Africa on top; Lisbon *(Lisboa)* on the far right; and the large city of Barcelona in between. The artist included himself holding the legend—with a scale in both leagues and miles.

Facing the map, head to the far-left end of the room, where the wall is filled by a dramatic portrayal of the Spanish Navy. Spain ruled the waves—and thereby an empire upon which the sun never set. Its reign lasted from 1492 until the defeat of the Spanish Armada in 1588; after that, Britannia's navy started to take over the helm, and it was her crown that controlled the next global empire.

• *Return to the Banquet Hall, then head outside at the far end to the...*

❿ Mercury Pond: The Mercury Pond, a reservoir fed by a 16th-century aqueduct, irrigated the palace's entire garden. As only elites had running water, the fountain was an extravagant show of power. Check out the bronze statue of Mercury, with his cute little winged feet. The wall defining the east side of the gar-den was part of the original Moorish castle wall. In the early 1600s, when

fortifications were no longer needed here, that end was redesigned to be a grotto-style gallery.

• *From the Mercury Pond, steps lead into the formal gardens. Just past the bottom of the steps, a tunnel on the right leads under the palace to the coolest spot in the city. Finally, explore the...*

⓫ Gardens: The intimate geometric zone nearest the palace

Christopher Columbus (1451-1506)

This Italian wool weaver ran off to sea, was shipwrecked in Portugal, married a captain's daughter, learned Portuguese and Spanish, and persuaded Spain's monarchs to finance his bold scheme to trade with the East by sailing west. On August 3, 1492, Columbus set sail from Palos (near Huelva, 60 miles west of Sevilla) with three ships and 90 men, hoping to land in Asia, which Columbus estimated was 3,000 miles away. Ten weeks—and yes, 3,000 miles—later, with a superstitious crew ready to mutiny after they'd seen evil omens (including a falling meteor and a jittery compass), Columbus landed on an island in the Bahamas, convinced he'd reached Asia. He and his crew traded with the "Indians" and returned home to Palos harbor, where they were received as heroes.

Columbus made three more voyages to the New World and became rich with gold. But he gained a bad reputation among the colonists, was arrested, and returned to Spain in chains. Though pardoned, Columbus fell out of favor with the court. On May 20, 1506, he died in Valladolid. His son said he was felled by "gout and by grief at seeing himself fallen from his high estate," but historians speculate that diabetes or syphilis may have contributed. Columbus died thinking he'd visited Asia, unaware he'd opened up Europe to a New World.

is the Moorish garden. The far-flung garden beyond that was the backyard of the Christian ruler.

Here in the gardens, as in the rest of the palace, the Christian and Islamic traditions merge. Both cultures used water and nature as essential parts of their architecture. The garden's pavilions and fountains only enhance this. Wander among palm trees, myrtle hedges, and fragrant roses. While tourists pay to be here, this is actually a public garden, and free to locals. It's been that way since 1931, when the king was exiled and Spanish citizens took ownership of royal holdings. In 1975, the Spanish people allowed the king back on the throne—but on their terms...which included keeping this garden.

• *Along the east wall is an air-conditioned **cafeteria** with a nice terrace overlooking the gardens. It's worth taking a few steps through the east wall to see the massive—and massively beautiful—bougainvillea that grows just on the other side of the wall.*

If you've booked a spot to visit the Upper Royal Apartments, return to the Courtyard of the Hunt, and head upstairs.

⓬ **Upper Royal Apartments** (Cuarto Real Alto): This is the royal palace of today's monarchs. Fifteen public reception rooms are open to visitors: the official dining room, Audience Hall, and so on. The rooms are amply decorated with Versailles-like furniture, chandeliers, carpets, and portraits of 19th-century nobility. The highlight is the Audience Room, a Mudejar-style room overlooking the Patio de la Montería.

• *Your Alcázar tour is over. From the Moors to Pedro I to Ferdinand and Isabel, and from Charles V to King Felipe VI, we've seen the home of a millennium of Spanish kings and queens. When you're ready to go, follow ⓭ **exit** signs and head out through the **Patio de Banderas**, once the entrance for guests arriving by horse carriage. Enjoy a classic Giralda bell tower view as you leave.*

NEAR THE CATHEDRAL
▲Archivo General de Indias
(General Archives of the Indies)

To the right of the Alcázar's main entrance, the Archivo General de Indias houses historic papers related to Spain's overseas territories. Its four miles of shelving contain 80 million pages documenting a once-mighty empire. While little of interest is actually on show, a visit is free, easy, and gives you a look at the Lonja Palace, one of the finest Renaissance edifices in Spain. Designed by royal architect Juan de Herrera, the principal designer of El Escorial, the building evokes the greatness of the Spanish empire at its peak (c. 1600).

Cost and Hours: Free, Mon-Sat 9:30-17:00, Sun 10:00-14:00, Avenida de la Constitución 3, tel. 954-500-528.

Visiting the Archives: Originally this spot was a market for traders—an early stock market. Back in the day, Sevilla was the only port licensed to trade with the New World, and merchants came here from all across Europe, establishing the city as a commercial powerhouse. But by the end of the 1600s, Sevilla had become a backwater (after suffering plagues and the silting up of its harbor, which allowed Cádiz to overtake Sevilla as Spain's main port), and in 1717, the building was abandoned. In 1785, it was put to new use as the storehouse for documents the country was quickly amassing from its discovery and conquest of the New World.

The ground floor houses a small exhibit on the building's history, with text in Spanish only. The lone items of interest here are a series of etchings showing how all those *archivos* were once stacked in the bookshelves upstairs, and a cannon discovered by American treasure hunter Mel Fisher. He used information in the archives to find a Spanish galleon that sank off the Florida coast in 1616—with a treasure of $450 million onboard. Fisher returned the cannon as a gesture of goodwill.

Continue your visit by climbing the extravagant marble staircase to the first floor. At the top, don't miss the huge 16th-century security chest—meant to store gold and important documents. Its elaborate locking mechanism (it fills the inner lid) could be opened only by following a set series of pushes, pulls, and twists—an effective way to keep prying eyes and greedy fingers from its valuable contents. Head left to find a curtained room where an interesting 15-minute video gives the historical context for Sevilla's New World connections and an overview of the archive's work. Then make a big circle through three galleries to check out the beautifully decorated domes and rotating exhibits.

Avenida de la Constitución

Old Sevilla is bisected by this grand boulevard. Its name celebrates the country's 1978 adoption of a democratic constitution, as the Spanish people moved quickly to reestablish their government after the 1975 death of longtime dictator Francisco Franco (an opportune change, since it was previously named for the founder of Spain's Fascist Party, José Antonio Primo de Rivera).

The busy avenue was converted into a pedestrian boulevard in 2007. Overnight, the city's paseo route took on a new dimension. Suddenly cafés and shops here had fresh appeal. (Three Starbucks moved in, strategically bookending the boulevard, but they've struggled to win over locals who prefer small €1 coffees to mammoth €4 ones.) The tram line (infamously short, only about a mile long) is controversial, as it violates what might have been a more purely pedestrian zone.

IN BARRIO SANTA CRUZ

Hospital de los Venerables

Buried in the Barrio Santa Cruz, this former charity-run old-folks home and hospital comes with a Baroque church and an exquisite painting gallery that includes the Centro Velázquez, which displays works by one of Spain's premier artists. It merges local history, art, and architecture in one building. Everything is well explained by the included audioguide.

Cost and Hours: €8, free on Sun after 14:00, open daily 10:00-18:00, Plaza de los Venerables 8, tel. 954-562-696, www.focus.abengoa.es.

Visiting the Hospital: In the courtyard, you get a sense of how retired priests and Sevilla's needy mingled around its sunken fountain.

The church, which takes you back to the year 1700, is bursting with Baroque decor, one of Spain's best pipe organs, and frescoes by Juan de Valdés Leal. Of note is the *trompe l'oeil* he painted on the sacristy ceiling, turning a small room into a piece of heaven. The decor exalts the priesthood and Spain's role as standard-bearer of the pope.

The top-notch **painting gallery** is dedicated to one of the world's greatest painters, Diego Velázquez (1599-1660), who was born here in Sevilla, where he also worked as a young man. Velázquez's *Vista de Sevilla* helps you imagine the excitement of this thriving city in 1649 when, with 120,000 people, it was the fourth largest in Europe. You'll recognize landmarks like the Giralda bell tower, the cathedral, and the Torre del Oro. The pontoon bridge leads to Triana—where citizens of all ranks strolled the promenade together, as they still do today.

The Sevilla that shaped Velázquez was the gateway to the New World. There was lots of stimulation: adventurers, fortune hunters, and artists passed through here, and many stayed for years. Of the few Velázquez paintings remaining in his hometown, three are in this gallery. Upstairs has little of interest, but the staircase dome is worth a look, as is the private box view into the church.

Centro de Interpretación Judería de Sevilla

This small, overpriced interpretive museum, standing in the heart of Barrio Santa Cruz, chronicles the history of Sevilla's Jews, who once called this neighborhood home. Bilingual placards and a few displays give visitors a glimpse of Sevilla's Sephardic heritage. However, most find the Casa de Sefarad in Córdoba more interesting.

Cost and Hours: €6.50, daily 11:00-19:00, longer hours in summer, all visits are guided—tours in English may be available on request, Calle Ximénez de Enciso 22, tel. 954-047-089, www.juderiadesevilla.es.

BETWEEN THE RIVER AND THE CATHEDRAL

▲▲Hospital de la Caridad

This charity hospital, which functioned as a place of final refuge for Sevilla's poor and homeless, was founded in the 17th century by the nobleman Don Miguel Mañara. Your visit includes an evocative courtyard, his office, a church filled with powerful art, and a good audioguide that explains it all. This is still a working charity, so when you pay your entrance fee, you're advancing the work Mañara started back in the 17th century.

Cost and Hours: €6, includes audioguide, daily 10:30-19:30, Calle Temprado 3, tel. 954-223-232, www.santa-caridad.es.

Background: The Hospice and Hospital of the Holy Charity in Sevilla was founded by Don Miguel Mañara (1626-1679), a big-time playboy and enthusiastic sinner who, late in life, had a massive change of heart. He spent his last years dedicating his life to strict worship and taking care of the poor. In 1674, Mañara acquired some empty warehouses in Sevilla's old shipyard and built this 150-ward "place of heroic virtues."

Mañara could well have been the inspiration for Don Juan, the quasi-legendary character from a play set in 17th-century Sevilla, popularized later by Lord Byron's poetry and Mozart's opera *Don Giovanni* ("Don Juan" in Spanish). While no one knows for sure, I think it makes sense...and it adds some fun to the visit.

One thing's for certain: Mañara is on the road to sainthood. His supporters request that you report any miraculous answers to prayers asking him to intercede—you need to perform miracles to become a saint.

Visiting the Hospital: The **courtyard** gives a sense of the origin of the building and its ongoing assistance to the poor. The statues come from Genoa, Italy, as Mañara's family were rich Genovese merchants who moved to Sevilla to get in on the wealth from New World discoveries. The Dutch tiles (from Delft), depicting scenes from the Old and New Testament, are a reminder that the Netherlands was under Spanish rule in centuries past.

The **Sala de Cabildos,** a small room at the end of the courtyard, is Mañara's former office. Here you'll see his original desk, a painting of him at work (busy preaching against materialism and hedonism), a treasure box with an elaborate lock mechanism, his sword (he killed several people in his wilder days), a whip that was part of his austere style of worship, and his death mask.

Exit right and walk to the corner gift shop to reach the highlight—the **chapel,** which Mañara had built. On entering, you are greeted by Juan de Valdés Leal's *In the Blink of an Eye (In ictu oculi).* In it, the Grim Reaper extinguishes the candle of life. Filling the canvas are the ruins of worldly goods, knowledge, power, and position. It's all gone in the blink of an eye—true in the 1670s...and true today.

Turn around to face the door you just entered and look up to find Leal's *The End of the Glories of the World.* The painting shows Mañara and a bishop decaying together in a crypt, with worms and assorted bugs munching away. Above, the hand of Christ—pierced by the nail—holds the scales of justice: sins (on the left) and good deeds (on the right). The placement of both paintings gave worshippers plenty to think about during and after their visit.

Sit in a front pew and take it in: This is Sevillian Baroque. Seven original or replica Murillo paintings celebrate good deeds and charity: feeding the hungry, tending the sick, and so on. The altar is carved wood with gold leaf. A dozen hardworking cupids support the Burial of Christ. The duty of the order of monks here was to give a Christian burial to the executed and drowned. See the dark-gray tombstone worked into the altar scene (on the right). Above are three female figures representing main Christian virtues (left to right): faith, charity, hope.

Before leaving the church, do Don Miguel Mañara a favor. Step on his **tombstone.** Located just outside the church's main entrance in the back, it's served as a welcome mat since 1679. He requested to be buried outside the church where everyone would step on him as they entered. It's marked "the worst man in the world."

Return to the courtyard, go straight across and around to the left. Wander around, noticing the brick Gothic arches of the huge halls of the 13th-century **shipyards,** whose original floors are 15 feet below. Overlooking the courtyard, immediately behind the church's altar, were the rooms where Mañara spent his last years. Here he could be close to his charity work and his intensely penitent place of worship.

Across the street from the entry is a park. Pop in and see Don Miguel—wracked with guilt—carrying a poor, sick person into his hospital.

Torre del Oro (Gold Tower) and Naval Museum

Sevilla's historic riverside Gold Tower was the starting and ending point for all shipping to the New World. It's named for the golden tiles that once covered it—not for all the New World booty that landed here. Ever since the Moors built it in the 13th century, it's been part of the city's fortifications, and long anchored a heavy chain that draped from here across the river to protect the harbor. Today, it houses a skippable, dreary naval museum with a mediocre river view.

NORTH OF THE CATHEDRAL
Plaza Nueva

This pleasant "New Square" is marked by a statue of King Ferdinand III, who liberated Sevilla from the Moors in the 13th century and was later sainted. For centuries afterward, a huge Franciscan monastery stood on this site; it was a spiritual home to many of the missionaries who colonized the California coast. (It was destroyed in 1840, following the disbanding of the monastic system under a government keen to take back power from the Church.) Today it's the end of the line for Sevilla's short tram system (which zips down Avenida de la Constitución to the San Bernardo train station).

Running along the city-center side of the square is the relatively modern **City Hall.** Couples use the grand salon upstairs for weekend weddings, then join their photographers on the front steps. For a more interesting look at this building, circle around to the other end (on the smaller square, called Plaza de San Francisco), where you can see how the structure has expanded right along with the city it governs: architectural styles evolve, from left to right, along the facade. The newest part of the facade, on the right, is more or less undecorated—a blank canvas for future artists to leave their mark. This square has been used for executions, bullfights, and (today) big city events.

▲Church of the Savior (Iglesia del Salvador)

Sevilla's second-biggest church, built on the site of a ninth-century mosque, gleams with freshly scrubbed Baroque pride. While the larger cathedral is a jumble of styles, this church is uniformly Andalusian Baroque—the architecture, decor, and statues are all from the same period. The church is home to some of the most beloved statues that parade through town during religious festivals.

Cost and Hours: €4, covered by cathedral combo-ticket (also sold here, with shorter lines), Mon-Sat 11:00-18:00, Sun 15:00-19:00, shorter hours in summer, audioguide-€2.50, Plaza del Salvador, tel. 954-211-679, www.iglesiadelsalvador.es.

Visiting the Church: If you've already bought the combo-ticket at the cathedral, walk through the exit, where a guard will let you skip the line.

The church's 14 richly decorated chapels and main altar, many from the 18th century, are its highlight. Start at the **high altar,** with the whirling pair of angels holding lamps with red ropes. Then look high above to see frescoes that, once long forgotten, were revealed by a recent cleaning. If you visit just before Holy Week (Semana Santa), you could see floats being assembled in the main nave and getting their silver polished.

In the right transept stands another venerable Mary; this one is **Our Lady of the Waters,** who predates this church by about 400 years. Though permanently parked now, for centuries she was paraded through Sevilla in times of drought.

In the left transept is the chapel with one of the city's most beloved statues (visible through the bars): the gripping **Christ of the Passion,** who is carrying the cross to his death (from 1619, by Juan Martínez Montañés). The statue is so revered by pilgrims and worshippers that the chapel has its own separate entrance (access through the courtyard, free, daily 10:00-14:00 & 17:00-21:00). For centuries the faithful have come here to pray, marvel at the sadness that fills the chapel, then kiss Jesus' heel (to join them, head up the stairs behind the altar). Jesus is flanked by a red-eyed John the Evangelist and a grieving María Dolorosa, with convincing tears and a literal dagger in her heart. Under the chapel's main altar, notice the skulls of two Jesuit missionaries who were martyred in Japan. In the adjacent shop, a wall tile shows the statue in a circa-1620 procession.

In the **courtyard,** you can feel the presence of the mosque that once stood on this spot. Its minaret is now the bell tower, and the mosque's arches are now halfway underground. What's left of the structure functions today as part of the church's crypt.

Nearby: Finish your visit by enjoying **Plaza del Salvador,** a favorite local meeting point. Strolling this square, you become part of the theater of life in Sevilla.

Casa de Pilatos

This 16th-century palace offers a scaled-down version of the royal Alcázar (with a similar mix of Gothic, Moorish, and Renaissance styles) and a delightful garden. The nobleman who built it was inspired by a visit to the Holy Land, where he saw the supposed mansion of Pontius Pilate. If you've seen the Alcázar, this might not be worth the time or money. Your visit comes in two parts: the stark ground floor and garden (a tile lover's fantasy, with good audioguide); and a plodding, 25-minute guided tour of the lived-in noble residence upstairs (English/Spanish spiel, 2/hour, check schedule at entry).

Cost and Hours: €10 includes entire house, audioguide, and guided tour; €8 covers just the ground floor and garden; daily 9:00-19:00, off-season until 18:00; Plaza de Pilatos 1, www.fundacionmedinaceli.org.

▲Museo Palacio de la Condesa de Lebrija

This aristocratic mansion takes you back to the 18th century like no other place in town. The Countess of Lebrija was a passionate collector of antiquities. Her home's ground floor is paved with Roman mosaics (which you can actually walk on) and lined with musty old cases of Phoenician, Greek, Roman, and Moorish artifacts—mostly pottery. The grand staircase and dining-room tiles came from a former Augustinian convent, and several rooms were even modified to fit the collectibles the countess bought (a good example is the octagonal room built to house an eight-sided Roman floor mosaic). To see a plush world from a time when the nobility had a private priest and their own chapel, take a quickie tour of the upstairs, which shows the palace as the countess left it when she died in 1938.

Cost and Hours: €5 for unescorted visit of ground floor (good English descriptions), €8 includes English/Spanish tour of "lived-in" upstairs offered every 45 minutes; July-Aug Mon-Fri 10:00-15:00, Sat until 14:00, closed Sun; Sept-June Mon-Fri 10:30-19:30, Sat 10:00-14:00 & 16:00-18:00, Sun 10:00-14:00; free and obligatory bag check, Calle Cuna 8, tel. 954-227-802, www.palaciodelebrija.com.

Plaza de la Encarnación

Several years ago, in an attempt to revitalize this formerly nondescript square, the city unveiled what locals call "the mushrooms": a gigantic, undulating canopy of five waffle-patterned, toadstool-esque, hundred-foot-tall wooden structures. Together, this struc-

ture (officially named *Metropol Parasol*) provides shade, a gazebo for performances, and a traditional market hall. While the market is busy each morning, locals don't know what to make of the avant-garde structure. A ramp under the canopy leads down to ancient-Roman-era street level, where a museum displays Roman ruins found during the building process. From the museum level, a €3 elevator takes you up top, where you can do a loop walk along the terrace to enjoy its commanding city views. It feels like walking on a roller-coaster track. I found it not worth the time or trouble. Other views in town are free, more central, and just as good (such as from the rooftop bar of the EME Catedral Hotel, across the street from the cathedral).

Cost and Hours: Plaza level always open and free; €3 viewpoint elevator ride includes beverage at the top and runs daily 10:00-23:30, shorter hours off-season; www.setasdesevilla.com.

▲Flamenco Dance Museum (Museo del Baile Flamenco)

Though small and pricey, this museum is worthwhile for anyone looking to understand more about the dance that embodies the spirit of southern Spain.

The main exhibition, on floor 1, takes about 45 minutes to see. It features well-produced videos, flamenco costumes, and other artifacts collected by the grande dame of flamenco, Christina Hoyos, including a collection of posters celebrating notable flamenco artists of yore (be sure to stand directly under the "sound showers"). The top floor and basement house temporary exhibits, mostly of photography and other artwork. On the ground floor and in the basement, you can watch flamenco lessons in progress—or even take one yourself (one hour, first person-€60, €20/person after that, shoes not provided).

Cost and Hours: €10, €24 combo-ticket includes evening concert, daily 10:00-19:00, pick up English booklet at front desk; hard to find—follow signs for *Museo del Baile Flamenco*, about 3 blocks east of Plaza Nueva at Calle Manuel Rojas Marcos 3; tel. 954-340-311, www.museoflamenco.com.

Performances: Live flamenco performances take place here nightly after the museum closes.

▲Museo de Bellas Artes

Sevilla's passion for religious art is preserved and displayed in its Museum of Fine Arts. While most Americans go for El Greco, Goya, and Velázquez (not a forte of this collection), this museum opens horizons and gives a fine look at other, less well-known

Spanish masters: Zurbarán and Murillo. Rather than exhausting, the museum is pleasantly enjoyable.

Cost and Hours: €1.50, mid-June–mid-Sept Tue-Sun 9:00-15:00; mid-Sept–mid-June Tue-Sat 9:00-20:00, Sun until 15:00; closed Mon year-round, tel. 955-542-942, www. museosdeandalucia.es.

Getting There: The museum is at Plaza Museo 9, a 15-minute walk from the cathedral, or a short ride on bus #C5 from Plaza Nueva. If coming from the Basílica de la Macarena, take bus #C4 to the Plaza de Armas bus station stop and walk inland four blocks.

Background: Sevilla was once Spain's wealthy commercial capital (like New York City) at a time when Madrid was a newly built center of government (like Washington, D.C.). Spain's economic Golden Age (the 1500s) blossomed into the Golden Age of Spanish painting (the 1600s), especially in Sevilla. Several of Spain's top painters—Zurbarán, Murillo, and Velázquez—lived here in the 1600s. Like their contemporaries, they labored to make the spiritual world tangible, and forged the gritty realism that marks Spanish painting. You'll see balding saints and monks with wrinkled faces and sunburned hands. The style suited Spain's spiritual climate, as the Catholic Church used this art in its Counter-Reformation battle against the Protestant rebellion.

In the early 1800s, Spain's government, in a push to take some power from the Church, began disbanding convents and monasteries. Secular fanatics had a heyday looting churches, but fortunately, much of Andalucía's religious art was rescued and hung safely here in this convent-turned-museum.

❍ Self-Guided Tour: The permanent collection features 20 rooms in neat chronological order. It's easy to breeze through once with my tour, then backtrack to what appeals to you. Pick up the English-language floor plan, which explains the theme of each room.

• *Enter and follow signs to the permanent collection, which begins in Sala I (Room 1).*

Rooms 1-4: Medieval altarpieces of gold-backed saints, Virgin-and-babes, and Crucifixion scenes attest to the religiosity that nurtured Spain's early art. Spain's penchant for unflinching realism culminates in Room 2 with Michaelangelo friend/rival Pietro Torrigiano's 1525 statue of an emaciated San Jerónimo, whose gaze never falters from the cross, and in Room 3 with the painted clay head of St. John the Baptist—complete with severed neck muscles, throat, and windpipe. This kind of warts-and-all naturalism would influence the great Sevillian painter Velázquez (two of his works are displayed in Room 4).

• *Continue through the pleasant outdoor courtyard to the grand, former church that is now Room 5.*

Room 5: *The Apotheosis of St. Thomas Aquinas* (*Apoteosis de Santo Tomás de Aquino,* 1631) by **Francisco de Zurbarán** (thoor-bar-AHN, 1598-1664) is considered to be the artist's most important work (at center-left as you look at the dome in this room). It was done at the height of his career, when stark realism was all the rage. In a believable, down-to-earth way, Zurbarán presents the pivotal moment when the great saint-theologian experiences his spiritual awakening. We'll see more of Zurbarán upstairs in Room 10.

An entire wall where the altar used to be shows off the works of another hometown boy, **Bartolomé Murillo** (1617-1682). His

signature subject is the Immaculate Conception, the doctrine that holds that Mary was exempt from original sin. Several *Inmaculadas* may be on display. Typically, Mary is depicted as young, dressed in white and blue, standing atop the moon (crescent or full). She clutches her breast and gazes up rapturously, surrounded by tumbling winged babies. Murillo's tiny *Madonna and Child* (*Virgen de la Servilleta,* 1665; at the end of the room in the center) shows the warmth and appeal of his work.

Murillo's sweetness is quite different from the harsh realism of his fellow artists, so his work was understandably popular. For many Spaniards, Mary is their main connection to heaven. They pray directly to her, asking her to intercede on their behalf with God. Murillo's Marys are always receptive and ready to help.

Besides his *Inmaculadas,* Murillo painted popular saints. They often carry sprigs of plants, and cock their heads upward, caught up in a heavenly vision of sweet Baby Jesus. Murillo is also known for his "genre" paintings—scenes of common folk and rascally street urchins—but the museum has few of these.

• *Now head back outside to enjoy the coolness of the cloister and the beauty of its tiles, then go up the Imperial Staircase to the first floor.*

Rooms 6-9: In Rooms 6 and 7, you'll see more Murillos and Murillo imitators. Room 8 is dedicated to yet another native Sevillian (and friend of Murillo), Juan de Valdés Leal (1622-1690). He adds Baroque motion and drama to religious subjects. His surreal colors and feverish, unfinished style create a mood of urgency.

Room 10: Here you'll find more Zurbarán saints and monks, and the miraculous things they experienced, with an unblinking, crystal-clear, brightly lit, highly detailed realism. Monks and nuns could meditate upon Zurbarán's meticulous paintings for hours, finding God in the details.

In Zurbarán's *St. Hugo Visiting the Refectory (San Hugo en el Refectorio)*, white-robed Carthusian monks gather together for their

simple meal in a communal dining hall. Above them hangs a painting of Mary, Baby Jesus, and John the Baptist. Zurbarán created paintings for monks' dining halls like this. His audience: celibate men and women who lived in isolation, as in this former convent, devoting their time to quiet meditation, prayer, and Bible study. Zurbarán shines a harsh spotlight on many of his subjects, creating strong shadows. Zurbarán's people often stand starkly isolated against a single-color background—a dark room or the gray-white of a cloudy sky. He was the ideal painter for the austere religion of 17th-century Spain.

Adjacent to *St. Hugo*, find *The Virgin of the Caves (La Virgen de las Cuevas)* and study the piety and faith in the monks' weathered faces. Zurbarán's Mary is protective, with her hands placed on the heads of two monks. Note the loving detail on the cape embroidery, the brooch, and the flowers at her feet.

The Rest of the Museum: Spain's subsequent art, from the 18th century on, generally followed the trends of the rest of Europe. Room 12 has creamy Romanticism and hazy Impressionism. You'll see typical Sevillian motifs such as matadors, cigar-factory girls, and river landscapes. Of particular interest is *Death of the Master* by José Villegas Cordero, in which bullfighters touchingly express their grief after their teacher, gored in the ring, dies in bed. Enjoy these painted slices of Sevilla, then exit to experience similar scenes today.

FAR NORTH OF THE CATHEDRAL
▲▲Basílica de la Macarena

Sevilla's Holy Week celebrations are Spain's grandest. During the week leading up to Easter, the city is packed with pilgrims witnessing 60 processions carrying about 100 religious floats. If you miss the actual event, you can get a sense of it by visiting the Basílica de la Macarena and its accompanying museum to see the two most impressive floats and the darling of Semana Santa, the statue of the Virgen de la Macarena. Although far from the city center, it's located on Sevilla's ring road and easy to reach. (While La Macarena is the big kahuna, for a more central look at beloved procession statues, consider stopping by the Church of the Savior, described earlier, or Triana's Church of Santa Ana, described later.)

Cost and Hours: Church-free, treasury museum-€5; church daily 9:00-13:30 & 17:00-20:30, treasury museum closes 30 minutes earlier; audioguide-€1. The museum closes a few weeks before Holy Week for float preparation.

Getting There: Wave down a taxi and say "Basílica Macarena" (about €6 from the city center). Buses #C1 through #C5 go there, but the quickest ride is on circular routes #C3 and #C4 from Puerta de Jerez (near the Torre de Oro) or Avenida de Menéndez Pelayo (the ring road east of the cathedral), tel. 954-901-800, www.hermandaddelamacarena.es.

☉ Self-Guided Tour: Despite the long history of the Macarena statue, the Neo-Baroque church was only built in 1949 to give the oft-moved sculpture a permanent home.

• *Grab a pew and study the...*

Weeping Virgin: La Macarena is known as the "Weeping Virgin" for the five crystal teardrops trickling down her cheeks. She's like a Baroque doll with human hair and articulated arms, and is even dressed in underclothes. Sculpted in the late 17th century (probably by Pedro Roldán), she's become Sevilla's most popular image of Mary.

Her beautiful expression—halfway between smiling and crying—is ambiguous, letting worshippers project their own emotions onto her. Her weeping can be contagious—look around you. She's also known as La Esperanza, the Virgin of Hope, and she promises better times after the sorrow.

Installed in the left side chapel is the **Christ of the Judgment** (from 1654), showing Jesus on the day he was condemned. This statue and La Macarena stand atop the two most important floats of the Holy Week parades. The side chapel on the right has an equally remarkable image of the **Virgen del Rosario** that's paraded around the city on the last Sunday of October.

• *To see the floats and learn more, visit the treasury museum. (The museum entrance is on the church's left side; to reach it, either exit the church or go through a connecting door at the rear of the church.)*

Tesoro (Treasury Museum): This small, three-floor museum tells the history of the Virgin statue and the Holy Week parades. Though rooted in medieval times, the current traditions developed around 1600, with the formation of various fraternities *(herman-dades)*. During Holy Week, they demonstrate their dedication to God by parading themed floats throughout Sevilla to retell the story of the Crucifixion and Resurrection of Christ. The museum displays ceremonial banners, scepters, and costumed mannequins; videos show the parades in action (some displays in English).

The three-ton float that carries the Christ of the Judgment is slathered in gold leaf and shows a commotion of figures acting out the sentencing of Jesus. (The statue of Christ—the one you saw in the church—is placed before this crowd for the Holy Week proces-sion.) Pontius Pilate is about to wash his hands. Pilate's wife cries as a man reads the death sentence. During the Holy Week procession, pious Sevillian women wail in the streets while relays of 48 men carry this float on the backs of their necks—only their feet showing under the drapes—as they shuffle through the streets from mid-night until 14:00 in the afternoon every Good Friday. The men rehearse for months to get their choreographed footwork in sync.

La Macarena follows the Christ of the Judgment in the pro-cession. Mary's smaller 1.5-ton float seems all silver and candles—"strong enough to support the roof, but tender enough to quiver in the soft night breeze." Mary has a wardrobe of three huge mantles, worn in successive years; these are about 100 years old, as is her six-pound gold crown/halo. This float has a mesmerizing effect on the crowds. They line up for hours, then clap, weep, and throw roses as it slowly sways along the streets, working its way through town. A Sevillian friend once explained, "She knows all the problems of Sevilla and its people; we've been confiding in her for centuries. To us, she is hope."

The museum collection also contains some matador parapher-nalia. La Macarena is the patron saint of bullfighters, and they give thanks for her protection. Copies of her image are popular in bullring chapels. In 1912, bullfighter José Ortega, hoping for protection, gave La Macarena the five emerald brooches she wears. It worked for eight years...until he was gored to death in the ring. For a month, La Macarena was dressed in widow's black—the only time that has happened.

Macarena Neighborhood: Outside the church, notice the best surviving bit of Sevilla's old walls. Originally Roman, what remains today was built by the Moors in the 12th century to (un-successfully) keep the Christians out. And yes, it's from this city that a local dance band (Los del Río) changed the world by giving us the popular 1990s song, "The Macarena." He-e-y-y, Macarena!

SOUTH OF THE CATHEDRAL
University
Today's university was yesterday's *fábrica de tabacos* (tobacco factory), which employed 10,000 young female *cigareras*—including the saucy femme fatale of Bizet's opera *Carmen*. In the 18th century, it was the second-largest building in Spain, after El Escorial. Skip the free, one-hour audioguide, and instead, wander through its halls on your way to Plaza de España, especially during a school day. The university's bustling café is a good place for cheap tapas, beer, wine, and conversation (Mon-Fri 8:00-20:00, Sat 9:00-13:00, closed Sun).

Plaza de España
This square, the surrounding buildings, and the adjacent María Luisa Park are the remains of the 1929 international fair, where

for a year the Spanish-speaking countries of the world enjoyed a mutual-admiration fiesta. With the restoration work here finished, this delightful area—the epitome of world's-fair-style architecture—is once again great for people-watching (especially during the 19:00-20:00 peak paseo hour). The park's highlight is this former Spanish Pavilion. Its tiles—a trademark of Sevilla—show historic scenes and maps from every province of Spain (arranged in alphabetical order, from Álava to Zaragoza). Climb to one of the balconies for a classic postcard view of Sevilla.

▲▲TRIANA, WEST OF THE RIVER
In Sevilla—as is true in so many other European cities that grew up in the age of river traffic—what was long considered the "wrong side of the river" is now the most colorful part of town. Sevilla's Triana is a proud neighborhood that identifies with its working-class origins and is famed for its flamenco soul (characterized by the statue that greets arrivals from across the river). Known for their independent spirit, locals describe crossing the bridge toward the city center as "going to Sevilla."

Visiting Triana: From downtown Sevilla, head to the river and cross over Puente de Isabel II to enter Triana. Note the bridge's distinctive design as you approach. It was inspired by an 1834 crossing over the Seine River in Paris—look for the circles under each span that lead the way into Triana.

While crossing the Guadalquivir River, to the right you can see Sevilla's single skyscraper—designed by Argentine architect César Pelli of Malaysia's Twin Towers fame. Locals lament the

Torre Sevilla because according to city law, no structure should be taller than the Giralda bell tower. But since this building doesn't sit within the city center, developers found a way to avoid that regulation. A bank and office building, the high-rise will also house a 159-room hotel in the near future. Surrounding the skyscraper are leftover buildings from the 1992 Expo.

The **Capilla del Carmen** sits at the end of the bridge. Designed by Expo '29 architect Aníbal González, the bell tower and chapel add glamour to the entrance to Triana. Inside the chapel is an image of Sevilla's patron saints, Justa and Rufina.

Just off the bridge and down the staircase is the **Castillo de San Jorge,** a 12th-century castle that in the 15th century was the headquarters for Sevilla's Inquisition (free small museum and TI kiosk). Explore the castle briefly, then retrace your steps to visit the neighborhood's covered **market.** Built in 2005 in the Moorish Revival style, it sits within the ruins of the castle (the remains of which you can see as you exit at the other side). The market bustles in the mornings and afternoons with traditional fruit and vegetable stalls as well as colorful tapas bars and cafés. This is a great spot to stop for coffee, watch produce being sold, and see locals catching up on the latest gossip.

Exit the market downstairs and left to discover the district's **ceramic history.** Do your best to ignore the shops and enter the **Museo de la Cerámica de Triana,** which focuses on tile and pottery production. Located in the remains of a former riverside factory, the museum explains the entire process—from selecting the right type of earth to kiln firing—with a small collection of ceramics and well-produced videos of interviews with former workers (good English translations). Another short video highlights Triana's neighborhood pride (€2.10, free with Alcázar ticket, Tue-Sat 11:00-17:30, Sun 10:00-14:30, closed Mon, Calle Antillano Campos 14, tel. 954-342-737).

After your visit to the museum, ponder what you can carry home from nearby shops. Walk along Calle Antillano Campos, then turn left on Calle Alfarería. This area is lined with the old facades of ceramic workshops that once populated this quarter. Most have either closed up or moved to the outskirts of town, where rent is cheaper. But a few stalwarts remain, including the lavishly decorated Santa Ana and the large showroom Santa Isabel (at Calle Alfarería 12). Several recommended bars are in this area (see "Eating in Sevilla," later).

You exit onto **Calle San Jacinto,** which is free from car traffic. It's the hip center of the people scene—a festival of life each evening. Venturing down side lanes, you find classic 19th-century facades with fine ironwork and colorful tiles.

Return down San Jacinto in the direction of the bridge. The

final cross-street, Calle Pureza, cuts (left) through the historic center of Triana. As you wander, pop into bars and notice how the decor mixes bullfighting lore with Virgin worship. It's easy enough to follow your nose into **Dulceria Manu Jara,** at Calle Pureza 5, where tempting artisan pastries are made on the spot.

Keep your eyes peeled for *abacerías,* traditional neighborhood grocers that also function as neighborhood bars (such as La Antigua Abacería, at Calle Pureza 12).

Stop at the **Church of Santa Ana,** nicknamed "the Cathedral of Triana." It's the home of the beloved Virgin statue called Nuestra Señora de la Esperanza de Triana (Our Lady of Hope of Triana). She's a big deal here—in Sevilla, upon meeting someone, it's customary to ask not only which football team they support, but which Virgin Mary they favor. The top two in town are the Virgen de la Macarena and La Esperanza de Triana. On the Thursday of Holy Week, it's a battle royale of the Madonnas, as Sevilla's two favorite Virgins are both in processions on the streets at the same time.

Continue down Calle Pureza until it intersects Calle Bernardo Guerra and Calle Duarte, then head toward the river. Peer into the traditional bars along Calle Betis, where local university students take advantage of affordable happy hours. (Don't be tempted to walk down to the riverside...the boardwalk leads to a dead-end.) Continue past some of my recommended restaurants to the Puente de San Telmo. You'll see the Torre del Oro across the river and end your Triana walk not far from the cathedral and the Alcázar. (The Metro stop at Plaza de Cuba is nearby, or you can catch bus #C3 toward the city center.)

NEAR SEVILLA
Itálica

One of Spain's most impressive Roman ruins is found outside the sleepy town of Santiponce, about six miles northwest of Sevilla. Founded in 206 B.C. for wounded soldiers recuperating from the Second Punic War, Itálica became a thriving town of great agricultural and military importance. It was the birthplace of the famous Roman emperors Trajan and Hadrian. Today its best-preserved ruin is its amphitheater—one of the largest in the Roman Empire—with a capacity for 30,000 spectators. Other highlights include beautiful floor mosaics, such as the one in Casa de los Pájaros (House of the Birds), with representations of more than 30 species of birds. In summer, plan your visit to avoid the midday heat—arrive either early or late in the day, and definitely bring water.

Cost and Hours: €1.50; Tue-Sun 9:00-15:00 (April-mid-June until 20:00 Tue-Sat), shorter hours off-season, closed Mon; tel. 955-123-847, www.museosdeandalucia.es.

Getting There: You can get to Itálica on bus #M-172A or

#M-172B from Sevilla's Plaza de Armas station (30-minute trip, 2/hour Mon-Sat, hourly on Sun). If you're driving, head west out of Sevilla in the direction of Huelva; after you cross the second branch of the river, turn north on SE-30, exit on to N-630, and after a few miles, get off at Santiponce. Drive past pottery warehouses and through the town to the ruins at the far (west) end.

Experiences in Sevilla

▲Bullfights

Some of Spain's most intense bullfighting happens in Sevilla's 14,000-seat bullring, Plaza de Toros. Fights are held (generally at 18:30) on most Sundays in May and June; on Easter and Corpus Christi; daily during the April Fair; and at the end of September (during the Feria de San Miguel). These serious fights, with adult matadors, are called *corrida de toros* and often sell out in advance. On many Thursday evenings in July, the *novillada* fights take place, with teenage novices doing the killing and smaller bulls doing the dying. *Corrida de toros* seats range from €25 for high seats looking into the sun to €150 for the first three rows in the shade under the royal box; *novillada* seats are half that—and easy to buy at the arena a few minutes before showtime (ignore scalpers outside; get information at a TI, your hotel, by phone, or online; tel. 954-501-382, www.plazadetorosdelamaestranza.com).

▲▲Bullring (Plaza de Toros) and Bullfight Museum (Museo Taurino)

Follow a bilingual (Spanish and English) 40-minute guided tour through the bullring's strangely quiet and empty arena, its museum, and the chapel where the matador prays before the fight. (Thanks to readily available blood transfusions, there have been no deaths in three decades.) The two most revered figures of Sevilla, the Virgen de la Macarena and the Jesús del Gran Poder (Christ of All Power), are represented in the chapel. In the museum, you'll see great classic scenes and the heads of a few bulls—awarded the bovine equivalent of an Oscar for a particularly good fight. The city was so appalled when the famous matador Manolete was killed in 1947 that even the mother of the bull that gored him was destroyed. Matadors—dressed to kill—are heartthrobs in their "suits of light." Many girls have their bedrooms wallpapered with posters of cute bullfighters.

Cost and Hours: €8, entrance with escorted tour only—no free time inside; 3/hour, daily 9:30-21:00, Nov-March until 19:00;

until 15:00 on fight days, when chapel and horse room are closed. While they take groups of up to 50, it's still wise to call or drop by to reserve a spot in the busy season (tel. 954-210-315, www. realmaestranza.com).

April Fair

Two weeks after Easter, much of Sevilla packs into its vast fairgrounds for a grand party (April 15-22 in 2018). The fair, seeming to bring all that's Andalusian together, feels friendly, spontaneous, and very real. The passion for horses, flamenco, and sherry is clear—riders are ramrod straight, colorfully clad girls ride sidesaddle, and everyone's drinking sherry spritzers. Women sport outlandish dresses that would look clownish elsewhere, but are somehow brilliant here en masse. Horses clog the streets in an endless parade until about 20:00, when they clear out and the streets fill with exuberant locals. The party goes on literally 24 hours a day.

Countless private party tents, called *casetas,* line the lanes. Each tent is the private party zone of a family, club, or association. You need to know someone in the group—or make friends quickly—to get in. Because of the exclusivity, it has a real family-affair feeling. In each *caseta,* everyone knows everyone. It seems like a thousand wedding parties being celebrated at the same time.

Any tourist can have a fun and memorable evening by simply crashing the party. The city's entire fleet of taxis (who can legally charge double) and buses seems dedicated to shuttling people from downtown to the fairgrounds. Given the traffic jams and inflated prices, you may be better off hiking: From the Torre del Oro, cross the San Telmo Bridge to Plaza de Cuba and hike down Calle Asunción. You'll see the towering gate to the fairgrounds in the distance. Just follow the crowds (there's no admission charge). Arrive before 20:00 to see the horses, but stay later, as the ambience improves after the *caballos* giddy-up on out. Some of the larger tents are sponsored by the city and open to the public, but the best action is in the streets, where party-goers from the livelier *casetas* spill out. Although private tents have bouncers, everyone is so happy that it's not tough to strike up an impromptu friendship, become a "special guest," and be invited in. The drink flows freely, and the food is fun and cheap.

Flamenco Classes

Energetic performances often leave people wanting more, so Concepción at Sevilla Walking Tours (described earlier, under "Tours in Sevilla") has teamed up with local experts to offer two ways to immerse yourself in flamenco culture.

Rhythm and Palmas introduces you to the origins of flamenco and its different styles *(palos)*. Learn to clap properly—technique is everything—in order to accompany flamenco music and song. Once you've got the beat down, you'll get more out of any show (Mon, Wed, and Fri at 16:00 and 17:45). **Flamenco Dance** is geared toward even the most beginning dancers, either women or men. If flamenco captivates you with its passion and tension, learn some of the basic movements to express those feelings. After basic foot and leg work, instructors will guide you through a unique routine—olé! (Mon, Wed, and Fri at 16:45 and 18:30). Reservations (required) for these 45-minute classes can be made online or by phone (€18 each, €34 for both, tel. 902-158-226, mobile 616-501-100, www.sevillawalkingtours.com).

Shopping in Sevilla

For the best local shopping experience in Sevilla, visit the popular pedestrian streets Sierpes and Tetuán/Velázquez. They, and the surrounding lanes near Plaza Nueva, are packed with people and shops. Popular souvenir items include ladies' fans, shawls, *mantillas* (ornate head scarves), other items related to flamenco (castanets, guitars, costumes), ceramics, and bullfighting posters.

Clothing and shoe stores stay open all day. Other shops generally take a siesta, closing between 13:30 and 16:00 or 17:00 on weekdays, as well as on Saturday afternoons and all day Sunday. Big department stores such as **El Corte Inglés** stay open (and air-conditioned) right through the siesta. El Corte Inglés also has a supermarket downstairs, a pricey cafeteria, and the Gourmet Experience food court on the fifth floor, with several international options and a view terrace (Mon-Sat 10:00-22:00, closed Sun).

Collectors' markets hop on Sunday: stamps and coins at Plaza del Cabildo (near the cathedral) and art on Plaza del Museo (by the Museo de Bellas Artes). The El Postigo **arts and crafts market,** in an architecturally interesting old building behind the Hospital de la Caridad, features artisan wares of all types (Mon-Sat 11:00-

14:00 & 16:00-20:00, Sun 16:00-20:00, at the corner of Calles de Arfe and Dos de Mayo, tel. 954-560-013).

Mercado del Arenal, the covered fish-and-produce market, is perfect for hungry photographers (Mon-Sat 9:00-14:30, closed Sun, least lively on Mon, on Calle Pastor y Landero at Calle Arenal, just beyond bullring).

▲▲Shopping Paseo

Although many tourists never get beyond the cathedral and Barrio Santa Cruz, the lively pedestrianized shopping area north of the cathedral is well worth a wander. The best shopping streets—Calle Tetuán, Calle Sierpes, and Calle Cuna—also happen to be part of the oldest section of Sevilla. A walk here is a chance to join one of Spain's liveliest paseos—that bustling celebration of life that takes place before dinner each evening, when everyone is out strolling, showing off their fancy shoes and checking out everyone else's. This walk, if done between 18:00 and 20:00, gives you a chance to experience the paseo scene while getting a look at the town's most popular shops. You'll pass windows displaying the best in both traditional and trendy fashion.

Start on the pedestrianized **Plaza Nueva**—the 19th-century square facing the ornate City Hall—which features a statue of Ferdinand III, a local favorite because he freed Sevilla from the Moors in 1248.

From here wander the length of **Calle Tetuán,** where old-time standbys bump up against fashion-right boutiques. **Juan Foronda** (#28) has been selling flamenco attire and *mantillas* since 1926. A few doors down, you'll find the flagship store of **Camper** (#24), the proudly Spanish shoe brand that's become a worldwide favorite. The rest of the street showcases mainly Spanish brands, such as Massimo Dutti, Zara, and Mango. Calle Tetuán (which becomes Calle Velázquez) ends at La Campana, a big intersection and popular meeting point, with the super department store, El Corte Inglés, just beyond, on Plaza del Duque de la Victoria. Keep your eyes peeled for ads made from *azulejos*—tile panels—to entice shoppers from an earlier era.

Turn right at the end of the street. At the corner of Calle Sierpes awaits a venerable pastry shop, **Confitería La Campana,** with a fine 1885 interior...and Sevilla's most tempting sweets (take a break at the outdoor tables, or head to the back of the shop, where you can grab a coffee and pastry at the stand-up bar).

Now head down **Calle Sierpes.** This is a great street for strolling, despite some signs of "*la crisis económica*"—empty storefronts. But there's nothing empty about the clock-covered, wood-paneled **El Cronómetro** shop (#19), where master watchmakers have been doing business since 1901. If you've got a problem with your Rolex, drop in—they're an official retailer of all the luxury brands. Otherwise, take a minute to set your watch by their precisely set display clocks. **Sombrereria Maquedano** (#40, at the corner of Calle Rioja) is a styling place for hats—especially for men. They claim to be the oldest hat seller in Sevilla, and maybe in all of Spain. Check out the great selection of wide-brimmed horse-rider hats, perfect for the April Fair.

At the corner of Sierpes and Jovellanos/Sagasta, you'll find several fine shops featuring Andalusian accessories. Drop in to see how serious local women are about their fans, shawls, *mantillas,* and *peinetas* (combs designed to secure and prop up the *mantilla*). The most valuable *mantillas* are silk, and the top-quality combs are made of tortoiseshell (though most women opt for much more affordable polyester and plastic). Andalusian women accessorize with fans, matching them to different dresses. The *mantilla* comes in black (worn only on Holy Thursday and by the mother of the groom at weddings) and white (worn at bullfights during the April Fair).

From here turn left down **Calle Sagasta.** Notice that the street has two names—the modern version and a medieval one: Antigua Calle de Gallegos ("Former Street of the Galicians"). With the Christian victory in 1248, the Muslims were given one month to evacuate. To consolidate Christian control during that time, settlers from Galicia, the northwest corner of Iberia, were planted here; this street was the center of their neighborhood.

Just before you hit the charming **Plaza del Salvador,** stop for a peek into the windows at **BuBi** (#6). This *boutique infantil* displays pricey but exquisitely made baby clothes—knit, embroidered, starched, and beribboned. Tiny crocheted booties are just affordable (€20). Now jump in to Plaza del Salvador—it's teeming with life at the foot of the Church of the Savior.

Backtrack left along **Calle Cuna,** famous for its exuberant flamenco dresses and classic wedding dresses. Local women save up to have flamenco dresses custom-made for the April Fair: They're considered an important status symbol. If all this shopping wasn't enough to make you feel like a countess, follow Calle Cuna to the Museo Palacio de la Condesa de Lebrija. Nearby is the mod, mushroom-shaped structure that towers over **Plaza de la Encarnación.**

Nightlife in Sevilla

▲▲▲FLAMENCO

This music-and-dance art form has its roots in the Roma (Gypsy) and Moorish cultures. Even at a packaged "flamenco evening," sparks fly. The men do most of the flamboyant machine-gun footwork. The women often concentrate on the graceful turns and smooth, shuffling step of the *soleá* version of the dance. Watch the musicians. Flamenco guitarists, with their lightning-fast finger-roll

strums, are among the best in the world. The intricate rhythms are set by castanets or the hand-clapping (called *palmas*) of those who aren't dancing at the moment. In the raspy-voiced wails of the singers, you'll hear echoes of the Muslim call to prayer.

Like jazz, flamenco thrives on improvisation. Also like jazz, good flamenco is more than just technical proficiency. A singer or dancer with "soul" is said to have *duende*. Flamenco is a happening, with bystanders clapping along and egging on the dancers with whoops and shouts. Get into it.

Hotels push tourist-oriented, nightclub-style flamenco shows, but they charge a commission. Fortunately, it's easy to book a place on your own.

Sevilla's flamenco offerings tend to fall into one of three categories: serious concerts (usually about €18 and about an hour long), where the singing and dancing take center stage; touristy dinner-and-drinks shows with table service (generally around €35—not including food—and two hours long); and—the least touristy option—casual bars with late-night performances, where for the cost of a drink you can catch impromptu (or semi-impromptu) musicians at play. Here's the rundown for each type of performance.

Serious Flamenco Concerts

While it's hard to choose among these three nightly, one-hour flamenco concerts, I'd say enjoying one is a must during your Sevilla visit. To the novice viewer, each company offers equal quality. They cost about the same, and each venue is small, intimate, and air-conditioned. For many, the concerts are preferable to the shows (listed next) because they're half the cost, length, and size (smaller audience), and generally start earlier in the evening.

My recommended concerts are careful to give you a good overview of the art form, covering all the flamenco bases. At each venue you can reserve by phone and pay upon arrival, or drop by early to pick up a ticket. While La Casa del Flamenco is the nicest and most central venue, the other two have exhibits that can add to the experience.

La Casa de la Memoria is a wide venue (just two rows deep), where everyone gets a close-up view and room to stretch out (€18, nightly at 19:30 and 21:00, no drinks, no children under age 6, 100 seats, Calle Cuna 6, tel. 954-560-670, www.casadelamemoria.es, flamencomemoria@gmail.com, run by Rosana). They also have an exhibit on one easy, well-described floor, with lots of photos and a few artifacts (free with concert ticket, open 10:30-14:00 & 17:00-19:00).

The **Flamenco Dance Museum,** while the most congested venue (with 115 tightly packed seats), has a bar and allows drinks, and you can visit the museum immediately before the show. It has festival seating—the doors open at 18:00, when you can grab the seat of your choice, then spend an hour touring the museum and enjoying a drink before the show (€20, nightly at 19:00 and 20:45, €24 combo-ticket includes the museum and a show, reservations smart, tel. 954-340-311, www.museoflamenco.com).

La Casa del Flamenco is in a delightful arcaded courtyard right in the Barrio Santa Cruz (€18, €2 discount for Rick Steves readers with this book who book directly and pay cash; shows nightly at 19:00 and 20:30 in April-May and Sept-Oct, one show rest of year, at 19:00 or 20:30—best to check their website for current times; no drinks, no kids under age 6, 60 spacious seats, reception at adjacent Hotel Alcántara serves as the box office, Calle Ximénez de Enciso 28, tel. 954-500-595, www.lacasadelflamencosevilla.com).

Razzle-Dazzle Flamenco Shows

These packaged shows can be a bit sterile—and an audience of tourists doesn't help—but I find both Los Gallos and El Arenal entertaining and riveting. While El Arenal may have a slight edge on talent, and certainly feels slicker, Los Gallos has a cozier setting, with cushy rather than hard chairs—and it's cheaper.

Los Gallos presents nightly two-hour shows at 20:30 and 22:30 (€35 ticket includes drink, €3/person discount with this book—limited to 2-3 people, arrive 30 minutes early for best seats, bar, no food served, Plaza de Santa Cruz 11, tel. 954-216-981, www.tablaolosgallos.com, owners José and Blanca promise goose bumps).

Tablao El Arenal has arguably more-professional performers and a classier setting for its show, but dinner customers get the preferred seating, and waiters are working throughout the performance (€38 ticket includes drink, €60 includes tapas, €72 includes dinner, 1.5-hour shows at 20:00 and 22:00, 30 minutes earlier off-season, near bullring at Calle Rodo 7, tel. 954-216-492, www.tablaoelarenal.com).

El Patio Sevillano is more of a variety show, with flamenco as well as other forms of song and dance. While hotels may recommend this, they're just working for kickbacks. I like the other two much better.

Impromptu Flamenco in Bars

Spirited flamenco singing still erupts spontaneously in bars throughout the old town after midnight—but you need to know where to look. Ask a local for the latest.

La Carbonería Bar, the sangria equivalent of a beer garden, is a few blocks north of the Barrio Santa Cruz. It's a big, open-tented area filled with young locals, casual guitar strummers, and nearly nightly flamenco music from about 22:30 to 24:00. Located just a few blocks from most of my recommended hotels, this is worth finding if you're not quite ready to end the day (no cover, daily 20:00-very late; near Plaza Santa María—find Hotel Fernando III, along the side alley Céspedes at #21; tel. 954-214-460).

While the days of Gypsies and flamenco throbbing throughout Triana are mostly long gone, a few bars still host live dancing; **Lo Nuestro** and **El Rejoneo** are favorites (at Calle Betis 31A and 31B).

OTHER NIGHTLIFE
▲▲Evening Paseo

Sevilla is meant for strolling. The paseo thrives every evening (except in winter) in these areas: along either side of the river between the San Telmo and Isabel II bridges (Paseo de Cristóbal Colón and Triana district), up Avenida de la Constitución, around Plaza Nueva, at Plaza de España, and throughout the Barrio Santa Cruz. The best paseo scene is about 18:00 to 20:00, but on hot summer nights, even families with toddlers are out and about past midnight. Spend some time rafting through this river of humanity.

Nighttime Views

Savor the view of floodlit Sevilla by night from the Triana side of the river—perhaps over dinner. For the best late-night drink with a cathedral view, visit the trendy top floor of **EME Catedral Hotel** (at Calle Alemanes 27). Ride the elevator to the top, climb the labyrinthine staircases to the bar, and sit down at a tiny table with a big view (daily 12:00-24:00).

Sleeping in Sevilla

All of my listings are centrally located, mostly within a five-minute walk of the cathedral. The first are near the charming but touristy Barrio Santa Cruz. The last group is just as central but closer to the river, across the boulevard in a more workaday, less touristy zone.

Room rates as much as double during the two Sevilla fiestas (Holy Week and the April Fair). In general, the busiest and most expensive months are April, May, September, and October. Hotels put rooms on the discounted push list in July and August—when people with good sense avoid this furnace—and from November through February.

If you do visit in July or August, you'll find the best deals in central, business-class places. They offer summer discounts and provide a (necessary) cool, air-conditioned refuge. But be warned that Spain's air-conditioning often isn't the icebox you're used to, especially in Sevilla.

BARRIO SANTA CRUZ

These places are off Calle Santa María la Blanca and Plaza Santa María. The most convenient parking lot is the underground Cano y Cueto garage. A self-service launderette is a couple of blocks away up Avenida de Menéndez Pelayo.

$$$$ Casa del Poeta offers peace, quiet, and a timeless elegance that seem contrary to its location in the heart of Santa Cruz. At the end of a side-street, Trinidad and Ángelo have lovingly converted an old family mansion with 17 rooms surrounding a large central patio into a home away from home. Evening guitar concerts plus a fantastic view terrace make it a worthwhile splurge (free breakfast if you reserve on their website, air-con, elevator, Calle Don Carlos Alonso Chaparro 3, tel. 954-213-868, www.casadelpoeta.es, info@casadelpoeta.es).

$$$$ Hotel Las Casas de la Judería has 178 quiet, classy rooms and junior suites, most of them tastefully decorated with hardwood floors and a Spanish flair. The service can be a little formal, but the rooms, which surround a series of peaceful courtyards, are a romantic splurge (RS% in low season, air-con, elevator, pool in summer, valet parking, Plaza Santa María 5, tel. 954-415-150, www.casasypalacios.com, juderia@casasypalacios.com).

$$$$ Hotel Casa 1800, well-priced for its elegance, is worth the extra euros. Located dead-center in the Barrio Santa Cruz (facing a boisterous tapas bar that quiets down after midnight), its 33 rooms are accessed via a lovely chandeliered patio lounge—it's here that the hotel hosts a daily free afternoon tea for guests. With a rooftop terrace and swimming pool offering an impressive cathedral view, and tastefully appointed rooms with high, beamed ceilings, it's a winner (air-con, elevator, Calle Rodrigo Caro 6, tel. 954-561-800, www.hotelcasa1800.com, info@hotelcasa1800.com).

$$$ Hotel Palacio Alcázar is the former home and studio of John Fulton, an American who moved here to become a bullfighter and painter. This charming boutique hotel has 12 crisp, modern rooms, and each soundproofed door is painted with a different scene of Sevilla. Triple-paned windows keep out the noise from the plaza (air-con, elevator, rooftop terrace with bar and cathedral views, Plaza de la Alianza 11, toll tel. 807-317-090, www.hotelpalacioalcazar.com, hotel@palacioalcazar.com).

$$ Hotel Amadeus is a classy and comfortable gem, with welcoming public spaces and a very charming staff. The 30 rooms, lovingly decorated with a musical motif, are situated around small courtyards. Elevators take you to a roof terrace with an under-the-stars hot tub. Breakfast comes on a trolley—enjoy it in your room, in the lounge, or on a terrace. Music lovers will appreciate the soundproof rooms with pianos—something I've seen nowhere else in Europe (air-con, elevator, iPads in some rooms, laundry service, pay parking nearby, Calle Farnesio 6, tel. 954-501-443, www.hotelamadeussevilla.com, reservas@hotelamadeussevilla.com, wonderfully run by María Luisa and her staff—Zaida and Cristina).

$$ El Rey Moro encircles its spacious, colorful patio (which tourists routinely duck into for a peek) with 19 rooms. Colorful, dripping with quirky Andalusian character, and thoughtful about including extras (such as free loaner bikes, a welcome drink, and private rooftop whirlpool-bath time), it's a class act (free breakfast if you reserve on their website, air-con, elevator, Reinoso 8, tel. 954-563-468, www.elreymoro.com, hotel@elreymoro.com).

$$ Hotel Alcántara offers clean and casual comfort in the heart of Santa Cruz. Well situated, it rents 23 slick rooms at a good price (RS%, nice buffet breakfast available, air-con, elevator, rentable laptop, outdoor patio, Calle Ximénez de Enciso 28, tel. 954-500-595, www.hotelalcantara.net, info@hotelalcantara.net). The hotel also functions as the box office for the nightly La Casa del Flamenco show, next door.

$$ Hotel Murillo enjoys one of the most appealing locations in Santa Cruz, along one of the very narrow "kissing lanes." Above its elegant, antiques-filled lobby are 57 nondescript rooms with marble floors (air-con, elevator, Calle Lope de Rueda 7, tel. 954-216-095, www.hotelmurillo.com, reservas@hotelmurillo.com). They also rent apartments with kitchens (see website for details).

$ Giralda Santa Cruz, once an 18th-century abbots' house, is now a homey 14-room hotel tucked away on a little street right off Calle Mateos Gago, just a couple of blocks from the cathedral. The exterior rooms have windows onto a pedestrian street, and a few of the interior rooms have small windows that look into the inner courtyard; all rooms are basic but neatly appointed (air-con, Calle Abades 30, tel. 954-228-324, www.alojamientosconencantosevilla.com, giralda@alojamientosconencantosevilla.com).

$ Pensión Córdoba, a homier and cheaper option, has 12 tidy, quiet rooms, solid modern furniture, and a showpiece tiled courtyard (cash only, air-con, on a tiny lane off Calle Santa María la Blanca

SEVILLA

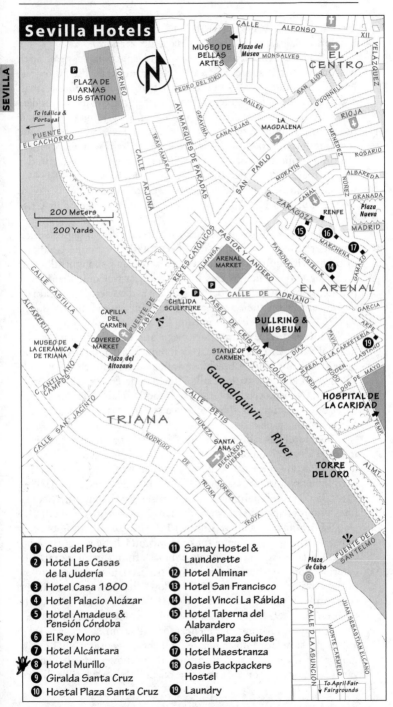

Sevilla Hotels

1. Casa del Poeta
2. Hotel Las Casas de la Judería
3. Hotel Casa 1800
4. Hotel Palacio Alcázar
5. Hotel Amadeus & Pensión Córdoba
6. El Rey Moro
7. Hotel Alcántara
8. Hotel Murillo
9. Giralda Santa Cruz
10. Hostal Plaza Santa Cruz
11. Samay Hostel & Launderette
12. Hotel Alminar
13. Hotel San Francisco
14. Hotel Vincci La Rábida
15. Hotel Taberna del Alabardero
16. Sevilla Plaza Suites
17. Hotel Maestranza
18. Oasis Backpackers Hostel
19. Laundry

Lope de Rueda # 7-9

SEVILLA

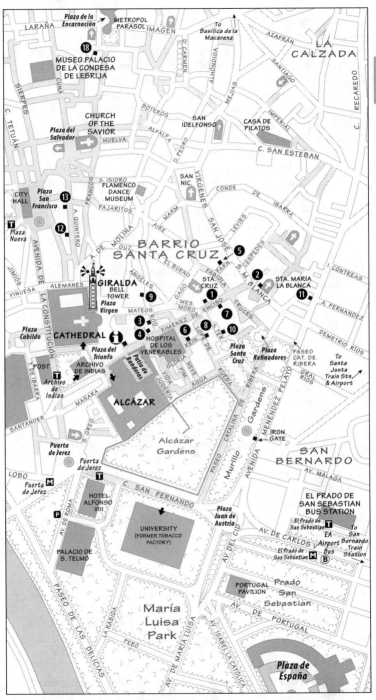

at Calle Farnesio 12, tel. 954-227-498, www.pensioncordoba.com, reservas@pensioncordoba.com, Ana and María).

$ Hostal Plaza Santa Cruz is a charming little place, with thoughtful touches that you wouldn't expect in this price range. The 17 clean, basic rooms surround a bright little courtyard that's buried deep in the Barrio Santa Cruz, just off Plaza Santa Cruz. They also have nine even-nicer rooms with a common terrace in a renovated residential palace on Calle Ximénez de Enciso (air-con, Calle Santa Teresa 15, tel. 954-228-808, www.alojamientosconencantosevilla. com, plaza@alojamientosconencantosevilla.com).

¢ Samay Hostel, on a busy avenue a block from the edge of the Barrio Santa Cruz, is a youthful, well-run slumbermill with 80 beds in 17 rooms (shared kitchen, air-con, elevator, laundry service, 24-hour reception, rooftop terrace, Avenida de Menéndez Pelayo 13, tel. 955-100-160, www.hostelsamay.com).

NEAR THE CATHEDRAL

$$ Hotel Alminar, plush and sophisticated, rents 11 fresh, slick, minimalist rooms. Double-pane windows keep it quiet at night, and two rooms have private terraces (air-con, elevator, loaner laptop, just 100 yards from the cathedral at Calle Álvarez Quintero 52, tel. 954-293-913, www.hotelalminar.com, reservas@hotelalminar. com, run by well-dressed, never-stressed Francisco).

$ Hotel San Francisco may have a classy facade, but inside its 17 rooms are sparsely decorated, with metal doors. It's centrally located, clean, and quiet, except for the noisy ground-floor room next to the TV and reception (air-con, elevator, small rooftop terrace with cathedral view, located on pedestrian Calle Álvarez Quintero at #38, tel. 954-501-541, www.sanfranciscoh.com, info@ sanfranciscoh.com, Carlos treats guests as part of the family).

WEST OF AVENIDA DE LA CONSTITUCIÓN

$$$$ Hotel Vincci La Rábida, part of a big, impersonal hotel chain, offers four-star comfort with its 81 rooms, huge and inviting courtyard lounge, and powerful air-conditioning. Its pricing is dictated by a computer that has it down to a science (elevator, Calle Castelar 24, tel. 954-501-280, www.vinccihoteles.com, larabida@ vinccihoteles.com).

$$$$ Hotel Taberna del Alabardero is unique, with only seven rooms occupying the top floor of a poet's mansion (above the classy recommended restaurant, Taberna del Alabardero). It's nicely located, a great value, and the ambience is perfectly circa-1900 (RS%, includes breakfast, air-con, elevator, pay parking, may close in Aug, Zaragoza 20, tel. 954-502-721, www.tabernadelalabardero. es, hotel.alabardero@esh.es).

$$$ Sevilla Plaza Suites rents 10 self-catering apartments with wood floors and kitchenettes. It's squeaky clean, family friendly, and well-located—and comes with an Astroturf sun terrace with a cathedral view. While service is scaled down, reception is open long hours (9:00-21:00) and rooms are cleaned daily (air-con, inside rooms are quieter, a block off Plaza Nueva at Calle Zaragoza 52, tel. 601-192-465, www.suitessevillaplaza.com, info@suitessevillaplaza.com, Javier).

$ Hotel Maestranza, sparkling with loving care and charm, has 17 simple, bright, clean rooms well-located on a street just off Plaza Nueva. It feels elegant for its price. Double-pane windows help to cut down on noise from the tapas bars below (family rooms available, 5 percent discount if you pay cash, air-con, elevator, Gamazo 12, tel. 954-561-070, www.hotelmaestranza.es, sevilla@hotelmaestranza.es, Antonio).

NEAR PLAZA DE LA ENCARNACIÓN

¢ Oasis Backpackers Hostel is a good place for cheap beds, and perhaps Sevilla's best place to connect with young backpackers. Each of the eight rooms, with up to eight double bunks, comes with a modern bathroom and individual lockers. The rooftop terrace—with lounge chairs, a small pool, and adjacent kitchen—is well-used (includes breakfast, just off Plaza de la Encarnación on the tiny and quiet lane behind the church at Compañía 1, reception hours vary—confirm check-in time when you book, tel. 955-262-696, www.oasissevilla.com, sevilla@hostelsoasis.com). Oasis also runs popular branches in Granada, Málaga, and Lisbon.

Eating in Sevilla

Eating in Sevilla is fun and affordable. People from Madrid and Barcelona find it a wonderful value. Make a point to get out and eat well when in Sevilla.

A clear dining trend in Sevilla is the rise of gourmet tapas bars, with spiffed-up decor and creative menus, at the expense of traditional restaurants. Even in difficult economic times, when other businesses are closing down, tapas bars are popping up all over. (Locals explain that with the collapse of the construction industry here, engineers, architects, and other professionals—eager for a business opportunity—are investing in trendy tapas bars.) Old-school places survive, but they often lack energy, and it seems that their clientele is aging with them. My quandary: I like the classic *típico* places. But the lively atmosphere and the best food are in the new places. One thing's for certain: if you want a good "restaurant" experience, your best value these days is to find a trendy tapas bar that offers good table seating, and sit down to enjoy some *raciones*.

TRIANA

Colorful Triana, across the river from the city center, offers a nice range of eating options. Its covered market is home to a world of tempting lunchtime eateries—take a stroll, take in the scene, and take your pick (busiest Tue-Sat morning through afternoon). Beyond the market, the neighborhood has three main restaurant zones to consider: trendy Calle San Jacinto, the neighborhood scene behind the Church of Santa Ana, and several riverside restaurants with views of central Sevilla.

On or near Calle San Jacinto

The area's pedestrianized main drag is lined with the tables of several easy-to-enjoy restaurants.

$$ Taberna Miami is a reliable bet for seafood. Grab a table with a good perch right on the street (daily 11:30-24:00, Calle San Jacinto 21, tel. 954-340-843).

$$ Blanca Paloma Bar is an untouristy classic that's a hit with the neighborhood crowd. It offers plenty of small tables for a sit-down meal, a delightful bar, and a fine selection of good Spanish wines by the glass, listed on the blackboard. They serve tasty tapa standards such as *pisto con huevo frito* (ratatouille with fried egg) that look and taste homemade (tapas at bar only, open daily at 8:30 but food served Mon-Sat 12:00-16:00 & 20:00-24:00, Sun 12:00-16:00, at the corner of Calle Pagés del Corro, tel. 954-333-640).

$$ Las Golondrinas Bar ("The Sparrows") is the talk of the Triana tapas scene, with a wonderful list of cheap and tasty tapas. Favorites here are the pork *solomillo* (tenderloin) and *champiñones* (mushrooms). Complement your meat with a veggie plate from the *aliños* section of the menu. Though they don't post a wine list, they serve plenty of nice wines by the glass. Cling to a corner of the bar and watch the amazingly productive little kitchen jam; you'll need to be aggressive to get an order in. To make a sit-down meal of it, nab one of the tables upstairs (Tue-Sun 13:00-16:00 & 20:00-24:00, may also be open Mon; one block down Calle San Jacinto from Isabel II Bridge—take the first right onto Calle Alfarería, then the first left onto Calle Antillano Campos to #26; tel. 954-331-626).

$ Dulcería Manu Jara satisfies the demanding sweet tooth. French pastry chef Manuel moved to Spain at age 27 after working in several Michelin-star restaurants and restored this 1873 shop to sell his creations. His local specialties, like *torrijas* (imagine French toast soaked in honey), are outstanding (Tue-Sun 10:00-14:00 & 16:30-20:30, no midday break on weekends, closed Mon, Pureza 5, tel. 675-873-674).

Behind the Church of Santa Ana

This is the best place in the area to take a break from the trendy dining scene. It offers a charming setting where you can sit down under a big tree to eat dinner along with local families.

$$ Bar Bistec, with most of the square's tables, does grilled fish with gusto. They're enthusiastic about their cod fritters and calamari, and brag about their pigeon, quail, and snails in sauce. Before taking a seat out on the square, consider the indoor seating and the fun action at the bar (daily 11:30-16:00 & 20:00-24:00, Plazuela de Santa Ana, tel. 954-274-759). **$$ Taberna La Plazuela,** which shares the square, is simpler, doing fried fish, grilled sardines, and *caracoles* (snails) in-season (spring-early summer).

$$ Bar Santa Ana, just a block away alongside the church, is a rustic neighborhood sports-and-bull bar with great seating on the street. Peruse the interior, draped in bullfighting and Weeping Virgin memorabilia. It's always busy with the neighborhood gang, who enjoy fun tapas like *delicia de solomillo* (pork tenderloin) and appreciate the bar's willingness to serve even cheap tapas at the outdoor tables. If you stand at the bar, they'll keep track of your bill by chalking it directly on the counter in front of you (facing the side of the church at Pureza 82, tel. 954-272-102).

Along the River

$$$ Kiosco de Las Flores started out serving fried fish from a simple green shack on the river in 1930, but has since become a Sevillian tradition. They serve up various *raciones* and meat dishes, but most diners come for the fried fish, which they gobble down either inside or on the terrace (Tue-Sat 11:00-16:00 & 19:00-23:30, Sun 11:00-16:00, closed Mon, on Calle Betis across from Torre del Oro, tel. 954-274-576).

$$$$ Abades Triana Ristorante is a hit for special occasions and fancy riverfront dining. It's a dressy restaurant with formal waiters serving modern Mediterranean cuisine. You'll sit in airconditioned comfort behind a big glass wall facing the river or on a classy outdoor terrace (daily 13:30-16:00 & 20:30-24:00, reservations smart but they don't reserve specific tables, directly across from Torre del Oro at Calle Betis 69, tel. 954-286-459, www. abadestriana.com).

$$$ Restaurante Río Grande is a stuffy, traditional, candlelit-fancy option, with properly attired waiters, a full menu, and lots of seafood. I'd skip the formal and more expensive dining room for the less expensive, more casual terrace with fine river views; in summer, they run a disco bar below the terrace (daily 13:00-16:00 & 19:30-24:00, air-con, next to the San Telmo Bridge, tel. 954-273-956).

Other Riverside Options: The little **$$ fish joints** fronting

SEVILLA

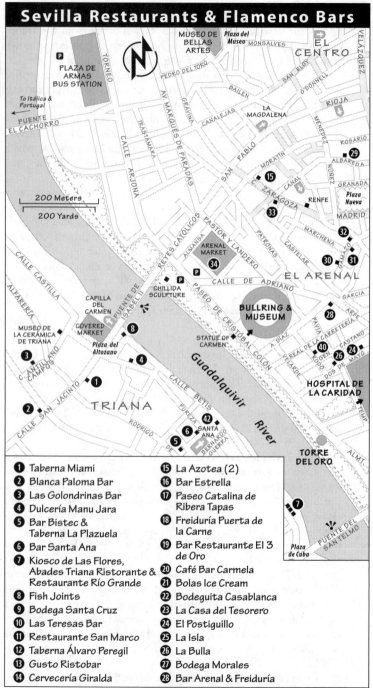

Sevilla Restaurants & Flamenco Bars

200 Meters
200 Yards

To Itálica &
Portugal

PUENTE EL CACHORRO

PLAZA DE ARMAS BUS STATION

MUSEO DE BELLAS ARTES

Plaza del Museo

MONSALVES

EL CENTRO

VELÁZQUEZ

TORNEO

PEDRO DEL TORO

AV. MARQUES DE PARADAS

GRAVINA

CANALEJAS

BAILEN

LA MAGDALENA

SAN PABLO

RIOJA

ROSARIO

ALBAREDA

29

GRANADA

15

MORATIN

C. ZARAGOZA

CANAL

NUÑEZ

Plaza Nueva

RENFE

MADRID

MARCHENA

33

CASTELAR

PATRONAS

32

30 **31**

REYES CATÓLICOS

PASTOR Y LANDERO

ALMANSA

ARENAL MARKET

34

CALLE DE ADRIANO

EL ARENAL

GARCIA

CALLE CASTILLA

ALFARERÍA

CAPILLA DEL CARMEN

PUENTE DE ISABEL II

CHILLIDA SCULPTURE

PASEO DE CRISTÓBAL COLÓN

BULLRING & MUSEUM

ARFE

FERIA

REAL DE LA CARRETERÍA

28

MUSEO DE LA CERÁMICA DE TRIANA

3

COVERED MARKET

Plaza del Altozano

8

STATUE OF CARMEN

A. DIAZ

VILARDE

40 **26** **24**

VIRGEN

DOS DE MAYO

CASTAÑO

C. ANTILLANO CAMPOS

1

4

CALLE BETIS

Guadalquivir River

HOSPITAL DE LA CARIDAD

2

TRIANA

CALLE SAN JACINTO

PUREZA

RODRIGO DE

42

6 SANTA ANA

5 BERNARDO GUERRA

TORRE DEL ORO

TEMP.

ALMT.

7

PUENTE DEL SAN TELMO

Plaza de Cuba

1 Taberna Miami	**15** La Azotea (2)
2 Blanca Paloma Bar	**16** Bar Estrella
3 Las Golondrinas Bar	**17** Paseo Catalina de Ribera Tapas
4 Dulcería Manu Jara	**18** Freiduría Puerta de la Carne
5 Bar Bistec & Taberna La Plazuela	**19** Bar Restaurante El 3 de Oro
6 Bar Santa Ana	**20** Café Bar Carmela
7 Kiosco de Las Flores, Abades Triana Ristorante & Restaurante Río Grande	**21** Bolas Ice Cream
8 Fish Joints	**22** Bodeguita Casablanca
9 Bodega Santa Cruz	**23** La Casa del Tesorero
10 Las Teresas Bar	**24** El Postiguillo
11 Restaurante San Marco	**25** La Isla
12 Taberna Álvaro Peregil	**26** La Bulla
13 Gusto Ristobar	**27** Bodega Morales
14 Cervecería Giralda	**28** Bar Arenal & Freiduría

SEVILLA

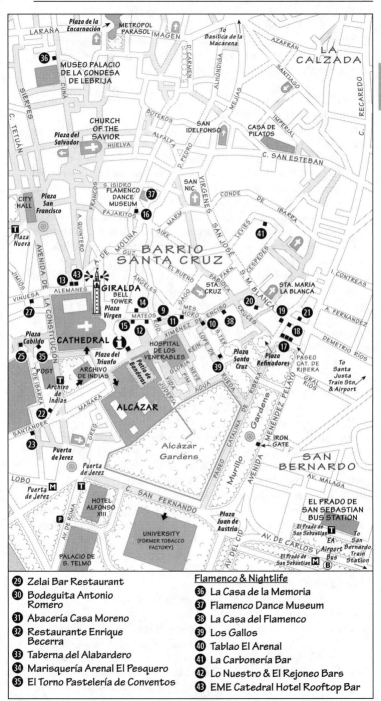

Flamenco & Nightlife

29 Zelai Bar Restaurant

30 Bodeguita Antonio Romero

31 Abacería Casa Moreno

32 Restaurante Enrique Becerra

33 Taberna del Alabardero

34 Marisquería Arenal El Pesquero

35 El Torno Pastelería de Conventos

Flamenco & Nightlife

36 La Casa de la Memoria

37 Flamenco Dance Museum

38 La Casa del Flamenco

39 Los Gallos

40 Tablao El Arenal

41 La Carbonería Bar

42 Lo Nuestro & El Rejoneo Bars

43 EME Catedral Hotel Rooftop Bar

the river just beyond the Isabel II Bridge—El Mero and Bodegón La Universal—change names like hats and charge a little extra for their scenic setting, but if you want to eat reasonably on the river, they're worth considering.

BARRIO SANTA CRUZ
Tapas with the Tourists

For tapas, the Barrio Santa Cruz is trendy and *romántico*. Plenty of atmospheric-but-touristy restaurants fill the neighborhood near the cathedral and along Calle Santa María la Blanca. From the cathedral, walk up Calle Mateos Gago, where several classic old bars—with the day's tapas scrawled on chalkboards—keep tourists and locals well fed and watered.

$$ Bodega Santa Cruz (a.k.a. **Las Columnas**) is a popular, user-friendly standby with cheap, unpretentious tapas. You're not coming here for the food (which is basic), but for the bustling atmosphere, as locals and tourists alike crowd the place, inside and out, for hours on end. You can keep an eye on the busy kitchen from the bar, or hang out like a cowboy at the tiny stand-up tables out front. To order you'll need to find your way to the bar—a fun experience in itself (there's no table service). Separate chalkboards list tapas and *montaditos* (daily 11:30-24:00, Calle de Rodrigo Caro 1A, tel. 954-213-246).

$$ Las Teresas is a characteristic small bar draped in festival posters and memorabilia. It serves good tapas from a tight little menu. Prices at the bar and outside tables (for fun tourist-watching) are the same, but tapas are only available inside. The hams (with little upside-down umbrellas that catch the dripping fat) are a reminder that the Spanish are enthusiastic about their cured meat (daily 10:00-24:00, Calle Santa Teresa 2, tel. 954-213-069).

$$$ Restaurante San Marco serves basic Italian cuisine under the arches of what was a Moorish bath in the Middle Ages (and a disco in the 1990s). The air-conditioned atmosphere may feel rather upscale, but it's also easygoing and family-friendly, with live Spanish guitar every night (daily 13:00-16:15 & 20:00-24:00, Calle Mesón del Moro 6, tel. 954-214-390, staff speaks English, welcoming Ángelo).

Near the Cathedral

I try to avoid the restaurants surrounding the cathedral, but if you can't take another step before finding a place to eat, here are a few decent options: The tiny **$$ Taberna Álvaro Peregil** is mixed in with the tourist jumble, but their small plates and *montaditos* are the real thing, along with *vino de naranja*—orange wine, a local specialty (daily 12:00-24:00, Calle Mateos Gago 20, tel. 954-218-966). If you can't face one more tapa, **$$ Gusto Ristobar,** just outside the cathedral's Court of the Orange Trees, has fresh-tasting *panini,* pizza, and salads (daily 8:30-23:30, Calle Alemanes 3, tel. 954-500-923). **$$ Cervecería Giralda,** a long-established meeting place for locals, is famous for its fine tapas, but may feel some-what touristy due to its location. The food is better quality than you would suspect, and prices are the same whether you sit outside, at an inside table, or at the bar (daily 9:00-24:00, Calle Mateos Gago 1, tel. 954-256-162).

$$$ La Azotea is a modern place that makes up for its lack of traditional character with gourmet tapas—made with native, sea-sonal ingredients—that have earned it a loyal following. It's run by Juan Antonio and his partner from San Diego, Jeanine, who've taken care to make the menu easy and accessible for English speak-ers. You can dine elegantly on tapas for reasonable prices (served only at the bar) or enjoy a sit-down meal—but you'll need to arrive early. They also serve breakfast (daily 9:00-24:00, Calle Mateos Gago 8, tel. 954-215-878). Another branch is not far from Plaza Nueva (daily 13:30-16:30 & 20:30-24:00, Calle Zaragoza 5, tel. 954-564-316).

$$ Bar Estrella sits only two blocks from the cathedral but seems far from the tourist buzz. Its homey vibe, traditional favor-ites, and good prices make this a nice spot to sample local dishes. The *flamenquín*—pork loin and ham rolled together, then deep-fried—as well as a pork tenderloin *(solomillo)* cooked in a whiskey sauce are worth trying (daily 12:00-24:00, Estrella 3, tel. 954-219-325).

On or near Calle Santa María la Blanca

This lively street, which defines the eastern boundary of the Barrio Santa Cruz, has an inviting concentration of eateries and is only slightly less touristy.

Tapas Restaurants on Paseo Catalina de Ribera: Two easy and good-value places located next to each other are worth consid-ering; they have similar prices, fine bars, happening and creative cuisine, good indoor seating, and wonderful tables outside on a busy sidewalk facing the Murillo Gardens. **$$ Vinería San Telmo** specializes in meaty tapas (the lamb with couscous and *rabo de toro* "wrap" are both winners) and offers lots of wine by the glass. Ask the speedy servers if there's something new on their often-updated menu (daily 13:00-24:00, tel. 954-410-600). **$$ Catalina Tapas Bar** is my favorite—like me, it's less hip than San Telmo but more creative than traditional tapas bars (daily 9:00-24:00, tel. 954-412-412).

$ Freiduría Puerta de la Carne and **$$ Bar Restaurante El 3 de Oro** are a two-for-one operation. The *freiduría* is a fried-fish-to-go place, with great outdoor seating, while El 3 de Oro is a fancier restaurant across the street that serves fine wine or beer to the fry shop's outdoor tables. First go into the fry shop and order a cheap cone of tasty fried fish (or incredibly delicious chicken wings). Study the photos of the options available; *un quarto* (250 grams, for €5-7) serves one person. Then head out front and flag down a server to order a drink and even a small salad (technically from the restaurant), all while enjoying a great outdoor setting—almost dining for the cost of a picnic (Freiduría open daily 13:00-17:00 & 20:00-24:30, usually no lunch service in summer; Santa María la Blanca 34, tel. 954-426-820).

Breakfast and Dessert on Plaza Santa María la Blanca: Several nondescript places work to keep travelers happy at breakfast time on the sunny main square near most of my recommended hotels. I like **$$ Café Bar Carmela.** For the cost of a continental breakfast at your hotel, you can be out on the square, with your choice of either a smaller, local-style breakfast, or a hearty American-style meal (breakfast served 9:00-13:00, easy menus, Calle Santa María la Blanca 6, tel. 954-540-590).

Bolas Ice Cream is the neighborhood favorite. *Maestro heladero* Antonino has been making ice cream in Sevilla for the past 40 years, with a focus on fresh, natural, and inventive products. They are generous with samples and creative with their offerings, so try a few wild flavors before choosing. Antonino's friendly wife, Cecilia, speaks English and doles out samples (daily 12:00-24:00, Puerto de la Carne 3, mobile 664-608-960).

BETWEEN THE CATHEDRAL AND THE RIVER

In the area between the cathedral and the river, just across Avenida de la Constitución, you can find tapas, cheap eats, and fine dining. Calle García de Vinuesa leads past several colorful and cheap tapas places to a busy corner surrounded by an impressive selection of happy eateries (where Calle de Adriano meets Calle Antonia Díaz).

$$$ Bodeguita Casablanca is famously the choice of bullfighters—and even the king. Just steps from the touristy cathedral area, this classy place seems a world apart, with stylish locals, a great menu, and a dressy interior complete with a stuffed bull's head. Sit inside for a serious meal of *raciones*. Be bold and experiment with your order—you can't go wrong here (Mon-Fri 12:30-17:00 & 20:00-24:00, Sat 12:30-17:30 except closed Sat in July, closed Sun and Aug, reservations smart, across the way from Archivo General de Indias at Calle Adolfo Rodríguez Jurado 12, tel. 954-224-114, www.bodeguitacasablanca.com).

$$$ La Casa del Tesorero creates its own world, with a calm, spacious, elegant interior built upon 12th-century Moorish ruins (look through the glass floor) and under historic arches of what used to be the city's treasury. It's a good, dressy Italian alternative to the tapas commotion, with mellow lighting and music (daily 12:30-16:00 & 19:30-23:30, Calle Santander 1, tel. 954-503-921).

At **$$ El Postiguillo,** the ambience combines bulls and *Bonanza*—stuffed heads decorate the walls of a fanciful wooden stable. Locals swear to its quality for traditional dishes, while tourists like the generous portions and easy menu. Prompt service is also a plus. Try the *carrillada* (stewed pork cheeks), *rabo de toro* (oxtail stew), or the chilled *salmorejo* (a thicker, Córdoba-style gazpacho). They can be busy at lunchtime, so go early to avoid a wait (daily 12:00-24:00, Calle Dos de Mayo 2, tel. 954-565-162).

$$ La Isla, tucked away in a narrow alley behind the Postigo craft market, would probably go unnoticed if their food and service weren't outstanding. A nautical theme reminds diners of seafood specialties—the *albóndigas de pescado* (fish meatballs) are delectable—but they also have decent grilled meats. Classy service is the norm whether dining outside, at the bar, or in the restaurant (daily 12:30-24:00, Calle Arfe 25, tel. 954-215-376).

$$ La Bulla feels like the brainchild of a gang of local foodies who, intent upon mixing traditional dishes, create an inventive international menu that's a welcome break from the usual fare. The place is bohemian-chic, with rickety tables gathered around a busy kitchen. The day's offerings are listed only on big chalkboards; ask for a stand-up English-language tour of what's available. While risotto is their signature dish, I prefer their other offerings. You'll enjoy gourmet presentation, a hip local crowd, easy jazz ambience, and good-looking servers. There's no bar—only table seating (and only indoors)—and dishes are easily splittable; three will stuff two people (daily 12:00-16:30 & 20:00-24:00, midway between cathedral and Torre del Oro at Calle 2 de Mayo 26, tel. 954-219-262, no reservations).

$$ Bodega Morales, farther up Calle García de Vinuesa (at #11), oozes old-Sevilla ambience. The front area is more of a drinking bar; for food, go in the back section (use the separate entrance around the corner). Here, sitting among huge adobe jugs, you can munch on affordable tiny sandwiches *(montaditos)* and tapas; both are just €2. Try the *salchicha al vino blanco*—tasty sausage braised in white wine (order at the bar, good wine selection, daily 13:00-16:00 & 19:30-24:00, tel. 954-221-242).

$$ Bar Arenal is a classic bull bar with tables spilling out onto a great street-corner setting. It's good for just a drink and to hang out with a crusty crowd. While they sell cheap, old-school tapas, you can complete the experience memorably by buying a load of fried fish from **$ El Arenal Freiduría** next door—this is perfectly permissible (fresh-fried portions can feed two, evenings only, bar is at Calle Arfe 2, tel. 954-223-686).

Near Plaza Nueva

$$$ Zelai Bar Restaurant is completely contemporary, without a hint of a historic-Sevilla feel or touristy vibe. Their pricey gourmet tapas and *raciones* are a hit with a smart local crowd, who enjoy the fusion of Basque, Andalusian, and international flavors. They also have a dressy little restaurant in back (reservations generally required) with a €40 tasting menu (Tue-Sat 13:00-16:30 & 21:00-23:30, closed Sun-Mon, just off Plaza Nueva at Calle Albareda 22, tel. 954-229-992, www.restaurantezelai.com).

$$ Bodeguita Antonio Romero has served so many *montaditos* (little sandwiches) over the years that they've lost count. They're known for their tasty *pringá* (a meaty mix of beef, pork, sausage, and fat simmered for hours), but my favorite is the *piripí* (mini mouthful of pork tenderloin, bacon, cheese, tomato, and mayo). They also offer many good wines by the glass (Tue-Sun 12:00-24:00, closed Mon, Gamazo 16, tel. 954-210-585).

$$ Abacería Casa Moreno is a classic *abacería*, a neighborhood grocery store that doubles as a standing-room-only tapas bar. Squeeze into the back room and you're slipping back in time—and behind a tall language barrier. They're proud of their top-quality *jamón serrano, queso manchego,* and super-tender *mojama* (cured, dried tuna). Rubbing elbows here with local eaters, under a bull's head, surrounded by jars of peaches and cans of sardines, you feel like you're in on a secret (Mon-Fri 9:45-15:30 & 18:30-22:30, Sat 10:30-16:00, closed Sun, 3 blocks off Plaza Nueva at Calle Gamazo 7, tel. 954-228-315).

$$$ Restaurante Enrique Becerra is a fancy little 10-table place popular with foodies. It's well-known for its gourmet Andalusian cuisine and fine wine. Muscle in among the well-dressed locals at the tiny bar for snacks like *albóndigas de cordero con yerbabuena* (minty lamb meatballs) and wine by the glass, or head to the quieter, fancier dining room in the restaurant upstairs (reservations essential). Its crowded quarters attest to its quality food (Mon-Sat 13:00-16:30 & 20:00-24:00, Sun 13:00-16:00, Gamazo 2, tel. 954-213-049, www.enriquebecerra.com).

$$$ Taberna del Alabardero, one of Sevilla's finest restaurants, serves refined Spanish cuisine in chandeliered elegance just a couple of blocks from the cathedral. If you order à la carte, it adds up to about €45 a meal, but for €55 you can have an elaborate, seven-course fixed-price meal with lots of little surprises from the chef. Or consider their €20/person (no sharing) starter sampler, followed by an entrée. The service in the fancy upstairs dining rooms gets mixed reviews (carefully read and understand your bill)...but the setting is stunning. Consider having tapas on their popular terrace while taking in views of the cathedral (daily 13:00-16:30 & 20:00-

23:30, terrace closed in bad weather, air-con, reservations smart, Zaragoza 20, tel. 954-502-721, www.tabernadelalabardero.es).

Taberna del Alabardero Student-Served Lunch: The ground-floor dining rooms (classy but nothing like upstairs) are popular with office workers for a great-value, student chef-prepared, fixed-price lunch sampler (three delightful courses—€14 Mon-Fri, €19 Sat-Sun; drinks not included, open daily 13:00-16:30). To avoid a wait at lunch, arrive before 14:00 (no reservations possible).

At the Arenal Market Hall

Mercado del Arenal, the covered fish-and-produce market, is ideal for snapping photos and grabbing a cheap lunch. As with most markets, you'll find characteristic little diners with prices designed to lure in savvy shoppers, not to mention a crispy fresh world of picnic goodies—and a riverside promenade with benches just a block away (Mon-Sat 9:00-14:30, closed Sun, sleepy on Mon, on Calle Pastor y Landero at Calle Arenal, just beyond bullring).

$$ Marisquería Arenal El Pesquero is a popular fish restaurant that thrives in the middle of the Arenal Market, but stays open after the market closes. In the afternoon and evening, you're surrounded by the empty Industrial Age market, with workers dragging their crates to and fro. It's a great family-friendly, finger-licking-good scene that's much appreciated by its enthusiastic local following. Fish is priced by weight, so be careful when ordering, and double-check the bill (Tue-Sat 13:00-17:00 & 21:00-24:00, Sun open for dinner only, closed Mon, reservations smart for dinner, enter on Calle Pastor y Landero 9, tel. 954-220-881).

Sevilla Connections

Note that many destinations are well served by both trains and buses.

BY TRAIN

Most trains arriving and departing Sevilla, including all high-speed AVE trains, leave from the larger, more distant **Santa Justa** station. But many *cercanías* and regional trains heading south to Granada, Jerez, Cádiz, and Málaga also stop at the smaller **San Bernardo** station a few minutes from Santa Justa, which is connected to downtown by tram. Hourly *cercanías* trains connect both stations (about a 4-minute trip). For tips on arrival at either station, see "Arrival in Sevilla," earlier.

Train Tickets: For schedules and tickets, visit a RENFE Travel Center, either at the train station (daily 8:00-22:00, take a number and wait, tel. 902-320-320 for reservations and info) or near Plaza Nueva in the city center (Mon-Fri 9:30-14:00 & 17:30-

20:00, Sat 10:00-13:30, closed Sun, Calle Zaragoza 29, tel. 954-211-455). You can also check schedules at www.renfe.com. Many travel agencies sell train tickets; look for a train sticker in agency windows.

From Sevilla by AVE Train to Madrid: The AVE express train is expensive but fast (2.5 hours to Madrid; hourly departures 7:00-23:00). Departures between 16:00 and 19:00 can book up far in advance, but surprise holidays and long weekends can totally jam up trains as well—reserve as far ahead as possible.

From Sevilla by Train to Córdoba: There are four options for this journey: slow and cheap regional, *media distancia* trains (7/day, 1.5 hours), fast and cheap regional high-speed **Avant** or **Alvia** trains (12/day, 45 minutes, requires reservation), and fast and expensive **AVE** trains (almost hourly, 45 minutes, requires reservation). Unless you must be on a particular departure, there's no reason to pay more for AVE; Avant or Alvia trains are just as quick and a third the price. However, promotional fares for the AVE can be as cheap as regional trains when booked in advance. (If you have a rail pass, you still must buy a reservation; Avant reservations cost about half as much as ones for AVE.)

Other Trains from Sevilla to: Málaga (14/day, 45 minutes on AVE; 7/day, 2 hours on Avant; 5/day, 2.5 hours on slower regional trains), **Ronda** (4/day, 3 hours, transfer in Bobadilla or Córdoba), **Granada** (4/day, 3.5 hours, transfer in Córdoba and Antequera), **Jerez** (nearly hourly, 1.25 hours), **Barcelona** (2/day direct, more with transfer in Madrid, 5.5 hours), **Algeciras** (3/day, 5-6 hours, transfer at Antequera or Bobadilla—bus is better). There are no direct trains to **Lisbon,** Portugal, so you'll have to take AVE to Madrid, then overnight to Lisbon; buses or a direct flight to Lisbon are far better (see later). Train info: Tel. 902-320-320, www.renfe.com.

BY BUS

Sevilla has two bus stations: The El Prado de San Sebastián station, near Plaza de España, primarily serves regional destinations; the Plaza de Armas station, farther north (near the bullring), handles most long-distance buses. Bus info: Tel. 954-908-040 but rarely answered, go to TI for latest schedule info.

From Sevilla's El Prado de San Sebastián station to Andalucía and the South Coast: Regional buses are operated by Comes (www.tgcomes.es), Los Amarillos (www.losamarillos.es), and Autocares Valenzuela (www.grupovalenzuela.com). Connections to **Jerez** are frequent, as many southbound buses head there first (7/day, 1.5 hours, run by all three companies; note that train is also possible—see earlier). Los Amarillos runs buses to some of Andalucía's hill towns, including **Ronda** (7/day, 2.5 hours, fewer on weekends) and **Arcos** (2/day, 2 hours; more departures possible with transfer in Jerez). For Spain's South Coast, a Comes bus departs Sevilla four times a day and heads for **Tarifa** (3 hours, but not timed well for taking a ferry to Tangier that same day—best to overnight in Tarifa), then **Algeciras** (3-4 hours), and ends at **La Línea/Gibraltar** (4.5 hours). However, if **Algeciras** is your goal, Autocares Valenzuela has a much faster direct connection (8/day, fewer on weekends, 2.5 hours). There are two buses a day from this station to **Granada** (3 hours); the rest depart from the Plaza de Armas station.

From Sevilla's Plaza de Armas station to: Madrid (9/day, 6 hours, www.socibus.es, tel. 902-229-292), **Córdoba** (7/day, 1-2 hours), **Granada** (7/day, 3 hours), **Málaga** (8/day direct, 3 hours), **Nerja** (2/day, 4-5 hours), **Barcelona** (2/day, 16.5 hours, including one overnight bus). Information: tel. 902-450-550.

By Bus to Portugal: The cheapest way to get to **Lisbon** is by bus (2/day, departures at 14:00 and 23:30, 8 hours, leaves from both Sevilla bus stations, tel. 954-905-102, www.alsa.es). The midnight departure continues past Lisbon to **Coimbra** (arriving 10:15) and **Porto** (arriving 12:00). Sevilla also has direct bus service to **Lagos,** on the Algarve (5/day in summer, 2/day off-season, 5.5 hours, buy ticket a day or two in advance May-Oct, tel. 954-907-737, www.damas-sa.es). The bus departs from Sevilla's Plaza de Armas bus station and arrives at the Lagos bus station. If you'd like to visit Tavira on the way to Lagos, purchase a bus ticket to Tavira (3-hour trip), have lunch there, then take the train to Lagos.

GRANADA

For a time, Granada was the grandest city in Spain. But after the tumult that came with the change from Moorish to Christian rule, it lost its power and settled into a long slumber. Today, Granada seems to specialize in evocative history and good living. Settle down in the old center and explore monuments of the Moorish civilization and its conquest. Taste the treats of a North African-flavored culture that survives here today.

Compared to other Spanish cities its size, Granada is delightfully cosmopolitan—it's worked hard to accept a range of cultures, and you'll see far more ethnic restaurants here than elsewhere in Andalucía. Its large student population (80,000, including more than 10,000 students from abroad) also lends it a youthful zest. The Grenadine people are serious about hospitality and have earned a reputation among travelers for being particularly friendly and eager to help you enjoy their historic city.

Granada's magnificent Alhambra fortress was the last stronghold of the Moorish kingdom in Spain. The city's exotically tangled Moorish quarter, the Albayzín, invites exploration. From its viewpoints, romantics can enjoy the sunset and evening views of the grand, floodlit Alhambra.

After visiting the Alhambra and then seeing a blind beggar, a Spanish poet wrote, "Give him a coin, for there is nothing worse in this life than to be blind in Granada." This city has much to see, yet it reveals itself in unpredictable ways; it takes a poet to sort through and assemble the jumbled shards of Granada. Peer through the intricate lattice of a Moorish window. Hear water burbling unseen among the labyrinthine hedges of the Generalife Gardens. Listen to a flute trilling deep in the swirl of alleys around the cathedral. Don't be blind in Granada—open all your senses.

PLANNING YOUR TIME

You could conceivably hit Granada's highlights in one very busy day, sandwiched between two overnights. With a more relaxed itinerary, Granada is worth two days and two nights. No matter what, reserve in advance for the Alhambra—up to three months ahead.

When you're ready to move on, consider heading to nearby Nerja, the Costa del Sol's best beach town (2.5 hours by car or bus). You can also get to White Hill Towns such as Ronda (3 hours by train). Sevilla is an easy 3.5-hour train ride away. The Madrid-Granada high-speed train service awaits completion, so riders are bused to Antequera and then continue on the AVE (4 hours).

Granada in One Day

With only one full day here, you could fit in the top sights by following this intense plan: In the morning, take my self-guided walk of the old town. After a quick lunch, do the Alhambra in the afternoon (reservation essential). Catch minibus #C1 into the Albayzín quarter (or hike the hippie lane if you still have energy) to the San Nicolás viewpoint for sunset, then find the right place for a suitably late dinner.

Granada in Two Days

Day 1: Stroll the Alcaicería market streets and follow my self-guided tour of the old town, including a visit to the cathedral and its Royal Chapel. Enjoy the vibe at Plaza Nueva, the town's main square. Wander up into the Albayzín Moorish quarter, stopping by a funky teahouse along the way. End your day at the San Nicolás viewpoint—the golden hour before sunset is best, when the Alhambra seems to glow with its own light.

Day 2: Follow my self-guided tour of the Alhambra; you'll see the elaborate and many-roomed Palacios Nazaríes, Charles V's Palace, the refreshing Generalife Gardens, and more.

On any **evening,** tapa-hop for dinner (consider Gayle's Granada Tapas Tours) or splurge on fine dining at a *carmen*. When the evening cools down, join the paseo. Take in a *zambra* dance in the Sacromonte district. Relax in an Arab bath (Hammam al Andalus) or a *tetería* (tea shop), or both. Slow down and smell the incense.

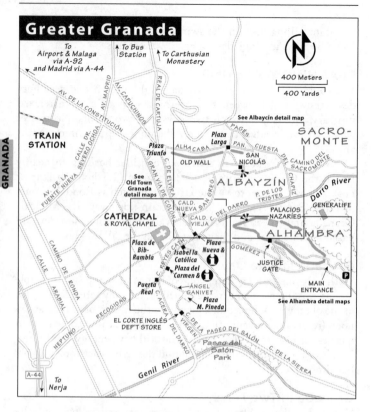

Greater Granada

To Airport & Malaga via A-92 and Madrid via A-44

↑ To Bus Station

↑ To Carthusian Monastery

400 Meters
400 Yards

See Albaycín detail map

TRAIN STATION

AV. DE LA CONSTITUCIÓN

AV. CAPUCHINOS

AV. DE MADRID

REAL DE CARTUJA

Plaza Triunfo

GRAN VÍA DE COLÓN

C. DE ELVIRA

Plaza Larga

ALHACABA

OLD WALL

PAGES

PAN

CUESTA

SAN NICOLÁS

ALBAYZÍN

C. DEL DARRO

P. DE LOS TRISTES

SACRO-MONTE

CAMINO DEL SACROMONTE

Darro River

GENERALIFE

See Old Town Granada detail maps

CATHEDRAL & ROYAL CHAPEL

CALD. NUEVA

SAN GREG.

CALD. VIEJA

PALACIOS NAZARÍES

ALHAMBRA

Plaza de Bib-Rambla

C. REYES CATH.

Isabel la Católica

Plaza Nueva &

GOMEREZ

JUSTICE GATE

Plaza del Carmen &

Puerta Real

ÁNGEL GANIVET

C. ACERA DEL DARRO

Plaza M. Pineda

MAIN ENTRANCE

See Alhambra detail maps

CAMINO DE RONDA

CALLE ARABIAL

NEPTUNO

RECOGIDAS

EL CORTE INGLÉS DEP'T STORE

C. DE LA VIRGEN

PASEO DEL SALÓN

Paseo del Salón Park

C. DE LA SIERRA

A-44
To Nerja

Genil River

Orientation to Granada

Modern Granada sprawls (235,000 people), but its main sights are all within a 20-minute walk of Plaza Nueva, where dogs wag their tails to the rhythm of modern hippies and street musicians. Most of my recommended hotels are within a few blocks of Plaza Nueva. Make this the hub of your Granada visit.

Plaza Nueva was a main square after Ferdinand and Isabel took Granada. This historic center is in the Darro River valley, which separates two hills (the river now flows under the square). On one hill is the great Moorish palace, the Alhambra, and on the other is the best-preserved Moorish quarter in Spain, the Albayzín. To the southwest are the cathedral, Royal Chapel, and Alcaicería (Moorish market), where the city's two main drags—Gran Vía

de Colón (often just called "Gran Vía" by locals) and Calle Reyes Católicos—lead away into the modern city.

TOURIST INFORMATION

The municipal TI, which covers only Granada, is inside City Hall on Plaza del Carmen, a short walk from the cathedral; they also sell the Granada Card Básico city pass (described below). Verify your Alhambra plans here (Mon-Sat 9:30-19:00, Sun until 14:00, longer hours in summer, tel. 958-248-280, www.granadatur.com). Another TI, tucked away just above Plaza Nueva, near the Santa Ana Church, covers not only Granada but also Andalucía, with good, free maps for destinations across the region. This TI also posts all of Granada's bus departures (Mon-Fri 9:00-19:30, Sat-Sun 9:30-15:00, tel. 958-575-202).

Alhambra Info: While any TI and every hotel has information on the Alhambra, the very helpful info desk inside the Corral del Carbón is your best resource, as it's run by the Alhambra administration and is located right in the heart of town (daily 9:00-19:00, Mariana Pineda s/n, tel. 958-575-131). It also has a Ticketmaster machine where you can collect your reserved Alhambra ticket (must use the same credit card with which you made the reservation).

Sightseeing Passes: The **Granada Card Básico** city pass gives you access to Alhambra reservations, covers the cost of your visit there, and also includes the cathedral, Royal Chapel, Carthusian Monastery, and five trips on city buses, plus minor sights and discounts on others (€37/3 days; a **Plus** version is not worth the extra €3 for most visitors).

The Granada Card is best purchased in advance online. When you buy it, schedule a time for your Alhambra visit. You can then pick up the card at the TI in City Hall on Plaza del Carmen. Purchasing the card on the same day you plan to visit the Alhambra is not a good option because Alhambra time slots are often already taken (www.granadatur.com/granada-card).

The **Dobla de Oro** card, available in advance on the Alhambra website (www.alhambra-tickets.es), is valid for three days and comes in three versions, all of which cover the Hammam El Bañuelo and other minor Albayzín sights: *Jardines* includes the Generalife Gardens, the Partal Palace, and the Alcazaba (€13); *General* includes the above plus a timed-entry visit to the Alhambra's Palacios Nazaríes (€21); *Nocturna* offers the same sights but with a nighttime Palacios Nazaríes visit (€16).

ARRIVAL IN GRANADA

By Train: Granada's modest train station is connected to the center by frequent buses, a €7 taxi ride, or a 30-minute walk down Avenida de la Constitución and Gran Vía. The train station does not have luggage storage.

Taxis wait out front. It's a two-minute walk to reach the bus stop: Exiting the train station, walk straight ahead up tree-lined Avenida Andaluces (following the Metro tracks). At the first major intersection, look right on Avenida de la Constitución and you'll see a covered bus stop. Wait there for the articulated LAC bus, which heads down Avenida de la Constitución to Gran Vía and a stop at the cathedral (Catedral)—the nearest stop to Plaza Nueva and most of my recommended hotels (stops are shown on monitors). Before boarding, buy a €1.20 ticket from a machine at the stop (or buy a Credibús pass to use throughout your stay). When you leave the bus, cross the busy Gran Vía and walk three short blocks to Plaza Nueva.

By Bus: Located on the city outskirts, Granada's bus station *(estación de autobuses)* has a good and cheap cafeteria, ATMs, luggage lockers, and a privately run tourist agency masquerading as an official TI. All of these services are downstairs, where you exit the buses.

Upstairs is the main arrivals hall with ticket windows, ticket machines, and a helpful information counter in the main hall that hands out printed schedules for each route. All buses are operated by Alsa (tel. 902-422-242, www.alsa.es).

To get from the bus station to the city center, it's either a 10-minute taxi ride (€8) or a 25-minute ride on bus #SN1 (€1.20, pay driver, change given). For Plaza Nueva, get off on Gran Vía at the Catedral stop (check monitors), a half-block before the grand square called Plaza Isabel La Católica. From here, it's a short three-block walk to Plaza Nueva and most of my recommended hotels. (Ignore the tram tracks outside the bus station—the tram stops nowhere near the city center.)

By Car: Driving in Granada's historic center is restricted to buses, taxis, and tourists with hotel reservations. Signs are posted to this effect, and entrances are strictly controlled. Hidden cameras snap a photo of your license plate as you enter the restricted zone. If you have a reservation, simply drive past the sign, check in, and make sure your hotel registers you with the local traffic police (this is routine for them, but if they don't do it within 48 hours, you'll be stuck with a steep ticket). Hotels provide parking or have a deal with a central-zone garage (such as Parking San Agustín, just off Gran Vía del Colón, €25/day).

If you're driving and don't have a hotel reservation in the center, find a place to park outside the prohibite[...] above the old town, has a huge lot where y[...] 24 hours (walk, catch the minibus, or taxi[...] are also garages just outside the restricted z[...] to the east (€23/day, Avenida de la Constit[...] garage to the south (Centro Comercial Neptuno, €15/day, on Calle Neptuno). To reach the city center from either parking garage, catch the articulated LAC bus nearby (on Avenida de la Constitución) and get off at the Catedral stop.

If you're driving directly to the Alhambra, you can easily avoid the historic center.

By Plane: Granada's relaxed airport is about 10 miles west of the city center.

HELPFUL HINTS

Theft Alert: Be on guard for pickpockets wherever there's a crowd, and especially late at night in the Albayzín. Your biggest threat is being conned while enjoying drinks and music in Sacromonte. Pushy women, usually hanging out near the cathedral and Alcaicería, may accost you with sprigs of rosemary, then demand payment for fortune-telling services—just say, *"No, gracias."*

Festivals and Concerts: From late June to early July, the **International Festival of Music and Dance** offers classical music, ballet, flamenco, and zarzuela (light opera) nightly in the Alhambra and other historic venues at reasonable prices. The ticket office is in the Corral del Carbón (open mid-April-Oct). Beginning in February, you can also book tickets online at www.granadafestival.org. This festival is one of the most respected and popular in Spain, and tickets for major performers typically sell out months in advance. During the festival, flamenco is free every night at midnight; ask the ticket office or TI for the venue.

From fall through spring, the **City of Granada Orchestra** offers popular concerts—mostly on weekends—that generally sell out quickly (€17-30, late Sept-mid-May only, Auditorio Manuel de Falla, best to purchase tickets in advance online, tel. 958-221-144, www.orquestaciudadgranada.es).

Wi-Fi: You'll find free Wi-Fi zones scattered throughout Granada, including in Plaza Nueva and on local buses.

Laundry: Tintorería-Lavandería Duquesa, a few blocks west of the cathedral area, will wash, dry, and fold your clothes (same-day service possible—drop off laundry early, no self-service, Mon-Fri 9:00-14:00 & 16:30-21:00, Sat 9:30-14:00, closed Sun, near the San Jerónimo Monastery at Duquesa 24, tel. 958-280-685).

T Lavo is a blessing for busy travelers: They'll pick up and deliver laundry to your hotel (€15/load). Have your hotel help with the phone call. Self-service is cheaper but probably not worth the trip to their location outside the center (Mon-Sat 10:00-15:00 & 17:00-20:00, closed Sun, Calle Real de Cartuja 67, tel. 958-279-659, www.lavanderiatlavo.com).

Post Office: It's at the big roundabout called Puerta Real (daily 8:30-20:30, tel. 958-221-138).

Travel Agencies: All travel agencies book flights, and many also sell long-distance bus and train tickets. Mega-chain **El Corte Inglés** sells plane, train, and bus tickets (Mon-Sat 10:00-21:30, closed Sun, ticket desk in basement level near supermarket, Acera del Darro, tel. 958-282-612).

GETTING AROUND GRANADA

With cheap taxis, frisky minibuses, good city buses, and nearly all points of interest an easy walk from Plaza Nueva, you'll get around Granada easily.

Tickets for minibuses and city buses cost €1.20 per ride (buy from driver except when riding the articulated LAC bus; machines with English instructions are at every LAC stop, change given; for schedules and routes, see www.transportesrober.com). Credibús cards save you money if you'll be riding often—or, since they're shareable, if you're part of a group (per-ride price drops to €0.79; can be loaded with €5, €10, or €20; plus refundable €2 card fee). Purchase the card from minibus drivers or from machines at any LAC bus stop (choose "contactless card," then "create card" options). To get a €5 card—likely all you'll need—ask for *"un bono de cinco."* These are valid on all buses (no fee for connecting bus if you transfer within 45 minutes).

By Minibus: Handy little made-for-tourists red minibuses—which cover the city center—depart every few minutes from Plaza Nueva, Plaza Isabel La Católica, and Gran Vía (Catedral stop) until late in the evening. Here are handy minibus routes to look for:

Bus #C1 departs from Plaza Nueva and winds around the Albayzín quarter (every 8-10 minutes, 7:00-23:00).

Bus #C2 follows a similar route as #C1 (although not to the San Nicolás viewpoint), delves deeper into the Albayzín, and also makes a side-trip into Sacromonte (every 20 minutes, 8:00-22:00).

Bus #C3 is the best for a trip up to the Alhambra, departing from the Catedral stop or just uphill from Plaza Isabel La Católica, with Alhambra stops at the main entrance and the shortcut Justice Gate (Puerta de la Justicia) entrance (every 5-7 minutes, 7:00-23:00).

Other Bus Lines: If you are heading beyond the tourist core (for instance, the train station or Carthusian Monastery), you'll likely ride the articulated LAC bus. This high-capacity bus runs a circuit through the center of town and connects to outbound routes (at Cruz del Sur, among other stops).

Tours in Granada

Walking Tours

Cicerone offers informative and spirited two-hour city tours describing the fitful and fascinating changes the city underwent as it morphed from a Moorish capital to a Christian one 525 years ago. While the tour doesn't enter any actual sights, it weaves together bits of the Moorish heritage that survive around the cathedral and the Albayzín. These basic Granada tours start at their office on Calle San Jerónimo 10; reservations are encouraged but not required. Tours are usually in both English and Spanish daily at 10:30 (€18, show this book for a discount, €14 for kids 10-13, free for kids under 10; to book a tour, call 958-561-810 or mobile 607-691-676; www.ciceronegranada.com, reservas@ciceronegranada.com). They also offer small group tours of the Alhambra that include an entry time to Palacios Nazaríes—handy if you have trouble getting a reservation on your own (€75, includes Alhambra ticket, ideally reserve at least 3-4 days ahead).

Local Guides

Margarita Ortiz de Landazuri (mobile 687-361-988, www.alhambratours.com, info@alhambratours.com) and **Miguel Ángel** (mobile 617-565-711, miguelangelalhambratours@gmail.com) are both good, English-speaking, licensed guides with lots of experience and a passion for teaching. Guide rates are standard (€130/2.5 hours, €260/day).

Olive Oil Tour

This company helps you explore Granada's countryside and taste some local olive oil. Choose between a three-hour tour that departs in the morning or afternoon (€38) or add a wine tasting and light tapas (€53). Tours are in English, and a driver will pick you up at your hotel (tel. 958-559-643, mobile 651-147-504, www.oliveoiltour.com, reservas@oliveoiltour.com).

Gayle's Granada Tapas Tours

After 21 years in Granada, Scottish-born Gayle Mackie knows where to find the best food in town. She and her team take small groups off the beaten path to characteristic tapas bars for a "food experience," providing cuisine tips and fascinating insights into Granada. The various routes offer a moveable feast (amounting to a filling meal) with good wine and craft beer (2.5 hours, €40/person, €5 discount/group with this book—not per person, tours for 2-6 people, daily at 13:30 or 20:00, family and group options, mobile

GRANADA

Granada at a Glance

▲▲▲**The Alhambra** The last and finest Moorish palace in Iberia, highlighting the splendor of that civilization in the 13th and 14th centuries. Reservations a must for a daytime visit. **Hours:** Entire complex open daily 8:30-20:00, mid-Oct-March until 18:00; Palacios Nazaríes and Generalife Gardens also open Tue-Sat for nighttime visits (Fri-Sat only in off-season). See page 96.

▲▲**Royal Chapel** Lavish 16th-century chapel with the tombs of Queen Isabel and King Ferdinand. **Hours:** Mon-Sat 10:15-19:30, Sun 11:00-18:30; Nov-March Mon-Sat 10:15-18:30, Sun from 11:00. See page 114.

▲▲**San Nicolás Viewpoint** Breathtaking vista over the Alhambra and the Albayzín. **Hours:** Best at sunset. See page 121.

▲**Granada Cathedral** The second-largest cathedral in Spain, unusual for its bright Renaissance interior. **Hours:** Mon-Sat 10:00-18:30, Sun 15:00-18:00. See page 117.

▲**The Albayzín** Spain's best old Moorish quarter. See page 120.

Alcaicería Tiny shopping lanes in what was once a Moorish silk market, now filled with tacky tourist shops. See page 90.

Corral del Carbón Granada's only surviving caravanserai (inn for traveling merchants), with impressive Moorish door. **Hours:** Door always viewable; office for Alhambra ticket pickup open daily 9:00-19:00. See page 89.

Paseo de los Tristes A prime strolling strip above the Darro River lined with eateries and peppered with Moorish history. **Hours:** Best in the evenings. See page 94.

Hammam El Bañuelo 11th-century ruins of Moorish baths. **Hours:** Daily 9:30-14:30 & 17:00-21:00, mid-Sept-March 10:00-17:00. See page 95.

Great Mosque of Granada Islamic house of worship featuring a minaret with a live call to prayer and a courtyard with commanding views. **Hours:** Daily 11:00-14:00 & 18:00-21:00, shorter hours in winter. See page 122.

Carthusian Monastery Lavish Baroque monastery on the outskirts of town. **Hours:** Daily 10:00-13:00 & 16:00-20:00, shorter hours Nov-March. See page 128.

619-444-984, www.granadatapastours.com). Gayle also offers a tour revealing how locals go about their daily lives through food (€60/person).

Granada Old Town Walk

This short self-guided walk, worth ▲▲, covers all the essential old town sights. Along the way, we'll see vivid evidence of the dramatic Moorish-to-Christian transition brought about by the Reconquista—the long and ultimately successful battle to retake Spain from the Moors and reestablish Christian rule. (Our first stop is a handy place to collect reserved Alhambra tickets.)

• *Start at Corral del Carbón, near Plaza del Carmen.*

❶ Corral del Carbón

A caravanserai (of Silk Road fame) was a protected place for mer-

chants to rest their animals, spend the night, get a bite to eat, and spin yarns. This, the only surviving caravanserai of Granada's original 14, was just a block away from the silk market (Alcaicería; the next stop on this walk). Stepping through the caravanserai's grand Moorish door, you find a square with 14th-century Moorish brickwork surrounding a water fountain. This plain-yet-elegant structure evokes the times when traders would gather here with exotic goods and swap tales from across the Muslim world.

It's a common mistake to think of the Muslim Moors as somehow not Spanish. They lived here for seven centuries and were really just as "indigenous" as the Romans, Goths, and Celts. While the Moors were Muslim, they were no more connected to Arabia than they were to France.

After the Reconquista, this space was used as a coal storage facility (hence "del Carbón"). These days it houses two offices where you can buy tickets for musical events. (And while here, you can pick up Alhambra tickets from a Ticketmaster machine...if you've reserved in advance.)

• *From the caravanserai, exit straight ahead down Puente del Carbón to the big street named Calle Reyes Católicos (for the "Catholic Monarchs" Ferdinand and Isabel, who finally conquered the Moors). The street covers a river that once ran openly here, with a series of bridges (like the "Coal Bridge," Puente del Carbón) lacing together the two parts of town. Today, the modern commercial center is to your left. Cross here and continue one block farther to the horseshoe-shaped gate marked* Alcaicería. *The pedestrian street you're crossing, Zacatín, was the main drag, which*

GRANADA

Granada's Old Town Walk

ALBAYZÍN

Walk

① Corral del Carbón
② Alcaicería
③ Plaza de Bib-Rambla
④ Granada Cathedral
⑤ Royal Chapel Square
⑥ Plaza Isabel La Católica
   (Bus to Alhambra)
⑦ Plaza Nueva
⑧ To Paseo de los Tristes
   & Hammam El Bañuelo

Other

⑨ Alhambra Bookstore
⑩ Gran Vía Cathedral Bus
   Stop (from Train & Bus Stations)
⑪ Gran Vía del Colón Bus Stop
   (to Train & Bus Stations)
⑫ Plaza Nueva Bus Stop
   (to Albayzín & Sacromonte)

ran parallel to the river before it was covered in the 19th century. Today it's a favorite paseo destination, busy each evening with strollers. Pass through the Alcaicería gate and walk 20 yards into the old market to the first intersection at Calle Ermita.

❷ Alcaicería

Originally a Moorish silk market with 200 shops, the Alcaicería (al-kai-thay-REE-ah) was filled with precious salt, silver, spices, and silk. It had 10 armed gates and its own guards. Silk was huge in Moorish times, and silkworm-friendly mulberry trees flourished in the countryside. It was such an important product that the sultans controlled and guarded it by constructing this fine, fortified market. After the Reconquista, the Christians realized this market was good for business and didn't mess with it. Later, the

more zealous Philip II had it shut down. A terrible fire in 1850 destroyed what was left. Today's Alcaicería was rebuilt in the late 1800s as a tourist souk (marketplace) to complement the romantic image of Granada popularized by the writings of Washington Irving.

Explore the mesh of tiny shopping lanes: overpriced trinkets, popcorn machines popping, men selling balloons, leather goods spread out on streets, kids playing soccer, barking dogs, dogged shoe-shine boys, and the whirring grind of bicycle-powered knife sharpeners. You'll invariably meet obnoxious and persistent women pushing their green rosemary sprigs on innocents in order to extort money. Be strong.

• *Turn left down Calle Ermita. After 50 yards, you'll leave the market via another fortified gate and enter a big square crowded with outdoor restaurants. Skirt around the tables to the Neptune fountain, which marks the center of the...*

❸ Plaza de Bib-Rambla

This exuberant square, just two blocks behind the cathedral (from the fountain you can see its blocky bell tower peeking above the big orange building) was once the center of Moorish Granada. While Moorish rule of Spain lasted 700 years, the last couple of those centuries were a period of decline as Muslim culture split under weak leadership and Christian forces grew more determined. The last remnants of the Moorish kingdom united and ruled from Granada. As Muslims fled south from reconquered lands, Granada was flooded with refugees. By 1400, Granada had an estimated 100,000 people—huge for medieval Europe. This was the main square,

the focal point for markets and festivals, but it was much smaller than now, pushed in by the jam-packed city.

Under Christian rule, Moors were initially tolerated (as they were considered good for business), and this area became the Moorish ghetto. Then, with the Inquisition (under Philip II, c. 1550), ideology trumped pragmatism, and Jews and Muslims were evicted or forced to convert. The elegant square you see today was built, and built big. In-your-face Catholic processions started here. To assert Christian rule, all the trappings of Christian power were layered upon what had been the trappings of Moorish power. Between here and the cathedral were the Christian University (the big orange building) and the adjacent archbishop's palace.

Today Plaza de Bib-Rambla is good for coffee or a meal amid the color and fragrance of flower stalls and the burbling of its Neptune-topped fountain. It remains a multigenerational hangout, where it seems everyone is enjoying a peaceful retirement.

With Neptune facing you, leave the plaza by the left corner (along Calle Pescadería) to reach a smaller, similarly lively square—little Plaza Pescadería, where families spill out to enjoy its many restaurants. For a quick snack, drop into tiny **Cunini Pescadería**—next to its namesake restaurant—for a takeaway bite of *pescaito frito*—fried fish.

• *Leave Plaza Pescadería on Calle Marqués de Gerona; within one block, you'll come to a small square fronting a very big church.*

❹ Granada Cathedral (Catedral de Granada)

Wow, the cathedral facade just screams triumph. That's partly because its design is based on a triumphal arch, built over a destroyed

mosque. Five hundred yards away, there was once open space outside the city wall with good soil for a foundation. But the Christian conquerors said, "No way." Instead, they destroyed the mosque and built their cathedral right here on difficult, sandy soil. This was the place where the people of Granada traditionally worshipped—and now they would worship as Christians.

The church—started in the early 1500s and not finished until the late 1700s—has a Gothic foundation and was built mostly in the Renaissance style, with

its last altars done in Neoclassical style. Hometown artist Alonso Cano (1601-1667) finished the building, at the king's request, in Baroque. Accentuating the power of the Roman Catholic Church, the emphasis here is on Mary rather than Christ. The facade declares *Ave Maria*. (This was Counter-Reformation time, and the Church was threatened by Protestant Christians. Mary was also more palatable to Muslim converts, as she is revered in the Quran.)

• *To tour the cathedral now, you can enter here. You'll exit on the far side, near the big street called Gran Vía de Colón.*

If you're skipping the cathedral interior for now, circle around the cathedral to the right, keeping the church on your left, until you reach the small square facing the Royal Chapel.

❺ Royal Chapel Square

This square was once ringed by important Moorish buildings. A hammam (public bath), a madrassa (school), a caravanserai (Days Inn), the silk market, and the leading mosque were all right here. With Christian rule, the madrassa (the faux-gray-stone building with the walls painted in 3-D Baroque style) became Granada's first City Hall (€2, daily 10:00-20:00 for short guided tour of 14th-century *mihrab* and Mudejar-era annex). Here, too, is the entrance to the Royal Chapel, where the coffins of Ferdinand and Isabel were moved in 1521 from the Alhambra.

• *Continue up the cobbled, stepped lane to Gran Vía. With the arrival of cars and the modern age, the people of Granada wanted a Parisian-style boulevard. In the early 20th century, they mercilessly cut through the old town and created Gran Vía and its French-style buildings—in the process destroying everything in its path, including many historic convents.*

Turn right and walk down Gran Vía toward the big square just ahead (near where minibus #C3 to the Alhambra stops). Face the statue above the fountain from across the busy intersection.

❻ Plaza Isabel La Católica

Granada's two grand boulevards, Gran Vía and Calle Reyes Católicos, meet here at Plaza Isabel La Católica. Above the fountain,

a beautiful statue shows Columbus unfurling a long contract with Isabel. It lists the terms of Columbus' MCCCCLXXXXII voyage: "For as much as you, Columbus, are going by our command to discover and subdue some Islands and Continents in the ocean...." The two reliefs show the big events in Granada of 1492: Isabel and Ferdinand accepting Columbus' proposal and a stirring battle scene (which never happened) at the walls of the Alhambra.

Isabel was driven by her desire to spread Catholicism. Spain, needing an alternate trade route to the Orient's spices after the Ottoman Empire cut off the traditional overland routes, was driven by trade. And Columbus was driven by his desire for money. As a reward for adding territory to Spain's Catholic empire, Isabel promised Columbus the ranks of Admiral of the Oceans and Governor of the New World. To sweeten the pot, she tossed in one-eighth of all the riches he brought home. Isabel died thinking that Columbus had found India or China. Columbus died poor and disillusioned.

Calle Reyes Católicos leads from this square downhill to the busy intersection called Puerta Real. From there, Acera del Darro takes you through modern Granada to the river, passing the huge El Corte Inglés department store and lots of modern commerce. This area erupts with locals out strolling each night. For one of the best Granada paseos, wander the streets here around 19:00.

• *Backtrack and cross over Gran Vía on a green light (don't cross against the light at this odd intersection). Follow Calle Reyes Católicos to the left for a couple of blocks until you reach . . .*

❼ Plaza Nueva

Plaza Nueva is dominated at the far end by the regional Palace of Justice (grand Baroque facade with green Andalusian flag). The fountain is capped by a stylized pomegranate—the symbol of the city, always open and fertile. The main action here is the comings and goings of the busy little shuttle buses serving the Albayzín. The local hippie community, nicknamed the *pies negros* (black feet) for obvious reasons, hangs out here and on Calle de Elvira. They squat—with their dogs and guitars—in abandoned caves above those the Roma (Gypsies) occupy in Sacromonte. Many are the children of rich Spanish families from the north, hell-bent on disappointing their high-achieving parents.

• *Our tour continues with a stroll up Carrera del Darro. Leave Plaza Nueva opposite where you entered, on the little lane that runs alongside the Darro River. This is particularly enjoyable in the cool of the evening.*

❽ Paseo de los Tristes

This stretch of road—Carrera del Darro—is also called Paseo de los Tristes—"Walk of the Sad Ones." It was once the route of funeral processions to the cemetery at the edge of town. As you leave Plaza Nueva, notice the small Church of Santa Ana on your right. This was originally a mosque—the church tower replaced a minaret. Notice the ceramic brickwork. This is Mudejar art by Moorish craftsmen, whose techniques were later employed by Christians.

Follow Carrera del Darro along the Darro River, which flows around the base of the Alhambra (look down by the river for a glimpse of feral cats). Six miles upstream, part of the Darro is diverted to provide water for the Alhambra's many fountains—a remarkable feat of Moorish engineering that made the grand fortress complex resistant to siege.

After passing two small, picturesque bridges, the road widens slightly for a bus stop. Here you'll see the broken nub of a once-grand 11th-century bridge that led to the Alhambra. Notice two slits in the column: One held an iron portcullis to keep bad guys from entering the town via the river. The second held a solid door that was lowered to build up water, then released to flush out the riverbed and keep it clean.

• *Across from the remains of the bridge is the brick facade of an evocative Moorish bath.*

Hammam El Bañuelo (Moorish Baths)

In Moorish times, hammams were a big part of the community (working-class homes didn't have bathrooms). Baths were strictly segregated and were more than places to wash: These were social meeting points where business was done. In Christian times it was assumed that conspiracies brewed in these baths—therefore, only a few of them survive. This place gives you the chance to explore the stark but evocative ruins of an 11th-century Moorish public bath.

Cost and Hours: €5, covered by Dobla de Oro card; daily 9:30-14:30 & 17:00-21:00, mid-Sept-March 10:00-17:00; Carrera del Darro 31, tel. 958-027-800.

Visiting the Baths: Upon entering, you pass the house of the keeper and the foyer, then visit the cold room, the warm room (where services like massage were offered), and finally the hot, or steam, room. Beyond that, you can see the oven that generated the heat, which flowed under the hypocaust-style floor tiles (the ones closest to the oven were the hottest). The romantic little holes in the ceiling once had stained-glass louvers that attendants opened and closed with sticks to regulate the heat and steaminess. Whereas Romans soaked in their pools, Muslims just doused. Rather than being totally immersed, people scooped and splashed water over themselves. Imagine attendants stoking the fires under the metal boiler...while people in towels and wooden slippers (to protect their feet from the heated floors) enjoyed all the spa services you can imagine as beams of light slashed through the mist.

This was a great social mixer. As all were naked, class distinctions disappeared—elites learned the latest from commoners. Mothers found matches for their kids. A popular Muslim phrase sums up the attraction of the baths: "This is where anyone would spend their last coin."

• *Just across from the baths is a stop for minibus #C1—the easy way to head up to the **Albayzín**. Otherwise, continue straight ahead. On your right is the **Church of San Pedro**, the parish church of Sacromonte's Roma community (across from the Mudejar Art Museum). Within its rich interior is an ornate oxcart used to carry the host on the annual* *pilgrimage to Rocío, a town near the Portuguese border. Just past this, on your left, is **Santa Catalina de Zafra**, a convent of cloistered nuns (they worship behind a screen that divides the church's rich interior in half).*

*This walk ends at **Paseo de los Tristes**—with its restaurant tables spilling out under the floodlit Alhambra. From here, the road arcs up to the Albayzín and into Sacromonte. If you've worked up a hunger, you can backtrack a few blocks to Calle de Gloria, where the **Convento de San Bernardo** sells cookies and monastic wine. Look for the Venta de Dulces sign on the corner; goods are sold from behind a lazy Susan.*

The Alhambra Tour

This last and greatest Moorish palace is one of Europe's top sights and worth ▲▲▲. Attracting up to 8,000 visitors a day, it's the reason most tourists come to Granada. Nowhere else does the splendor of Moorish civilization shine so beautifully.

The last Moorish stronghold in Europe is, with all due respect, really a symbol of retreat. For centuries, Granada was merely a regional capital. Gradually the Christian Reconquista moved south, taking Córdoba (1237) and Sevilla (1248). The Nazarids, one of the many diverse ethnic groups of Spanish Muslims, held together the last Moorish kingdom, which they ruled from Granada until 1492. As you tour their grand palace, remember that while Europe slumbered through the Dark Ages, Moorish magnificence blossomed—ornate stucco, plaster "stalactites," colors galore, scalloped windows framing Granada views, exuberant gardens, and water, water everywhere. Water—so rare and precious in most of the Islamic world—was the purest symbol of life to the Moors. The Alhambra is decorated with water: standing still, cascading, masking secret conversations, and drip-dropping playfully.

The Alhambra consists of four sights clustered together atop a hill, all covered by the following self-guided tour:

Palacios Nazaríes: Exquisite Moorish palace, the Alhambra's must-see sight.

Charles V's Palace: Christian Renaissance palace plopped on top of the Alhambra after the Reconquista, with the fine Alhambra Museum.

Generalife Gardens: Fragrant, lovely manicured gardens with small summer palace.

Alcazaba: Empty but evocative old fort with tower and views.

It's crucial to make **advance reservations** for the Alhambra, where daytime tickets to the Palacios Nazaríes often sell out.

GETTING THERE

You have four options for getting to the Alhambra.

On Foot: From Plaza Nueva, hike 20-25 minutes up Cuesta de Gomérez. Keep going straight—you'll see the Alhambra high on your left. Along the way, after about 10 minutes, look for the Justice Gate shortcut. The ticket pavilion is on the far side of the Alhambra, near the entrance to the Generalife Gardens.

For walking directions back to town, see the end of the Alhambra tour.

By Bus: Just uphill from Plaza de Isabel La Católica, catch a red #C3 minibus, marked *Alhambra* (€1.20 per trip or use Credibús card). There are three Alhambra stops: Generalife (main ticket office and the gardens), Charles V, and Justice Gate (best if you already have a printed ticket or are using a Granada Card or Dobla de Oro card).

By Taxi: It's a €7 ride from the taxi stand on Plaza Nueva.

By Car: If you're coming from outside the city by car, you can drive to the Alhambra without passing through Granada's historic center. From the freeway, take the exit marked *Ronda Sur-Alhambra*. Signs will lead you to a public parking lot, located near the main entrance (€2.70/hour). Overnight parking here is perfectly permissible (€18/24 hours, guarded at night). When you leave, be careful to go out the same way you came in, avoiding the driving ban in Granada's historic center.

PLANNING YOUR TIME

Daytime "Alhambra General" tickets are sold with a specific 30-minute time slot for admission to the Palacios Nazaríes (first entry to palaces at 8:30, last entry one hour before closing). You must enter the palaces within your 30-minute window, but once inside, you can linger as long as you like. Morning time slots sell out the quickest. But for most travelers, an afternoon is ample time to see the site—not only is the light perfect later in the day, there are fewer tour groups.

Be sure to arrive at the Alhambra with enough time to make it to the palace within your allotted half-hour entry time. Ticket checkers at the Palacios Nazaríes are strict. Be aware that if you are picking up your tickets at the main entrance (at the top end), or you start with the gardens, you're a 15-minute walk away from Palacios Nazaríes at the other end. Plan accordingly.

Although you can see the sights in any order, to minimize walking, I recommend seeing Charles V's Palace and the Alcazaba fort before your visit to Palacios Nazaríes (these three sights are at the lower end of the hill). When you finish touring the palace, you'll leave through the Partal Gardens, a pleasant 15-minute walk from the Generalife Gardens. If you have a long time to wait for your Palacios Nazaríes appointment, you could do the gardens first, then head down to the other three. Or you can kill time luxuriously on the breezy view terrace of the parador bar (within the Alhambra walls).

ORIENTATION TO THE ALHAMBRA
Cost and Hours

Cost: Various paid tickets, listed below, cover the sights of the Alhambra (prices listed do not include Ticketmaster surcharge). For many travelers, the first option is best. A portion of the grounds is free to visit, as is Charles V's Palace (and the Alhambra Museum inside it).

- **Alhambra General:** €14, covers the Alcazaba fort, Palacios Nazaríes, and Generalife Gardens. This is the only ticket that allows you to see Palacios Nazaríes during the day.
- **Alhambra Gardens, Generalife, and Alcazaba:** €7, covers daytime admission to everything but the Palacios Nazaríes
- **Alhambra Nocturna—Palaces:** €8, nighttime visit to the Palacios Nazaríes
- **Alhambra Nocturna—Generalife:** €8, nighttime visit to the gardens and summer palace
- **Alhambra Experiences:** €14, nighttime visit to Palacios Nazaríes, then (the next morning) entry to the Alcazaba and Generalife Gardens

Hours: The entire Alhambra complex is open daily 8:30-20:00, mid-Oct-March until 18:00. Ticket office opens at 8:00, last entry one hour before closing, toll tel. 902-441-221, www.alhambra-patronato.es.

The Palacios Nazaríes and Generalife Gardens are also open most **evenings** (Tue-Sat 22:00-23:30, closed Sun-Mon; mid-Oct-March Fri-Sat 20:00-21:30 only, last entry one hour before closing).

Getting In with a Reservation

Reserving in Advance: Reservations are essential to be assured of seeing the entire sight, because on most days, the highlight of the Alhambra—the popular Palacios Nazaríes—is sold out completely. Reserve an entry time up to three months before your visit (€1.40 Ticketmaster surcharge), and pick up your tickets in Spain. For most of the year, booking one month in advance is sufficient—but reserve farther out for Holy Week, weekends, and major holidays. Off-season (July-Aug and winter), you can generally book a few days ahead. Everyone who visits the palaces, even children, must have their own ticket (kids under 12 are free; discount for kids 12-15).

You can reserve online or by phone:

Order **online** at www.alhambra-tickets.es. Select the "Alhambra General" ticket, choose your date, then select a half-hour time slot for entry to Palacios Nazaríes (*agotado* means "sold out").

By **phone,** an English-speaking operator walks you through the process. Within Spain, dial 902-888-001. From the US, dial 011-34-958-926-031. The line is open Mon-Fri 8:00-24:00 Spanish time, closed Sat-Sun.

Picking Up Reserved Tickets: No matter how you make your reservation, you'll need to convert it to a printed ticket in Spain (bring the same credit card you used to reserve).

Save time by retrieving your ticket *before* you reach the Alhambra: Collect it from the Ticketmaster machines at the Alhambra office in town (inside the Corral del Carbón). Picking up your ticket in advance lets you use the Justice Gate shortcut, avoiding the mob at the main entrance.

If you do pick up your ticket at the main entrance, follow *Bookings collection with credit card* signs to the windows marked *Retirada de Reservas,* or use the Ticketmaster machines (in the less-crowded pavilion behind the bookstore). Allow up to a half-hour to pick up tickets and walk from there to the Palacios.

Getting In Without a Reservation

If you arrive in Granada without an "Alhambra General" reservation, you have these options:

- Buy the Granada Card Básico city pass, which even on late notice lets you choose an entry time, although not likely for the same day. Another option is the Dobla de Oro card.
- Take a guided tour, which admits you without reservations.
- See if your hotel can wrangle a reservation.
- Try for a last-minute reservation online or by phone, or visit the in-town Alhambra office at the Corral del Carbón (they sell tickets for future dates, not same-day tickets).
- Be in line by 7:30 at the Alhambra's main entrance in the hopes of snaring a same-day ticket.
- Purchase a ticket online or at the main entrance to visit everything except Palacios Nazaríes. Or stroll through just the free parts (Charles V's Palace, Alhambra Museum, and the grounds) and enjoy the views.
- See the Alhambra by moonlight, and skip the reservation hassles altogether.

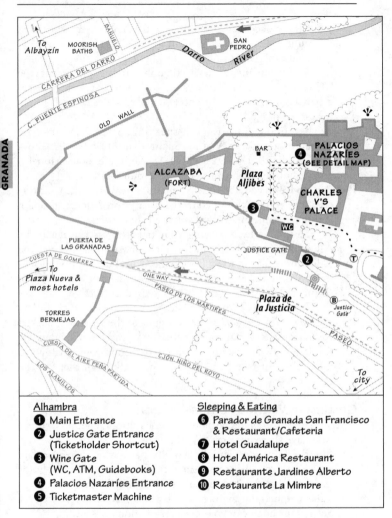

Alhambra
1 Main Entrance
2 Justice Gate Entrance
(Ticketholder Shortcut)
3 Wine Gate
(WC, ATM, Guidebooks)
4 Palacios Nazaríes Entrance
5 Ticketmaster Machine

Sleeping & Eating
6 Parador de Granada San Francisco
& Restaurant/Cafeteria
7 Hotel Guadalupe
8 Hotel América Restaurant
9 Restaurante Jardines Alberto
10 Restaurante La Mimbre

At the Alhambra

Entering: If you already have your ticket in hand, you can take a shortcut to the core of the complex by entering through the closer-to-town **Justice Gate** (if you're walking, this saves about 15 minutes of uphill climbing; you can also get off the minibus here).

If you want to see the Generalife Gardens first, or don't yet have a ticket, use the upper, **main entrance.** The ticket pavilion has a cash-only line for same-day ticket purchases and a line for picking up reserved tickets. If these lines are long, or to pay by credit card, head to the smaller pavilion just past the bookstore—you'll find Ticketmaster machines

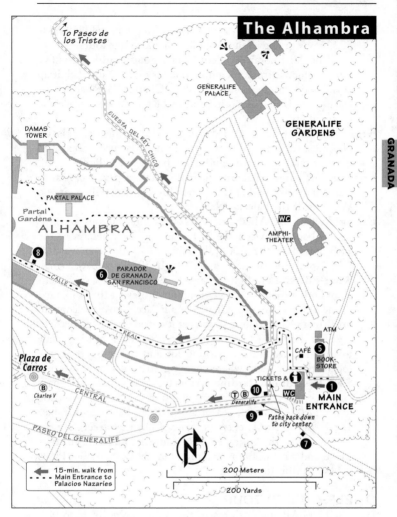

The Alhambra

To Paseo de los Tristes

GENERALIFE PALACE

GENERALIFE GARDENS

DAMAS TOWER

CUESTA DEL REY CHICO

PARTAL PALACE

Partal Gardens

ALHAMBRA

WC

AMPHI-THEATER

❽

PARADOR DE GRANADA SAN FRANCISCO

❻

CALLE

REAL

ATM

CAFÉ

❺ BOOKSTORE

Plaza de Carros

❽ Charles V

CENTRAL

TICKETS & ❶

❿

T B
Generalife

WC

❶ MAIN ENTRANCE

❾

Paths back down to city center

PASEO DEL GENERALIFE

❼

N

← 15-min. walk from Main Entrance to Palacios Nazaríes

200 Meters

200 Yards

GRANADA

for collecting reserved tickets as well as machines for purchasing tickets. Those with tickets in hand can thread their way between the ticket pavilion and the bookstore to the entrance.

Visitor Information: I recommend the slick and colorful *Alhambra and Generalife in Focus,* sold at bookstores in town; to make the most of your visit, buy and read it before you tour the sight. Alhambra bookstores push the pricey *Official Guide,* a well-produced, scholarly tome—but it weighs a ton.

Tours: Various companies run tours that include transportation to the Alhambra and a **guided tour** of Palacios Nazaríes (for example, GranaVisión has tours from €49, tel. 958-535-872, www.granavision.com; Cicerone also has tours).

The Alhambra's excellent €7 tablet **audioguide** offers five tours to choose from, including one for night visits. Pick it up at the main entrance or the kiosk by Charles V's Palace (must leave photo ID as a deposit; return tablet to the same place you picked it up).

Bags: To prevent damage to delicate stucco inside the Palacios Nazaríes, staff request that if you bring a day pack, wear it in front or carry it in your hand. Even better, travel light.

Services: WCs are available at the main entrance pavilion, next to the Wine Gate, and at the Generalife Gardens. There are no WCs inside the Palacios Nazaríes.

Eating: Within the Alhambra walls, your food options are limited. Choose between the restaurant or the cafeteria at the **$$$ parador;** the peaceful ambience of the courtyard at **$$$ Hotel América** (Sun-Fri 12:30-16:30, closed Sat); a small **$ bar-café kiosk** in front of the Alcazaba fort (basic sandwiches and other snacks); and **vending machines** (at the WC) next to the Wine Gate, near Charles V's Palace. You're welcome to bring in a **picnic** as long as you eat it outside ticketed areas.

For better-value (but touristy) options, head outside to the area around the parking lot and ticket booth at the top of the complex, where there's a strip of handy eateries. **$$$ Restaurante Jardines Alberto,** across from the main entrance, has a nice courtyard and offers a charming setting (daily 12:00-23:30, off-season until 18:00; Paseo de la Sabica 1, tel. 958-221-661, enter up stairs from the street). By the #C3 bus stop, the breezy **$$$ Restaurante La Mimbre** offers shade and a break from the crowds (daily 12:00-17:00, Paseo del Generalife 18, tel. 958-222-276).

❍ SELF-GUIDED TOUR

I've listed the Alhambra sights in the order you're likely to visit them. The first three cluster at the bottom/far end of the complex, while the Generalife Gardens are about a 15-minute walk away, at the top (main entrance).

▲▲Charles V's Palace and the Alhambra Museum

While it's only natural for a conquering king to build his own palace over his foe's palace, the Christian Charles V (the Holy Roman Emperor, who ruled as Charles I over Spain) respected the splendid Moorish palace. And so, to make his mark, he built a modern Renaissance palace for official functions and used the existing Palacios Nazaríes as a royal residence. With a unique circle-within-a-square design by Pedro Machuca, a pupil of Michel-

angelo, this is Spain's most impressive Renaissance building. Stand in the circular courtyard surrounded by mottled marble columns, then climb the stairs. Perhaps Charles' palace was designed to have a dome, but it was never finished—his son, Philip II, abandoned it to build his own, much more massive palace outside Madrid, El Escorial (the final and most austere example of Spanish Renaissance architecture). Even without a dome, acoustics are perfect in the center—stand in the middle and sing your best aria. The palace doubles as a venue for the popular International Festival of Music and Dance.

The **Alhambra Museum** (Museo de la Alhambra, on the ground floor of Charles V's Palace), worth ▲, shows off some of the Alhambra's best surviving Moorish art. The museum's beautifully displayed and well-described artifacts—including tiles, characteristic green, blue, and black pottery, lion fountains even bigger than ones you'll see in the palaces, and a beautiful carved-wood door—help humanize the Alhambra (free, Wed-Sat 8:30-20:00, Sun and Tue until 14:30, shorter hours off-season, closed Mon year-round). The **Fine Arts Museum** (Museo de Bellas Artes, upstairs) is of little interest to most.

• *From the front of Charles V's Palace (as you face the Alcazaba fort), the entrance to Palacios Nazaríes is to the right (look for the line snaking along the outside edge of the garden), while the Alcazaba is across a moat straight ahead (to get there, go through the keyhole-shaped Wine Gate, then hook right and walk up to the open area in front of the fort).*

Alcazaba

This fort—the original "red castle" ("Alhambra")—is the oldest and most ruined part of the complex, offering exercise and fine city views. What you see is from the mid-13th century, but there was probably a fort here in Roman times. Once upon a time, this tower defended a medina (town) of 2,000 Muslims living within the Alhambra walls. It's a huge, sprawling complex—wind your way through passages and courtyards, over uneven terrain, to reach the biggest tower at the tip of the complex. Then climb stairs steeply up to the very top. From there (looking north), find Plaza Nueva and the San Nicolás viewpoint in

The Alhambra by Moonlight

If you prefer doing things after dark, you can avoid the Alhambra reservation hassle. Late-night visits to the Alhambra are easy (see "Cost and Hours" on page 98)—just buy your ticket upon arrival, as night-visit tickets hardly ever sell out. Keep in mind that combining two separate tickets (daytime "Alhambra Gardens," evening "Alhambra at Night—Palaces") offers more flexibility than the "Alhambra Experiences" ticket, which locks you into a visit over two days.

You can't see the Alcazaba fort at night, but, hey, Palacios Nazaríes provides 80 percent of the Alhambra's thrills anyway. Although a few small sections of both the palace and the gardens are closed at night, you'll see most of what the daytime visitors see. While some find the Alhambra disappointing at night, others find it even more magical (less crowded and beautifully lit); either way, it's better than not seeing it at all.

the Albayzín. To the south are the Sierra Nevada Mountains. Is anybody skiing today? Notice the tower's four flags: the blue of the European Union, the green and white of Andalucía, the red and yellow of Spain, and the red and green of Granada.

Speaking of flags, imagine that day in 1492 when the Christian cross and the flags of Aragon and Castile were raised on this tower, and (according to a probably fanciful legend) the fleeing Moorish king Boabdil (Abu Abdullah, in Arabic) looked back and wept. His mom chewed him out, saying, "You weep like a woman for what you couldn't defend like a man." With this defeat, more than seven centuries of Muslim rule in Spain came to an end. Much later, Napoleon stationed his troops at the Alhambra, contributing substantially to its ruin when he left.

• If you're going from the Alcazaba to Palacios Nazaríes, backtrack through the Wine Gate, then look for the people lined up along the gardens by Charles V's Palace.

▲▲▲Palacios Nazaríes

During the 30-minute entry time stamped on your ticket, enter the jewel of the Alhambra: the Moorish royal palace. If you show up at the start of your entry window and the place seems particularly crowded, consider lingering outside and enjoying the views for about 15 minutes to give crowds time to dissipate inside. Once you're in, you can relax—you're no longer under any time constraints. You'll walk through three basic sections: royal offices, ceremonial rooms, and private quarters. Built mostly in the 14th

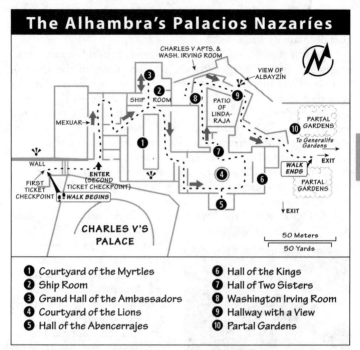

The Alhambra's Palacios Nazaríes

CHARLES V APTS. &
WASH. IRVING ROOM

VIEW OF
ALBAYZÍN

❸

SHIP ❷ ROOM

❽

❾

PATIO
OF
LINDA-
RAJA

MEXUAR→

❶

PARTAL
GARDENS

❿

To Generalife
Gardens

GRANADA

WALL

❼

WALK
ENDS

EXIT

ENTER
(SECOND
TICKET CHECKPOINT)

❹

❻

FIRST
TICKET
CHECKPOINT

PARTAL
GARDENS

WALK BEGINS

↓ EXIT

**CHARLES V'S
PALACE**

50 Meters

50 Yards

❶ Courtyard of the Myrtles
❷ Ship Room
❸ Grand Hall of the Ambassadors
❹ Courtyard of the Lions
❺ Hall of the Abencerrajes

❻ Hall of the Kings
❼ Hall of Two Sisters
❽ Washington Irving Room
❾ Hallway with a View
❿ Partal Gardens

century, this palace offers your best possible look at the refined, elegant Moorish civilization of Al-Andalus (the Arabic word for the Moorish-controlled Iberian Peninsula).

You'll visit rooms decorated from top to bottom with carved wood ceilings, stucco "stalactites," ceramic tiles, molded-plaster walls, and filigree windows. Open-air courtyards feature fountains with bubbling water, which give the palace a desert-oasis feel. A garden enlivened by lush vegetation and peaceful pools is the Quran's symbol of heaven. The palace is well-preserved and well-restored, but the trick to fully appreciating it is to imagine it furnished and filled with Moorish life...sultans with hookah pipes lounging on pillows upon Persian carpets, heavy curtains on the windows, and ivory-studded wooden furniture. The whole place was painted with bright colors, many suggested by the Quran—red (blood), blue (heaven), green (oasis), and gold (wealth). Throughout the palace, walls, ceilings, vases, carpets, and tiles were covered with decorative patterns and calligraphy, mostly poems and verses of praise from the Quran and from local poets. Much of what is known about the Alhambra is known simply from reading the inscriptions that decorate its walls.

As you wander, keep the palace themes in mind: water, a near absence of figural images (they're frowned upon in the Quran), "stalactite" ceilings—and few signs telling you where you are. As tempting as it might be to touch the stucco, don't—it is very susceptible to damage from the oils from your hand. Use this book's map to locate the essential stops listed below.

• *Begin by walking through a few administrative rooms (the* mexuar) *with a stunning Mecca-oriented prayer room (the oratorio, with a niche on the right facing Mecca) and a small courtyard with a round fountain, until you hit the big rectangular courtyard with a fish pond lined by two myrtle-bush hedges.*

❶ **Courtyard of the Myrtles** (Patio de Arrayanes): The standard palace design included a central courtyard like this. Moors

loved their patios—with a garden and water, under the sky. In accordance with medieval Moorish mores, women rarely went out, so they stayed in touch with nature in courtyards like the Courtyard of the Myrtles—named for the two fragrant myrtle hedges that added to the courtyard's charm. Notice the wooden screens (erected by jealous husbands) that allowed the cloistered women to look out without being clearly seen. The upstairs was likely for winter use, and the cooler ground level was probably used in summer.

• *Head left from the entry through gigantic wooden doors into the long narrow antechamber to the throne room, called the...*

❷ **Ship Room** (Sala de la Barca): It's understandable that many think the Ship Room is named for the upside-down-hull shape of its fine cedar ceiling. But the name is actually derived from the Arab word *baraka,* meaning "divine blessing and luck." As you passed through this room, blessings and luck are exactly what you'd need—because in the next room, you'd be face-to-face with the sultan.

• *Oh, it's your turn. Enter the ornate throne room.*

❸ **Grand Hall of the Ambassadors** (Gran Salón de los Embajadores): The palace's largest room, also known as the Salón de Comares, functioned as the throne room. It was here that the sultan, seated on a throne opposite the entrance, received foreign emissaries. Ogle the room—a perfect cube—from top to bottom. The star-studded, domed wooden ceiling (made from 8,017 inlaid pieces like a giant jigsaw puzzle) suggests the complexity of Allah's infinite universe. Wooden "stalactites" form the cornice, running

around the entire base of the ceiling. The stucco walls, even without their original paint and gilding, are still glorious. The filigree windows once held stained glass and had heavy drapes to block out the heat. Some precious 16th-century tiles survive in the center of the floor.

A visitor here would have stepped from the glaring Courtyard of the Myrtles into this dim, cool, incense-filled world, to meet the silhouetted sultan. Imagine the alcoves functioning busily as work stations, and the light at sunrise or sunset, rich and warm, filling the room.

Let your eyes trace the finely carved Arabic script. Muslims avoided making images of living creatures—that was God's work. But they could carve decorative religious messages. One phrase— "only Allah is victorious"—is repeated 9,000 times throughout the palace. Find the character for "Allah"—it looks like a cursive W with a nose on its left side, with a vertical line to the right. The swoopy toboggan blades underneath are a kind of artistic punctuation used to set off one phrase.

In 1492, two historic events likely took place in this room. Culminating a 700-year-long battle, the Reconquista was completed here as the last Moorish king, Boabdil, signed the terms of his surrender before eventually leaving for Africa.

And it was here that Columbus made one of his final pitches to Isabel and Ferdinand to finance a sea voyage to the Orient. Imagine the scene: The king, the queen, and the greatest minds from the University of Salamanca gathered here while Columbus produced maps and pie charts to make his case that he could sail west to reach the East. Ferdinand and the professors laughed and called Columbus mad—not because they thought the world was flat (most educated people knew otherwise), but because they thought Columbus had underestimated the size of the globe, and thus the length and cost of the journey.

But Isabel said, *"Sí, señor."* Columbus fell to his knees (promising to pack light, wear a money belt, and use the most current guidebook available).

Opposite the Ship Room entrance, photographers pause for a picture-perfect view of the tower reflected in the Courtyard of the Myrtles pool. This was the original palace entrance (before Charles V's Palace was built).

• *Continue deeper into the palace, to a courtyard where, 600 years ago, only the royal family and their servants could enter. It's the much-photographed...*

❹ **Courtyard of the Lions** (Patio de los Leones): This de-

GRANADA

Islamic Art

Rather than making paintings and statues, Islamic artists expressed themselves with beautiful but functional objects. Ceramics (most of them blue and white, or green and white), carpets, glazed tile panels, stucco-work ceilings, and glass tableware are covered with complex patterns. The intricate interweaving, repetition, and unending lines suggest the complex, infinite nature of God, known to Muslims as Allah.

You'll see few pictures of humans, since Islamic doctrine holds that the creation of living beings is God's work alone. However, secular art by Muslims for their homes and palaces was not bound by this restriction; you'll get an occasional glimpse of realistic art featuring men and women enjoying a garden paradise, a symbol of the Muslim heaven.

Look for floral patterns (twining vines, flowers, and arabesques) and geometric designs (stars and diamonds). The decorative motifs (Arabic script, patterns, flowers, shells, and so on) that repeat countless times throughout the palace were made by pressing wet plaster into molds. The most common pattern is calligraphy—elaborate lettering of an inscription in Arabic, the language of the Quran. A quote from the Quran on a vase or lamp combines the power of the message with the beauty of the calligraphy.

lightful courtyard is named for the famous fountain at its center with its ring of 12 marble lions—originals from the 14th century. Conquering Christians disassembled the fountain to see how it worked, rendering it nonfunctional; it finally flowed again in 2012. From the center of the courtyard, four channels carry water outward—figuratively to the corners

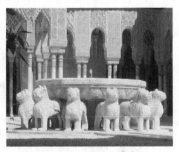

of the earth and literally to various more private apartments of the royal family. The arched gallery that surrounds the courtyard is supported by 124 perfectly balanced columns. The craftsmanship is first-class. For example, the lead fittings between the precut sections of the columns allow things to flex during earthquakes, preventing destruction during shakes.

Six hundred years ago, the Muslim Moors could read the

Quranic poetry that ornaments this court, and they could understand the symbolism of this lush, enclosed garden, considered the
embodiment of paradise or truth. ("How beautiful is this garden /
where the flowers of Earth rival the stars of Heaven. / What can
compare with this alabaster fountain, gushing crystal-clear water? /
Nothing except the fullest moon, pouring light from an unclouded
sky.") They appreciated this part of the palace even more than we do
today.

*• On the right, off the courtyard, the only original door still in the palace
leads into a square room called the...*

❺ Hall of the Abencerrajes (Sala de los Abencerrajes): This
was the sultan's living room, with an exquisite ceiling based on
the eight-sided Muslim star. The
name of the room comes from a
legend of the 16th century. The
father of Boabdil took a new wife
and wanted to disinherit the children of his first marriage—one
of whom was Boabdil. To deny
power to Boabdil and his siblings,
the sultan killed nearly all the pre-
Boabdil Abencerraje family members. He thought this would pave
the way for the son of his new wife
to be the next sultan. He is said to
have stacked 36 Abencerraje heads
in the pool, under the sumptuous
honeycombed stucco ceiling in this

hall. But his scheme failed, and Boabdil ultimately assumed the
throne. Bloody power struggles like this were the norm here in
the Alhambra.

• At the end of the court opposite where you entered is the...

❻ Hall of the Kings (Sala de los Reyes): This hall has been
undergoing restoration for several years and will be partially closed
off during your visit. If the side vaults were visible, you'd see paintings on the goat-leather ceiling depicting scenes of the sultan and
his family. The center room's group portrait shows the first 10 of
the Alhambra's 22 sultans. The scene is a fantasy, since these people
lived over a span of many generations. The two end rooms display
scenes of princely pastimes, such as hunting and shooting skeet. In
a palace otherwise devoid of figures, these offer a rare look at royal
life in the palace.

*• Continue around the lion fountain. Before entering the next room,
you'll pass doors leading right and left to a 14th-century WC plumbed by
running water and stairs up to the harem. Next is the...*

❼ Hall of Two Sisters (Sala de Dos Hermanas): The Sala

de Dos Hermanas—nicknamed for the giant twin slabs of white marble on the floor flanking the fountain—has another oh-wow stucco ceiling lit by clerestory windows. This is a typical royal bedroom, with alcoves for private use and a fountain. Running water helped cool and humidify the room but also added elegance and extravagance, as running water was a luxury most could only dream of.

The room features geometric patterns and stylized Arabic script quoting verses from the Quran. If the inlaid color tiles look "Escher-esque," you've got it backward: Escher is Alhambra-esque. M. C. Escher was inspired by these very patterns on his visit. Study the patterns—they remind us of the Moorish expertise in math. The sitting room (farthest from the entry) has low windows, because Moorish people sat on the floor. Some rare stained glass survives in the ceiling. From here the sultana enjoyed a grand view of the medieval city (before the 16th-century wing was added, which blocks the view today).

• *That's about it for the palace. From here, we enter the later, 16th-century Christian section, and wander past the domed roofs of the old baths down a hallway to a pair of rooms decorated with mahogany ceilings. Marked with a large plaque is the...*

❽ Washington Irving Room: While living in Spain in 1829, Washington Irving stayed in the Alhambra, and he wrote *Tales of the Alhambra* in this room. It was a romantic time, when the palace was home to Roma and donkeys. His "tales" rekindled interest in the Alhambra, causing it to be recognized as a national treasure. A plaque on the wall thanks Irving, who later served as the US ambassador to Spain (1842-1846). Here's a quote from Irving's *The Alhambra by Moonlight:* "On such heavenly nights I would sit for hours at my window inhaling the sweetness of the garden, and musing on the checkered fortunes of those whose history was dimly shadowed out in the elegant memorials around."

• *As you leave, stop at the open-air...*

❾ Hallway with a View: Here you'll enjoy the best-in-the-palace view of the labyrinthine Albayzín—the old Moorish town on the opposite hillside. Find the famous San Nicolás viewpoint (below where the white San Nicolás church tower breaks the horizon). Creeping into the mountains on the right are the Roma neighborhoods of Sacromonte. Still circling old Granada is the Moorish wall (built in the 1400s to protect the city's population, swollen by Muslim refugees driven south by the Reconquista).

The Patio de Lindaraja (with its garden of maze-like hedges) marks the end of the palace visit. Before exiting, you can detour right into the "Secrets Room"—a domed brick room of the former baths with fun acoustics. Whisper into a corner, and your friend—with an ear to the wall—can hear you in the opposite corner. Try talking in the exact center.

• *Step outside into our last stop...*

❿ **The Partal Gardens** (El Partal): The Partal Gardens are built upon the ruins of the Partal Palace. Imagine a palace like the one you just toured, built around this reflecting pond. A fragment of it still stands—once the living quarters—on the cooler north side. Its Mecca-facing oratory has been recently restored, so you can peek inside. The Alhambra was the site of seven different palaces in 150 years. You have toured parts of just two or three.

• *Leaving the palace, climb a few stairs, continue through the gardens, and follow signs directing you left to the Generalife Gardens or right to the Alcazaba (and the rest of the Alhambra grounds).*

The path to the Generalife Gardens is a delightful 15-minute stroll through lesser (but still pleasant) gardens, along a row of fortified towers—just follow signs for Generalife. *Just before reaching the Generalife, you'll cross over a bridge and look down on the dusty lane called Cuesta del Rey Chico (a handy shortcut for returning to downtown later).*

▲▲Generalife Gardens

The sultan's vegetable and fruit orchards and summer palace retreat, called the Generalife (*h*eh-neh-rah-LEE-fay), was outside the pro-

tection of the Alhambra wall—and, today, a short hike uphill past the ticket office. The thousand-or-so residents of the Alhambra enjoyed the fresh fruit and veggies grown here. But most important, this little palace provided the sultan with a cool and quiet summer escape.

Follow the simple one-way path through the sprawling gardens. You'll catch glimpses of a sleek, modern outdoor theater, built in the 1950s. It continues to be an important concert venue for Granada. Its cypress-lined stage sees most activity during the International Festival of Music and Dance. Many of the world's greatest artists have performed here, including Andrés Segovia, Bobby McFerrin, and Jessye Norman.

From the head of the theater, signs will lead you through manicured-hedge gardens, along delightful ponds and fountains, to the palace.

Before arriving at the bright white palace, pass through the

GRANADA

The Alhambra Grounds

As you wander the grounds, remember that the Alhambra was once a city of a thousand people fortified by a 1.5-mile rampart and 30 towers. The zone within the walls was the **medina,** an urban town. As you stroll from the ticket booth down the garden-like Calle Real de la Alhambra to the palace, you're walking through the ruins of the medina (destroyed by the French in 1812). This path traces the wall, with its towers on your left. In the distance are the snowcapped Sierra Nevada peaks—the highest mountains in Iberia. The Palacios

Nazaríes, Alcazaba fort, and Generalife Gardens all have entry fees and ticket checkpoints. But the medina—with Charles V's Palace, a church, a line of shops showing off traditional wood-working techniques, and the fancy Alhambra parador—is wide open and free to everyone.

It's especially fun to snoop around the historic **Parador de Granada San Francisco,** which—as a national monument—is open to the public. Once a Moorish palace within the Alhambra, it was later converted into a Franciscan monastery, with a historic claim to fame: Its church is where the Catholic Monarchs (Ferdinand and Isabel) chose to be buried. For a peek, step in through the front door leading to a small garden area and reception. Continue straight to see the burial place, located in the open-air ruins of the

dismounting room (imagine dismounting onto the helpful stone ledge, and letting your horse drink from the trough here). Show your ticket and enter the most accurately re-created Arabian garden in Andalucía.

Here in the retreat of the Moorish kings, this garden is the closest thing on earth to the Quran's description of heaven. It was planted more than 600 years ago—that's remarkable longevity for a European garden. While there were originally only eight water jets, most of the details in today's garden closely match those lovingly described in old poems. The flowers, herbs, aromas, and water are exquisite...even for a sultan. Up the Darro River, the royal aqueduct diverted a life-giving stream of water into the Alhambra. It was channeled through this extra-long decorative fountain to irrigate the bigger garden outside, then along an aqueduct into the Alhambra for its thirsty residents. And though the splashing fountains are a delight, they are a 19th-century addition. The Moors liked a peaceful pond instead.

At the end of the pond, you enter the sultan's tiny three-church (passing the reception-desk area and a delightful former cloister; the history is described in English). The slab on the ground near the altar—a surviving bit from the mosque that was here before the church—marks the place where the king and queen rested until 1521 (when they were moved to the Royal Chapel downtown). Now a hotel, the parador has a restaurant and terrace café—with lush views of the Generalife—open to non-guests.

The medina's main road dead-ended at the **Wine Gate** (Puerta del Vino), which protected the fortress. When you pass through the Wine Gate, you enter a courtyard that was originally a moat, then a reservoir (in Christian times). The well—now encased in a bar-kiosk—is still a place for cold drinks. If you're done with your Alhambra visit, you can exit down to the city from the Wine Gate via the Justice Gate, immediately below. From there you'll walk

past a Renaissance fountain and pass through the **Pomegranate Gate** (Puerta de las Granadas) into the modern city, close to Plaza Nueva.

room summer retreat. From the last room, climb 10 steps into the upper Renaissance gardens (c. 1600). The ancient tree rising over the pond inspired Washington Irving, who wrote that this must be the "only surviving witness to the wonders of that age of Al-Andalus."

Climbing up and going through the turnstile, you enter the Romantic 19th-century garden. Your visit to the Alhambra is complete, and you've earned your reward. "Surely Allah will make those who believe and do good deeds enter gardens beneath which rivers flow; they shall be adorned therein with bracelets of gold and pearls, and their garments therein shall be of silk" (Quran 22.23).

• *From here you have two options: If you're exhausted, just head to the right and follow* salida *signs toward the gardens' exit (next to the Alhambra's main entrance).*

But if you want a little more exercise (and views), turn left at the sign for "continuación de la visita", *and take the half-mile loop up and around to see the staircase called Escalera del Agua, whose banisters double as little water canals. From the top, you'll have a chance to enter the*

"Romantic Viewpoint"—climb up the stairs for a top-floor view over the gardens (pleasant enough, but less impressive than other views at the Alhambra). Then hike back down through the garden and follow *salida* signs, through the long oleander trellis tunnel, to the exit.

There are two direct and **scenic routes to town.** One is the easily overlooked Cuesta del Rey Chico pathway. It starts not far from the main entrance, by Restaurante La Mimbre and the minibus stop—a sign just past the restaurant entrance will confirm you're on the right path. You'll walk downhill on a peaceful, cobbled lane scented with lavender and rock rose, beneath the Alhambra ramparts and past the sultan's horse lane leading up to Generalife Gardens. In 10-15 minutes you're back in town at Paseo de los Tristes, where you can stroll along a level road to Plaza Nueva or continue walking into the Albayzín district (walking downhill on this trail from the Alhambra, you can't get lost). The other route is a straight walk along the base of the fortress wall until you reach a fountain on the left. Follow the shady canopy of trees down, down, down until reaching Cuesta de Gomérez and Plaza Nueva.

More Sights in Granada

IN THE OLD TOWN
▲▲Royal Chapel (Capilla Real)
Without a doubt Granada's top Christian sight, this lavish chapel in the old town holds the dreams—and bodies—of Queen Isabel and King Ferdinand. The "Catholic Monarchs" were all about the Reconquista. Their marriage united the Aragon and Castile kingdoms, allowing an acceleration of the Christian and Spanish push south. In its last 10 years, the Reconquista snowballed. This last Moorish capital—symbolic of their victory—was their chosen burial place. While smaller and less architecturally striking than the cathedral (described later), the chapel is far more historically significant.

Cost and Hours: €5; Mon-Sat 10:15-19:30, Sun 11:00-18:30; Nov-March Mon-Sat 10:15-18:30, Sun from 11:00; no photos, entrance on Calle Oficios, just off Gran Vía del Colón—go through iron gate, tel. 958-227-848, www.capillarealgranada.com.

Visiting the Chapel: In the lobby, before you show your ticket and enter the chapel, notice the **painting of Boabdil** (on the black horse) giving the key of Granada to the conquering King Ferdinand. Boabdil wanted to fall to his knees, but the Spanish king, who had great respect for his Moorish foe, embraced him instead. They fought a long and noble war (for instance, respectfully returning the bodies of dead soldiers). Ferdinand is in red, and Isabel is behind him wearing a crown. The painting is flanked by **glass-enclosed exhibits** comparing wood sculptures of the four royal family members buried here with their marble tomb sculptures (their faces are too high up to see clearly inside the chapel).

Isabel decided to make Granada the capital of Spain (and burial place for Spanish royalty) for three reasons: 1) With the conquest of this city, Christianity had finally overcome Islam in Europe; 2) her marriage with Ferdinand, followed by the conquest of Granada, had marked the beginning of a united Spain; and 3) in Granada, she agreed to sponsor Columbus.

Show your ticket and step into the **chapel.** It's Plateresque Gothic—light and lacy silver-filigree style, named for and inspired by the fine silverwork of the Moors. The chapel's interior was originally austere, with fancy touches added later by Ferdinand and Isabel's grandson, Emperor Charles V. Five hundred years ago, this must have been the most splendid space imaginable. Because of its speedy completion (1506-1521), the Gothic architecture is unusually harmonious.

In the center of the chapel (in front of the main altar), the **four royal tombs** are Renaissance-style. Carved in Italy in 1521

from Carrara marble, they were sent by ship to Spain. The faces—based on death masks—are considered accurate. **Ferdinand** and **Isabel** are the lower, more humble of the two couples. (Isabel fans attribute the bigger dent she puts in the pillow to her larger brain.) Isabel's contemporaries described the queen as being of medium height, with auburn hair and blue eyes, and possessing a serious, modest, and gentle personality. (Compare Ferdinand and Isabel's tomb statues with the painted and gilded wood statues of them kneeling in prayer, flanking the altarpiece.)

Philip the Fair and **Juana the Mad** (who succeeded Ferdinand and Isabel) lie on the left. Philip was so "Fair" that it drove the insanely jealous Juana "Mad." Philip died young, and Juana, crazy like a fox, used her "grief" over his death to forestall a second marriage, thereby ensuring that their son Charles would inherit the throne. Charles was a key figure in European history, as his coronation merged the Holy Roman Empire (Philip the Fair's Habsburg domain) with Juana's Spanish empire. Charles V ruled a vast empire stretching from Holland to Sicily, from Bohemia to Bolivia (1519-1556). But today's Spaniards reflect that the momentous marriage that created their country also sucked them into centuries of European squabbling, eventually leaving Spain impoverished.

Granada lost power and importance when Philip II, the son of

Charles V, built his El Escorial palace outside Madrid, establishing that city as the single capital of a single Spain. This coincided with the beginning of Spain's decline, as the country squandered its vast wealth trying to maintain an impossibly huge empire. Spain's rulers were defending the romantic, quixotic dream of a Catholic empire—ruled by one divinely ordained Catholic monarch—against an irrepressible tide of nationalism and Protestantism that was sweeping across the vast Habsburg holdings in Central and Eastern Europe. Spain's relatively poor modern history can be blamed, in part, on its people's stubborn unwillingness to accept the end of this old-regime notion. Even Franco borrowed symbols from the Catholic Monarchs to legitimize his dictatorship and keep the 500-year-old legacy alive.

Look at the intricate **carving** on the Renaissance tombs. It's a humanistic statement, with these healthy, organic, realistic figures rising out of the Gothic age. Charles V thought it wasn't dazzling enough to honor his grandparents' importance, so he funded decorative touches like the iron screen and the Rogier van der Weyden painting *The Deposition* (to the left after passing through the screen; this is a copy—the original is at the Prado in Madrid). Immediately to the right, with the hardest-working altar boys in Christendom holding up gilded Corinthian columns, is a chapel with a locked-away relic (an arm) of John the Baptist.

From the feet of the marble tombs, step downstairs to see the actual **coffins.** They are plain. Ferdinand and Isabel were originally buried in the Franciscan monastery (in what is today the parador, up at the Alhambra). You're standing in front of the two people who created Spain. The fifth coffin (on right, marked *Príncipe Miguel*) belongs to a young Prince Michael, who would have been king of a united Spain and Portugal. (A sad—but too-long—story...)

The **high altar** is one of the finest Renaissance works in Spain. It's dedicated to two Johns: the Baptist and the Evangelist. In the center you can see the Baptist and the Evangelist chatting as if over tapas—an appropriately humanistic scene. Scenes from the Baptist's life are on the left: John beheaded after Salomé's fine dancing, and (below) John baptizing Jesus. Scenes from the Evangelist's life are on the right: John's martyrdom (a failed attempt to boil him alive in oil), and, below, John on Patmos (where he may have written the last book of the Bible, Revelation). John is talking to the eagle that, according to tradition, flew him to heaven. Flanking both Johns, statues of Ferdinand and Isabel kneel in prayer. A colorful series of reliefs at the bottom level recalls the Christian conquest of the Moors (left to right): a robed processional figure, Boabdil with army and key to Alhambra, Moors expelled from Alhambra, conversion of Muslims by tonsured monks (two panels, right of altar table), and another robed figure.

A finely carved Plateresque arch, with the gilded royal initials *F* and *Y*, leads to a small glass pyramid in the **treasury.** This

holds Queen Isabel's silver crown ringed with pomegranates (symbolizing Granada), her scepter, and King Ferdinand's sword. Do a counterclockwise spin around the room to see it all, starting to the right of the entry arch. There you'll see the devout Isabel's prayer book, in which she followed the Mass. The book and its sturdy box date from 1496. According to legend, the fancy box on the other side of the door is supposedly the one that Isabel filled with jewels and gave to bankers as collateral for the cash to pay Columbus. In the corner (also behind glass) is the ornate silver-and-gold cross that Cardinal Mendoza, staunch supporter of Queen Isabel, carried into the Alhambra on that historic day in 1492—and used as the centerpiece for the first Christian Mass in the conquered fortress. Next, the big silver-and-gold silk tapestry is the altar banner for the mobile campaign chapel of Ferdinand and Isabel, who always traveled with their army. In the case to its left, you'll see the original Christian army flags raised over the Alhambra in 1492. Finally, as you complete your spin, view the original funeral vestments worn by Ferdinand and Isabel.

The next zone of this grand hall holds the first great **art collection** established by a woman. Queen Isabel amassed more than 200 important paintings. After Napoleon's visit, only 31 remained. Even so, this is an exquisite collection, all on wood, featuring works by Sandro Botticelli, Pietro Perugino, the Flemish master Hans Memling, and some less-famous Spanish masters.

Finally, at the end of the room are two **carved sculptures** of Ferdinand and Isabel, the originals from the high altar. Charles V considered these primitive (I disagree) and replaced them with the ones you saw earlier.

To reach the cathedral (described next), exit the treasury behind Isabel, and walk around the block to the right.

▲Granada Cathedral (Catedral de Granada)

One of only two Renaissance churches in Spain (the other is in Córdoba), Granada's cathedral is the second-largest church in the country (after Sevilla's). While it was started as a Gothic church, it was built using Renaissance elements, and then decorated in Baroque style.

Cost and Hours: €5, includes audioguide, Mon-Sat 10:00-

18:30, Sun 15:00-18:00, tel. 958-222-959, www.catedraldegranada.com.

Visiting the Cathedral: Enter the church from Plaza de las Pasiegas. Before exploring the interior, step into the cathedral's little **museum** (tucked into the corner behind the ticket counter). Filling the ground floor of the big bell tower, it's worth seeking out for two pieces of art: a Gothic, hexagonal-shaped monstrance with a Renaissance-era base given to the cathedral by Isabel, and a beautiful sculpture of San Pablo (Paul, with a flowing beard)—a kneeling self-portrait by hometown great Alonso Cano. Remember his face, because you'll see it again soon.

Leave the museum and stand in the back of the **nave** for an overview. Survey the church. It's huge. It was designed to be the national church when Granada was the capital of a newly reconquered-from-the-Muslims Spain. High above the main altar are square niches originally intended for the burial of Charles V and his family. But King Philip II changed focus and abandoned Granada for El Escorial, so the niches are now plugged with paintings, including seven from the life of Mary by Cano.

The cathedral's cool, spacious interior is mostly Renaissance—a refreshing break from the closed-in, dark Gothic of so many Spanish churches. In a move that was modern back in the 18th century, the walls of the choir (the big, heavy wooden box that dominates the center of most Spanish churches) were taken out so that people could be involved in the worship. (Back when a choir clogged the middle of the church, regular people only heard the Mass.) At about the same time, a bishop ordered the interior painted with lime (for hygienic reasons, during a time of disease). The people liked it, and it stayed white.

Notice that the two rear chapels (sand-colored, on right and left) are Neoclassical in style—a reminder that the church took 300 years to finish. As you explore, remember that the abundance of Marys is all part of the Counter-Reformation. Most of the side chapels are decorated in Baroque style. Behind you to the left (as you face the altar) is the tomb of Cano, the artist. His face should look familiar from the San Pablo sculpture in the museum. Although an equally-as-gifted contemporary of Velázquez and Murillo, Cano has yet to achieve their level of recognition.

Now, as you walk to the front for a closer look at the **altar,** take a small detour to the scale model of the entire complex (left of pews). Examine the cathedral's immensity. The Royal Chapel (right side) is shaped like a small church would be, complete with mini transepts and fitting perfectly into the corner of the cathedral. Resume your walk to the altar, passing two fine Baroque organs with horizontal trumpet pipes, unique to Spain.

Standing before the altar, notice the abundance of gold leaf. It's from the Darro River, which originally attracted Romans here for its gold. As this is a seat of the local bishop, there's a fine wooden bishop's throne on the right.

Between the pairs of Corinthian columns on both sides of the altar are **sculptures** with a strong parenting theme: Inside the thick, round frames at the top are busts of Adam and Eve, from whom came mankind. Around them are the four gold-covered evangelists, who—with the New Testament—brought the Good News of salvation to believers. Completing the big parenting picture are Ferdinand and Isabel, kneeling in prayer, who brought Catholicism to the land. Their complex coat of arms (beneath each respective statue) celebrates how their marriage united two influential kingdoms to create imperial Spain.

To your right is the ornate carved-stone Gothic door to the **Royal Chapel** (described earlier), with 15th-century decorations that predate the cathedral. The chapel holds the most important historic relics in town—the tombs of the Catholic Monarchs. And, because the chapel and cathedral are run by two different religious orders, this door is always closed and there are separate admission fees for each. In the chapel, immediately to the left of the door, is a politically incorrect version of St. James the Moor-Slayer, with his sword raised high and an armored Moor trampled under his horse's hooves.

Strolling behind the altar, look for the **giant music sheets:** They're mostly 16th-century Gregorian chants. Notice the sliding C clef. Rather than a fixed G or F clef, the monks knew that this clef—which could be located wherever it worked best on the staff—marked middle C, and they chanted to notes relative to that. Go ahead—try singing a few verses of the Latin.

The **sacristy** (between the exit and the St. James altarpiece, in the right corner) is worth a look. It's lush and wide open; its gilded ceilings, mirrors, and wooden cabinets give it a light, airy feel. Two grandfather clocks made in London (one with Asian motifs) ensured that everyone got dressed on time. The highlight of this room is another work by Cano—a small, delicate painted wood statue of the *Immaculate Conception,* under the Crucifixion.

Exit the cathedral through its little **shop** (with a nicely curated selection of religious and secular souvenirs). If you walk straight out, you'll come directly to Gran Vía and the stop for minibus #C1 for the Albayzín (to walk to the Albayzín, head left up Gran Vía for two blocks, then turn right on Calle Cárcel Baja). But first, for a fun detour, make a quick left into the little lane immediately upon exiting the cathedral—you'll be just steps from Medievo, a fine purveyor of bulk spices and teas.

NEAR PLAZA NUEVA
Hammam al Andalus (Arab Baths)

For an intimate and subdued experience, consider some serious relaxation at these Arab baths, where you can enjoy three different-temperature pools and a steam room. Up to 35 people are allowed in the baths at one time.

Cost and Hours: €30 for 90-minute soak in the baths (more if you add a massage), daily 10:00-24:00, appointments scheduled every even-numbered hour, coed with mandatory swimsuits, quiet atmosphere encouraged, free lockers and towels available, no loaner swimsuits but you can buy one, just off Plaza Nueva—follow signs a few doors down from the TI to Santa Ana 16, paid reservation required (refunded if cancelled up to 48 hours before the appointment), tel. 958-229-978, www.hammamalandalus.com.

THE ALBAYZÍN

Spain's best old Moorish quarter, with countless colorful corners, flowery patios, and shady lanes, is worth ▲. While the city center of Granada feels more or less like many other pleasant Spanish cities, the Albayzín is unique. You can't say you've really seen Granada until you've at least strolled a few of its twisty lanes. Climb high to the San Nicolás church for the best view of the Alhambra. Then wander through the mysterious back streets.

Getting to the Albayzín: Ride the bus, hike up, or take a taxi to the San Nicolás viewpoint. From there, follow my tips for "Exploring the Albayzín," later.

The handy Albayzín **minibus #C1** makes a 20-minute loop through the quarter, getting you scenically and sweatlessly to the San Nicolás viewpoint (departs about every 10 minutes from Gran Vía or Plaza Nueva). While good for a lift to the top of the Albayzín (buzz when you want to get off), I'd stay on for an entire circle and return to the Albayzín later for dinner—either on foot or by bus again. (Note: The less frequent minibus #C2, departing every 20 minutes, does a similar but longer route, with a side-trip up into Sacromonte—but it does not go past the San Nicolás viewpoint.)

Here's the #C1 route: The minibus leaves Plaza Nueva, heads along the Paseo de los Tristes, and turns up (left) to climb into the thick of the Albayzín, with stops below the San Nicolás church (famous viewpoint, and the midpoint in my Albayzín walk, described next; the driver generally calls out this stop for tourists) and at Plaza San Miguel el Bajo (cute square with recommended eateries). From here, you can ride back down through residential neighborhoods before turning down the city's main drag, Gran Vía, and returning to Plaza Nueva.

It's a steep but fascinating 20-minute **walk** up: Leave the west end of Plaza Nueva on Calle de Elvira. After about 50 yards, at the pharmacy and newsstand, bear right on Calle Calderería Vieja. Follow this stepped street past Moroccan eateries and pastry shops, vendors of imported North African goods, halal butchers, and *teterías* (Moorish tea rooms). Turn right at the recommended Arrayanes restaurant, then continue to the left of the church on Cuesta de San Gregorio as the street slants, winds, and zigzags uphill. Cuesta de San Gregorio eventually curves left and is regularly signposted. When you reach the Moorish-style house, La Media Luna (with the tall palm trees and keyhole-style doorway), stop for a photo and a breather, then follow the wall, continuing uphill. At the next intersection (with the black cats), turn right on Aljibe del Gato. A bit farther on, look for a 90-degree turn to the left; at this point, turn onto the stepped Cuesta de María de la Miel. It's signposted behind you, but even if you miss it, keep going up, up, up. At the crest, turn right on Camino Nuevo de San Nicolás, then walk to the street that curves up left (look for a bus-stop sign—this is where the minibus would have dropped you off). Continue up the curve, and soon you'll see feet hanging from the plaza wall. More steps lead up to the viewpoint. Whew! You made it!

You can also **taxi** to the San Nicolás church and explore from there.

▲▲San Nicolás Viewpoint (Mirador de San Nicolás)

For one of Europe's most romantic viewpoints, be here at sunset, when the Alhambra glows red and Albayzín widows share the benches with local lovers, hippies, and tourists (free, always open). In 1997, President Clinton made a point to bring his family here—a favorite spot from a trip he made as a student. But this was hardly an original idea; generations of visitors have been drawn here. For an affordable drink with the same million-euro view, step into the El Huerto de Juan Ranas Bar (just below and to the left, at Calle de Atarazana 8). Enjoy

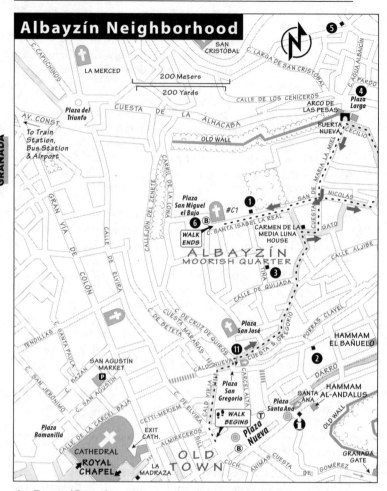

Albayzín Neighborhood

the Roma (Gypsy) musicians who perform here for tips. Order a drink, tip them, settle in, and consider it a concert.

Great Mosque of Granada (Mezquita Mayor de Granada)

Granada's Muslim population is on the rebound, and now numbers 8 percent of the city's residents. A striking and inviting mosque is just next to the San Nicolás viewpoint (to your left as you face the Alhambra). Local Muslims write, "The Great Mosque of Granada signals, after a hiatus of 500 years, the restoration of a missing link with a rich and fecund Islamic contribution to

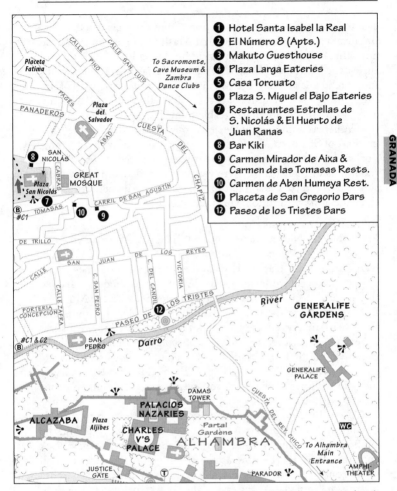

1. Hotel Santa Isabel la Real
2. El Número 8 (Apts.)
3. Makuto Guesthouse
4. Plaza Larga Eateries
5. Casa Torcuato
6. Plaza S. Miguel el Bajo Eateries
7. Restaurantes Estrellas de S. Nicolás & El Huerto de Juan Ranas
8. Bar Kiki
9. Carmen Mirador de Aixa & Carmen de las Tomasas Rests.
10. Carmen de Aben Humeya Rest.
11. Placeta de San Gregorio Bars
12. Paseo de los Tristes Bars

all spheres of human enterprise and activity." Built in 2003 (with money from the local community and Islamic Arab nations), it has a peaceful view courtyard and a minaret that comes with a live call to prayer five times a day (printed schedule inside). It's stirring to hear the muezzin holler "God is Great" from the minaret. Visitors are welcome in the courtyard, which offers Alhambra views without the hedonistic ambience of the more famous San Nicolás viewpoint.

Cost and Hours: Free, daily 11:00-14:00 & 18:00-21:00, shorter hours in winter, tel. 958-202-526, www.mezquitadegranada. com.

Background: While tourists come to Granada to learn about its complex cultural history, local Muslims are sometimes frustrated by the misperceptions and misinformation that more passive tourists accept without question. From their perspective, it is important for visitors to know that Muslims are as indigenous as any other cultural group in Spain. After living here for seven centuries, the Muslims of Granada and Andalucía are as Iberian as any modern Spaniard today. For Muslims, Islam is not a religion of immigrants, nor is it a culture of the Arabian Middle East. ("Muslim" and "Arab" are not interchangeable terms.)

Whereas some might perceive the Reconquista as the "liberation" of Spain, to Muslims it has an entirely different meaning. For them, the Reconquista was a brutal experience, when tens of thousands of their people were viciously expelled and many more suffered forced conversion in the 16th century. Five centuries later, there are almost 2 million Muslims in Spain.

Exploring the Albayzín

From the San Nicolás viewpoint and the Great Mosque, you're at the edge of a hilltop neighborhood even the people of Granada recognize as a world apart. Each of the district's 20 churches sits on a spot once occupied by a mosque. When the Reconquista arrived in Granada, the Christians attempted to coexist with the Muslims. But after seven years, this idealistic attempt ended in failure, and the Christians forced the Muslims to convert. In 1567, Muslims were expelled, leading to 200 years of economic depression for the city. Eventually, large, walled, noble manor houses with private gardens were built here in the depopulated Albayzín. These survive today in the form of the characteristic *carmen* restaurants so popular with visitors.

From the San Nicolás viewpoint, turn your back to the Alhambra and walk north (passing the church on your right and the Biblioteca Municipal on your left). A lane leads past a white brick arch (on your right)—now a chapel built into the old Moorish wall. You're walking by the scant remains of the pre-Alhambra fortress of Granada. At the end of the lane, step down to the right through the 11th-century "New Gate" (Puerta Nueva—older than the Alhambra) and into **Plaza Larga.** In medieval times, this tiny square (called "long," because back then it was) served as the local marketplace. It still is a busy market each morning. Casa Pasteles, at the near end of the square, serves good coffee and cakes.

From Plaza Larga look up **Calle Agua de Albayzín** (as you face Casa Pasteles, it's to your right). The street, named for the public baths that used to line it, shows evidence of the Moorish plumbing system: gutters. Back when Europe's streets were filled with muck, Granada actually had Roman Empire-style gutters with drains leading to clay and lead pipes.

You're in the heart of the Albayzín. Explore. Poke into an old

Safety in the Albayzín

With tough economic times, young ruffians are hanging out in the dark back lanes of the labyrinthine Albayzín quarter. While

this charming Moorish district is certainly safe by day, it can be edgy after dark. Most of the area is fine to wander, though many streets are poorly lit, and the maze of lanes can make it easy to get lost and wind up somewhere you don't want to be. Some nervous travelers choose to avoid the neighborhood entirely after dark, but I recommend venturing into the Albayzín to enjoy its restaurants, ideal sunset views, and charming ambience. Just be sure to exercise normal precautions: Leave your valuables at your hotel, stick to better-lit streets, and take a minibus or taxi home if you're unsure of your route. Violent crime is rare, but pickpocketing is common. Keep a very close eye on your stuff.

Locals say the biggest hazard when walking in the Albayzín is the many deposits left by its four-legged inhabitants (and not cleaned up by their poorly trained owners). If you bury your nose in a guidebook while you walk, you may wind up burying your shoe in something else.

church. They're plain by design to go easy on the Muslim converts, who weren't used to being surrounded by images as they worshipped. You'll see lots of real Muslim culture living in the streets, including many recent Spanish converts. When you are finished exploring, walk back down Placeta de las Minas (which becomes Cuesta de María la Miel) to Camino Nuevo de San Nicolás, where you walked up. Turn right, and wander to **Plaza San Miguel el Bajo,** where you can stop for a meal or a refreshing snack (see "Eating in Granada," later) before catching minibus #C1 back into town.

SACROMONTE

The Sacromonte district is home to Granada's thriving Roma community. Marking the entrance to Sacromonte is a statue of Chorrohumo (literally, "exudes smoke," and a play on the slang word for "thief": *chorro*). He was a Roma from Granada, popular in the 1950s for guiding people around the city.

While the neighboring Albayzín is a sprawling zone blanketing a hilltop, Sacromonte is much smaller—very compact and very steep. Most houses are burrowed into the wall of a cliff. Sacromonte has one main street: Camino del Sacromonte, which is lined with caves primed for tourists and restaurants ready to fight over the bill. (Don't come here expecting to get a deal on anything.) Intriguing lanes run above and below this main drag—a steep hike above Camino del Sacromonte is the cliff-hanging, parallel secondary street, Vereda de Enmedio, which is less touristy, with an authentically residential vibe.

Cave Museum of Sacromonte
(Museo Cuevas del Sacromonte)

This hilltop complex, also known as the Center for the Interpretation of Sacromonte (Centro de Interpretación del Sacromonte), is a kind of open-air folk museum about Granada's unique Roma cave-dwelling tradition (though it doesn't have much on the people themselves). Getting there is a bit of a slog for what you'll end up seeing—but if you can combine your visit with one of their flamenco and/or guitar concerts (described later), it may be worth your while. The exhibits (with adequate, if not insightful, English descriptions) are spread through a series of whitewashed caves along a ridge, with spectacular views to the Alhambra. As you stroll from cave to cave, you'll see displays on the native habitat (rocks, flora, and fauna); crafts (basket-weav-ing, potterymaking, metalworking, and weaving); and lifestyles (including a look into a typical home and kitchen). There's also an exhibit about other cave-dwelling cultures from around the "troglodyte world," and one about Sacromonte's vital role in the development of Granada's brand of flamenco. As you wander, imagine this in the 1950s, when it was still a bustling community of Roma cave-dwellers.

Cost and Hours: €5, daily 10:00-20:00, off-season until 18:00, Barranco de los Negros, tel. 958-215-120, www.sacromontegranada.com, info@sacromontegranada.com.

Getting There: You can ride minibus #C2 from Plaza Nueva (ask driver, *"¿Museo cuevas?"*; departs every 20 minutes) or take a taxi. Get off at the "Sacromonte 2" bus stop, next to the big Venta El Gallo restaurant, along the main road (several *zambra* performance caves line up along here, too—see next). From here, it's a steep 10-minute hike past cave dwellings up to the top of the hill—follow the signs.

Granada's Roma (Gypsies)

Both the English word "Gypsy" and its Spanish counterpart, *gitano,* come from the word "Egypt"—where Europeans once believed these nomadic people had originated. Today the preferred term is "Roma," since "Gypsy" has acquired negative connotations (though for clarity's sake, I've used both terms throughout this book).

After migrating from India in the 14th century, the Roma people settled mostly in the Muslim-occupied lands in southern Europe (such as the Balkan Peninsula, then controlled by the Ottoman Turks). Under medieval Muslims, the Roma enjoyed relative tolerance. They were traditionally good with crafts and animals.

The first Roma arrived in Granada in the 15th century—and they've remained tight-knit ever since. Today 50,000 Roma call Granada home, many of them in the district called Sacromonte. In most of Spain, Roma are more assimilated into the general population, but Sacromonte is a large, distinct Roma community. (After the difficult Spanish Civil War era, they were joined by many farmers who, like the Roma, appreciated Sacromonte's affordable, practical cave dwellings—warm in the winter and cool in the summer.)

Spaniards, who generally consider themselves to be tolerant and not racist, claim that in maintaining such a tight community, the Roma segregate themselves. The Roma call Spaniards *payos* ("whites"). Recent mixing of Roma and *payos* has given birth to the term *gallipavo* (rooster-duck), although who's who depends upon whom you ask.

Are Roma thieves? Sure, some of them are. But others are honest citizens, trying to make their way in the world just like anyone else. Because of the high incidence of theft, it's wise to be cautious when dealing with a Roma person—but it's also important to keep an open mind.

Performances: In summer (July-Aug), the center also features flamenco shows and classical guitar concerts in its wonderfully scenic setting (prices and schedules vary—see website mentioned earlier for details).

Zambra Dance

A long flamenco tradition exists in Granada, and the Roma of Sacromonte are credited with developing this city's unique flavor of the Andalusian art form. Sacromonte is a good place to see *zambra,* a flamenco variation in which the singer also dances. A half-dozen cave-bars offering *zambra* in the evenings line Sacromonte's main drag. Hotels are happy to book you a seat and arrange the included transfer.

Two well-established venues are **Zambra Cueva de la Rocio**

(€30, includes a drink and bus ride from and to your hotel, €20 without transport, daily show at 22:00, 1 hour, Camino del Sacromonte 70, tel. 958-227-129, www.cuevalarocio.com) and **María la Canastera,** an intimate venue where the Duke of Windsor and actor Yul Brynner came to watch *zambra* (€28, includes drink and bus from hotel, €22 without transport, daily show at 22:00, 1 hour, Camino del Sacromonte 89, tel. 958-121-183, www.granadainfo.com/canastera). The biggest operation here is the restaurant **Venta El Gallo,** which has performances of more straightforward flamenco (not specifically *zambra*, €33 with bus from hotel, €26 without transport, daily shows at 21:00 and 22:30, dinner possible beforehand on outdoor terrace, Barranco de los Negros 5, tel. 958-228-476, www.ventaelgallo.com). Or consider the summer performances at the Cave Museum (explained earlier).

If you don't want to venture to Sacromonte, try **Casa del Arte Flamenco,** which performs one-hour shows just off Plaza Nueva (€18, €3 discount for booking online, at 19:30 and 21:00, Cuesta de Gomérez 11, tel. 958-565-767, www.casadelarteflamenco.com).

NEAR GRANADA
Carthusian Monastery (Monasterio de la Cartuja)
A church with an interior that looks as if it squirted out of a can of whipped cream, La Cartuja is nicknamed the "Christian Alhambra" for its elaborate white Baroque stucco work. In the rooms just off the cloister, notice the gruesome paintings of martyrs placidly meeting their grisly fates.

Cost and Hours: €4, daily 10:00-13:00 & 16:00-20:00, shorter hours Nov-March, tel. 958-161-932.

Getting There: The monastery is a mile north of town on the way to Madrid. Catch the articulated LAC bus and transfer to #N7 (ask at TI for specifics). Drivers take the *Méndez Núñez* exit from the A-44 expressway and follow signs.

Sleeping in Granada

In July and August, when Granada's streets are littered with sunstroke victims, rooms are plentiful and prices soft. In the crowded months of April, May, September, and October, prices can spike up 20 percent. Most places offer breakfast for an additional charge.

If you're traveling by car, you're free to drive into the prohibited center zone, but be sure your hotel registers you immediately with the traffic police.

ON OR NEAR PLAZA NUEVA

Each of these (except the hostel) is professional, plenty comfortable, and perfectly located within a 5- to 10-minute walk of Plaza Nueva.

$$$ Hotel Casa 1800 Granada sets the bar for affordable class. Its 25 rooms face the beautiful, airy courtyard of a 17th-century mansion in the lower part of the Albayzín (just steps above Plaza Nueva). Tidy, friendly, and well-run, it offers special extras, such as a complimentary tea and coffee bar each afternoon (pricier rooms not much different except for the Alhambra views and patios, air-con, elevator, Benalúa 11, tel. 958-210-700, www.hotelcasa1800granada.com, info@hotelcasa1800granada.com).

$$$ Hotel Maciá Plaza, right on the colorful Plaza Nueva, has 44 smallish, clean, modern, and classy rooms. Choose between an on-the-square view or a quieter interior room (RS%, air-con, elevator, Plaza Nueva 5, tel. 958-227-536, www.maciahoteles.com, maciaplaza@maciahoteles.com, friendly Pedro).

$$ Casa del Capitel Nazarí, just off the church end of Plaza Nueva, is a restored 16th-century Renaissance palace transformed into 18 small but tastefully decorated rooms, all facing a courtyard that hosts changing art exhibits. Insomniacs have a choice of five different pillows (RS%, includes afternoon tea/coffee, air-con, loaner laptop, pay parking, Cuesta Aceituneros 6, tel. 958-215-260, www.hotelcasacapitel.com, info@hotelcasacapitel.com).

$$ Hotel Anacapri is a bright, cool marble oasis with 53 modern rooms and a peaceful lounge (family rooms, non-promotional direct rates include breakfast, air-con, elevator, pay parking, 2 blocks toward Gran Vía from Plaza Nueva at Calle Joaquín Costa 7, just a block from cathedral bus stop, tel. 958-227-477, www.hotelanacapri.com, reservas@hotelanacapri.com, friendly and helpful staff, plus Kathy speaks Iowan).

$ Hotel Inglaterra, with 36 rooms, is a little rough around the edges but in an ideal location. Exterior rooms come with some noise from the popular bars below (air-con, elevator to third floor only, pay parking, Cetti Merien 6, tel. 958-221-559, www.hotelinglaterragranada.com, info@hotel-inglaterra.es).

¢ Oasis Hostel Granada offers 90 beds in 12 coed rooms and lots of backpacker bonding, including daily tours and activities on request. It's just a block above the lively Moorish-flavored tourist drag (includes welcome drink; at the top end of Placeta Correo Viejo at #3, tel. 958-215-848, www.oasisgranada.com, granada@hostelsoasis.com).

CHEAP SLEEPS ON CUESTA DE GOMÉREZ

These lodgings, all inexpensive and some ramshackle, are on this street leading from Plaza Nueva up to the Alhambra. Sprinkled among the knickknack stores are the storefront workshops of several guitar makers, who are renowned for their handcrafted instruments.

$ Hotel Puerta de las Granadas has 16 crisp, clean rooms with an Ikea vibe, an inviting and peaceful courtyard, and a handy location (RS%, air-con, elevator, free tea and coffee in cafeteria all day, pay parking, Cuesta de Gomérez 14, tel. 958-216-230, www.hotelpuertadelasgranadas.com, reservas@hotelpuertadelasgranadas.com).

$ Pensión Landazuri is run by friendly English-speaking Matilde Landazuri, her son Manolo, and daughters Margarita and Elisa. Their characteristic old house has 18 rooms—some are well-worn, while others are renovated. It boasts hardworking, helpful management and a great roof garden with an Alhambra view (family rooms, no elevator or air-con, pay parking, Cuesta de Gomérez 24, tel. 958-221-406, www.pensionlandazuri.com, info@pensionlandazuri.com). The Landazuris also run a good, cheap café open for breakfast and lunch.

$ Pensión Al Fin is located just up the street from Pensión Landazuri and run by the same family. Its five high-ceilinged rooms feature antique wooden beams and marble columns, with bright, Cuban-style flair. A glass floor in the lobby lets you peer into a well from an ancient house (some rooms with balconies, pay parking, reception at Pensión Landazuri, Cuesta de Gomérez 31, tel. 958-221-406, www.pensionalfin.com, info@pensionalfin.com).

¢ Hostal Navarro Ramos is a small cheapie, renting seven quiet, clean rooms (5 with private baths) facing away from the street (no elevator, Cuesta de Gomérez 21, tel. 958-250-555, www.pensionnavarroramos.com, Carmen).

¢ Pensión Austria, owned by Austrian Irene (ee-RAY-nay), rents 15 basic but tidy backpacker-type rooms (family rooms, air-con, Cuesta de Gomérez 4, tel. 958-227-075, www.pensionaustria.com, pensionaustria@pensionaustria.com).

NEAR THE CATHEDRAL

$ Hotel Los Tilos offers 30 comfortable, business-like rooms (some with balconies) on the charming traffic-free Plaza de Bib-Rambla. Guests are welcome to use the fourth-floor terrace with views of the cathedral and the Alhambra (free breakfast for Rick Steves readers—get details when booking, air-con, pay parking, Plaza de Bib-Rambla 4, tel. 958-266-712, www.hotellostilos.com, clientes@hotellostilos.com, friendly José María).

On or near Plaza de la Trinidad

The charming, park-like square called Plaza de la Trinidad, just a

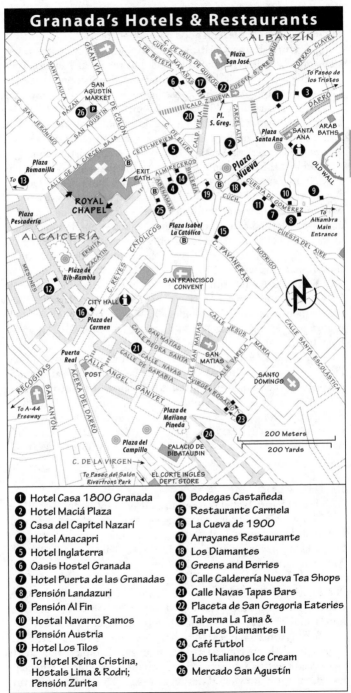

Granada's Hotels & Restaurants

1. Hotel Casa 1800 Granada
2. Hotel Maciá Plaza
3. Casa del Capitel Nazarí
4. Hotel Anacapri
5. Hotel Inglaterra
6. Oasis Hostel Granada
7. Hotel Puerta de las Granadas
8. Pensión Landazuri
9. Pensión Al Fin
10. Hostal Navarro Ramos
11. Pensión Austria
12. Hotel Los Tilos
13. To Hotel Reina Cristina, Hostals Lima & Rodri; Pensión Zurita
14. Bodegas Castañeda
15. Restaurante Carmela
16. La Cueva de 1900
17. Arrayanes Restaurant
18. Los Diamantes
19. Greens and Berries
20. Calle Calderería Nueva Tea Shops
21. Calle Navas Tapas Bars
22. Placeta de San Gregoria Eateries
23. Taberna La Tana & Bar Los Diamantes II
24. Café Futbol
25. Los Italianos Ice Cream
26. Mercado San Agustín

short walk west of the cathedral area (Pescadería and Bib-Rambla squares), is home to several good accommodations.

$$ Hotel Reina Cristina has 55 quiet, homey rooms a few steps off Plaza de la Trinidad. Check out the great Mudejar ceiling at the top of the stairwell. The famous Spanish poet Federico García Lorca hid out in this house before being captured and executed by the Guardia Civil during the Spanish Civil War (includes breakfast, cheaper rate without breakfast, air-con, elevator, pay parking, near Plaza de la Trinidad at Tablas 4, tel. 958-253-211, www.hotelreinacristina.com, clientes@hotelreinacristina.com).

$ Hostal Lima, run with class by Manolo and Carmen, has 25 well-appointed rooms (some small) in two buildings a block off the square. The public areas and rooms are flamboyantly decorated with medieval flair—colorful tiles, wood-carved life-sized figures, and swords (home-cooked dinner available—book in advance, air-con, elevator in one building only, pay parking, Laurel de las Tablas 17, tel. 958-295-029, www.hostallimagranada.eu, info@hostallimagranada.eu).

$ Hostal Rodri, run by Manolo's brother José, has 10 similarly good rooms a few doors down that feel new and classy for their price range. Take in the sun on an "L"-shaped terrace (air-con, elevator, pay parking, Laurel de las Tablas 9, tel. 958-288-043, www.hostalrodri.com, info@hostalrodri.com).

$ Pensión Zurita, well-run by personable Francisco and Loli, faces Plaza de la Trinidad. Twelve of the 14 rooms—all remodeled—have modern, in-room baths and small exterior balconies. Even with double-pane windows, some rooms may come with night noise from cafés below (air-con, kitchen nook available for guest use, pay parking, Plaza de la Trinidad 7, tel. 958-275-020, mobile 685-843-745, www.pensionzurita.es, pensionzurita@gmail.com).

IN THE ALBAYZÍN

$$$ Hotel Santa Isabel la Real, a handsome 16th-century edifice, has 11 rooms ringing a charming courtyard. Each room is a bit different; basic rooms look to the patio, while pricier rooms have better exterior views. Furnished in a way that gives you the old Moorish Granada ambience, it offers a warm welcome and rich memories (air-con, elevator, pay parking, midway between San Nicolás viewpoint and Plaza San Miguel el Bajo on Calle Santa Isabel la Real, minibus #C1 stops in front, tel. 958-294-658, www.hotelsantaisabellareal.com, info@hotelsantaisabellareal.com).

$ El Número 8 is a traditional house in the heart of the Albayzín that's been converted into four small, funky kitchenette apartments with an eclectic, ever-evolving artistic feel. Chicago-raised, easygoing owner Rafa lives on-site. You'll share two tiny patios and a rooftop terrace with a spectacular, in-your-face view of the Alhambra. Contact Rafa in advance to set up a time to check in. He'll ease your arrival by meeting you at a taxi or bus drop-off point and walking you back to the apartment (air-con in one room, others have fans, laundry facilities, 5-minute walk from Plaza Nueva at tiny Plaza Virgen del Carmen, tel. 958-220-682, mobile 610-322-216, www.elnumero8.com, casaocho@gmail.com).

¢ **Makuto Guesthouse,** a hostel tucked deep in the Albayzín, feels like a hippie commune you can pay to join for a couple of days. With 42 beds in seven rooms clustered around a lush garden courtyard that's made for hanging out—including several hammock-and-lounge-sofa "hang-out zones"—it exudes a young, easygoing Albayzín vibe (private rooms available, includes breakfast, dinners available, Calle Tiña 18, tel. 958-805-876, www.makutohostel.com, info@makutohostel.com). From the minibus #C1 stop on Calle Santa Isabel la Real, it's a long block down Calle Tiña and on the left.

IN OR NEAR THE ALHAMBRA

To stay on the Alhambra grounds, choose between a famous, over-priced parador (generally booked up long in advance) and a practical and economical hotel above the parking lot. Both are a half-mile up the hill from Plaza Nueva.

$$$$ Parador de Granada San Francisco offers 40 designer rooms in a former Moorish palace that was later transformed into a 15th-century Franciscan monastery. It's considered Spain's premier parador—and that's saying something (air-con, free parking, Calle Real de la Alhambra, tel. 958-221-440, www.parador.es, granada@parador.es). You must book months ahead to spend the night in this lavishly located, stodgy, and historic palace. Any peasant, however, can drop in for a coffee, drink, snack, or meal.

$ Hotel Guadalupe, big and modern with 58 sleek rooms, is quietly and conveniently located overlooking the Alhambra parking lot. While it's a 30-minute hike above the town, many—especially drivers—find this to be a practical option (air-con, elevator, special parking rate in Alhambra lot, Paseo de la Sabica 30, tel. 958-225-730, www.hotelguadalupe.es, info@hotelguadalupe.es).

Eating in Granada

Restaurants generally serve lunch from 13:00 to 16:00 and dinner from 20:00 until very late (remember, Spaniards don't start dinner until about 21:00). Granada's bars pride themselves on serving a small tapas plate free with any beverage—a tradition that's dying out in most of Spain. Save on your food expenses by doing a tapas crawl (but avoid touristy Calle Navas, right off Plaza del Carmen)

GRANADA

and claim your "right" to a free tapa with every drink. (Order your drink and wait for the free tapa before ordering food. If you order food with your drink, you likely won't get the freebie.) For more budget-eating thrills, buy picnic supplies near Plaza Nueva, and schlep them up into the Albayzín. This makes for a great

cheap date at the San Nicolás viewpoint or on one of the scattered squares and lookout points.

In search of an edible memory? A local specialty, *tortilla de Sacromonte,* is a spicy omelet with lamb's brain and other organs. *Berenjenas fritas* (fried eggplant) and *habas con jamón* (small green fava beans cooked with cured ham) are worth seeking out. *Tinto de verano*—a red-wine spritzer with lemon and ice—is refreshing on a hot evening.

IN THE ALBAYZÍN

The food scene in the Albayzín can be a mixed bag. To find a particular square, ask any local, or follow my directions and the full-color Granada map at the front of this book. If dining late, take the minibus or a taxi back to your hotel; Albayzín back streets can be poorly lit and confusing to follow. Part of the charm of the quarter is the lazy ambience on its squares. My two favorites are Plaza Larga and Plaza San Miguel el Bajo.

Plaza Larga is extremely characteristic, with tapas bar tables spilling out onto the square, a morning market, and a much-loved pastry shop. A few blocks beyond Plaza Larga, **$$ Casa Torcuato** is a hardworking eatery serving creative food in a smart upstairs dining room. Or grab a table on the little square out front or in the downstairs bar. They serve a good fixed-price lunch, plates of fresh fish, and prizewinning, thick, *salmorejo*-style gazpacho (closed Sun night and Mon, Calle Pagés 31, tel. 958-202-818). Minibus #C2 stops right in front of the restaurant.

Plaza San Miguel el Bajo, the farthest hike into the Albayzín, boasts my favorite funky local scene—kids kicking soccer balls, old-timers warming benches, and women gossiping under the facade of a humble church. It's circled by half a dozen inviting little bars and restaurants—each very competitive with cheap lunch deals, more expensive à la carte and evening meals, and good seating right on the square. Drop by for lunch or dinner and spend a few minutes surveying your options: **$$ Bar Casa María,** run with pride by friendly María, promises "Andalusian flavor with a light dash of the Orient" (open daily). **$$ Rincón de la Aurora** feels more comfortable and has tapas (closed Wed and Sun afternoon).

$$ El Ají is a sit-down restaurant with a mod vibe and a bit of Argentinian flair (closed Tue). This square is a nice spot to end your Albayzín visit, as there's a viewpoint overlooking the modern city a block away. Minibus #C1 rumbles by every few minutes, ready to zip you back to Plaza Nueva. Or just walk five minutes down from the viewpoint.

Near the San Nicolás Viewpoint

This area is thoroughly touristy, so don't expect any local hangouts. But these options are suitable for a good meal with a view you'll never forget.

$$$ Restaurante Estrellas de San Nicolás, in the former home of a well-loved Albayzín bigwig, immediately next to the view terrace, features dreamy Alhambra views from its two floors of indoor seating. Serving a mix of French and Spanish cuisine, this place keeps its mostly tourist clientele very happy (smart to reserve a view table, Atrazana Vieja 1, tel. 958-288-739, www. estrellasdesannicolas.es).

$$$ El Huerto de Juan Ranas Restaurante is a higher-priced venue, but at their simple terrace bar you can order off their "casual" menu at half the price. It's immediately below the San Nicolás viewpoint and has amazing Alhambra views (Calle de Atarazana 8, tel. 958-286-925).

$$ Bar Kiki, a laid-back and popular bar-restaurant on an unpretentious square with no view but plenty of people-watching, serves both simple and updated tapas. Try their tasty fried eggplant (Thu-Tue 9:00-24:00, closed Wed, just behind viewpoint at Plaza de San Nicolás 9, tel. 958-276-715).

Carmens in the Albayzín

For a more memorable but pricey experience, consider fine dining with Alhambra views in a *carmen*, a typical Albayzín house with a garden (buzz to get in). After the Reconquista, the Albayzín became depopulated. Wealthy families took larger tracts of land and built fortified mansions with terraced gardens within their walls. Today, the gardens of many of these *carmens* host dining tables and romantic restaurants.

$$$ Carmen Mirador de Aixa, small and elegant, has the dreamiest Alhambra views among the *carmens*. You'll pay a little more, but the food is exquisitely presented and the view makes the price worthwhile. Try the codfish or ox (Tue-Sat 20:00-23:00, also open for lunch Wed-Sun 13:30-15:30, closed Mon all day; next to Carmen de las Tomasas at Carril de San Agustín 2, tel. 958-223-616, www.miradordeaixa.com).

$$$ Carmen de las Tomasas serves seasonal, gourmet Andalusian cuisine with killer views in a slightly formal atmosphere

(July-Sept Tue-Sat 20:30-24:00, closed Sun-Mon; Oct-June Tue-Sun 13:00-16:00 & 20:00-23:30 except closed Sun dinner and Tue lunch; closed Mon; reservations required, Carril de San Agustín 4, tel. 958-224-108, www.lastomasas.com, Joaquín and Cristina).

$$ Carmen de Aben Humeya is the least expensive and least stuffy, but no less romantic. Its outdoor-only seating lets you enjoy a meal or just a long cup of coffee while gazing at the Alhambra. This is a rare place that's enthusiastic about dinner salads (daily 12:00-16:00 & 19:00-23:00, Cuesta de las Tomasas 12, tel. 958-226-665, www.abenhumeya.com).

NEAR PLAZA NUEVA

For people-watching, consider the many restaurants on Plaza Nueva or Plaza de Bib-Rambla. For a happening scene, check out the bars on and around Calle de Elvira. It's best to wander and see where the biggest crowds are.

$$ Bodegas Castañeda, just a block off Plaza Nueva, is the best mix of lively, central, and cheap among the tapas bars I visited. When it's crowded, you need to power your way to the bar to order. When it's quiet, you can order at the bar and grab a little table (same prices). Consider their *tablas combinadas*—variety plates of cheese, meat, and *ahumados* (four different varieties of smoked fish)—and tasty *croquetas de jamón* (breaded and fried béchamel sauce with cured ham). Order a glass of their gazpacho. The big kegs tempt you with different local vermouths, and wine comes with a free tapa (daily 11:30-16:30 & 19:00-24:00, Calle Almireceros 1, tel. 958-215-464). They've recently expanded with extra tables across the alley, but don't be confused by the neighboring, similar "Antigua Bodega Castañeda" restaurant (run by a relative and not as good).

$$ Restaurante Carmela is owned by a local culinary star who consistently participates in annual tapas contests. The flavors are complex, while the presentation is kept clean and simple. You can dine on the outside terrace or take a table in the fresh, modern interior. If breakfast isn't included at your hotel, consider starting your day here (daily 8:00-24:00, just up from Plaza Isabel La Católica at Calle Colcha 13, tel. 958-225-794).

$$ La Cueva de 1900, a family-friendly deli-like place on the main drag, is appreciated for its simple dishes and quality ingredients. Though it lacks character, it's reliable and low-stress. They're proud of their homemade hams, sausages, and cheeses—sold in 100-gram lots and served on grease-proof paper (daily 8:00-23:00, Calle Reyes Católicos 42, tel. 958-229-327).

$$ Arrayanes is a good Moroccan restaurant a world apart from anything else listed here. Mostafa will help you choose among the many salads, the *briwat* (a chicken-and-cinnamon pastry appetizer), the *pastela* (a first-course version of *briwat*), the couscous, or *tajin* dishes. He treats his guests like old friends...especially the ladies (Wed-Mon 13:30-16:30 & 19:30-23:30, closed Tue, Cuesta Marañas 4, where Calles Calderería Nueva and Vieja meet, tel. 958-228-401).

$$ Los Diamantes is a modern, packed, high-energy local favorite for fresh seafood (free tapa with drink, only *raciones* and half-*raciones* on the menu, prices the same at picnic-bench seating as at the bar, Mon-Fri 12:00-18:00 & 20:00-24:00, Sat-Sun 11:00-24:00, facing Plaza Nueva at #13, tel. 958-075-313).

$ Greens and Berries anchors Plaza Nueva, serving fresh salads, sandwiches, and real fruit smoothies to go (no seating). Try one of their combos—such as the *queso de cabra y tomate* sandwich (goat cheese and tomato with caramelized onions) paired with a Caribbean smoothie—and enjoy it on a sunny plaza bench (daily 9:00-22:00, Plaza Nueva 1, tel. 633-895-086).

Laid-Back Options on Calle Calderería Nueva: From Plaza Nueva, walk two long blocks down Calle de Elvira and turn right onto the wonderfully hip and Arabic-feeling Calle Calderería Nueva, which leads uphill into the Albayzín. The street is lined with trendy *teterías*. These small tea shops are good places to linger, chat, and imagine you're in Morocco. They're open all day but are most interesting at tea time—17:00-19:30. Many offer the opportunity to rent a hookah (water pipe) to smoke some fruit-flavored tobacco with friends. Some are conservative and unmemorable, and others are achingly romantic, filled with incense, beaded cushions, live African music, and effervescent young hippies. They sell light meals such as crêpes, and a worldwide range of teas, all marinated in a candlelit snake-charmer ambience.

Placeta de San Gregorio: This tiny junction at the top of Calle Calderería Nueva has a special hang-loose character. Grab a rickety seat here (at **$$ Taverna 22** or **$$ Bar las Cuevas**), under the classic church facade with potted plants and a commotion of tiled roofs, and enjoy the steady stream of hippies (and people who wish they were hippies) flowing by.

Paseo de los Tristes: This spot is like a stage set of outdoor bars on a terrace over the river gorge. While it lacks a serious restaurant and the food values are mediocre at best, the scene is a winner—cool, along a stream under trees, with the floodlit Alhambra high above and a happy crowd of locals enjoying a meal or drink out. From here, it's a simple, level, five-minute walk back to Plaza Nueva.

Tapas Beyond Plaza del Carmen, Away from the Tourist Zone: Granada is a wonderland of happening little tapas bars. As the scene changes from night to night, it's best to simply wander

The Paseo Without the Tourists

While Granada's old town is great for strolling, it's also fun to leave the aura of the Alhambra and just be in workaday Granada with everyday locals. A five-minute walk from Plaza Nueva gets you into a delightful and untouristy urban slice of Andalucía.

To enjoy an evening paseo without tourists, start with a tapas crawl along any of the streets beyond Plaza del Carmen (see page 137), then stroll down Carrera de la Virgen, off Plaza del Campillo. This is the town's mini Ramblas, leading gracefully down to the Paseo del Salón riverbank park (and passing the useful El Corte Inglés department store).

and see what appeals. You'll be amazed at how the vibe changes when you venture just five minutes from the historic and touristic center. Everything mentioned below lies within a few neighboring, parallel streets.

From Plaza del Carmen, wander down Calle Navas for a tight little gauntlet of competing tapas joints—try the bright and busy **$$ Fogón de Galicia** (just off Plaza del Carmen), which specializes in seafood. If you want something quieter, consider a side-trip down Calle San Matías. Another good street to explore is the arcaded Ángel Ganivet, off Puerta Real (stop at any of the wine bars, such as **Tinta Fina** at #8).

Don't miss my favorite stretch, where Calle Navas becomes Calle Virgen del Rosario. On Virgen del Rosario, consider **$$ Taberna La Tana** (for fine wine, funky decor, and large *raciones*) and **$$ Bar Los Diamantes II** (across the street, for seafood).

Then head to **$$ Café Fútbol** on Plaza Mariana Pineda for chocolate and *churros*—it's the best place in town for the local coffee and doughnut-dunking ritual. Two blocks away (to the southwest) is a good paseo street, Carrera de la Virgen, leading to the river (see sidebar).

Ice Cream: Italian-run and teeming with locals, **Los Italianos** is popular for its ice cream, *horchata* (*chufa*-nut drink), and shakes. When Michelle Obama visited Granada in 2010, this is where she got her ice-cream fix. For something special, try their *cassata*, a slice (not scoop) of mixed flavors with frozen fruit in a cone (daily 9:00-24:00, shorter hours and sometimes closed off-season, across the street from cathedral and Royal Chapel at Gran Vía 4, tel. 958-224-034).

Markets: Though heavy on fresh fish and meat, **Mercado San Agustín** also sells fruits and veggies. Throughout the EU, people lament the loss of the authentic old market halls as they are replaced with new hygienic versions. If nothing else, it's as refreshingly cool as a meat locker (Mon-Sat 9:00-15:00, closed Sun, very quiet on Mon, a block north of cathedral and a half-block off Gran Vía on Calle Cristo San Agustín). Tucked away in the back of the market is a very cheap and colorful little eatery: **Cafetería San Agustín.** They make their own *churros* and give a small tapa free with each drink (menu on wall). If you are waiting for the cathedral or Royal Chapel to open, kill time in the market.

Granada Connections

BY PLANE

Though Granada airport—officially Federico García Lorca Granada-Jaén Airport—is far from the city center, it still provides faster connections to Spain's big cities than current train and bus services. Iberia and low-cost carrier Vueling offer several direct flights daily to Madrid and Barcelona (airport code: GRX, tel. 902-404-704, www.aena.es, select "Granada-Jaén F.G.L.").

To get between the airport and downtown, you can take a taxi (€35) or, much cheaper, the airport bus, timed to leave from directly outside the terminal when flights arrive and depart (€3, 16/day, 45 minutes). Get off at the Gran Vía stop. To reach the airport from the town center, use the bus stop at the end of Gran Vía, just after the Jardines del Triunfo stop.

BY PUBLIC TRANSPORTATION

Although tracks are laid, high-speed train service from Granada isn't running yet. Instead, you'll go by bus to Antequera (1.25 hours), then continue on the AVE train. Regular-speed train service has also been interrupted of late. Expect to take a bus to Antequera and transfer there, regardless of your destination.

From Granada by Train to: Barcelona (2/day, 8 hours), **Madrid** (5/day, 4 hours), **Toledo** (all service is via Madrid, with nearly hourly AVE connections to Toledo), **Algeciras** (3/day, 4-5 hours), **Ronda** (3/day, 3 hours), **Sevilla** (4/day, 3.5 hours), **Córdoba** (7/day, 2 hours), **Málaga** (6/day, 2.5 hours with 1 transfer—bus is better). Train info: Toll tel. 902-320-320, www.renfe.com. Many of these connections have a more frequent (and sometimes much faster) bus option.

From Granada by Bus to: Nerja (6/day, 2.5 hours), **Sevilla** (7/day to Plaza de Armas station, 2/day to El Prado station, 3 hours *directo*), **Córdoba** (6/day *directo,* 3 hours; 2/day *ruta,* 4 hours),

Madrid (hourly, 5-6 hours; most to Estación Sur, a few to Avenida de América, 2 direct to T4 Barajas Airport), **Málaga** (hourly, 2 hours, several direct to Málaga airport), **Algeciras** (4/day, 4 hours, change here to continue to La Línea de la Concepción/Gibraltar), **Barcelona** (4/day, 14 hours, often at odd times, only one fully daytime connection departs Granada at 10:00 and arrives Barcelona at 24:15). To reach **Ronda,** change in Málaga or Antequera (train is direct and better option); to reach **Tarifa,** change in Algeciras or Málaga. Bus info: Main bus station tel. 913-270-540; all of these routes are run by Alsa (tel. 902-422-242, www.alsa.es). If there's a long line at the ticket windows, you can use the machines (press the flag for English)—but these only sell tickets for some major routes (such as Málaga). There is almost always an Alsa representative at the machines to help and answer questions.

CÓRDOBA

Straddling a sharp bend of the Guadalquivir River, Córdoba has a glorious Roman and Moorish past, once serving as a regional capital for both empires. It's home to Europe's best Islamic sight after Granada's Alhambra: the Mezquita, a splendid and remarkably well-preserved mosque that dates from A.D. 784. When you step inside the mosque, which is magical in its grandeur, you can imagine Córdoba as the center of a thriving and sophisticated culture. During the Dark Ages, when much of Europe was barbaric and illiterate, Córdoba was a haven of enlightened thought—famous for religious tolerance, artistic expression, and dedication to philosophy and the sciences. To this day, you'll still hear the Muslim call to prayer in Córdoba.

Beyond the magnificent Mezquita, the city of Córdoba has two sides: the touristy maze of old town streets immediately surrounding the giant main attraction (lined with trinket shops, hotels, and restaurants); and the workaday but interesting modern city (centered on Plaza de las Tendillas). In between are the side lanes of the Jewish Quarter, humming with history. Just a quick walk takes you from a commercialized vibe into real-life Córdoba.

PLANNING YOUR TIME

Ideally, Córdoba is worth two nights and a day. Don't rush the magnificent Mezquita, but also consider sticking around to experience the city's other pleasures: wander the evocative Jewish Quarter, enjoy the tapas scene, and explore the modern part of town.

However, if you're tight on time, it's possible to do Córdoba more quickly—especially since it's conveniently located on the AVE bullet-train line (and because, frankly, Córdoba has fewer major sights than the other two big Andalusian cities, Sevilla and Granada). To see Córdoba as an efficient stopover between Madrid and Sevilla (or as a side-trip from Sevilla—frequent trains, 45-minute trip), focus on the Mezquita: taxi from the station, spend one hour there, explore the old town for an hour or two...and then get on your way.

Orientation to Córdoba

Córdoba's big draw is the mosque-turned-cathedral called the Mezquita (meth-KEE-tah). Most of the town's major sights are nearby, including the Alcázar, a former royal castle. And though the town seems to ignore its marshy Guadalquivir River (a prime bird-watching area), the riverbank sports a Renaissance triumphal arch next to a stout "Roman Bridge." The bridge leads to the town's old fortified gate (which houses a museum on Moorish culture, the Museum of Al-Andalus Life). The Mezquita is buried in the characteristic medieval town. Around that stretches the Jewish Quarter, then the modern city—with some striking Art Deco buildings at Plaza de las Tendillas and more modern architecture lining Avenida del Gran Capitán.

TOURIST INFORMATION

Córdoba has helpful TIs at the train station and Plaza de las Tendillas (both open daily 9:00-14:00 & 17:00-18:30, slightly longer hours in summer, tel. 902-201-774, www.turismodecordoba.org). Another TI, near the Mezquita, is run separately and covers both Córdoba and the Andalucía region (Mon-Fri 9:00-19:30, Sat-Sun 9:30-15:00, free WCs in basement along with a few ruins and a reproduction of how the Moorish city of "Qurtuba" looked 1,000 years ago, Plaza del Triunfo, tel. 957-355-179).

A ticket for Córdoba's **hop-on, hop-off bus** is good for a "panoramic" circuit that stops mostly in places you won't want to see; an "intimate" route that stops at the Alcázar, Mezquita, Plaza de las Tendillas, and Palacio de Viana (and elsewhere); and two one-hour walking tours—one through the Jewish Quarter and San Basilio neighborhood and one into the central shopping area around Plaza de las Tendillas (confirm tour times when purchasing ticket). This could be worth the money for an ambitious day-tripper coming in by train or bus, as the station is also a stop and the tour includes an excursion to far-flung Madinat Al-Zahra, the ruins of a Moorish palace (€17; purchase at orange City Expert booth in train station or from vendor by Triumphal Arch; buses depart about every 30 minutes from 9:30-21:00, more tours in May, shorter hours off-season; www.city-sightseeing.com).

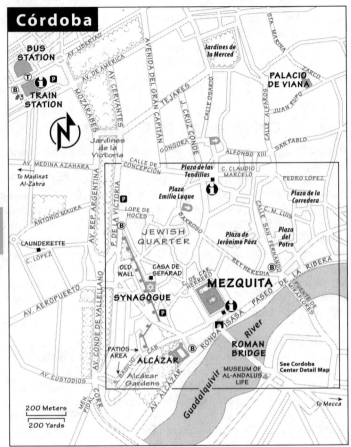

Córdoba

BUS STATION

PALACIO DE VIANA

Jardines de la Merced

AV. LIBERTAD

AV. DE AMÉRICA

AV. CERVANTES

MOZÁRABES

AVENIDA DEL GRAN CAPITÁN

STA. MARINA

ZARCO

JUAN RUFO

CALLE ALFAROS

SAN PABLO

TEJARES

J. CRUZ CONDE

GÓNGORA

ALFONSO XIII

TRAIN STATION
#3

Jardines de la Victoria

To Madinat Al-Zahra

AV. MEDINA AZAHARA

CALLE DE CONCEPCIÓN

Plaza de las Tendillas

C. CLAUDIO MARCELO

PEDRO LÓPEZ

Plaza Emilio Luque

Plaza de la Corredera

AV. REP. ARGENTINA

LOPE DE HOCES

BARROSO

Plaza de Jerónimo Páez

CALLE SAN FERNANDO

C. M. LUIS

Plaza del Potro

ANTONIO MAURA

JEWISH QUARTER

LAUNDERETTE

C. LÓPEZ

OLD WALL

CASA DE SEFARAD

C. DE CÁR HERRERO

REY HEREDIA

DE LA RIBERA

PASEO DE LA FUENTE DE MIRAFLORES

MEZQUITA

AV. AEROPUERTO

AV. CONDE DE VALLELLANO

P. DE LA VICTORIA

SYNAGOGUE

RONDA ISASA

River

ROMAN BRIDGE

PATIOS AREA

S. BASILIO

CAP.

ALCÁZAR

Alcázar Gardens

AV. CUSTODIOS

MEN. FIDAL

CORK

AV. ALCÁZAR

MUSEUM OF AL-ANDALUS LIFE

Guadalquivir

See Cordoba Center Detail Map

To Mecca

200 Meters
200 Yards

ARRIVAL IN CÓRDOBA

By Train or Bus: Córdoba's train station is located on Avenida de América. Built in 1991 to accommodate the high-speed AVE train line, the modern glass-and-steel station has ATMs, restaurants, a variety of shops, a TI booth (mixed in with the shops), an information counter, and a small lounge for first-class AVE passengers. Taxis and local buses are just outside, to the left as you come up the escalators from the platforms.

The bus station is across the street from the train station (on Avenida Vía Augusta, to the north). There's no luggage storage at the train station, but the bus station has lockers (look for *consigna* sign and buy token at machine, security guards can help you find the lockers). All car rental agencies are located here.

To get to the old town, hop a **taxi** (€7 to the Mezquita) or catch **bus #3** (stop is at back corner of train station near archaeological ruins of Palatium Maximiani, buy €1.30 ticket on board, ask driver for *"mezquita,"* get off at Calle San Fernando, and take Calle del Portillo, following the twists and turns—and occasional signs—to the Mezquita).

It's about a 25-minute **walk** from either station to the old town. To walk from the train station to the Mezquita, turn left onto Avenida de América, then right through the pleasantly manicured Jardines de la Victoria park. Near the end of the park, on the left, you'll see a section of the old city walls. The Puerta de Almodóvar gate and a statue of Seneca mark the start of Calle de Cairuán (sometimes signposted as Kairuán)—follow this street downhill, with the wall still on your left, until you reach Plaza Campo de los Santos Mártires. Then head left, past the Alcázar, down Calle Amador de los Rios, which leads directly to the Mezquita and the river.

By Car: The easiest way to enter the city center from Madrid or Sevilla on A-4/E-5 is to follow signs for *Córdoba sur* and Plaza de Andalucía, following palm-tree-lined A-431 (a.k.a. Avenida del Corregidor). Unless your hotel offers parking, avoid driving near the Mezquita. Instead, head for public parking: half a mile after crossing the Guadalquivir River, veer right onto Paseo de la Victoria, then look for a blue parking sign on the left (just before Calle Concepción) and a ramp down to an underground lot. To reach the bus and train stations (with car rental agencies), continue north on Paseo de la Victoria.

HELPFUL HINTS

Closed Days: The synagogue, Alcázar, Madinat Al-Zahra, and Palacio de Viana are closed on Monday. The Mezquita is open daily.

Festivals: May is busy with festivals. During the first half of the month, Córdoba hosts the Concurso Popular de Patios Cordobeses—a patio contest.

Laundry: Solymar Tintoreria has self-service machines (Mon-Fri 9:00-13:00 & 17:00-20:30, closed Sat afternoon and all day Sun, Calle Maestro Priego López 2, tel. 957-233-818).

Supermarket: Día has a large branch in the modern part of town, near Plaza de las Tendillas (Mon-Sat 9:00-21:30, closed Sun, Sevilla 6).

Local Guides: Isabel Martínez Richter is a charming archaeologist who loves to make the city come to life for curious Americans (weekday €135/3 hours, €30 more on weekends and holidays, mobile 669-369-645, isabmr@gmail.com). **Ángel Lucena** is a good teacher and a joy to be with (€100/3 hours, mobile 607-898-079, lucenaangel@hotmail.com).

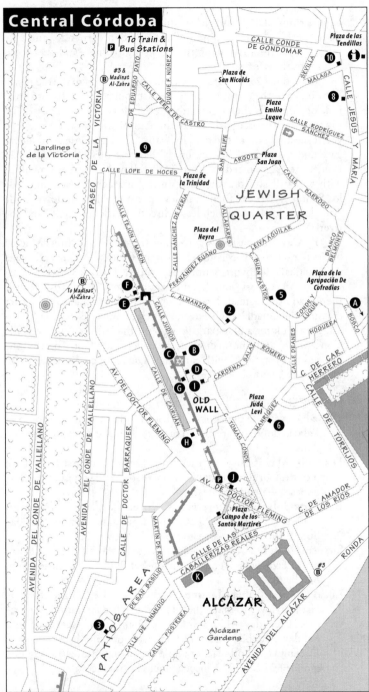

Central Córdoba

To Train & Bus Stations

#3 & Madinat Al-Zahra

Plaza de las Tendillas

CALLE CONDE DE GONDOMAR

Plaza de San Nicolás

Plaza Emilio Luque

CALLE RODRÍGUEZ SÁNCHEZ

Plaza San Juan

JEWISH QUARTER

Jardines de la Victoria

PASEO DE LA VICTORIA

CALLE LOPE DE HOCES

Plaza de la Trinidad

Plaza del Neyra

Plaza de la Agrupación De Cofradias

To Madinat Al-Zahra

Plaza Judá Levi

OLD WALL

Plaza Campo de los Santos Martires

CALLE DE LAS CABALLERIZAS REALES

ALCÁZAR

PATIOS AREA

Alcázar Gardens

AVENIDA DEL ALCÁZAR

CÓRDOBA

Sights

- **A** Calleja de las Flores
- **B** Casa de Sefarad
- **C** Synagogue
- **D** Artisan Market
- **E** Puerta de Almodóvar Gate
- **F** Seneca Statue
- **G** Maimonides Statue
- **H** Averroes Statue
- **I** Museo Taurino Córdoba
- **J** Baths of the Caliphate Alcázar
- **K** Caballerizas Reales
- **L** Museo Julio Romero de Torres

Hotels

- **1** Balcón de Córdoba
- **2** La Llave de la Judería
- **3** El Patio de la Costurera
- **4** Hotel Mezquita
- **5** Hotel Albucasis
- **6** Hotel González
- **7** Al-Katre Backpacker Hostel
- **8** Hotel Córdoba Centro
- **9** Hotel Califa
- **10** Hotel Boston
- **11** Funky Córdoba Hostel

Sights in Córdoba

▲▲▲Mezquita

This massive former mosque—now with a 16th-century church rising up from the middle—was once the center of Western Islam and the heart of a cultural capital that rivaled Baghdad and Constantinople. A wonder of the medieval world, it's remarkably well-preserved, giving today's visitors a chance to soak up the ambience of Islamic Córdoba in its 10th-century prime.

Cost: €10, ticket kiosk and machines inside the Patio de los Naranjos, Mon-Sat free entry 8:30-9:30 (because they don't want to charge a fee to attend the 9:30 Mass; no access to altar, choir, or treasury during free entry period), detailed but dry audioguide-€3.50.

Hours: March-Oct Mon-Sat 8:30-19:00, Sun 8:30-11:30 & 15:00-19:00; in winter closes daily at 18:00; Christian altar accessible only after 11:00 unless you attend Mass; usually less crowded after 15:00. During religious holidays, particularly Holy Week, the Mezquita may close to sightseers at some times of day—check the online events calendar before you go. You can also enjoy the Mezquita on a sound-and-light tour on most summer evenings.

Information: Tel. 957-470-512, www.catedraldecordoba.es.

Bell Tower Climb: €2, limited to 20 people every half-hour, daily 9:30-18:30, until 17:30 in winter. Reserve a time for your climb when you buy your ticket. Inside you'll see a few remnants of the original minaret that became the base structure for the bell tower, and as you climb, you'll have progressively better views of the mosque-cathedral and the city itself.

Planning Your Time: Usually one hour is enough to visit the interior of the Mezquita. If you plan to climb the bell tower, save it for last.

❸ Self-Guided Tour: Before entering the patio, take in the exterior of the Mezquita. The mosque's massive footprint is clear when you survey its sprawling walls from outside. At 600 feet by 400 feet, it dominates the higgledy-piggledy medieval town that surrounds it.

❶ Patio de los Naranjos: The Mezquita's big, welcoming courtyard is free to enter. When this was a mosque, the Muslim faithful would gather in this courtyard to perform ablution—ritual washing before prayer, as directed by Muslim law. The courtyard walls display many of the former mosque's carved and painted ceiling panels and beams, which date from the 10th century.

❷ Bell Tower/Minaret: Gaze up through the trees for views of the bell tower (c. 1600), built over the remains of the original

Muslim minaret. For four centuries, five times a day, a singing cleric (the muezzin) would ride a donkey up the ramp of the minaret, then call to all Muslims in earshot that it was time to face Mecca and pray.

• *Buy your ticket (and, if you wish, rent an audioguide at a separate kiosk to the right). Enter the building during regular hours by passing through the keyhole gate at the far-right corner (pick up an English map-brochure as you enter). During the free entry period, enter through the Puerta de las Palmas.*

❸ Entrance: Walking into the former mosque from the patio, you pass from an orchard of orange trees into a forest of delicate columns (erected here in the eighth century). The more than 800 red-and-blue columns are topped with double arches—a round Romanesque arch above a Visigothic horseshoe arch—made from alternating red brick and white stone. The columns and capitals (built

of marble, granite, and alabaster) were recycled from ancient Roman ruins and conquered Visigothic churches. (Golden Age Arabs excelled at absorbing both the technology and the building materials of the peoples they conquered—no surprise, considering the culture's nomadic roots; centuries of tentmaking didn't lend much stoneworking expertise.) The columns seem to recede to infinity, as if reflecting the immensity and complexity of Allah's creation.

Although it's a vast room, the low ceilings and dense columns create an intimate and worshipful atmosphere. The original mosque was brighter, before Christians renovated the place for their use and closed in the arched entrances from the patio and street. The giant cathedral sits in the center of the mosque. For now, pretend it doesn't exist. We'll visit it after exploring the mosque.

• *From either entrance, count five columns into the building and look for two small walls. Between them, find a glass floor covering a section of mosaic floor below. Look in.*

❹ Visigothic Mosaic: The mosque stands on the site of the early-Christian Church of San Vicente, built during the Visigothic period (sixth century). Peering down, you can see a mosaic that

CÓRDOBA

Mezquita

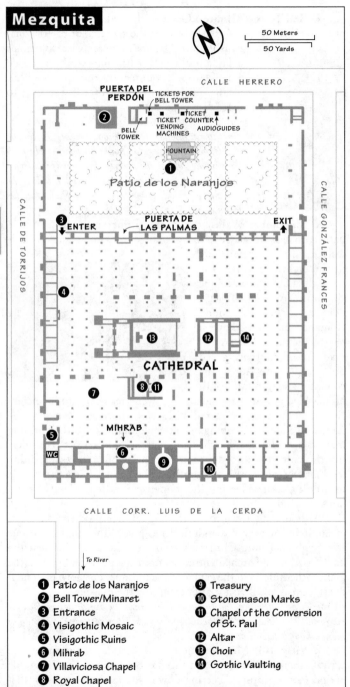

50 Meters
50 Yards

CALLE HERRERO

PUERTA DEL PERDÓN

TICKETS FOR BELL TOWER

Bell Tower

TICKET VENDING MACHINES

TICKET COUNTER

AUDIOGUIDES

FOUNTAIN

❶

Patio de los Naranjos

CALLE DE TORRIJOS

CALLE GONZÁLEZ FRANCES

❷

❸ ENTER

PUERTA DE LAS PALMAS

EXIT

❹

❼

❺

WC

MIHRAB

❻

❾

❿

❽ ❶❶

CATHEDRAL

❶❸

❶❷

❶❹

CALLE CORR. LUIS DE LA CERDA

To River

CÓRDOBA

❶ Patio de los Naranjos
❷ Bell Tower/Minaret
❸ Entrance
❹ Visigothic Mosaic
❺ Visigothic Ruins
❻ Mihrab
❼ Villaviciosa Chapel
❽ Royal Chapel

❾ Treasury
❿ Stonemason Marks
❶❶ Chapel of the Conversion of St. Paul
❶❷ Altar
❶❸ Choir
❶❹ Gothic Vaulting

remains from that original church. This is important to Catholic locals, as it proves there was a church here before the mosque—thereby giving credence to those who see the modern-day church on this spot as a return to the site's original purpose, rather than a violation of the mosque.

• *Continue ahead to the wall opposite the entrance, where you'll find more...*

❺ **Visigothic Ruins:** On display in the corner are rare bits of carved stone from that same sixth-century church. (Most other stonework here had been scrubbed of its Christian symbolism by Muslims seeking to reuse them for the mosque.) Prince Abd Al-Rahman bought the church from his Christian subjects before leveling it to build his mosque. From here, pan to the right to take in the sheer vastness of the mosque. (A hidden WC and drinking fountain are in the corner.)

CÓRDOBA

• *Walk to your left until you come to the mosque's focal point, the...*

❻ **Mihrab:** The mosque equivalent of a church's high altar, this was the focus of the mosque and remains a highlight of the Mezquita today. Picture the original mosque at prayer time, with a dirt floor covered by a patchwork of big carpets...more than 20,000 people could pray at once here. Imagine the multitude kneeling in prayer, facing the mihrab, rocking forward to touch their heads to the ground, and saying, *"Allahu Akbar, la ilaha illa Allah, Muhammad rasul Allah"*—"Allah is great, there is no God but Allah, and Muhammad is his prophet."

The mihrab, a feature in all mosques, is a decorated niche—in this case, more like a small room with a golden-arch entrance.

During a service, the imam (prayer leader) would stand here to read scripture and give sermons. He spoke loudly into the niche, his back to the assembled crowd, and the architecture worked to amplify his voice so all could hear. Built in the mid-10th century by Al-Hakam II, the exquisite room reflects the wealth of Córdoba in its prime. Three thousand pounds of shimmering multicolored glass-and-enamel cubes panel the walls and domes in mosaics designed by Byzantine craftsmen, depicting flowers and quotes from the Quran. Gape up. Overhead rises a colorful, starry dome with skylights and interlocking lobe-shaped arches.

• *Now turn around so that you're facing away from the mihrab. Ahead of you, and a bit to the left, is a roped-off open area. Gaze into the first chapel built within the mosque after the Christian Reconquista.*

❼ **Villaviciosa Chapel:** In 1236, Saint-King Ferdinand III

Islamic Córdoba (756-1236): Medieval Europe's Cultural Capital

After political rivals slaughtered his family in 750, the 20-year-old Umayyad prince Abd Al-Rahman fled the royal palace at Damascus, headed west across North Africa, and went undercover among the Berber tribesmen of Morocco. For six years he avoided assassination while building a power base amongst his fellow Arab expatriates and the local Muslim Berbers. As an heir to the title of "caliph" (a civil and religious leader), he sailed north and claimed Moorish Spain as his own, confirming his power by decapitating his enemies and sending their salted heads to the rival caliph in Baghdad. This split in Islam was somewhat like the papal schism that stirred up medieval Christian Europe, when the Church split into factions over who was the rightful pope.

Thus began an Islamic flowering in southern Spain under the Umayyads. They dominated Sevilla and Granada, ruling the independent state of "Al-Andalus," with their capital at Córdoba.

By the year 950—when the rest of Europe was mired in poverty, ignorance, and superstition—Córdoba was Europe's greatest city, rivaling Constantinople and Baghdad. It had well over 100,000 people (Paris had a third that many), with hundreds of mosques, palaces, and public baths. The streets were paved and lit at night with oil lamps, and running water was piped in from the outskirts of the city. Medieval visitors marveled at the size and luxury of its mosque (the Mezquita), a symbol that the Umayyads of Spain were the equals of the caliphs of Baghdad.

This Golden Age was marked by a remarkable spirit of tolerance and cooperation in this region among the three great monotheistic religions: Islam, Judaism, and Christianity. As a proudly Andalusian guide once explained to me, "Umayyad Al-Andalus was not one country with three cultures. It was one culture with

conquered the city and turned the mosque into a church. The higher ceiling allowed for clerestory windows and more light, which

were key to making it feel more church-like. Still, the locals continued to call it "la Mezquita," and left the structure virtually unchanged (70 percent of the original mosque structure survives to this day). Sixteen columns were removed and replaced by Gothic arches to make this first chapel. It feels as if the church architects appreciated the opportunity to incorporate the sublime architecture of the preexisting mosque into their church. Notice how the floor was once almost entirely covered with three religions...its people shared the same food, dress, art, music, and language. Different religious rituals within the community were practiced in private. But clearly, Muslims ruled. No church spire could be taller than a minaret, and while the call to prayer rang out five times daily, there was no ringing of church bells."

The university rang with voices in Arabic, Hebrew, and Latin, sharing their knowledge of medicine, law, literature, and *al-jibra*. The city fell under the enlightened spell of the ancient Greeks, and Córdoba's 70 libraries bulged with translated manuscripts of Plato and Aristotle, works that would later inspire medieval Christians.

Ruling over the Golden Age were two energetic leaders— Abd Al-Rahman III (912-961) and Al-Hakam II (961-976)—who conquered territory, expanded the Mezquita, and boldly proclaimed themselves caliphs.

Córdoba's Y1K crisis brought civil wars that toppled the caliph (1031), splintering Al-Andalus into several kingdoms. Córdoba came under the control of the Almoravids (Berbers from North Africa), who were less sophisticated than the Arab-based Umayyads. Then a wave of even stricter Islam swept through Spain, bringing the Almohads to power (1147) and driving Córdoba's best and brightest into exile. The city's glory days were over, and it was replaced by Sevilla and Granada as the center of Iberian Islam. On June 29, 1236, Christians conquered the city. That morning Muslims said their last prayers in the great mosque. That afternoon, the Christians set up their portable road altar and celebrated the church's first Mass. Córdoba's days as a political and cultural superpower were over.

the tombs of nobles and big shots eager to make this their final resting place.

• *Immediately to your right (as you face the main entrance of the Mezquita), you'll see the...*

❾ **Royal Chapel:** The chapel—designed for the tombs of two Christian kings of Castile, Fernando IV and Alfonso XI—is completely closed off. Peek through the windows here or wander to the right side for the best views. While it was never open to the public, the tall, well-preserved Mudejar walls and dome are easily visible. Notice the elaborate stucco and tile work. The lavish Arabic-style decor dates from the 1370s, done by Muslim artisans after the Reconquista of the city. The floor is above your head to accommodate tombs buried beneath it. The fact that a Christian king chose to be buried in a tomb so clearly Moorish in design indicates the mutual respect between the cultures (before the Inquisition changed all that). The remains of both Castilian kings were moved to another Córdoba church in the 1700s, so it remains a mystery why this chapel is still closed to visitors.

• *Return to the mihrab, then go through the big, pink marble door to your immediate left, which leads into the Baroque...*

❾ Treasury (Tesoro): The treasury is filled with display cases of religious artifacts and the enormous monstrance that is paraded through the streets of Córdoba each Corpus Christi, 60 days after Easter (notice the handles).

The monstrance was an attempt by 16th-century Christians to create something exquisite enough to merit being the holder of the Holy Communion wafer. As they believed the wafer actually was the body of Christ, this trumped any relics. The monstrance is designed to direct your gaze to heaven. While the bottom is silver-plated 18th-century Baroque, the top is late Gothic—solid silver with gold plating courtesy of 16th-century conquistadors. Gaze up at an equally spectacular ceiling.

The big canvas nearest the entrance shows Saint-King Ferdinand III, who conquered Córdoba in 1236, accepting the keys to the city's fortified gate from the vanquished Muslims. The victory ended a six-month siege and resulted in a negotiated settlement: The losers' lives were spared, providing they evacuated. Most went to Granada, which remained Muslim for another 250 years. The same day, the Spaniards celebrated Mass in a makeshift chapel right here in the great mosque.

The black-and-white marble tomb at the entrance opposite Ferdinand III belongs to Fray Pedro de Salazar y Toledo. After studies in Salamanca, Salazar had the honor of being the main preacher to two Spanish kings, Philip IV and Charles II. In 1686, he was named cardinal by Pope Innocent XI, but his local claim to fame is as founder of one of the first public hospitals in Córdoba, in use today as the School of Philosophy for the local university.

Among the other Catholic treasures, don't miss the ivory crucifix (next room, body carved from one tusk, arms carefully fitted on) from 1665. Get close to study Jesus' mouth—it's incredibly realistic. The artist? No one knows.

• *Just outside the treasury exit, a glass case holds casts that show many...*

❿ Stonemason Marks: These casts bear the marks and signatures left by those who cut them to build the original Visigothic church and later, the mosque. Try to locate the actual ones on nearby columns. (I went five for six.) This part of the mosque has the best light for photography, thanks to skylights put in by 18th-century Christians.

The mosque grew over several centuries under a series of rulers. Remarkably, each ruler kept to the original vision—rows and rows of multicolored columns topped by double arches. Then came the Christians.

⓫ Chapel of the Conversion of St. Paul: Sharing a back wall with the Royal Chapel, the church ceded this space for the burial of Pedro Muñiz de Godoy—Grand Master of the Order of Santiago who fought several battles for Castile against the Portuguese in the 1300s. Godoy's descendants recently spent a fortune to painstakingly clean and restore the chapel, which drips with gold and 17th-century sculpture. The chapel is likely by the same architect as the choir you are about to see.

• *Find the towering church in the center of the mosque and step in.*

⓬ Altar: Rising up in the middle of the forest of columns is the bright and newly restored cathedral, oriented in the Christian tradition, with its altar at the east end. Gazing up at the rich, golden decoration, it's easy to forget that you were in a former mosque just seconds ago. While the mosque is about 30 feet high, the cathedral's space soars 130 feet up. Look at the glorious ceiling.

In 1523 Córdoba's bishop proposed building this grand church in the Mezquita's center. The town council opposed it, but Charles

V (called Charles I in Spain) ordered it done. If that seems like a travesty to you, consider what some locals will point out: Though it would have been quicker and less expensive for the Christian builders to destroy the mosque entirely, they respected its beauty and built their church into it instead.

As you take in the styles of these two great places of worship, ponder how they reflect the differences between Catholic and Islamic aesthetics and psychology: horizontal versus vertical, intimate versus powerful, fear-inspiring versus loving, dark versus bright, simple versus elaborate, feeling close to God versus feeling small before God.

The basic structure is late Gothic, with fancy Isabelline-style columns. The nave's towering Renaissance arches and dome emphasize the triumph of Christianity over Islam in Córdoba. The twin pulpits feature a marble bull, eagle, angel, and lion—symbols of the four evangelists. The modern *cátedra* (the seat of the bishop) is made of Carrara marble.

While churches and mosques normally both face east (to Jerusalem or Mecca), this space holds worship areas aimed 90 degrees from each other, since the mihrab faces south. Perhaps it's because from here you have to go south (via Gibraltar) to get to Mecca. Or maybe it's because this mosque was designed by the

Umayyad branch of Islam, whose ancestral home was Damascus—from where Mecca lies to the south.

• *Facing the high altar is a big, finely decorated wooden enclosure.*

❸ **Choir:** The Baroque-era choir stalls were added much later—made in 1750 of New World mahogany. While cluttering up a previously open Gothic space, the choir is considered one of the masterpieces of 18th-century Andalusian Baroque. Each of the 109 stalls (108 plus the throne of the bishop) features a scene from the Bible: Mary's life on one side facing Jesus' life on the other. The lower chairs feature carved reliefs of the 49 martyrs of Córdoba (from Roman, Visigothic, and Moorish times), each with a palm frond symbolizing martyrdom and the scene of their death in the background.

The medieval church strayed from the inclusiveness taught by Jesus: choirs (which were standard throughout Spain) were for clerics (canons, priests, and the bishop). The pews in the nave were for nobles. And the peasants listened in from outside. (Lay people didn't understand what they were hearing anyway, as Mass was held in Latin until the 1960s.) Those days are long over. Today, a public Mass is said—in Spanish—right here most mornings (Mon-Sat at 9:30, Sun at 12:00 and 13:30).

• *Before leaving, walk to the back of the altar to admire the* ❹ *Gothic vaulting mingled with Moorish arches—a combination found nowhere else in the world.*

NEAR THE MEZQUITA
These sights are all within a few minutes' walk of the Mezquita.

On and near the River
Just downhill from the Mezquita is the Guadalquivir River, which flows on to Sevilla and eventually out to the Atlantic. While silted up today, it was once navigable from here. The town now seems to turn its back on the Guadalquivir, but the arch next to the Roman Bridge (with its ancient foundation surviving) and the fortified gate on the far bank (now housing a museum, described later) evoke a day when the river was key to the city's existence.

Triumphal Arch and Plague Monument
The unfinished Renaissance arch was designed to give King Philip II a royal welcome, but he arrived before its completion—so the

job was canceled. ("Very Andalusian," according to a local friend.) The adjacent monument with the single column is an 18th-century plague monument dedicated to St. Raphael (he was in charge of protecting the region's population from its main scourges: plague, hunger, and floods).

Roman Bridge

The ancient bridge sits on its first-century-A.D. foundations and retains its 16th-century arches. It was the first bridge built over this river and established Córdoba as a strategic place. As European bridges go, it's a poor stepchild (its pedestrian walkway was unimaginatively redone in 2009), but Cordovans still stroll here nightly. Walk across the bridge for a fine view of the city—especially the huge mosque with its cathedral busting through the center. You'll be steps away from the museum described next.

▲Museum of Al-Andalus Life and Calahorra Tower (Museo Vivo de Al-Andalus)

This museum fills the fortified gate (built in the 14th century to protect the Christian city) at the far side of the Roman Bridge. Its worthy mission—to explain the thriving Muslim Moorish culture of 9th- to 12th-century Córdoba and Al-Andalus—is undermined by its obligatory but clumsy audioguide system. You'll don a headset and wander through simple displays as the gauzy commentary lets you sit at the feet of the great poets and poke into Moorish living rooms. The scale models of the Alhambra and the Mezquita are fun, as are the dollhouse tableaus showing life in the market, mosque, university, and baths. It's worth the climb up to the rooftop terrace for the best panoramic view of Córdoba.

Cost and Hours: €4.50, includes one-hour audio tour, daily May-Sept 10:00-14:00 & 16:30-20:30, Oct-April 10:00-18:00, Torre de la Calahorra, tel. 957-293-929, http://www.torrecalahorra.es.

Jewish Córdoba

Córdoba's Jewish Quarter dates from the late Middle Ages, after Muslim rule and during the Christian era. Now little remains. For a sense of the neighborhood in its thriving heyday, first visit the Casa de Sefarad, then the synagogue located a few steps away. For a pretty picture, find **Calleja de las Flores** (a.k.a. "Blossom Lane"). This narrow flower-bedecked street frames the cathedral's bell tower as it hovers in the distance (the view is a favorite for local guidebook covers).

Casa de Sefarad

Set inside a restored 14th-century home directly across from the synagogue, this interpretive museum brings to life Córdoba's rich

Córdoba's Jewish Quarter: A Ten-Point Scavenger Hunt

Whereas most of the area around the Mezquita is commercial and touristy, the neighborhood to the east seems somehow almost untouched by tourism and the modern world (as you leave the Mezquita, turn right and exit the orange-grove patio, then wander into the lanes immediately behind Hotel Mezquita). To catch a whiff of Córdoba as it was before the onslaught of tourism and the affluence of the 21st century, explore this district. Just meander and observe. Here are a few characteristics to look for:

1. **Narrow streets.** Skinny streets make sense in hot climates, as they provide much-appreciated shade. The ones in this area are remnants from the old Moorish bazaar, crammed in to fit within the protective city walls.

2. **Thick, whitewashed walls.** Both features serve as a kind of natural air-conditioning—and the chalk ingredient in the whitewash "bugs" bugs.

3. **Colorful doors and windows.** In this famously white city, what little color there is—mostly added in modern times—helps counter the boring whitewash.

4. **Iron grilles.** Historically, these were more artistic, but modern ones are more practical. Their continued presence is a reminder of the persistent gap through the ages between rich and poor.

Jewish past. Exhibits in the rooms around a central patio recount Spanish Jewish history, focusing on themes such as domestic life, Jewish celebrations and holidays, and Sephardic musical traditions. Upstairs is an interpretive exhibit about the synagogue, along with rooms dedicated to the philosopher Maimonides and the Inquisition. Along with running this small museum, the Casa de Sefarad is a cultural center for Sephardic Jewish heritage (Sephardic Jews are those from Spain or Portugal). They teach courses, offer a library, and promote an appreciation of Córdoba's Jewish past.

Cost and Hours: €4, daily 10:00-19:00, opens and closes one hour later in winter, 30-minute guided tours in English by request if guide is available, across from synagogue at corner of Calle de los Judíos and Calle Averroes, tel. 957-421-404, www.casadesefarad.es.

Concerts: The Casa de Sefarad hosts occasional concerts—acoustic, Sephardic, Andalusian, and flamenco—on its patio (€15, usually at 19:00, confirm schedule).

The wooden latticework covering many windows is a holdover from days when women, held to extreme standards of modesty, wanted to be able to see out while still keeping their privacy.

5. **Stone bumpers on corners.** These protected buildings against reckless drivers. Scavenged secondhand ancient Roman pillars worked well.

6. **Scuff guards.** Made of harder materials, these guards sit at the base of the whitewashed walls—and, from the looks of it, are serving their purpose.

7. **Riverstone cobbles.** These stones were cheap and local, and provided drains down the middle of a lane. They were flanked by smooth stones that stayed dry for walking (and now aid the rolling suitcases of modern-day tourists).

8. **Pretty patios.** Cordovans are proud of their patios. Walk up to the inner iron gates of the wide-open front doors and peek in (see "Patios" sidebar, later).

9. **Remnants of old towers from minarets.** Muslim Córdoba peaked in the 10th century with an estimated 600,000 people, which meant lots of neighborhood mosques.

10. **A real neighborhood.** People really live here. There are no tacky shops, and just about the only tourist is...you.

Synagogue (Sinagoga)

This small yet beautifully preserved synagogue was built between 1314 and 1315, and was in use right up until the final expulsion of the Jews from Spain in 1492.

Cost and Hours: Free, mid-June-mid-Sept Tue-Sun 9:00-15:00; mid-Sept-mid-June Tue-Sat 9:00-20:30, Sun until 15:00; closed Mon year-round, Calle de los Judíos 20, tel. 957-202-928.

Visiting the Synagogue: The synagogue was built by Mudejar craftsmen during a period of religious tolerance after the Christian Reconquista of Córdoba (1236). During Muslim times, Córdoba's sizable Jewish community was welcomed in the city, though its members paid substantial taxes—money that enlarged the Mezquita and generated goodwill. That goodwill came in handy when Córdoba's era of prosperity and mutual respect ended with the arrival of the intolerant Almohad Berbers. Christians and Jews were repressed, and

brilliant minds—such as the philosopher Maimonides, whose statue sits nearby—fled for their own safety.

Its relatively small dimensions lead historians to believe this was a private or family synagogue. It's one of only three medieval synagogues that still stand in Spain (and the only one in Andalucía). That it survived at all is due to its having been successively converted into a church (look for the cross painted into a niche), a hospital, and a shoemakers' guild. The building's original purpose was only rediscovered in the late 19th century.

Rich Mudejar decorations of intertwined flowers and arabesques plaster the walls. The inscriptions in the main room are nearly all from the Bible's Book of Psalms (in Hebrew, with translations posted on each wall). On the east wall (the symbolic direction of Jerusalem), find the niche for the Ark, which held the scrolls of the Torah (the Jewish scriptures). The upstairs gallery was reserved for women.

Artisan Market (Zoco Municipal)

This charming series of courtyards off Calle de los Judíos was the first craft market in Spain. More than a dozen studios cluster around the pretty patios, where artists work in leather, glass, textiles, mosaics, and pottery. Their products—tiles, notecards, jewelry, leather bracelets, and bags—are sold in the associated retail shop.

Cost and Hours: Free to enter, daily 10:00-20:00, Calle de los Judíos s/n, tel. 957-204-033, www.artesaniadecordoba.com.

City Walls

Built upon the foundation of Córdoba's Roman walls, these fortifications date mostly from the 12th century. While the city stretched beyond the walls in Moorish times, these fortifications protected its political, religious, and commercial center. Of the seven original gates, the Puerta de Almodóvar (near the synagogue) is best-preserved today. Along this wall, you'll find statues honoring Córdoba's great thinkers.

Statues of Seneca, Maimonides, and Averroes

Among Córdoba's deepest-thinking homeboys were a Roman philosopher forced to commit suicide, and a Jew and a Muslim who were both driven out during the wave of intolerance after the fall of the Umayyad caliphate. (Seneca is right outside the Puerta de Almodóvar; Maimonides is 30 yards downhill from the synagogue; Averroes is outside the old wall, where Cairuán and Doctor Fleming streets meet.)

Lucius Annaeus Seneca the Younger (c. 3 B.C.-A.D. 65) was born into a wealthy Cordovan family, but was drawn to Rome early in life. He received schooling in Stoicism and made a name for himself in oration, writing, law, and politics. Exiled to Corsica by Emperor Claudius, a remarkable reversal brought him into the role of trusted advisor to Emperor Nero, but eventually Nero accused Seneca of plotting against him and demanded Seneca kill himself. In true Stoic fashion, Seneca complied with this request in A.D. 65, leaving behind a written legacy that includes nine plays, hundreds of essays, and numerous philosophical works that influenced the likes of Calvin, Montaigne, and Rousseau.

Moses Maimonides (1135-1204), "the Jewish Aquinas," was born in Córdoba and raised on both Jewish scripture and the phi-

losophy of Aristotle. Like many tolerant Cordovans, he saw no conflict between the two. An influential Talmudic scholar, astronomer, and medical doctor, Maimonides left his biggest mark as the author of *The Guide for the Perplexed,* in which he asserted that secular knowledge and religious faith could go hand-in-hand (thereby inspiring the philosophy of St. Thomas Aquinas). In 1148, Córdoba was transformed when the fundamentalist Almohads assumed power, and young Maimonides and his family were driven out. Today tourists, Jewish scholars, and fans of Aquinas rub the statue's foot in the hope that some of Maimonides' genius and wisdom will rub off on them.

The story of **Averroes** (1126-1198) is a near match of Maimonides', except that Averroes was a Muslim lawyer, not a Jewish physician. He became the medieval world's number-one authority on Aristotle, also influencing Aquinas. Averroes' biting tract *The Incoherence of the Incoherence* attacked narrow-mindedness, asserting that secular philosophy (for the elite) and religious faith (for the masses) both led to truth. The Almohads banished him from the city and burned his books, ending four centuries of Cordovan enlightenment.

Museo Taurino Córdoba

This museum, in a beautiful old palatial home of brick arcades and patios, examines Córdoba's bullfighting tradition. Displays explore the landscape where bulls are bred and raised, and pay tribute to great bullfighters of the past (and their remarkably tiny waistlines) and to the tempo and aesthetics of the bullfight. It's high-tech, spacious, and merits a visit if you're interested in learning about an important local tradition. But if you've already seen the bullfight museums in Ronda or Sevilla, give this one a pass.

Cost and Hours: €4; open Sept-June Tue-Fri 8:30-20:45, Sat until 16:30, Sun until 14:30; July-Aug Tue-Sat 8:30-15:00; Sun until 14:30; closed Mon year-round; Plaza de Maimonides s/n, tel. 957-201-056, www.museotaurinodecordoba.es.

Alcázar (Alcázar de los Reyes Cristianos)

Tourists line up to visit Córdoba's overrated fortress, the "Castle of the Christian Monarchs," which sits strategically next to the Guadalquivir River. (I think they confuse it with the much more worthy Alcázar in Sevilla.) Upon entering, look to the right to see a big, beautiful garden rich with flowers and fountains. To the left is a modern-feeling, unimpressive fort. While it was built along the Roman walls in Visigothic times, constant reuse and recycling has left it sparse and barren (with the exception of a few interesting Roman mosaics on the walls). Crowds squeeze up and down the congested spiral staircases of "Las Torres" for meager views. Ferdinand and Isabel donated the castle to the Inquisition in 1482, and it became central in the church's effort to discover "false converts to Christianity"—mostly Jews who had decided not to flee Spain in 1492.

Cost and Hours: €4.50, open mid-Sept-mid-June Tue-Fri 8:30-20:45, Sat until 16:30, Sun until 14:30; shorter hours in summer; closed Mon year-round; tel. 957-204-333. On Fridays and Saturdays, you're likely to see people celebrating civil weddings here.

Baths of the Caliphate Alcázar (Baños del Alcázar Califal)

The scant but evocative remains of these 10th-century royal baths are all that's left from the caliph's palace complex. They date from a time when the city had hundreds of baths to serve a population of several hundred thousand. The exhibit teaches about Arabic baths in general and the caliph's in particular. A 10-minute video (normally in Spanish, English on request) tells the story well.

Cost and Hours: €2.50, open same hours as Alcázar, on Plaza Campo de los Santos Mártires, just outside the wall—near the Alcázar.

AWAY FROM THE MEZQUITA

Plaza de las Tendillas

While most tourists leave Córdoba having seen only the Mezquita and the cute medieval quarter that surrounds it, the modern city offers a good peek at urban Andalucía. Perhaps the best way to sample this is to browse Plaza de las Tendillas and the surrounding streets. The square, with an Art Deco charm, acts like there is no tourism in Córdoba. On the hour, a clock here chimes the chords of flamenco guitarist Juan Serrano—a Cordovan classic since 1961.

Characteristic cafés and shops abound. For example, **Café La Gloria** provides an earthy Art Nouveau experience. Located just down the street from Plaza de las Tendillas, it has an unassuming entrance, but a sumptuous interior. Carved floral designs wind around the bar, mixing with *feria* posters and bullfighting memories. Pop in for a quick beer or coffee with the locals (Mon-Sat 9:00-24:00, closed Sun, quiet after lunch crowd clears out, Calle Claudio Marcelo 15, tel. 957-477-780).

Museo Julio Romero de Torres

A city rich in mystical monuments and colorful patios, Córdoba has produced several fine artists during its long history. Well-to-do Julio Romero de Torres began painting at the age of 10 in 1884, under the tutelage of his father who was also a painter and director of the city's fine-arts museum. Early works resembled those of fellow Impressionists like Joaquín Sorolla, but in the 1920s Julio developed a distinct style—the dreamy-eyed, melancholic gaze of the women he loved to paint. After he died in 1930, his family donated many works to the city government and this museum opened one year later. Stroll through six small rooms and discover the spirit of Córdoba through this captivating artist's eyes.

Cost and Hours: €4.50, mid-June-mid-Sept Tue-Sat 8:30-15:00, Sun until 14:30; off-season Tue-Fri 8:30-20:45, Sat until 16:30, Sun until 14:30; closed Mon year-round; Plaza del Potro 1, tel. 957-470-356, www.museojulioromero.cordoba.es.

Palacio de Viana

Decidedly off the beaten path, this former palatial estate is a 25-minute walk northeast from the cluster of sights near the Mezquita. The complex's many renovations over its 500-year history are a case study in changing tastes. A guided tour whisks you through each room of an exuberant 16th-century estate, while an English handout trudges through the dates and origin of each important piece. But the house is best enjoyed by ignoring the guide and gasping at the massive collection of—for lack of a better word—stuff. Decorative-art fans will have a field day. If your interests run more to flowers,  skip the house and buy a "patio" ticket: 12 connecting garden patios, each with a different theme, sprawl around and throughout the residence. It's no Alhambra, but if you won't see the gardens in Granada, these are a wee taste of the Andalusian style.

Cost and Hours: House—€8, patios only—€5; Sept-June Tue-Sat 10:00-19:00, Sun until 15:00; July-Aug Tue-Sun 9:00-15:00; closed Mon year-round, last entry one hour before closing; Plaza Don Gome 2, tel. 957-496-741.

CÓRDOBA

NEAR CÓRDOBA
Madinat Al-Zahra (Medina Azahara)

Five miles northwest of Córdoba, these ruins of a once-fabulous palace of the caliph were completely forgotten until excavations began in the early 20th century.

Extensively planned, with an orderly design, Madinat Al-Zahra was meant to symbolize and project a new discipline on an increasingly unstable Moorish empire in Spain. It failed. Only 75 years later, the city was looted and destroyed.

Cost and Hours: €1.50; mid-April–mid-June Tue-Sat 9:00-20:30, mid-June–mid-Sept until 17:00, mid-Sept–mid-April until 18:00; Sun 10:00-17:00 and closed Mon year-round; tel. 957-104-933, www.museosdeandalucia.es.

Getting There: Madinat Al-Zahra is located on a back road five miles from Córdoba. By **car,** head to Avenida de Medina Azahara (one block south of the train station), following signs for *A-431;* the site is well-signed from the highway. The TI runs a **shuttle bus** that leaves several times a day and returns 2.5 hours later (€9, buy ticket at any TI; runs year-round Tue-Sat at 10:15, 11:00, and 15:00 plus extra Sat bus at 13:45, Sun at 10:15, 11:00, and 11:45; confirm current bus schedule at TI, informative English booklet). Catch the shuttle on Paseo de la Victoria at either of two stops shared with the Bus Turístico route.

Visiting Madinat Al-Zahra: Check at the TI before committing to a trip, as the most interesting sections of the site may be closed for restoration. Built in A.D. 929 as a power center to replace Córdoba, Madinat Al-Zahra was both a palace and an entirely new capital city—the "City of the Flower"—covering nearly half a square mile (only about 10 percent has been uncovered).

The site is underwhelming—a jigsaw puzzle waiting to be reassembled by patient archaeologists. Upper terrace excavations have

uncovered stables and servants' quarters. Farther downhill, the house of a high-ranking official has been partially reconstructed. At the lowest level, you'll come to the remains of the mosque—placed at a diagonal, facing true east. The highlight of the visit is an elaborate re-

Patios

In Córdoba, patios are taken very seriously, as shown by the fiercely fought contest, the Concurso Popular de Patios Cor-

dobeses, which takes place the first half of every May to pick the city's most picturesque. Patios, a common feature of houses throughout Andalucía, have a long history here. The Romans used them to cool off, and the Moors added lush, decorative touches. The patio functioned as a quiet outdoor living room, an oasis from the heat. Inside elaborate ironwork gates, roses, geraniums, and jasmine spill down whitewashed walls, while fountains play and caged birds sing. Some patios are owned by individuals, some are communal courtyards for several homes, and some grace public buildings like museums or convents.

Today homeowners take pride in these miniparadises, and have no problem sharing them with tourists. Keep an eye out for square metal signs that indicate historic homes. As you wander Córdoba's back streets, pop your head into any wooden door that's open. The proud owners (who keep inner gates locked) enjoy showing off their picture-perfect patios.

A concentration of patio-contest award-winners runs along Calle de San Basilio and Calle Martín Roa, just across from the Alcázar gardens. Seven of these winners have banded together to open their patios to the public for a small entry fee (€7; Mon and Wed-Sat 10:00-14:00 & 17:00-20:00, Sun 10:00-14:00, patios closed Tue; get tickets at office on Calle de San Basilio 14, tel. 654-530-377). Many other nearby patios are free to visit.

construction of the caliph's throne room, capturing a moody world of horseshoe arches and delicate stucco. Legendary accounts say the palace featured waterfall walls, lions in cages, and—in the center of the throne room—a basin filled with mercury, reflecting the colorful walls. The effect likely humbled anyone fortunate enough to see the caliph.

Entertainment in Córdoba

Caballerizas Reales de Córdoba

This equestrian show at the royal stables (just beyond the Alcázar) combines an artful demonstration of different riding styles with flamenco dance (€15; 1-hour shows Wed, Fri, and Sat at 21:00; Sun at 12:00; no shows Mon-Tue or Thu; outside in summer, inside in winter, tel. 957-497-843, www.cordobaecuestre.com). During the day, you can tour the stables for free (Mon-Sat 10:00-13:30 & 16:00-19:30, Sun 10:00-11:00, Caballerizas Reales 1).

Flamenco

While flamenco is better in nearby Sevilla, you can see it in Córdoba, too. **Tablao Flamenco Cardenal** is the city's most popular and awarded show, with 120 seats in a beautifully decorated private patio. They also offer a preshow dinner with typical dishes from Córdoba (€23, includes one drink, dinner—€11 extra, 1.5-hour shows Mon-Thu at 20:15, Fri-Sat at 21:00, no shows Sun, confirm schedule online, Buen Pastor 2, mobile 691-217-922, www.tablaocardenal.es).

El Alma de Córdoba

To experience "the soul of Córdoba"—or at least the Mezquita by night—you can take this pricey one-hour audio tour, joining about 80 people to be shepherded around the complex listening via headset to an obviously Christian-produced sound-and-light show (€18, March-Oct Mon-Sat, off-season Fri-Sat only, 1-2 shows a night, hours vary according to sunset; book at Mezquita or online; www.catedraldecordoba.es).

Sleeping in Córdoba

My price ratings are for high season; most of these places are cheaper outside peak times.

NEAR THE MEZQUITA

These are all within a five-minute stroll of the Mezquita.

$$$$ Balcón de Córdoba is an elegant little boutique hotel buried in the old town, just steps away from the Mezquita. With 10 stylish rooms, charming public spaces, plenty of attention to detail, and a magnificent rooftop terrace, it's a lot of luxury for the price. It feels both new and steeped in tradition. The restaurant serves wonderful cuisine, enhanced by evening views of the Mezquita from the terrace (includes breakfast, air-con, pay parking, restaurant open daily 12:30-15:00 & 19:30-22:00, Calle Encarnación 8, tel. 957-498-478, www.balcondecordoba.com, reservas@balcondecordoba.com).

$$$ La Llave de la Judería is a nine-room jewel box of an inn, featuring plush furniture, tasteful traditional decor, and attentive service. Quiet and romantic, it's tucked in the old quarter just far enough away from the tourist storm, yet still handy for sightseeing (website shows each room, includes generous breakfast, air-con, midway between Puerta de Almodóvar and the Mezquita at Calle Romero 38, tel. 957-294-808, www.lallavedelajuderia.es, info@

lallavedelajuderia.es). Managers Rocío and Alberto make you feel right at home.

$$ El Patio de la Costurera offers a uniquely Cordovan experience: sleeping in one of the city's prize-winning patios. Araceli and her sister rent four homey and colorful apartments, each with a kitchenette. While some noise might come from patio visitors during the day, the neighborhood is quiet at night and close to several recommended restaurants (air-con, Calle de San Basilio 40, tel. 654-530-377, www.elpatiodelacosturera.com).

$$ Hotel Mezquita, just across from the Mezquita, rents 32 modern and comfortable rooms. The grand entrance lobby elegantly recycles an upper-class mansion (air-con, elevator, Plaza Santa Catalina 1, tel. 957-475-585, www.hotelmezquita.com, recepcion@hotelmezquita.com).

$ Hotel Albucasis, at the edge of the tourist zone, features 15 basic, clean rooms, all of which face quiet interior patios. The friendly, accommodating staff and cozy setting make you feel right at home (air-con, elevator, pay parking but free off-season, Buen Pastor 11, tel. 957-478-625, www.hotelalbucasi.com, hotelalbucasis@hotmail.com).

$ Hotel González, with many of its 29 basic rooms facing a cool and peaceful patio, is spartan but very sleepable. It's clean and well-run, with a good location and price. Streetside rooms come with a bit of noise at night (air-con, elevator, Calle de los Manríquez 3, tel. 957-479-819, www.hotelgonzalez.com, recepcion@hotelgonzalez.com).

¢ Al-Katre Backpacker is a fun hostel run in a homey way by three energetic girlfriends. Its rooms gather around a cool courtyard (Calle Martínez Rucker 14, tel. 957-487-539, www.alkatre.com, alkatre@alkatre.com).

IN THE MODERN CITY

While still within easy walking distance of the Mezquita, these places are outside of the main tourist zone—not buried in all that tangled medieval cuteness.

$$ Hotel Córdoba Centro sits at a good crossroads between the historic center around the Mezquita and the modern part of the city. Most of its 27 simple but comfortable rooms are interior, assuring a solid night's sleep, while nine rooms face the pedestrian street and coffee shop below. Good deals can be found on their website with advance booking (air-con, elevator, Jesús y María 8, tel. 957-497-850, www.hotel-cordobacentro.es).

$ Hotel Califa, a modern 65-room business-class hotel belonging to the NH chain, sits on a quiet street a block off busy Paseo Victoria, on the edge of the jumbled old quarter. Still close enough to the sights, its slick modern rooms can be a great value if you get a deal (air-con, elevator, pay parking, Lope de Hoces 14, tel. 957-299-400, www.nh-hotels.com, nhcalifa@nh-hotels.com).

$ Hotel Boston, with 39 rooms, is a decent budget bet if you want a reliable, basic hotel away from the touristy Mezquita zone. It's a taste of workaday Córdoba (air-con, elevator, Calle Málaga 2, just off Plaza de las Tendillas, tel. 957-474-176, www.hotel-boston. com, info@hotel-boston.com).

¢ Funky Córdoba Hostel rents beds in a great neighborhood (air-con, terrace, right by Plaza del Potro bus stop—take #3 from station—at Calle Lucano 12, tel. 957-492-966, www. funkycordoba.com, funkycordoba@funkyhostels.es).

Eating in Córdoba

Córdoba has a reputation among Spaniards as a great dining town, with options ranging from obvious touristy bars in the old center to enticing, locals-only hangouts a few blocks away. Specialties include *salmorejo,* Córdoba's version of gazpacho. It's creamier, with more bread and olive oil and generally served with pieces of ham and hard-boiled egg on top. Look for winners of the city's yearly oxtail stew *(rabo de toro)* contest and find your favorite. Most places serve white wines from the nearby Montilla-Moriles region; these *finos* are slightly less dry but more aromatic than the sherry produced in Jerez de la Frontera. Ask for a *fino fresquito* (chilled) and you'll fit right in.

NEAR THE MEZQUITA

Touristy options abound near the Mezquita. By walking a couple of blocks north or east of the Mezquita, you'll find plenty of cheap, accessible little places offering a better value.

$$ Bodegas Mezquita is one of the touristy places, but it's easy and handy—a good bet for a bright, air-conditioned place near the mosque. They have a good *menú del día,* or you can order from their menu of tapas, half-*raciones,* and *raciones* (daily 12:30-23:30, one block above the Mezquita patio at Calle Céspedes 12, tel. 957-490-004). They have one other location near the Mezquita, at Calle Corregidor Luis de la Cerda 73.

$ Bar Santos, facing the Mezquita, supplies the giant *tortilla de patatas* (potato omelette) that you see locals happily munching on the steps of the mosque. All of their "fast" food is served to-go in disposable containers. A hearty tortilla and a beer make for a very cheap meal; add a *salmorejo* and it feels complete (daily 10:00-24:00, Calle Magistral González Francés 3, tel. 957-484-975).

BARRIO SAN BASILIO

This delightful little quarter outside the town wall, just a couple of minutes' walk west of the Mezquita and behind the royal stables, is famous for its patios. It's traffic-free, quaint as can be, and feels perfectly Cordovan without the crush of tourists around the Mezquita. Things start late here—don't go before 21:00.

$$ La Posada del Caballo Andaluz is a fresh, modern restaurant with tables delightfully scattered around a courtyard (no bar area). Enjoy tasty traditional Cordovan cuisine at great prices while sitting amid flowers and under the stars (daily 12:30-16:30 & 20:00-23:30, Calle de San Basilio 16, tel. 957-290-374).

$$ Mesón San Basilio, just across the street, is the longtime neighborhood favorite, with no tourists and no pretense. Although there's no outside seating, it still offers a certain patio ambience, with a view of the kitchen action and lots of fish and meat dishes (classic fixed-priced meal, lunch special weekdays, Mon-Sat 13:00-16:00 & 20:00-24:00, closed Sun, Calle de San Basilio 19, tel. 957-297-007).

$ Bodega San Basilio, around the corner, is rougher, serving rustic tapas and good meals to workaday crowds. The bullfight decor gives the place a crusty character—and you won't find a word of English here (closed Tue, on the corner of Calle de Enmedio and small street leading to Calle de San Basilio at #29, tel. 957-297-832).

BETWEEN PUERTA DE ALMODÓVAR AND THE JEWISH QUARTER

The evocative Puerta de Almodóvar gate connects a park-like scene outside the wall with the delightfully jumbled Jewish Quarter just inside it, where cafés and restaurants take advantage of the neighborhood's pools, shady trees, and dramatic face of the wall. The first two recommendations are immediately inside the gate; the others are on or near Calle de los Judíos, which runs south from there.

$$ Taberna Restaurante Casa Rubio serves reliably good traditional dishes with smart, prompt service and several zones to choose from: a few sidewalk tables, with classic people-watching; inside, with a timeless interior; or on the rooftop, with dressy white tablecloths and a view of the old wall (daily 13:00-16:00 & 19:30-23:30, easy English menu, Puerta de Almodóvar 5, tel. 957-420-853).

$$ Taberna Casa Salinas is a more basic place with a fine reputation for quality food at a good price (run by the same people who run the highly recommended Taberna Salinas in the modern city, Mon-Sat 12:30-16:00 & 20:00-23:00, closed Sun, near gate at Puerta de Almodóvar 2, tel. 957-290-846).

$$$ Restaurante El Choto is a bright, formal, and dressy

Restaurants in Central Córdoba

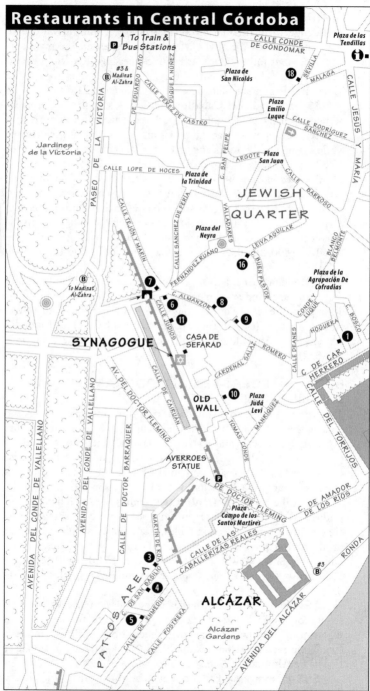

CÓRDOBA

1 Bodegas Mezquita (2)
2 Bar Santos
3 La Posada del Caballo Andaluz
4 Mesón San Basilio
5 Bodega San Basilio
6 Taberna Restaurante Casa Rubio
7 Taberna Casa Salinas
8 Restaurante El Choto
9 El Churrasco Restaurante
10 Casa Mazal
11 Bodega Guzmán
12 Bodegas Campos
13 Macsura Gastrotaberna
14 Taberna Salinas
15 To Taberna San Miguel (Casa el Pisto)
16 Tablao Flamenco Cardenal
17 Café La Gloria
18 Día Supermarket

steak house buried deep in the Jewish Quarter. With a small leafy patio, it's touristy yet intimate, serving well-presented international dishes with an emphasis on grilled meat. The favorite is kid goat with garlic—*choto al ajillo* (closed Sun evening year-round and all day Mon in summer, Calle Almanzor 10, tel. 957-760-115).

$$$ El Churrasco Restaurante is a charmingly old-fashioned place, where longtime patrons are greeted by name. The specialty is grilled meat and seafood, cooked simply and deliciously over oak-charcoal braziers in the open kitchen, but it's a fun place for tapas, too (daily 13:00-16:00 & 20:30-23:30, Calle Romero 16, tel. 957-290-819).

$$ Casa Mazal, run by the nearby Casa de Sefarad Jewish cultural center, serves updated, modern Jewish cuisine. Small dining rooms sprawl around the charming medieval courtyard of a former house. With a seasonal menu that includes several vegetarian options, it offers a welcome dose of variety from the typical Spanish standards (daily 12:30-17:00 & 20:00-24:00, Calle Tomás Conde 3, tel. 957-941-888).

$ Bodega Guzmán could hardly care less about attracting tourists. This rough, dark holdover from a long-gone age proudly displays the heads of brave-but-unlucky bulls, while serving cold, very basic tapas to locals who burst into song when they feel the flamenco groove. Notice how everyone seems to be on a first-name basis with the waiters. It may feel like a drinks-only place, but they do serve rustic tapas and *raciones* (ask for the list in English). Choose a table or belly up to the bar and try a glass of local white wine, either dry *(blanco seco)* or sweet *(blanco dulce)*. If it's grape juice you want, ask for *mosto* (closed Thu, Calle de los Judíos 7, tel. 957-290-960).

JUST EAST OF THE MEZQUITA ZONE

$$$ Bodegas Campos, my favorite place in town, is a historic and venerable house of eating, attracting so many locals it comes with its own garage. It's worth the 10-minute walk from the tourist zone. They have a stuffy and expensive formal restaurant upstairs, but I'd eat in the more relaxed and affordable tavern on the ground floor. The service is great, portions are large, and the menu is inviting. Experiment—you can't go wrong. House specialties are bull-tail stew (*rabo de toro*—rich, tasty, and a good splurge) and anything with *pisto,* the local ratatouille-like vegetable stew. Don't leave without exploring the sprawling complex, which fills 14 old houses that have been connected to create a network of dining rooms and patios, small and large. The place is a virtual town history museum: look for the wine barrels signed by celebrities and VIPs, the old refectory from a convent, and a huge collection of classic, original *feria* posters and great photos (Mon-Sat 13:30-

16:30 & 20:30-23:00, Sun 12:00-17:00 only; Calle de Lineros 32; tel. 957-497-500, www.bodegascampos.com).

$$ Macsura Gastrotaberna serves beautifully presented international dishes for anyone who might need a break from *jamón*—think Asian-Spanish fusion. Choose between bright and white inside seating or watch the locals go by on a triangular patio outside (Mon-Fri 11:30-16:30 & 19:00-24:00, Sat-Sun 11:30-24:00, Calle Cardenal González, tel. 957-486-004).

IN THE MODERN CITY

These places are worth the 10- to 15-minute walk from the main tourist zone—walking here, you feel a world apart from the touristy scene. Combine a meal here with a paseo through the Plaza de las Tendillas area to get a good look at modern Córdoba. If Taberna Salinas is full, as is likely, there are plenty of characteristic bars nearby in the lanes around Plaza de la Corredera.

$$ Taberna Salinas seems like a movie set designed to give you the classic Córdoba scene. Though all the seating is indoors, it's still pleasantly patio-esque and popular with locals for its traditional cuisine and exuberant bustle. The seating fills a big courtyard and sprawls through several smaller, semiprivate rooms. The fun menu features a slew of enticing *raciones* (spinach with chickpeas is a house specialty). Study what locals are eating before ordering. There's no drink menu—just beer, *fino*, or inexpensive wine. If there's a line (as there often is later in the evening), leave your name and throw yourself into the adjacent tapas-bar mosh pit for a drink (Mon-Sat 12:30-16:00 & 20:00-23:30, closed Sun and Aug; from Plaza de las Tendillas walk 3 blocks to the Roman temple, then go 1 more block and turn right to Tundidores 3; tel. 957-480-135).

$$ Taberna San Miguel is nicknamed "Casa el Pisto" for its famous vegetable stew *(pisto)*. Well-respected, it's packed with locals who appreciate regional cuisine, a good value, and a place with a long Cordovan history. There's great seating in its charming interior or on the lively square (tapas at bar only, closed Sun and Aug, 2 blocks north of Plaza de las Tendillas at Plaza San Miguel 1, tel. 957-478-328).

Córdoba Connections

From Córdoba by Train: Córdoba is on the slick **AVE** train line (reservations required), making it an easy stopover between **Madrid** (almost hourly, 2 hours) and **Sevilla** (45 minutes). The **Avant** train connects Córdoba to Sevilla just as fast for nearly half the price (12/day, 45 minutes; rail pass reservations also about half-price). The slow *media distancia* train to Sevilla takes about twice as long, but doesn't require a reservation and is even cheaper (7/day, 1.5 hours).

Other trains go to **Barcelona** (2/day direct, 5 hours, many more with transfer in Madrid), **Granada** (6/day but with bus transfer in Antequera; bus is more frequent, cheaper, and nearly as fast), **Ronda** (2/day direct on Altaria, 2 hours), **Jerez** (to transfer to Arcos; 8/day, 2.5 hours), **Málaga** (fast and cheap Avant train, 6/day, 1 hour; fast and expensive AVE train, 10/day, 1 hour), and **Algeciras** (2/day direct, 3 hours, more with transfer, 4 hours). Train info: toll tel. 902-320-320, www.renfe.com.

By Bus to: Granada (6/day *directo*, 3 hours; 2/day *ruta*, 4 hours), **Sevilla** (7/day, 2 hours), **Madrid** (6/day, 5 hours), **Málaga** (4/day, 3 hours *directo*), **Barcelona** (2/day, 14 hours). The efficient staff at the information desk prints bus schedules for you—or you can check all schedules at www.estacionautobusescordoba.es. Bus info: tel. 957-404-040.

ANDALUCÍA'S WHITE HILL TOWNS

Arcos de la Frontera • Ronda • Zahara and Grazalema •
Jerez de la Frontera

Just as the American image of Germany is Bavaria, the Yankee dream of Spain is Andalucía. This is the home of bullfights, flamenco, gazpacho, pristine whitewashed hill towns, and glamorous Mediterranean resorts. The big cities of Andalucía (Granada, Sevilla, and Córdoba) and the South Coast (Costa del Sol) are covered in separate chapters. This chapter explores Andalucía's hill-town highlights.

The Route of the White Hill Towns (Ruta de los Pueblos Blancos), Andalucía's charm bracelet of cute villages perched in the sierras, gives you wonderfully untouched Spanish culture. Spend a night in the romantic queen of the white towns, Arcos de la Frontera. (Towns with "de la Frontera" in their names were established on the front line of the centuries-long fight to recapture Spain from the Muslims, who were slowly pushed back into Africa.) Farther east, the larger town of Ronda stuns visitors with its breathtaking setting—straddling a gorge that thrusts deep into the Andalusian bedrock. Ronda's venerable old bullring, smattering of enjoyable sights, and thriving tapas scene round out its charms. Smaller hill towns, such as Zahara and Grazalema, offer plenty of beauty. As a whole, the hill towns—no longer strategic, no longer on any frontier—are now just passing time peacefully. Join them.

West of the hill towns, the city of Jerez de la Frontera—teeming with traffic and lacking in charm—is worth a peek for its famous dancing horses and a glass of sherry on a bodega tour.

To study ahead, visit www.andalucia.com for information on hotels, festivals, museums, nightlife, and sports in the region.

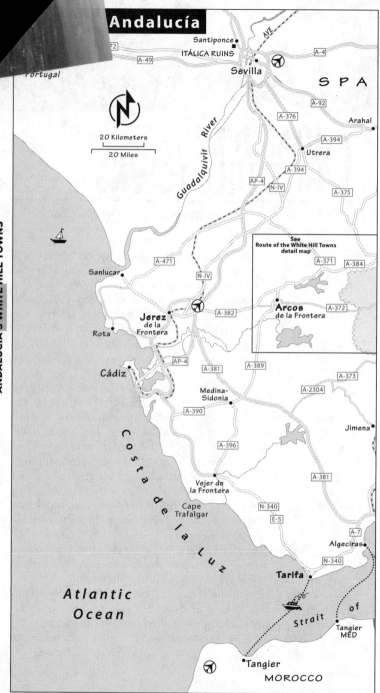

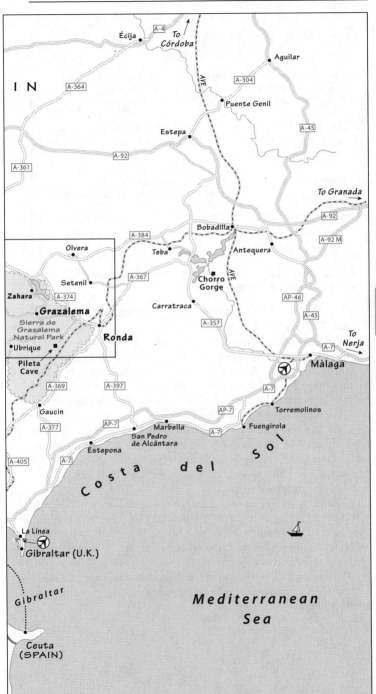

Andalucía's White Hill Towns at a Glance

▲▲▲**Arcos de la Frontera** Queen of the Andalusian hill towns, with a cliff-perched old town that meanders down to a vibrant modern center; well-suited as a home base.

▲▲**Ronda** Midsize town dramatically overhanging a deep gorge, and home to Spain's oldest bullring, with nearby prehistoric paintings at Pileta Cave.

▲**Jerez de la Frontera** Proud equestrian mecca and birthplace of sherry, with plenty of opportunities to enjoy both in a relatively urban setting.

Zahara de la Sierra Tiny whitewashed village scenically set between a rocky Moorish castle and a turquoise reservoir.

Grazalema Bright-white town nestled in the green hills of the Sierra de Grazalema Natural Park.

PLANNING YOUR TIME

On a three-week vacation in Spain, Andalucía's hill towns are worth at least one night and one day sandwiched between visits to Sevilla and Tarifa. Arcos makes the best home base, as it's close to interesting smaller towns, near Jerez, and conveniently situated halfway between Sevilla and Tarifa. The towns can also be accessed from the Costa del Sol resorts via Ronda.

See Jerez on your way in or out, spend a day hopping from town to town in the more remote interior (including Grazalema and Zahara), and overnight in Arcos, enjoying the town early and late in the day. With more time, the larger town of Ronda offers a full day of sightseeing.

Unlike most hill towns, Arcos, Jerez, and Ronda are conveniently reached by public transportation: They have bus connections with surrounding towns, and Ronda is on a train line. For more details on exploring this region by car, see "Route Tips for Drivers" at the end of this chapter.

Spring and fall are high season throughout this area. In summer you'll encounter intense heat, but empty hotels, lower prices, and no crowds.

Arcos de la Frontera

Arcos smothers its long, narrow hilltop and tumbles down the back of the ridge like the train of a wedding dress. It's larger than most other Andalusian hill towns, but equally atmospheric. The old center is a labyrinthine wonderland, a photographer's feast. Viewpoint-hop through town. Feel the wind funnel through the narrow streets as cars inch around tight corners. Join the kids' soccer game on the churchyard patio. Enjoy the moonlit view from the main square.

Though it tries, Arcos doesn't have much to offer other than its basic whitewashed self. The locally produced English guidebook on Arcos waxes poetic and at length about very little. You can arrive late and leave early and still see it all.

Orientation to Arcos

Arcos consists of two parts: the fairy-tale old town on top of the hill and the more commercial lower, or new, town. The **main TI** is on the skinny one-way road leading up into the old town—park up top or down below and walk to it (Mon-Sat 9:30-14:00 & 15:00-19:30, Sun 10:00-14:00; Cuesta de Belén 5, tel. 956-702-264). On the floors above the TI is a skippable local history museum (sparse exhibits described only in Spanish).

ARRIVAL IN ARCOS

By Bus: The bus station is on Calle Corregidores, at the foot of the hill. To get up to the old town, catch the shuttle bus marked *Centro* from the bus stalls behind the station (€1, pay driver, 2/hour, runs roughly Mon-Fri 8:00-21:00, Sat from 9:00, none on Sun), hop a taxi (€5 fixed rate; if there are no taxis waiting, call 956-704-640), or hike 20 uphill minutes (see map).

By Car: The old town is a tight squeeze with a one-way traffic flow from west to east (coming from the east, circle south under town). The TI and my recommended hotels are in the west. If you miss your target, you must drive out the other end, double back, and try again. Driving in Arcos is like threading needles (many drivers pull in their side-view mirrors to buy a few extra precious inches). Turns are tight, parking is frustrating, and congestion can lead to long jams.

Small cars capable of threading the narrow streets of the old town can park in the main square at the top of the hill (Plaza del Cabildo). Buy a ticket from the machine (€0.70/hour, 2-hour maximum, only necessary Mon-Fri 9:00-14:00 & 17:00-21:00 and Sat 9:00-14:00—confirm times on machine). Hotel guests parking

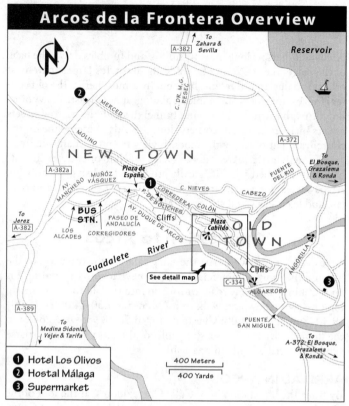

Arcos de la Frontera Overview

❶ Hotel Los Olivos
❷ Hostal Málaga
❸ Supermarket

here overnight must obtain a €5 dashboard pass from their hotelier; daytime parking charges still apply.

It's less stressful (and better exercise) to park in the Paseo de Andalucía modern underground pay lot (€15/day) at Plaza de España in the new town and hike 15 uphill minutes to the old town. Or catch a taxi or the *Centro* shuttle bus—see "By Bus" earlier (as you're looking uphill, the bus stop is to the right of the traffic circle). Many hotels offer discounts at this lot; inquire when booking your room.

GETTING AROUND ARCOS

The old town is easily walkable, but it's fun to take a circular **minibus** joyride. The little shuttle bus constantly circles through the town's one-way system and around the valley (see "Arrival in Arcos," earlier, for details). For a 30-minute tour, hop on. You can catch it just below the main church in the old town near the mystical stone circle (generally departs at roughly :20 and :50 past the hour). Sit in the front seat for the best view of the tight squeezes and the school kids hanging out in the plazas as you wind through the old town. After passing under a Moorish gate, you enter a modern residential neighborhood, circle under the eroding cliff, and return to the old town by way of the bus station and Plaza de España.

HELPFUL HINTS

Money: There are no ATMs in the old town. To reach one, take the main street below the Church of Santa María toward Plaza de España; you'll find several ATMs along Calle Corredera and near the Paseo de Andalucía underground parking lot.

Post Office: It's at the lower end of the old town at Paseo de los Boliches 24, a few doors up from Hotel Los Olivos (Mon-Fri 8:30-14:30, Sat 9:30-13:00, closed Sun).

Supermarket: The Spanish chain **Mercadona** is along the mini-bus route, downhill in the new town on Calle Hernan de San Pedro (Mon-Sat 9:00-21:30, closed Sun).

Walking Tours: Infotur, run by local guides Carmen and Luisa, give walking tours of the old town, covering Arcos' history, lifestyles, and Moorish influences (€5/person; Mon-Sat— call or email to reserve, none on Sun; 5-person minimum, in Spanish and/or English, tel. 687-944-299, www.infoturarcos. es, infoturarcos@yahoo.es).

Views: For drivers, the best town overlook is from a tiny park just beyond the new bridge on the El Bosque road. In town, there are some fine viewpoints (for instance, from the main square), but the church towers are no longer open to the public.

Arcos Old Town Walk

This self-guided walk will introduce you to virtually everything worth seeing in Arcos. (Avoid this walk during the hot midday siesta.)

• *Start at the top of the hill, in the main square dominated by the church.*

Plaza del Cabildo

Stand at the viewpoint opposite the church on the town's main square. Survey the square, which in the old days doubled as a bull-ring. On your right is the parador, a former palace of the governor. It flies three flags: green for Andalucía, red-and-yellow for Spain, and blue-and-yellow for the European Union. On your left is City

Arcos de la Frontera

OLD TOWN

VIEWPOINT

CASTLE (NOT OPEN)

SANTA MARIA

Plaza Cabildo

CLOISTERED NUNS

ST. PETER

Cliffs

Río Guadalete

MIRADOR

MARKET

PEÑA VIEJA

MONTERO

AV. DEL DUQUE DE ARCOS

C-334

To
A-372: El Bosque,
Grazalema
& Ronda

To
Paseo de
Andalucía &
Bus Stn.

To
Bus Stn.

100 Meters
100 Yards

❶ Parador
❷ Hotel El Convento
❸ La Casa Grande
❹ Rincón de las Nieves
❺ Hostal El Patio
❻ Hostal & Bar San Marcos
❼ Bar La Cárcel
❽ Alcaraván
❾ Restaurante Café Babel
❿ Mesón Los Murales
⓫ Tapas-Bar Bluebell
⓬ El Tablao de Manuela (Flamenco)

ANDALUCÍA'S WHITE HILL TOWNS

Hall, below the 11th-century Moorish castle where Ferdinand and Isabel held Reconquista strategy meetings (castle privately owned and closed to the public).

Now belly up to the railing and look down. The people of Arcos boast that only they see the backs of the birds as they fly. Ponder the parador's erosion concerns (it lost part of its lounge in the 1990s when it dropped right off), the orderly orange groves, and the fine views toward the southernmost part of Spain. The city council considered building an underground parking lot to clear up the square, but nixed it because of the land's fragility. You're 330 feet above the Guadalete River. This is the town's suicide departure point for men (women jump from the other side).

• *Looming over the square is the...*

Church of Santa María

After Arcos was retaken from the Moors in the 13th century, this church was built atop a mosque. Notice the church's fine but

chopped-off bell tower. The old one fell in the earthquake of 1755 (famous for destroying Lisbon). The replacement was intended to be the tallest in Andalucía after Sevilla's—but money ran out. It looks like someone lives on an upper floor. Someone does—the church guardian resides there in a room strewn with bell-ringing ropes.

Cost and Hours: €2, Mon-Fri 10:00-13:00 & 16:00-19:00, Sat 10:00-14:00, shorter hours in winter, closed Sun and Jan-Feb.

Visiting the Church: Buy a ticket and step inside, where you can see they've packed a lot of decoration into a small space. Work your way between the pews to examine the beautifully carved choir. Its organ was built in 1789 with that many pipes. At the very front of the church, the nice Renaissance high altar—carved in wood—covers up a Muslim prayer niche that survived from the older mosque. The altar shows God with a globe in his hand (on top), and scenes from the life of Jesus (on the right) and Mary (left).

Continue circling the church and notice the elaborate chapels. Although most of the architecture is Gothic, the chapels are decorated in the Baroque and Rococo styles that were popular when the post-earthquake remodel began. The ornate statues are used in Holy Week processions. Sniff out the "incorruptible body" (miraculously never rotting) of St. Felix—a third-century martyr (directly across from the entry). Felix may be nicknamed "the incorruptible," but take a close look at his knee. He's no longer skin and bones...just bones and the fine silver mesh that once covered his skin. Rome sent his body here in 1764, after recognizing this church as the most important in Arcos. In the back of the church, near a huge fresco of St. Christopher (carrying his staff and Baby Jesus), is a gnarly Easter candle from 1767.

• *Back outside, examine the...*

Church Exterior

Circle clockwise around the church, down four steps, to find the third-century Roman votive altar with a carving of the palm tree of life directly in front of you. Though the Romans didn't build this high in the mountains, they did have a town and temple at the foot of Arcos. This carved stone was discovered in the foundation of the original Moorish mosque, which stood here before the first church was built.

Head down a few more steps and come to the main entrance (west portal) of the church (always closed). This is a good example of Plateresque Gothic—Spain's last and most ornate kind of Gothic.

In the pavement, notice the 15th-century magic circle with 12 red and 12 white stones—the white ones have various "constellations" marked (though they don't resemble any of today's star charts). When a child would come to the church to be baptized, the parents stopped here first for a good Christian exorcism. The exorcist would stand inside the protective circle and cleanse the baby of any evil spirits. While locals no longer do this (and a modern rain drain now marks the center), many Sufi Muslims still come here in a kind of pilgrimage every November. (Down a few more steps, you can catch the public minibus for a circular joyride through Arcos; see "Getting Around Arcos," earlier.)

Go down the next few stairs to the street, and just past the recommended Hostal El Patio peer down a narrow path called Cuesta de las Monjas. The security grille (over the window above) protected cloistered nuns when this building was a convent. Look at the arches that prop up the houses downhill; all over town, arches *(arcos)* support earthquake-damaged structures and give the town its distinctive name.

Continue straight under the **flying buttresses.** Notice the scratches of innumerable car mirrors on each wall (and be glad you're walking). The buttresses were built to shore up the church when it was damaged by an earthquake in 1699. (Thanks to these supports, most of the church survived the bigger earthquake of 1755.)

• *Now make your way...*

From the Church to the Market

Completing your circle around the church (huffing back uphill), turn left under more arches built to repair earthquake damage and walk east down the bright, white Calle Escribanos. From now to the end of this walk, you'll basically follow this lane until you come to the town's second big church (St. Peter's). After a block, you hit Plaza Boticas.

On your right is the last remaining **convent** in Arcos. Notice the no-nunsense, spiky window grilles high above, with tiny peepholes in the latticework for the cloistered nuns to see through. If you're hungry, check out the list and photos of the treats the nuns provide. Then step into the lobby under the fine portico to find their one-way mirror and a spinning cupboard that hides the nuns from view. Push the buzzer, and one of the eight sisters (several are from Kenya and speak English well) will spin out some boxes of excellent, freshly baked cookies—made from pine nuts, peanuts, almonds, and other nuts—for you to consider buying (€7-8, open daily but not reliably 8:30-14:30 & 17:00-19:00; be careful—if you stand big and tall to block out the light, you might see the sister through the glass). If you ask for *magdalenas,* bags of cupcakes will swing around (€3.50). These are traditional goodies made from natural ingredients. Buy some treats to support their church work, and give them to kids as you complete your walk.

The **covered market** *(mercado)* at the other end of the plaza (down from the convent) resides in an unfinished church. At the entry, notice half of a church wall. The church was being built for the Jesuits, but construction stopped in 1767 when King Charles III, tired of the Jesuit appetite for politics, expelled the order from Spain. The market is closed on Sunday and Monday—they rest on Sunday, so there's no produce, fish, or meat ready for Monday. Poke inside. It's tiny but has everything you need. Pop into the *servicio público* (public WC)—no gender bias here.

• *As you exit the market, turn right and continue straight down Calle Botica...*

From the Market to the Church of St. Peter

As you walk, peek discreetly into private patios. These wonderful, cool-tiled courtyards filled with plants, pools, furniture, and happy family activities are typical of Arcos. Except in the mansions, these patios are generally shared by several families. Originally, each courtyard served as a catchment system, funneling rainwater to a drain in the middle, which filled the well. You can still see tiny wells in wall niches with now-decorative pulleys for the bucket.

Also notice the ancient columns on each corner. All over town, these columns—many actually Roman, appropriated from their original ancient settlement at the foot of the hill—were put up to protect buildings from reckless donkey carts and tourists in rental cars.

As you continue straight, notice that the walls are scooped out on either side of the windows. These are a reminder of the days when women stayed inside but wanted the best possible view of any action in the streets. These "window ears" also enabled boys in a more modest age to lean inconspicuously against the wall to chat up eligible young ladies.

Across from the old chapel facade ahead, find the **Association of San Miguel.** Duck right, past a bar, into the oldest courtyards in town—you can still see the graceful Neo-Gothic lines of this noble home from 1850. The bar is a club for retired men—always busy when a bullfight's on TV or during card games. The guys are friendly, and drinks are cheap. You're welcome to flip on the light and explore the old-town photos in the back room.

Just beyond, facing the elegant front door of that noble house, is Arcos' second church, **St. Peter's** (€2, enter through small door left of main entrance; Mon-Fri 10:00-13:00 & 16:00-19:00, Sat 10:00-14:00, shorter hours in winter, closed Sun and Jan-Feb). You know it's St. Peter's because St. Peter, mother of God, is the centerpiece of the facade. Let me explain. It really is the second church, having had  an extended battle with Santa María for papal recognition as the leading church in Arcos. When the pope finally favored Santa María (he declared it a minor basilica in 1993), St. Peter's parishioners changed their prayers. Rather than honoring "María," they wouldn't even say her name. They prayed "St. Peter, mother of God." Like Santa María, it's a Gothic structure, filled with Baroque decor (including a stunning organ covered with cherubs), many Holy Week procession statues, and humble English descriptions. Santa María may have won papal recognition, but St. Peter's has more relic skeletons in glass caskets (flanking both sides of the main altar are St. Fructuoso and St. Víctor, martyrs from the third century A.D.).

In the cool of the evening, the tiny square in front of the church—about the only flat piece of pavement around—serves as the old-town soccer field for neighborhood kids. Until a few years ago, this church also had a resident bellman—notice the cozy balcony halfway up. He was a basket-maker and a colorful character, famous for bringing a donkey into his quarters that grew too big to get back out. Finally, he had no choice but to kill and eat the donkey.

Twenty yards beyond the church, step into the nice **Galería de Arte San Pedro,** featuring artisans in action and their reasonably priced paintings and pottery (Mon-Fri 10:00-21:00, Sat-Sun until 19:00, shorter hours in winter). Walk inside. Find the water drain and the well.

Across the street, signs direct you to a **mirador**—a tiny square 100 yards downhill that affords a commanding view of Arcos. The reservoir you see to the northeast of town is used for water sports in the summertime. Looking south, among the rolling fields you'll see a power plant that local residents protested—to no avail—based on environmental concerns. Wind-driven generators blink along the horizon at night. Relax on a bench and take in this spectacular view.

Return to the Church of St. Peter, circle down and left to return to the main square, wandering the tiny neighborhood lanes. Just below St. Peter's (on Calle Maldonado) is a delightful little Andalusian garden (formal Arabic style, with aromatic plants such as jasmine, rose, and lavender, and water in the center). A bit farther along on Maldonado, peek into the **Belén Artístico,** a little cave-like museum, which highlights a popular Spanish tradition of setting up a Nativity scene during Christmas using miniature figures (free, but donations accepted). The lane called Higinio Capote, below the Church of Santa María, is particularly picturesque with its many geraniums. Peek into patios, kick a few soccer balls, and savor the views.

Nightlife in Arcos

The newer part of Arcos has a modern charm. In the cool of the evening, all generations enjoy life out around Plaza de España (15-minute walk from the old town). Several good tapas bars border the square or are nearby.

The **big park** (Recinto Ferial) below Plaza de España is the late-night fun zone in the summer (June-Aug) when *carpas* (restaurant tents) fill with merrymakers, especially on weekends. The scene includes open-air tapas bars, disco music, and dancing.

In the old town, the bar **El Tablao de Manuela** has flamenco, tapas, and homemade sangria most nights (€5 cover, 21:00-late, Calle Deán Espinosa 10, tel. 671-176-851).

Sleeping in Arcos

Hotels in Arcos consider April, May, August, September, and October to be high season. Note that some hotels double their rates during the motorbike races in nearby Jerez de la Frontera (usually April or May, varies yearly, call TI or ask your hotel) and during Holy Week before Easter.

IN THE OLD TOWN

Drivers should obtain a parking pass (€5) from your hotel to park overnight on the main square. (The pass does not exempt you from daytime rates.) Otherwise, park in the Paseo de Andalucía lot at Plaza de España in the new town and walk or catch a taxi or the shuttle bus up to the old town (see "Arrival in Arcos," earlier).

$$$ Parador de Arcos de la Frontera is royally located, with 24 elegant, recently refurbished and reasonably priced rooms (eight have balconies). If you want to experience a parador, this is a good one (air-con, elevator, Plaza del Cabildo, tel.

956-700-500, www.parador.es, arcos@parador.es).

$$ Hotel El Convento, deep in the old town just beyond the parador, is the best value in town. Run by a hardworking family and their wonderful staff, this cozy hotel offers 13 fine rooms—all with great views, most with balconies. In 1998 I enjoyed a big party with most of Arcos' big shots as they dedicated a fine room with a grand-view balcony to "Rick Steves, Periodista Turístico." Guess where I sleep when in Arcos...(RS%, usually closed Nov-Feb, Maldonado 2, tel. 956-702-333, www.hotelelconvento.es, reservas@hotelelconvento.es).

$$ La Casa Grande is a lovingly appointed *Better Homes and Moroccan Tiles* kind of place that rents eight rooms with big-view windows. As in a lavish yet very authentic old-style inn, you're free to enjoy its fine view terrace and homey library, or have a traditional breakfast (extra) on the atrium-like patio. They also offer massage services (family rooms, air-con, Wi-Fi in public areas only, Maldonado 10, tel. 956-703-930, www.lacasagrande.net, info@lacasagrande.net, Elena).

$ Rincón de las Nieves, with simple Andalusian style, has a cool inner courtyard filled with plants and ceramics surrounded by three rooms. Two rooms have their own outdoor terraces with obstructed views, and all have access to the rooftop terrace. One apartment is also available (air-con, Boticas 10, tel. 956-701-528, mobile 656-886-256, www.rincondelasnieves.com, info@rincondelasnieves.com, Paqui).

¢ Hostal El Patio offers the best cheap beds in the old town. With a tangled floor plan and eight simple rooms, it's on a sometimes-noisy street behind the Church of Santa María (air-con, Calle Callejón de las Monjas 4, tel. 956-702-302, mobile 605-839-995, www.elpatio-arcos.com, reservas@elpatio-arcos.com, staff speak a bit of English). The bar-restaurant with bullfighting posters in the cellar serves affordable breakfast, tapas, and several fixed-priced meals.

¢ Hostal San Marcos, above a neat little bar in the heart of the old town, offers four air-conditioned rooms and a great sun terrace with views of the reservoir (air-con, Marqués de Torresoto 6, best to reserve by phone, tel. 956-105-429, mobile 675-459-106, reservas@elpatio-arcos.com, José speaks some English).

IN THE NEW TOWN

$$ Hotel Los Olivos is a bright, cool, and airy place with 19 rooms, an impressive courtyard, roof garden, generous public spaces, bar, view, friendly folks, and easy parking. The five view rooms can be a bit noisy in the afternoon, but—with double-paned windows—are usually fine at night (RS%, includes buffet breakfast, Paseo de Boliches 30, tel. 956-700-811, www.hotel-losolivos.es, reservas@hotel-losolivos.es, Raquel, Marta, and Miguel Ángel).

¢ **Hostal Málaga** is surprisingly nice and a very good value if for some reason you want to stay on the big road at the Jerez edge of town. Nestled on a quiet lane between truck stops off A-393, it offers 17 clean, attractive rooms and a breezy two-level terrace (air-con, easy parking, Avenida Ponce de León 5, tel. 956-702-010, www.hostalmalaga.com, hostalmalaga@hotmail.com, Josefa and son Alejandro speak a *leetle* English).

Eating in Arcos

VIEW DINING

$$$ The **Parador** (described earlier, under "Sleeping in Arcos") has a restaurant with a cliff-edge setting. Its tapas and *raciones* are reasonably priced but mediocre; still, a drink and a snack on the million-dollar-view terrace at sunset is a nice experience (daily 12:00-16:00 & 20:00-23:00, shorter hours off-season, on main square).

CHEAPER EATING IN THE OLD TOWN

Several decent, rustic bar-restaurants are in the old town, within a block or two of the main square and church. Most serve tapas at the bar and *raciones* at their tables.

$$ Bar La Cárcel ("The Prison") is run by a hardworking family that brags about its exquisite tapas and small open-faced sandwiches. I would, too. The menu is accessible; prices are the same at the bar or at the tables—including at terrace seating across the street—and the place has a winning energy, giving the traveler a fun peek at this community (Tue-Sun 12:00-24:00, closed Mon—except open Mon and closed Sun July-Aug, Calle Deán Espinosa 18, tel. 956-700-410).

$$ Alcaraván tries to be a bit trendier yet *típico*. A funky and fun ambience fills its medieval vault in the castle's former dungeon. This place attracts French and German tourists who give it a cool, cozy vibe (Wed-Sun 12:00-16:00 & 20:00-23:00, closed Mon-Tue, Calle Nueva 1, tel. 956-703-397).

$$ Restaurante Café Babel offers authentic Moroccan dishes in a tasteful spot at the end of the old town. Grilled kebabs are a favorite, along with the *pastela* (slightly sweet puff pastry filled with minced chicken and savory spices). Oscar and Nadia are perfect

ANDALUCÍA'S WHITE HILL TOWNS

hosts whether you come in for a full meal or stop by for a drink at the bar (daily 13:00-16:00 & 20:00-23:00, Calle Corredera 11, tel. 671-138-256).

$$ Bar San Marcos is a tiny, homey bar with five tables and an easy-to-understand menu offering hearty, simple home cooking (kitchen open long hours Mon-Sat, closed Sun, Marqués de Torresoto 6, tel. 956-700-721).

$$ Mesón Los Murales serves tasty, affordable tapas, *raciones,* and fixed-price meals in their rustic bar or at tables in the square outside (Fri-Wed 10:00-24:00, closed Thu, at Plaza Boticas 1, tel. 956-700-607).

$ Tapas-Bar Bluebell, run by outgoing Tracey from the UK, adds international flavor to the traditional bar scene in Arcos. Hang out at the beautiful blue bar or grab a streetside table to enjoy a drink or light tapas, such as a smoked salmon tostada with goat cheese (Wed-Mon 10:00-24:00, closed Tue, shorter hours off-season, Calle Botica 7, tel. 654-639-767).

Arcos Connections

BY BUS
Leaving Arcos by bus can be frustrating (especially if you're going to Ronda)—buses generally leave late, the schedule information boards are often inaccurate, and the ticket window usually isn't open (luckily, you can buy your tickets on the bus). But local buses do give you a glimpse at *España profunda* ("deep Spain"), where everyone seems to know each other, no one's in a hurry, and despite any language barriers, people are quite helpful when approached.

Two bus companies—Los Amarillos and Comes—share the Arcos bus station. If your Spanish is good, you could call the Jerez offices for departure times—otherwise ask your hotelier or the TI for help. To find out about the Arcos-Jerez schedule, make it clear you're coming from Arcos (Los Amarillos tel. 902-210-317, www.losamarillos.es; Comes tel. 956-291-168, www.tgcomes.es). Also try the privately run www.movelia.es for bus schedules and routes.

From Arcos by Bus to: Jerez (hourly, 40 minutes), **Ronda** (2-3/day, 2 hours), **Sevilla** (1-2/day, 2 hours, more departures with transfer in Jerez). Buses run less frequently on weekends. The closest train station to Arcos is Jerez.

ROUTE TIPS FOR DRIVERS
The trip to **Sevilla** takes about 1.5 hours if you pay €7 for the toll road that starts near Jerez. To reach **southern Portugal,** follow the freeway to Sevilla, and skirt the city by turning west on the SE-30 ring road in the direction of Huelva. It's a straight shot from there on A-49/E-1.

For more driving tips for the region, see the end of this chapter.

Ronda

With more than 34,000 people, Ronda is one of the largest white hill towns. It's also one of the most spectacular, thanks to its gorge-straddling setting. Approaching the town from the train or bus station, it seems flat...until you reach the New Bridge and realize that it's clinging to the walls of a canyon.

While day-trippers from the touristy Costa del Sol clog Ronda's streets during the day, locals retake the town in the early evening, making nights peaceful. If you liked Toledo at night, you'll love the local feeling of evenings in Ronda. Since it's served by train and bus, Ronda makes a relaxing break for nondrivers traveling between Granada, Sevilla, and Córdoba. Drivers can use Ronda as a convenient base from which to explore many of the other *pueblos blancos*.

Ronda's main attractions are its gorge-spanning bridges, the oldest bullring in Spain, and an intriguing old town. The cliff-side setting, dramatic today, was practical back in its day. For the Moors, it provided a tough bastion, taken by the Spaniards only in 1485, seven years before Granada fell. Spaniards know Ronda as the cradle of modern bullfighting and the romantic home of 19th-century *bandoleros*. The real joy of Ronda these days lies in exploring its back streets and taking in its beautiful balconies, exuberant flowerpots, and panoramic views. Walking the streets, you feel a strong local pride and a community where everyone seems to know everyone.

Orientation to Ronda

Ronda's breathtaking ravine divides the town's labyrinthine Moorish quarter and its new, noisier, and more sprawling Mercadillo quarter. A massive-yet-graceful 18th-century bridge connects these two neighborhoods. Most things of touristic importance (TI, post office, hotels, bullring) are clustered within a few blocks of the bridge. The paseo (early evening stroll) happens in the new town, on Ronda's major pedestrian and shopping street, Carrera Espinel.

ANDALUCÍA'S WHITE HILL TOWNS

TOURIST INFORMATION

Ronda's hardworking TI, across the square from the bullring, covers not only the town but all of Andalucía. It gives out good, free maps of the town, Andalusia's roads, Granada, Sevilla, and the Route of the White Towns. It also sells the Bono Turístico city pass, has listings of the latest museum hours, and organizes walking tours—see details under "Tours in Ronda," later (TI open Mon-Fri 10:00-19:00, Sat until 17:00, Sun until 14:30, shorter hours Oct-late March, Paseo Blas Infante, tel. 952-187-119, www.turismoderonda.es).

Sightseeing Pass: An avid sightseer should consider the €8 **Bono Turístico** city pass, which gets you into four sights—the Arab Baths, Joaquín Peinado Museum, Mondragón Palace, and the New Bridge Interpretive Center. It's valid for one week and sold at the TI and all participating sights except the Joaquín Peinado Museum.

ARRIVAL IN RONDA

By Train: The small station has ticket windows, a train information desk, and a café, but no baggage lockers (there is storage at the nearby bus station; for details, see "Helpful Hints" below).

From the station, it's a 15-minute **walk** to the center: Turn right out of the station on Avenida de Andalucía, and walk to the large roundabout (you'll see the bus station on your right). Continue straight down the street (now called San José) until you reach its end at Calle Jerez. Turn left and walk downhill past a church and the Alameda del Tajo park. Keep going down this street, passing the bullring, to get to the TI and the famous bridge. A **taxi** to the center costs about €7.

By Bus: To get to the center from the bus station, leave the station walking to the right of the roundabout, then follow the directions for train travelers described above. Baggage storage is available (see "Helpful Hints" below).

By Car: Street parking away from the center is often free. The handiest place for paid parking is the underground lot at Plaza del Socorro (one block from bullring).

HELPFUL HINTS

Baggage Storage: The WC attendant at the bus station can store your luggage in a locked room (daily 8:00-20:00).

Laundry: HigienSec has one machine for self-service. Full-service options for several extra euros can include delivery to your hotel (same-day service if you drop off early enough; Mon-Fri 10:00-14:00 & 17:00-20:30, Sat 10:00-14:00, closed Sun, two blocks east of the bullring at Calle Molino 6, tel. 952-875-249).

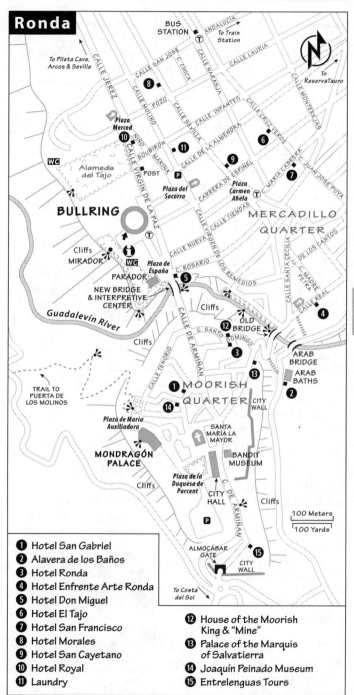

Ronda

BUS STATION

To Pileta Cave, Arcos & Sevilla

CALLE JEREZ

ANDALUCÍA
To Train Station

CALLE LAURIA

To ReservaTauro

CALLE SAN JOSÉ
C. CHICA
CALLE NARANJA

CALLE MONTEREJAS

8

CALLE MOLINO
POZO

CALLE SEVILLA

CALLE INFANTES

CALLE CRUZ VERDE

Plaza Merced

10

NIÑO SOUBIRÓN

CALLE VIRGEN DE LA PAZ

CALLE MARINA

CALLE DE LA ALMENDRA

11

9

6

MARÍA CABRERA

C. JUAN JOSÉ PUYA

7

WC

Alameda del Tajo

POST

Plaza del Socorro

P

CARRERA DE ESPINEL

Plaza Carmen Abela

BULLRING

Cliffs
MIRADOR

i

WC

PARADOR

Plaza de España

CALLE NUEVA
CALLE TIENDAS

CALLE VIRGEN DE LOS REMEDIOS

MERCADILLO QUARTER

CALLE SANTA CECILIA

C. DE LOS CANTOS

C. MADRE PETRA

5

C. ROSARIO

CALLE REAL

NEW BRIDGE & INTERPRETIVE CENTER

Guadalevín River

Cliffs

Cliffs

C. SANTO DOMINGO

OLD BRIDGE

12

ARAB BRIDGE

4

3

CALLE DE ARMIÑÁN

ARAB BATHS

13

2

TRAIL TO PUERTA DE LOS MOLINOS

CALLE TENORIO

1 MOORISH
14 QUARTER

CITY WALL

Plaza de María Auxiliadora

SANTA MARÍA LA MAYOR

MONDRAGÓN PALACE

BANDIT MUSEUM

Cliffs

Plaza de la Duquesa de Parcent

CITY HALL

C. DE ARMIÑÁN

Cliffs

P

100 Meters
100 Yards

ALMOCÁBAR GATE

15

CITY WALL

To Costa del Sol

1 Hotel San Gabriel
2 Alavera de los Baños
3 Hotel Ronda
4 Hotel Enfrente Arte Ronda
5 Hotel Don Miguel
6 Hotel El Tajo
7 Hotel San Francisco
8 Hotel Morales
9 Hotel San Cayetano
10 Hotel Royal
11 Laundry

12 House of the Moorish King & "Mine"
13 Palace of the Marquis of Salvatierra
14 Joaquín Peinado Museum
15 Entrelenguas Tours

ANDALUCÍA'S WHITE HILL TOWNS

Souvenirs: Worth a browse is **Taller de Grabados Somera,** a printmaking studio near the New Bridge. Their inexpensive, charming prints of Ronda's iconic scenery and famous bulls are hand-pulled right in their shop (Mon-Fri 10:00-19:00, Sat-Sun 10:30-18:00, Calle Rosario 4, just across from the parador, www.grabadossomera.com).

Tours in Ronda

Walking Tours
Many local guides work in conjunction with the TI to offer two-hour guided walks of the city (call to confirm route and price, can range from €20-45 for afternoon visits, often a 4-person minimum). Reserve and pay at the TI. The language used on the tour depends on the guide.

    Entrelenguas is a cultural center in Ronda that offers much more than Spanish-language lessons. Alex, Mar, and Javier guide visitors around Ronda, focusing on monuments (€35) or cultural immersion and showcasing local businesses (€75). They can do wine tastings on request (€35) or even put together a cooking class for a small group (Calle Espíritu Santo 9, tel. 951-083-862, www.entrelenguas.es).

Local Guide
Energetic and knowledgeable **Antonio Jesús Naranjo** will take you on a two-hour walking tour of the city's sights. He showed Michelle Obama around when she was in town (€120, reserve early, mobile 639-073-763, www.guiaoficialderonda.com, guiajesus@yahoo.es). The TI has a list of other local guides.

Sights in Ronda

IN THE NEW TOWN
▲▲▲Bullring (Real Maestranza de Caballería de Ronda)
Ronda is the birthplace of modern bullfighting, and this was the first great Spanish bullring. Philip II initiated bullfighting as war training for knights in the 16th century. Back then, there were two kinds of bullfighting: the type with noble knights on horseback, and the coarser, man-versus-beast entertainment for the commoners (with no rules...much like when WWF wrestlers bring out the folding chairs). Ronda practically worships Francisco Romero, who

melded the noble and chaotic kinds of bullfighting with rules to establish modern bullfighting right here in the early 1700s. He introduced the scarlet cape, held unfurled with a stick. His son Juan further developed the ritual (local aficionados would never call it a "sport"—you'll read newspaper coverage of fights not on the sports pages but in the culture section), and his grandson Pedro was one of the first great matadors (killing nearly 6,000 bulls in his career).

Ronda's bullring and museum are Spain's most interesting (even better than Sevilla's). To tour the ring, stables, chapel, and museum, buy a ticket at the back of the bullring.

Cost and Hours: €7, daily April-Sept 10:00-20:00, March and Oct until 19:00, Nov-Feb until 18:00, tel. 952-874-132, www.rmcr.org. The excellent €1.50 audioguide describes everything and is essential to fully enjoy your visit.

Bullfights: Bullfights are scheduled only for the first weekend of September during the *feria* (fair) and occur very rarely in the spring. Whereas every other *feria* in Andalucía celebrates a patron saint, the Ronda fair glorifies legendary bullfighter Pedro Romero. For September bullfights, tickets go on sale the preceding July. (As these sell out immediately, Sevilla and Madrid are more practical places for a tourist to see a bullfight.)

 ❍ **Self-Guided Tour:** I'd visit in this order. Disobey *exit* signs and enter directly to the right to see the bullfighters' **chapel.** Before going into the ring, every matador would stop here to pray to Mary for safety—and hope to see her again.

• *Just beyond the chapel are the doors to the museum exhibits: horse gear and weapons on the left, and the story of bullfighting on the right, all with English translations.*

The **horse gear and guns exhibit** makes the connection with bullfighting and the equestrian upper class. Examine the fine

stable gear along the narrow hallway before diving into the gun display. As throughout Europe, "chivalry" began as a code among the sophisticated, horse-riding gentry. (In Spanish, the word for "gentleman" is the same as the word for "horseman"—*caballero.*) And, of course, nobles are into hunting and dueling, hence the fancy guns. Don't miss the well-described dueling section in a room at the end, with gun cases for two, as charming as a picnic basket with matching wine glasses.

Return to the hallway with the chapel to see Spain's best **bullfighting exhibit.** It's a shrine to bullfighting and the historic Romero family. First it traces the long history of bullfighting, going all the way back to the ancient Minoans on Crete. Historically, there were only two arenas built solely for bullfighting: in Ronda and Sevilla. Elsewhere, bullfights were held in town squares—you'll see a painting of Madrid's Plaza Mayor filled with spectators for a bullfight. (For this reason, to this day, even a purpose-built bullring is generally called *plaza de toros*—"square of bulls.") You'll also see stuffed bull heads, photos, "suits of light" worn by bullfighters, and capes (bulls are actually colorblind, but the traditional red cape was designed to disguise all the blood). One section explains some of the big "dynasties" of fighters. At the end of the hall are historical posters from Ronda's bullfights (all originals except the Picasso). Running along the left wall are various examples of artwork glorifying bullfighting, including original Goya engravings.

• *Exit at the far end of the bullfighting exhibit and take advantage of the opportunity to walk in the actual arena.*

Here's your chance to play *toro*, surrounded by 5,000 empty seats. The two-tiered **arena** was built in 1785—on the 300th anniversary of the defeat of the Moors in Ronda. Notice the 136 classy Tuscan columns, creating a kind of 18th-century Italian theater. Lovers of the "art" of bullfighting will explain that the event is much more than the actual killing of the bull. It celebrates noble heritage and Andalusian horse culture. When you leave the museum and  walk out on the sand, look left to see the ornamental columns and painted doorway where the dignitaries sit (over the gate where the bull enters). On the right is the place for the band (marked *música*), which, in the case of a small town like Ronda, is most likely a high school band.

• *Just beyond the arena are more parts of the complex. Find the open gate beneath the dignitaries' seats.*

Walk through the bulls' entry into the bullpen and the **stables**. There are six bulls per fight (plus two backups)—and three matadors. The bulls are penned up here beforehand, and ropes and pulleys safely open the right door at the right time. Climb the skinny staircase and find the indoor arena *(picadero)* and see Spanish thoroughbred horses training from the **Equestrian School** of the Real Maestranza (often during weekdays). Explore the spectators' seating before exiting through the gift shop.

Alameda del Tajo Park

One block away from the bullring, the town's main park is a great breezy place for a picnic lunch, people-watching, a snooze in the shade, or practicing your Spanish with seniors from the nearby old-folks' home. Don't miss its view balcony overlooking the scenic Serranía de Ronda mountains (daily 8:00-24:00, closes at 22:00 off-season).

▲▲▲The Gorge and New Bridge (Puente Nuevo)

The ravine, called El Tajo—360 feet deep and 200 feet wide—divides Ronda into the whitewashed old city (Moorish Quarter) and

the new town (El Mercadillo) that was built after the Christian reconquest in 1485. The New Bridge mightily spans the gorge. A different bridge was built here in 1735, but it fell after six years. This one was built from 1751 to 1793. Look down...carefully.

You can see the foundations of the original bridge and a super view of the New Bridge from a walkway that was recently named the Paseo de Kazunori Yamauchi (after the Japanese race-car driver and video-game designer who included a hyperrealistic version of Ronda in his latest release). It skirts the parador—the town's former town hall turned hotel—which overlooks the gorge and bridge from the new-town side. For the price of a drink, you can enjoy the view from inside the parador's lobby bar or on its terrace.

From the new-town side of the bridge, on the right (just outside the parador), you'll see the entrance to the **New Bridge Interpretive Center,** where you can pay to climb down and enter the structure of the bridge itself (€2; Mon-Fri 10:00-19:00, Sat-Sun until 15:00, closes earlier off-season; mobile 649-965-338). Inside the empty-feeling hall are modest audiovisual displays about the bridge's construction and the famous visitors to Ronda—worth a quick look only if you have the Bono Turístico pass. The views of the bridge and gorge from the outside are far more thrilling than anything you'll find within.

IN THE OLD TOWN

▲Church of Santa María la Mayor (Iglesia de Santa María)

This 15th-century church with a fine Mudejar bell tower shares a park-like square with orange trees and City Hall. It was built on and around the remains of Moorish Ronda's main mosque (which was itself built on the site of a temple to Julius Caesar). With a pleasantly eclectic interior that features some art with unusually

ANDALUCÍA'S WHITE HILL TOWNS

modern flair, and a good audioguide to explain it all, it's worth a visit.

Cost and Hours: €4.50, daily April-Sept 10:00-20:00, closed Sun 13:00-14:00 for Mass, may close earlier off-season, includes audioguide, Plaza Duquesa de Parcent in the old town.

Visiting the Church: In the room where you purchase your ticket, look for the only surviving mosque **prayer niche** (that's a mirror; look back at the actual mihrab, which faces not Mecca, but Gibraltar—where you'd travel to get to Mecca). Partially destroyed by an earthquake, the reconstruction of the church resulted in the Moorish/Gothic/Renaissance/Baroque fusion (or confusion) you see today.

After entering the church, turn around to see the magnificent Baroque **Altar del Sagrario** with a statue of the Immaculate Conception in the center. The smaller altar directly to the right is a good example of Churrigueresque architecture, a kind of Spanish Rococo in which the decoration consumes the architecture—notice that you can hardly make out the souped-up columns. Its fancy decor provides a frame for an artistic highlight of the town, the "Virgin of the Ultimate Sorrow." The big fresco of St. Christopher with Baby Jesus on his shoulders (on the left, above the door where you entered) shows the patron saint both of Ronda and of travelers.

In the center of the church is an elaborately carved **choir** with a series of modern reliefs depicting scenes from the life of the Virgin Mary. Similar to the Via Crucis (Way of the Cross), this is the Via Lucis (Way of the Light), with 14 stations focusing on the Resurrection and its aftermath (such as #13—the Immaculate Conception, and #14—Mary's assumption into heaven) that serve as a worship aid to devout Catholics. The centerpiece is Mary as the

light of the world (with the moon, stars, and sun around her).

Head to the left around the choir, noticing the bright **paintings** along the wall by French artist Raymonde Pagegie, who gave sacred scenes a fresh twist—like the Last Supper attended by female servants, or the scene of Judgment Day, when the four horsemen of the apocalypse pause to adore the Lamb of God.

The **treasury** (at the far-right corner, with your back to the choir) displays vestments that look curiously like matadors' brocaded outfits—appropriate for this bullfight-crazy town. Before exiting, look for a spiral staircase with 73 steps leading to a U-shaped **terrace** around the church's rooftop. Enjoy more spectacular views of the city, even if you have to duck down to go from side to side. If you aren't afraid of heights, one interior balcony looks down on the elaborate main altar.

Mondragón Palace (Palacio de Mondragón)

This beautiful, originally Moorish building was erected in the 14th century and is the legendary (but not actual) residence of Moorish kings. The building was restored in the 16th century (notice the late Gothic tiled courtyard), and its facade dates only from the 18th century. The rest of the building houses Ronda's Municipal Museum, focusing on prehistory and geology. Wander through its many kid-friendly rooms to find the prehistory section, with exhibits on Neolithic toolmaking and early metallurgy (described in English). Local Roman history is also briefly described. If you plan to visit the Pileta Cave, find the panels that describe the cave's formation and shape. Even if you have no interest in your ancestors or speleology, the building's architecture is impressive; linger in the two small gardens with wonderful panoramic views, especially the shaded one.

Cost and Hours: €3.50; Mon-Fri 10:00-19:00, Sat-Sun until 15:00, closes earlier off-season; on Plaza Mondragón in old town, tel. 952-870-818.

Nearby: Leaving the palace, wander left a few short blocks to the nearby Plaza de María Auxiliadora for more views and a look at the two rare *pinsapos* (resembling extra-large Christmas trees) in the middle of the park; this part of Andalucía is the only region in Europe where these ancient trees still grow. For an intense workout but a picture-perfect view, find the tiled *Puerta de los Molinos* sign and head down, down, down. (Just remember you have to walk back up, up, up.) Not for the faint of heart or in the heat of the afternoon sun, this pathway leads down to the viewpoint where windmills once stood. Photographers go crazy reproducing the most famous postcard view of Ronda—the entirety of the New Bridge. Wait until just before sunset for the best light and cooler temperatures.

Bandit Museum (Museo del Bandolero)

This tiny museum, while not as intriguing as it sounds, has an interesting assembly of *bandolero* photos, guns, clothing, knickknacks, and old documents and newspaper clippings. The Jesse Jameses and Billy el Niño of Andalucía called this remote area home. One brand of romantic bandits fought Napoleon's army—often more effectively than the regular Spanish troops. The exhibits profile specific *bandoleros* and display books (from comics to pulp fiction) that helped romanticize these heroes of Spain's "Old West." The museum feels a bit like a tourist trap—with every available space packed full of memorabilia, and a well-stocked gift shop—but brief and helpful English descriptions make this a fun stop. Next door is a free 22-minute movie about *bandoleros* (only in Spanish).

Cost and Hours: €3.75, daily May-Sept 11:00-20:30, Oct-April until 19:00, across main street below Church of Santa María la Mayor at Calle Armiñan 65, tel. 952-877-785, www.museobandolero.com.

▲Joaquín Peinado Museum (Museo Joaquín Peinado)

Housed in an old palace, this fresh museum features an overview of the life's work of Joaquín Peinado (1898-1975), a Ronda na-

tive and pal of Picasso. Because Franco killed creativity in Spain for much of the last century, nearly all of Peinado's creative work was done in Paris. His style evolved through the big "isms" of the 20th century, ranging from Expressionism to Cubism, and even to eroticism. Peinado's works follow the major trends of his time—understandable, as he was friends with one of the art world's biggest talents. The nine-minute movie that kicks off the display is only in Spanish, though there are good English explanations throughout the museum. Find a famous Cubist version of Don Quixote upstairs and a few Picasso pieces downstairs. You'll have an interesting modern-art experience here, without the crowds of Madrid's museums. It's fun to be exposed to a lesser-known but very talented artist in his hometown.

Cost and Hours: €4, Mon-Fri 10:00-17:00, Sat until 15:00, closed Sun, Plaza del Gigante, tel. 952-871-585, www.museojoaquinpeinado.com.

Walk Through Old Town to Bottom of Gorge

From the New Bridge you can descend down Cuesta de Santo Domingo (cross the bridge from the new town into the old, and take the first left just beyond the former Dominican convent, once the headquarters of the Inquisition in Ronda) into a world of white-washed houses, tiny grilled balconies, and winding lanes—the old town. (Be ready for lots of ups and downs—this is not a flat walk.)

A couple of blocks steeply downhill (on the left), you'll see the **House of the Moorish King** (Casa del Rey Moro). It was never the home of any king; it was given its fictitious name by the grandson of President McKinley, who once lived here. Although the house is closed and its once-fine belle époque garden is overgrown, it does offer visitors entry to the **"Mine,"** an exhausting series of 280 slick, dark, and narrow stairs (like climbing down and then up a 20-story building) leading to the floor of the gorge. The Moors cut this zig-zag staircase into the wall of the gorge in the 14th century to access water when under siege, then used Spanish slaves to haul water up to the thirsty town (€5, daily 10:00-20:00).

Fifty yards downhill from the garden is the **Palace of the Marquis of Salvatierra** (Palacio del Marqués de Salvatierra, closed to public). As part of the "distribution" of spoils following the Reconquista here in 1485, the Spanish king gave this grand house to the Salvatierra family (who live here to this day). The facade is rich in colonial symbolism from Spanish America—note the pre-Columbian-looking characters (four Peruvian Indians) flanking the balcony above the door and below the family coat of arms.

Just below the palace, stop to enjoy the view terrace. Look below. There are two old bridges, with the Arab Baths just to the right.

Twenty steps farther down, you'll pass through the Philip V gate, for centuries the main gate to the fortified city of Ronda.

Continuing downhill, you come to the **Old Bridge** (Puente Viejo), rebuilt in 1616 upon the ruins of an Arabic bridge. Enjoy the views from the bridge (but don't cross it yet), then continue down the old stairs past a small, Moorish-inspired electric substation. Swing around the little chapel at the bottom of the staircase to look back up to the highly fortified Moorish city walls. A few steps ahead is the oldest bridge in Ronda, the Arab Bridge (also called the San Miguel Bridge). Sometimes given the misnomer of Puente Romano (Roman Bridge), it was more likely built long after the Romans left. For centuries, this was the main gate to the fortified city. In Moorish times, you'd purify both your body and your soul here before entering the city, so just outside the gate was a little mosque (now the chapel) and the Arab Baths.

The **Arab Baths** (Baños Árabes), worth ▲, are evocative ruins that warrant a quick look. They were located half underground to maintain the temperature and served by a horse-powered water tower. You can still see the top of the shaft (30 yards beyond the bath rooftops, near a cypress tree, connected to the baths by an aqueduct). Water was hoisted from the river below to the aqueduct by ceramic containers that were attached to a belt powered by a horse walking in circles. Inside, two of the original eight columns scavenged from the Roman ruins still support brick vaulting. A delightful 10-minute video brings the entire complex to life—Spanish and English versions run alternately (€3.50, free Tue 15:00-19:00; open Mon-Fri 10:00-19:00, Sat-Sun until 15:00; shorter hours off-season, may change hours unpredictably—confirm at TI before visiting).

From here, hike back to the new town along the other side of the gorge: Climb back up to the Old Bridge, cross it, and take the brick stairs immediately on the left, which lead scenically along the gorge through the Jardines de Cuenca park. Leave the park going left on Calle Virgen de los Remedios to the recommended Bar El Lechuguita. Stop for a much-deserved break here; continue down Calle Rosario to return to the New Bridge.

Sights near Ronda

Pileta Cave (Cueva de la Pileta)

The Pileta Cave, set in a dramatic, rocky limestone ridge at the eastern edge of Sierra de Grazalema Natural Park, offers Spain's most intimate look at Neolithic and Paleolithic paintings that are up to 25,000 years old. Farmer José Bullón and his family live down the hill from the cave—which was discovered by Bullón's grandfather in 1905. Señor Bullón and his son lead up to 25 people at a time through it. Because the number of cave visitors is strictly limited, Pileta's rare paintings are among the best-preserved in the world.

Cost and Hours: €8, one-hour tours go between 10:30-13:00 and 16:30-18:00 when enough people gather (Nov-mid-April until 17:00), closing times indicate last tour, arrive at least 15 minutes before your reserved time, €10 guidebook, mobile 687-133-338, www.cuevadelapileta.org.

Getting There: Pileta Cave is 14 miles from Ronda, past the town of Benaoján, at the end of an access road. It's particularly handy if you're driving between Ronda and Grazalema.

From Ronda, you can get to the cave by taxi—it's about a half-hour drive on twisty roads—and have the driver wait (€70 round-trip). If you're driving, it's easy: Leave Ronda through the new part of town, and take A-374 towards Sevilla. After a few miles and a really large curve, exit left toward Benaoján on MA-7401. Go through Benaoján (MA-7401 changes names to MA-8400), then take a sharp left onto MA-8401 and follow the numerous signs (reading *Cueva de la Pileta*) to the cave. Leave nothing of value in your car.

Visiting the Cave: Call the night before to see if there's a tour and space available at the time you want. Note that if you simply show up for the 13:00 tour, you'll risk not getting a spot—and it'll be over three hours before the next one starts. Arrive early, and be flexible. Bring a sweater and sturdy, grippy shoes. You need a good sense of balance to take the tour. The 10-minute hike, from the parking lot up a trail with stone steps to the cave entrance, is moderately steep. Inside the cave, there are no handrails, and it can be difficult to keep your footing on the slippery, uneven floor while being led single-file, with only a lantern light illuminating the way.

Señor Bullón is a master at hurdling the language barrier. As you walk the cool half-mile, he'll spend an hour pointing out lots of black, ochre, and red drawings, which are five times as old as the Egyptian pyramids. Mostly it's just lines or patterns, but there are also horses, goats, cattle, and a rare giant fish, made from a mixture of clay and fat by finger-painting prehistoric *hombres*. The 200-foot main cavern is impressive, as are some weirdly recognizable natural formations such as the Michelin man and a Christmas tree.

Eating near the Cave: Nearby Montejaque has several good restaurants clustered around the central square.

ReservaTauro

As the birthplace of modern bullfighting, Ronda attracts plenty of *aficionados* and even bullfighters themselves. Rafael Tejada worked as an engineer for many years but eventually switched gears to train as a bullfighter. In 2011, he bought land in the nearby *serranía* to raise horses, cows, and stud bulls, and now welcomes visitors to experience his working farm. An hour-long visit allows you to get up close and personal with bulls and horses, as well as try out some matador skills in a practice ring (no bulls, no worries...just the capes). The two-hour option lets you also help the herdsman in one of his daily tasks, such as feeding the free-range bulls, and concludes with local wine and tapas.

Cost and Hours: €25/1 hour, €40/2 hours; 10:00-19:00, until 18:00 off-season; reservations recommended, tel. 951-166-008, www.reservatauro.com.

Getting There: Drivers should leave Ronda through the new part of town, and take A-367 (Carretera Ronda-Campillos) to-wards Campillos. After about 5.5 miles, turn right into a stone gate marked by a small black-and-white, arrow-shaped sign labeled *RESERVATAURO*. If you're visiting in spring or autumn without a car, they may be able to pick you up from the Ronda TI and drop you back off. Call to confirm availability (€24, pick-up at 16:00, request at info@reservatauro.com).

Sleeping in and near Ronda

Ronda has plenty of reasonably priced, decent-value accommodations. It's crowded only during Holy Week (the week leading up to Easter) and the first week of September (for bullfighting season). Most of my recommendations are in the new town, a short stroll from the New Bridge and about a 10-minute walk from the train station. In the cheaper places, ask for a room with a *ventana* (window) to avoid the few interior rooms. Breakfast is usually not included.

IN THE OLD TOWN

Clearly the best options in town, these hotels are worth reserving early. The first two are right in the heart of the old town, while the Alavera de los Baños is a steep 15- to 20-minute hike below, but still easily walkable to all the sights (if you're in good shape) and in a bucolic setting.

$$ Hotel San Gabriel has 22 pleasant rooms, a kind staff, public rooms filled with art and books, a cozy wine cellar, and a fine garden terrace. It's a large 1736 townhouse, once the family's home, that's been converted to a characteristic hotel, marinated in history. If you're a cinephile, kick back in the charming TV room—with seats from Ronda's old theater and a collection of DVD classics—then head to the breakfast room to check out photos of big movie stars (and, ahem, bespectacled travel writers) who have stayed here (air-con, incognito elevator, double-park in front and they'll direct you to a pay parking spot, follow signs on the main street of old town to Calle Marqués de Moctezuma 19, tel. 952-190-392, www.hotelsangabriel.com, info@hotelsangabriel.com, family-run by José Manuel and Ana).

$$ Alavera de los Baños, a delightful oasis located next to ancient Moorish baths at the bottom of the hill, has 11 small rooms, two spacious suites, and big inviting public places, with appropriately Moorish decor. This hotel offers a swimming pool, a peaceful Arabic garden, and a selection of sandwiches for lunch. The artistic ambience urges, "Relax!" You're literally in the countryside, with sheep and horses outside near the garden (includes breakfast, some rooms have balconies, free and easy parking, closed Jan, steeply below the heart of town at Calle Molino de Alarcón, tel. 952-879-143, www.alaveradelosbanos.com, hotel@alaveradelosbanos.com, well run by personable Christian and Inma).

$ Hotel Ronda provides an interesting mix of minimalist and traditional Spanish decor in this refurbished mansion, which is both quiet and homey. Although its five rooms are without views, the small, lovely rooftop deck overlooks the town (air-con, ask for parking directions when you book, Ruedo Doña Elvira 12, tel. 952-872-232, www.hotelronda.net, reservas@hotelronda.net, some English spoken).

IN THE NEW TOWN

More convenient than charming (except the Hotel Enfrente Arte Ronda—in a class all its own), these hotels put you in the thriving new town.

$$ Hotel Enfrente Arte Ronda, on the edge of things a steep 10- to 15-minute walk below the heart of the new town, is relaxed and funky. The 12 rooms are spacious and exotically decorated, but dimly lit. It features a sprawling maze of public spaces with creative decor, a peaceful bamboo garden, a game and reading room, small swimming pool, sauna, and terraces with sweeping countryside views. Guests can help themselves to free drinks from the self-service bar or have their feet nibbled for free by "Dr. Fish." This one-of-a-kind place is in all the guidebooks, so reserve early—Madonna even stayed here (includes buffet breakfast with home-baked bread, air-con, elevator, Calle Real 40, tel. 952-879-088, www.enfrentearte.com, reservations@enfrentearte.com).

$$ Hotel Don Miguel, facing the gorge next to the bridge, can seem like staying in a cave, but it couldn't be more central. Of its 30 sparse but comfortable rooms, 20 have gorgeous views at no extra cost. Street rooms come with a little noise (buffet breakfast, air-con, elevator, pay parking a block away, Plaza de España 4, tel. 952-877-722, www.hoteldonmiguelronda.com, reservas@dmiguel.com).

$ Hotel El Tajo has 54 modern and quiet rooms with updated bathrooms. Although lacking in charm, the hotel is popular with Spanish tour groups because of its central location (air-con, elevator, pay parking, Calle Cruz Verde 7, a half-block off the pedestrian street, tel. 952-874-040, www.hoteleltajo.com, reservas@hoteleltajo.com).

$ Hotel San Francisco offers 27 small, nicely decorated rooms a block off the main pedestrian street in the town center (family rooms available, air-con, elevator, pay parking, María Cabrera 20, tel. 952-873-299, www.hotelsanfrancisco-ronda.com, recepcion@hotelsanfrancisco-ronda.com).

$ Hotel Morales has 18 simple but prim-and-proper rooms, and friendly Lola helps you feel right at home. Interior rooms can be a bit dark, so request to be street-side. There's little traffic at night (air-con, elevator, pay parking nearby, Sevilla 51, tel. 952-871-538, www.hotelmorales.es, reservas@hotelmorales.es).

$ Hotel San Cayetano puts you in the heart of the evening paseo. With 22 basic but clean and comfy rooms, it provides easy access to recommended restaurants on a pedestrian offshoot of the main drag (buffet breakfast, air-con, elevator, pay parking nearby, Sevilla 16, tel. 952-161-212, www.hotelsancayetano.com, reservas@hotelsancayetano.com).

¢ **Hotel Royal** has a dark reception hall but friendly staff and 29 clean, spacious, simple rooms—many on the main street that runs between the bullring and bridge. Thick glass keeps out most of the noise, while the tree-lined Alameda del Tajo park across the street is a treat (air-con, pay parking, Calle Virgen de la Paz 42, tel. 952-871-141, www.ronda.net/usuar/hotelroyal, hroyal@ronda. net).

IN THE COUNTRYSIDE NEAR PILETA CAVE

A good base for visiting Ronda and the Pileta Cave (as well as Grazalema) is **$$ Cortijo las Piletas.** Nestled at the edge of Sierra de Grazalema Natural Park (just a 15-minute drive from Ronda, with easy access from the main highway), this spacious family-run country estate has eight rooms and plenty of opportunities for exploring the surrounding area (includes breakfast, dinner offered some days—book in advance, mobile 605-080-295, www.cortijolaspiletas.com, info@cortijolaspiletas.com, Pablo and Elisenda). Another countryside option is **$ Finca La Guzmana,** run by Peter, an expat Brit. Six beautifully appointed pastel rooms surround an open patio at this renovated estate house (includes breakfast, mobile 600-006-305, www.laguzmana.com, info@ laguzmana.com). Both hotels offer bird-watching, swimming, and hiking.

Eating in Ronda

Plaza del Socorro, a block in front of the bullring, is an energetic scene, bustling with tourists and local families enjoying the square and its restaurants. The pedestrian-only **Calle Nueva** is lined with hardworking eateries. To enjoy a drink or a light meal with the best view in town, consider the terraces of Hotel Don Miguel just under the bridge. For coffee and pastries, locals like the elegant little **$ Confitería Daver** (café open daily 8:00-20:30, three locations—Calle Virgen de los Remedios 6, Calle Padre Mariano Soubiron 8, and Calle Espinel 58). Picnic shoppers find the **Alameda Market** (Mon-Sat 8:30-21:00, Sun 9:00-15:00, Calle Virgen de La Paz 23) conveniently located next to Alameda del Tajo park, which has benches and a WC. The **Día** supermarket, opposite Hotel El Tajo, is also very central (Mon-Sat 9:15-21:15, closed Sun, Calle Cruz Verde 18).

TAPAS IN THE CITY CENTER

Ronda has a fine tapas scene. You won't get a free tapa with your drink as in some other Spanish towns, but these bars have accessible tapas lists, and they serve bigger plates. Each of the following

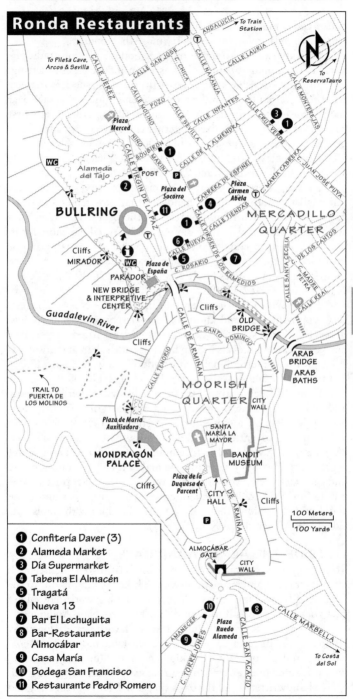

Ronda Restaurants

To Train Station

ANDALUCÍA

To Pileta Cave, Arcos & Sevilla

CALLE JEREZ

CALLE SAN JOSÉ

C. CHICA

CALLE NARANJA

CALLE LAURIA

To ReservaTauro

CALLE MONTEREJAS

Plaza Merced

CALLE MOLINO POZO

NIÑO SOUBIRON

CALLE SEVILLA

CALLE INFANTES

CALLE CRUZ VERDE

3

1

WC

Alameda del Tajo

CALLE VIRGEN DE LA PAZ

POST

CALLE MARINA

CALLE DE LA ALMENDRA

1

P

Plaza del Socorro

CARRERA DE ESPINEL

Plaza Carmen Abela

C. MARÍA CABRERA

C. JUAN JOSÉ PUYA

BULLRING

2

11

4

T

MERCADILLO QUARTER

DE LOS CANTOS

CALLE SANTA CECILIA

Cliffs

MIRADOR

WC

Plaza de España

1

CALLE NUEVA

CALLE VIRGEN DE LOS REMEDIOS

CALLE TIENDAS

6

5

7

C. MADRE

C. PETRA

PARADOR

C. ROSARIO

CALLE REAL

NEW BRIDGE & INTERPRETIVE CENTER

Guadalevín River

Cliffs

CALLE DE ARMIÑÁN

C. SANTO DOMINGO

Cliffs

OLD BRIDGE

ARAB BRIDGE

ARAB BATHS

TRAIL TO PUERTA DE LOS MOLINOS

MOORISH QUARTER

CITY WALL

Plaza de María Auxiliadora

SANTA MARÍA LA MAYOR

MONDRAGÓN PALACE

BANDIT MUSEUM

Cliffs

Plaza de la Duquesa de Parcent

CITY HALL

C. DE ARMIÑÁN

Cliffs

100 Meters

100 Yards

P

ALMOCÁBAR GATE

CITY WALL

10

8

CALLE MARBELLA

C. AMANECER

Plaza Ruedo Alameda

CALLE SAN ACACIO

9

C. TORREJONES

To Costa del Sol

1 Confitería Daver (3)
2 Alameda Market
3 Día Supermarket
4 Taberna El Almacén
5 Tragatá
6 Nueva 13
7 Bar El Lechuguita
8 Bar-Restaurante Almocábar
9 Casa María
10 Bodega San Francisco
11 Restaurante Pedro Romero

places could make a fine solo destination for a meal, but they're close enough that you can easily try more than one.

$$ Taberna El Almacén offers a modern take on traditional tapas from many Spanish regions in an industrial chic setting. Friendly, approachable staff can explain the day's specials that are *fuera de carta* (not listed on the menu). Even veggie haters rave over their *pisto*—a type of ratatouille where all ingredients are first cooked separately, then mixed together and served with a fried egg on the side. This is a good spot to try local wines as well (Tue-Sat 13:00-16:00 & 20:30-23:00, Sun 13:00-16:00, closed Mon, Calle Virgen de los Remedios 7, tel. 951-489-818).

$$ Tragatá serves creative and tasty tapas in a stainless-steel minimalist bar. There's just a handful of tall tiny tables and some bar space inside, with patio seating on the pedestrian street, and an enticing blackboard of the day's specials. You'll pay more for it, but if you want to sample Andalusian gourmet (such as asparagus on a stick sprinkled with grated manchego cheese), this is the place to do it. They love chives (daily 13:00-16:00 & 20:00-23:00, Calle Nueva 4, tel. 952-877-209).

$$ Nueva 13, the latest entrant in the Calle Nueva tapa fest, serves up admirable and affordable *raciones*. Specials such as *rabo de toro* (bull's-tail stew) and *calamares* (squid) are listed on the giant blackboard inside. Locals love to hang out at the bar, and postcards from previous international visitors adorn the walls (daily 13:00-17:00 & 20:00-24:00, Calle Nueva 13, tel. 952-190-090).

$ Bar El Lechuguita, a traditional hit with older locals early and younger ones later, serves a long and tasty list of tapas for a good price. Rip off a tapas inventory sheet and mark which ones you want. Be adventurous and don't miss the bar's namesake, *lechuguita* (#16, a wedge of lettuce with vinegar, garlic, and a secret ingredient). The order-form routine makes it easy to communicate and get exactly what you like, plus you know the exact price (Mon-Sat 13:00-15:00 & 20:15-23:30, closed Sun, just a bar and some stand-up ledges along the wall, some rustic tables with stools outside, Calle Virgen de los Remedios 35).

OUTSIDE THE ALMOCÁBAR GATE

To entirely leave the quaint old town and bustling city center with all of its tourists and grand gorge views, hike 10 minutes out to the far end of the old town, past City Hall, to a big workaday square that goes about life as if the world didn't exist outside Andalucía.

$$ Bar-Restaurante Almocábar is a favorite eatery for many Ronda locals. Its restaurant—a cozy eight-table room with Moorish tiles and a window to the kitchen—serves up tasty, creative, well-presented meals from a menu that's well described in English (plus a handwritten list of the day's specials). Many opt for the good salads—rare in Spain. At the bar up front, choose from gourmet tapas like the *serranito* (a pork, roast pepper, and tomato mini sandwich) or you can order from the dining-room menu (Wed-Mon 13:00-16:00 & 19:30-23:00, closed Tue, reservations smart, Calle Ruedo Alameda 5, tel. 952-875-977).

$$ Casa María is a small tapas bar offering typical Andalusian fare in a homey, if crowded, setting. In summer, their tables spill out onto the plaza (Wed-Mon 12:30-24:00, closed Tue, facing Plaza Ruedo Alameda at #27, tel. 676-126-822).

$$ Bodega San Francisco is a rustic bar with tables upstairs, a homey restaurant across the street, and tables out front and on the square. They offer an accessible list of *raciones* and tapas, as well as serious plates and big splittable portions (same menu in bar and restaurant). This place is great for people-watching and a favorite with visitors from all over (long hours, closed Thu, Ruedo de Alameda 32, tel. 952-878-162).

DINING IN THE CITY CENTER

Ronda is littered with upscale-seeming restaurants that toe the delicate line between a good dinner spot and a tourist trap. For a more authentic dining experience, do a tapas crawl through town, or head for the far more characteristic eateries just outside the Almocábar Gate (both described earlier).

$$$ Restaurante Pedro Romero, though touristy and overpriced, is a venerable institution in Ronda. Assuming a shrine to bullfighting draped in *el toro* memorabilia doesn't ruin your appetite, it gets good reviews. Rub elbows with the local bullfighters or dine with the likes (well, photographic likenesses) of Orson Welles, Ernest Hemingway, and Francisco Franco daily 12:00-16:00 & 19:30-23:00, air-con, across from bullring at Calle Virgen de la Paz 18, tel. 952-871-110).

Ronda Connections

Note that some destinations are linked with Ronda by both bus and train. Direct bus service to other hill towns can be sparse (as few as one per day), and train service usually involves a transfer in Bobadilla. It's worth spending a few minutes in the bus or train station on arrival to plan your departure. Your options improve from major transportation hubs such as Málaga.

From Ronda by Bus to: Algeciras (1/day, 3.5 hours, Comes), **La Línea/Gibraltar** (no direct bus, transfer in Algeciras; Algeciras to Gibraltar—2/hour, 45 minutes, buy ticket on bus, Comes), **Arcos** (3/day, 2 hours, Comes), **Grazalema** (2/day, 45 minutes, Los Amarillos), **Zahara** (2/day, Mon-Fri only, 45 minutes, Comes), **Sevilla** (7/day, 2-2.5 hours, fewer on weekends, Los Amarillos;

also see trains, next), **Málaga** (*directo* 10/day Mon-Fri, 6/day Sat-Sun, 2 hours, Los Amarillos; other bus companies take twice as long; access other Costa del Sol points from Málaga), **Marbella** (2/day, 1.5 hours, Los Amarillos), **Fuengirola** (3/day, 2 hours, Los Amarillos), **Nerja** (4 hours, transfer in Málaga; can take train or bus from Ronda to Málaga, bus is better). If traveling to **Córdoba,** it's easiest to take the train since there are no direct buses (see next). Bus info: Los Amarillos (tel. 902-210-317, www.losamarillos.es), Portillo (tel. 902-450-550, http://portillo.avanzabus.com), and Comes (tel. 956-291-168, www.tgcomes.es). It's more efficient to pick up a bus timetable from the city TI. Or you can drop by and compare schedules (at the station on Plaza Concepción García Redondo, several blocks from train station).

By Train to: Algeciras (5/day, 1.5 hours), **Málaga** (1/day, 2 hours, 2 more with transfer in Bobadilla), **Sevilla** (4/day, 3 hours, transfer in Bobadilla, Córdoba, or Antequera), **Granada** (3/day, 3 hours, transfer to bus in Antequera due to AVE construction, buses will wait for you), **Córdoba** (2/day direct, 2 hours; 2 more with transfer in Antequera, 2 hours), **Madrid** (2/day direct, 4 hours; more with transfer in Antequera). Any transfer is a snap and time-coordinated; with four trains arriving and departing simultaneously, double-check that you're jumping on the right one. Train info: tel. 902-320-320, www.renfe.com.

Zahara and Grazalema

There are plenty of interesting hill towns to explore. Public transportation is frustrating, so I'd do these towns only by car. Useful information on the area is rare. Fortunately, a good map, the tourist brochure (pick it up in Sevilla or Ronda), and a spirit of adventure work fine.

Along with Arcos, Zahara de la Sierra and Grazalema are my favorite white villages. While Grazalema is a better overnight stop, Zahara is a delight for those who want to hear only the sounds of the wind, birds, and elderly footsteps on ancient cobbles.

ZAHARA DE LA SIERRA

This tiny town in a tingly setting under a Moorish castle (worth ▲ and the climb) has a spectacular view over a turquoise reservoir. While the big church facing the town square is considered one of the richest in the area, the smaller church has the most-loved statue. The Virgin of Dolores is Zahara's answer to Sevilla's Virgin of Macarena (and is similarly paraded through town during Holy Week).

The **TI** is located in the main plaza (closed Mon, gift shop, Plaza del Rey 3, tel. 956-123-114). Upstairs from the TI are Spanish-only displays about the flora and fauna of nearby Sierra de Grazalema Natural Park. A map posted nearby shows the tour and trail system.

Drivers can park for free in the main plaza, or continue up the hill to the parking lot at the base of the castle, just past the recommended Hotel Arco de la Villa. It's one way up and one way down, so follow *salida* signs to depart. The street that connects both churches, Calle de San Juan, is lined with tapas bars and cafés.

Sights in Zahara: During Moorish times, Zahara lay within the fortified castle walls above today's town. It was considered the gateway to Granada and a strategic stronghold for the Moors by the Christian forces of the Reconquista. Locals tell of the Spanish conquest of the Moors' castle (in 1482) as if it happened yesterday: After the Spanish failed several times to seize the castle, a clever Spanish soldier noticed that the Moorish sentinel would check if any attackers were hiding behind a particular section of the wall by tossing a rock and setting the pigeons in flight. If they flew, the sentinel figured there was no danger. One night a Spaniard hid there with a bag of pigeons and let them fly when the sentinel tossed his rock. Upon seeing the birds, the guard assumed he was clear to enjoy a snooze. The clever Spaniard then scaled the wall and opened the door to let in his troops, who conquered the castle. Ten years later Granada fell, the Muslims were back in Africa, and the Reconquista was complete.

Skip the church, but it's a fun climb up to the remains of the **castle** (free, tower always open). Start at the paved path across from the town's upper parking lot. It's a moderately steep 15-minute hike past some Roman ruins and along a cactus-rimmed ridge to the top, where you can enter the tower. Use your phone's flashlight or feel along the stairway to reach the roof, and enjoy spectacular views from this almost impossibly high perch far above the town. As you pretend you're defending the tower, realize that what you see is quite different from what the Moors saw: the huge lake dominating the valley is a reservoir—before 1991, the valley had only a tiny stream.

Sleeping and Eating in Zahara: $ **Hotel Arco de la Villa** is the town's only real hotel (16 small modern rooms, Wi-Fi in com-

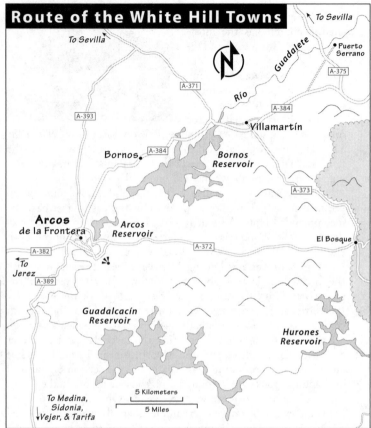

Route of the White Hill Towns

To Sevilla

To Sevilla

Río Guadalete

Puerto Serrano

A-375

A-371

A-384

A-393

Villamartín

Bornos

A-384

Bornos Reservoir

A-373

Arcos de la Frontera

Arcos Reservoir

A-372

El Bosque

A-382

To Jerez

A-389

Guadalcacín Reservoir

Hurones Reservoir

5 Kilometers

5 Miles

To Medina, Sidonia, Vejer, & Tarifa

mon areas only, tel. 956-123-230, www.tugasa.com, arco-de-la villa@tugasa.com). Its very good **$ restaurant** offers a €10 *menú del día,* along with reservoir and mountain views.

GRAZALEMA

A beautiful postcard-pretty hill town, Grazalema offers a royal balcony for a memorable picnic, a square where you can watch old-

timers playing cards, and plenty of quiet whitewashed streets and shops to explore. Situated within Sierra de Grazalema Natural Park, Grazalema is graced with lots of scenery and greenery. Driving here from Ronda on A-372, you pass through a beautiful parklike grove of cork trees. While the park is known as the

rainiest place in Spain, it's often just covered in a foggy mist. If you want to sleep in a small Andalusian hill town, this is a good choice.

The **TI** is located at the car park at the cliffside viewpoint, Plaza de los Asomaderos. It has WCs and a small gift shop featuring local products (tel. 956-132-052, www.grazalemaguide.com). Enjoy the view, then wander into the town.

A tiny lane leads a block from the center rear of the square to Plaza de Andalucía (filled by the tables of a commotion of tapas bars). Shops sell the town's beautiful and famous handmade wool blankets and good-quality leather items from nearby Ubrique. A block farther uphill takes you to the main square with the church, Plaza de España. A coffee on the square here is a joy. Small lanes stretch from here into the rest of the town.

Popular with Spaniards, the town makes a good home base for exploring Sierra de Grazalema Natural Park—famous for its spectacularly rugged limestone landscape of cliffs, caves, and gorges. For outdoor gear and adventures, including hiking, caving, and

canoeing, contact **Horizon** (summer Tue-Sat 9:00-14:00 & 17:00-20:00, shorter afternoon hours rest of year, closed Sun-Mon year-round, off Plaza de España at Corrales Terceros 29, tel. 956-132-363, mobile 655-934-565, www.horizonaventura.com).

Sleeping in Grazalema: $ La Mejorana Guesthouse is your best bet—if you can manage to get one of its six rooms. This beautifully perched garden villa, with royal public rooms, overlooks the valley from the top of town (includes breakfast, pool, on tiny lane below Guardia Civil headquarters at Santa Clara 6, tel. 956-132-327, mobile 649-613-272, www.lamejorana.net, info@lamejorana.net, Ana and Andrés can help with local hiking options).

$ Hotel Peñón Grande, named for a nearby mountain, is just off the main square and rents 16 comfortable business-class rooms (air-con, Plaza Pequeña 7, tel. 956-132-434, www.hotelgrazalema.com, hotel@hotelgrazalema.com).

¢ Casa de Las Piedras, just a block from the main square, has 16 comfortable rooms with private baths; two other rooms that share a single bathroom and have access to a kitchen and washing machine; and 14 super-cheap basic rooms sharing five bathrooms (and no kitchen/washing machine access). The beds feature the town's locally made wool blankets (RS%, Calle de las Piedras 32,

To Zahara
(via CA-531)
& Ronda

A-372

1 La Mejorana Guesthouse
2 Hotel Peñón Grande
3 Casa de Las Piedras
4 Plaza de Andalucía Eateries
5 El Torreón Restaurante
6 Mesón El Simancón
7 La Maroma Bar
8 Día Market
9 Horizon Adventure Tours

CALLE DE LOS ANGELES

PUERTA DE LA VILLA

ARRIBA

C. DE LA EMPEDRADA

CALLE DEL DOCTOR MATEOS GAGO

CALLE M. JIMENEZ

CALLE DE LAS PIEDRAS

CALLE DE CORRALES SEGUNDOS

C. CORRALES TERCEROS

CALLE DE LAS PARRAS

Plaza de los
Asomaderos

CALLE DEL AGUA

Plaza de
España

CALLE DE LAGUNETA

CALLE JUAN DE LA ROSA

A-372

100 Meters
100 Yards

ANDALUCÍA'S WHITE HILL TOWNS

tel. 956-132-014, mobile 627-415-047, www.casadelaspiedras.es, reservas@casadelaspiedras.net, Caty and Rafi).

Eating in Grazalema: Grazalema offers many restaurants and bars. Tiny Plaza de Andalucía has several good bars for tapas with umbrella-flecked tables spilling across the square, including **$$ Zulema** (big salads), **$ La Posadilla,** and **$ La Cidulia.** The recommended **Casa de Las Piedras** has an adjacent **$** restaurant (same name) that offers tapas, fixed-price meals, and several vegetarian options. To pick up picnic supplies, head to the **Día** supermarket (Mon-Sat 9:00-14:00 & 17:00-21:00, Sun 9:00-14:00, on Calle Corrales Terceros 3).

$$ El Torreón specializes in local cuisine such as lamb and game dishes, and also has many vegetarian options. Diners are warmed by the woodstove while deer heads keep watch (daily 12:00-16:00 & 19:00-23:00, Calle Agua 44, tel. 956-132-313).

$$ Mesón El Simancón serves well-presented cuisine typical of the region in a romantic setting. While a bit more expensive, it's considered the best restaurant in town (Wed-Mon 12:00-16:00 & 19:00-23:00, closed Tue, facing Plaza de los Asomaderos and the car park, tel. 956-132-421).

$ La Maroma Bar serves home-cooked regional specialties, three meals a day, at affordable prices (daily 8:00 until late, Calle Santa Clara, near La Mejorana Guesthouse, tel. 617-543-756, José & María).

Grazalema Connections: By Bus to Ronda (2/day, 45 minutes), **El Bosque** (2/day, 45 minutes). Bus service is provided by Los Amarillos (www.losamarillos.es).

Jerez de la Frontera

With more than 200,000 people, Jerez de la Frontera is your typical big-city mix of industry and dusty concrete suburbs, but it has a lively old center and two claims to touristic fame: horses and sherry. Jerez is ideal for a noontime visit on a weekday. See the famous horses, sip some sherry, wander through the old quarter, and swagger out. For the most efficient visit if arriving by bus or train, taxi from the train station right to the Royal Andalusian School for the equestrian performance, then walk around the corner to Sandeman's for the next English tour.

Orientation to Jerez

Thanks to its complicated medieval street plan, there is no easy way to feel oriented in Jerez—so ask for directions liberally.

The helpful **TI** is on Plaza del Arenal (Mon-Fri 9:00-15:00 & 17:00-19:00, Sat-Sun 9:30-14:30; shorter evening hours Oct-May; tel. 956-338-874, www.turismojerez.com). If you're walking to see the horses, ask here for detailed directions, as the route is a bit confusing.

ARRIVAL IN JEREZ

By Bus or Train: The bus and train stations are located side by side, near the Plaza del Minotauro (with enormous headless statue). Unfortunately, you can't store luggage at either one. You can stow bags for free in the Royal Andalusian School's *guardaropa* (coat room) if you attend their equestrian performance, but only for the duration of the show.

Cheap and easy **taxis** wait in front of the train station (€5 to TI; about €7 to the horses).

It's a 20-minute **walk** from the stations to the center of town and the TI: Angle across the brick plaza (in front of the stations, with two black smokestacks) to find Calle Diego Fernández de Herrera (look for the awning for the *churros* bar). Follow this street faithfully for several blocks until you reach a little square (Plaza de las Angustias). Continue in the same direction, leaving the square

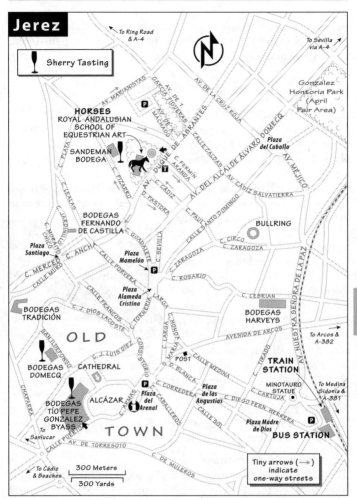

at the far left side down Calle Corredera. In a few minutes you will arrive at Plaza del Arenal (ringed with palm trees, with a large fountain in the center)—the TI is in the arcaded building across the plaza.

By Car from Arcos: Driving in Jerez can be frustrating. The outskirts are filled with an almost endless series of roundabouts. Continuing straight through each one will eventually bring a rail bridge into sight. Continue to follow traffic and signs to *Centro Ciudad*. The route may seem circuitous (it is), but it will ultimately take you into Plaza Alameda Cristina. From here, it's best to park in one of the many underground garages (at Plaza Alameda Cristina or Plaza Arenal, €1.30/hour) and catch a cab or walk. For street parking, blue-line zones require prepaid parking tickets on your dashboard (Mon-Fri 9:00-13:30 & 17:00-20:00, Sat 9:00-14:00, free on Sun and July-Aug afternoons).

Sights in Jerez

▲▲Royal Andalusian School of Equestrian Art

If you're into horses, a performance of the Royal Andalusian School of Equestrian Art (Fundación Real Escuela Andaluza del Arte Ecuestre) is a must. Even if you're not, this is art like you've never seen.

Getting There: On **foot,** from the TI at Plaza del Arenal, it's about a half-hour walk down mostly pedestrianized shopping streets to the horses. Leave the plaza on Calle Lanceria, heading to the left of the rounded Fino La Ina Fundador building to Calle Larga. It will bend gently left, depositing you at the foot of a tree-lined boulevard (Plaza Alameda Christina/Plaza Mamelón). From here, veer right and follow the *Real Escuela de Arte Ecuestre* signs.

From the bus or train stations to the horses, it's about a €7 **taxi** ride. Taxis wait at the exit of the school for the return trip.

One-way streets mean there is only one way to arrive by **car.** Follow signs to *Real Escuela de Arte Ecuestre.* Expect to make at least one wrong turn, so allow a little extra time. You'll find plenty of free parking behind the school.

Equestrian Performances

This is an equestrian ballet with choreography, purely Spanish music, and costumes from the 19th century. The stern riders and their talented, obedient steeds prance, jump, hop on their hind legs, and do-si-do in time to the music, all to the delight of an arena filled with mostly tourists and local horse aficionados.

The riders cue the horses with subtle dressage commands, either verbally or with body movements. You'll see both purebred Spanish horses (of various colors, with long tails, calm personalities, and good jumping ability) and the larger mixed breeds (with short tails and a walking—not prancing—gait). The horses must be three years old before their three-year training begins, and most performing horses are male (stallions or geldings), since mixing the sexes brings problems.

The equestrian school is a university, open to all students in the EU, and with all coursework in Spanish. Although still a male-

Sherry

Spanish sherry is not just the sweet dessert wine sold in the States as sherry. In Spain, sherry is (most commonly) a chilled and very dry fortified white wine, often served with appetizers such as tapas, seafood, and cured meats.

British traders invented the sherry-making process as a way of transporting wines so they wouldn't go bad on a long sea voyage. Some of the most popular brands (such as Sandeman and Osbourne) were begun by Brits, and for years it was a foreigners' drink. But today, sherry is typically Spanish.

Sherry is made by blending wines from different grapes and vintages, all aged together. Start with a strong, acidic wine (from grapes that grow well in the hot, chalky soil around Jerez). Mature it in large vats until a yeast crust *(flor)* forms on the surface, protecting the wine from the air. Then fortify it with distilled alcohol.

Next comes sherry-making's distinct *solera* process. Pour the young fortified wine into the top barrel of a unique contraption—a stack of oak barrels called a *criadera.* Every year, one-third of the oldest sherry (in the barrels on the ground level) is bottled. To replace it, one-third of the sherry in the barrel above is poured in, and so on. This continues until the top barrel is one-third empty, waiting to be filled with the new year's vintage.

Fino is the most popular type of sherry (and the most different from Americans' expectations)—white, dry, and chilled. The best-selling commercial brand of *fino* is Tío Pepe; *manzanilla* is a regional variation of *fino,* as is *montilla* from Córdoba. Darker-colored and more complex varieties of sherry include *amontillado* and *oloroso.* And yes, Spain also produces the thick, sweet cream sherries served as dessert wines. A good raisin-y, syrupy-sweet variety is Pedro Ximénez (often marked just "PX"), made from sun-dried grapes of the same name.

dominated activity, there have recently been a few female graduates. Tightly fitted mushroom hats are decorated with different stripes to show each rider's level. Professors often team with students and evaluate their performance during the show.

Cost and Hours: General seating—€21, "preference" seating—€27; 1.5-hour show runs Tue and Thu at 12:00 most of the year (also one Sat show per month year-round and on Fri in Aug and Oct, Jan-Feb Thu only); tel. 956-318-008, tickets available online at www.realescuela.org. General seating is fine; some "preference" seats are too close for good overall views. The show explanations are in Spanish.

Training Sessions

The public can get a sneak preview at training sessions on nonperformance days. Sessions can be exciting or dull, depending on what the trainers are working on. Afterward, you can take a 1.5-hour guided tour of the stables, horses, multimedia and carriage museums, tack room, gardens, and horse health center. Sip sherry in the arena's bar to complete this Jerez experience.

Cost and Hours: €11; Mon, Wed, and Fri—except no Fri in Aug-Sept, also on Tue in Jan-Feb; arrive anytime between 10:00 and 14:00—they'll start a tour when they have a large-enough group (but avoid 11:00, when tour groups crowd in). A shorter €6.50 tour covers only the museums and saddlery.

▲▲Sherry Bodega Tours

Spain produces more than 10 million gallons per year of the fortified wine known as sherry. The name comes from English attempts to pronounce Jerez. Although sherry was traditionally the drink of England's aristocracy, today's producers have left the drawing-room vibe behind. Your tourist map of Jerez is speckled with *venencia* symbols, each representing a sherry bodega that offers tours and tasting. (*Venencias* are specially designed ladles for dipping inside the sherry barrel, breaking through the yeast layer, and getting to the good stuff.) For all the bodegas, it's smart to confirm tour times before you go, as schedules can be changeable.

Bodegas Tradición

Although founded in 1998, this winery continues family winemaking traditions that date back to 1650. Their guided tours do a remarkable job of explaining the sometimes difficult-to-understand method of producing sherry. Aficionados claim that their award-winning sherries are not to be missed. Art lovers will get an extra treat: a museum-worthy private collection of works by Velázquez, El Greco, Zurburán, Goya, and many others.

Cost and Hours: €20 for 4 sherries and 2 brandies; English tours always available; open Sept-June Mon-Fri 9:00-17:00, Sat 10:00-14:00; July-Aug 8:00-15:00; closed Sun year-round; reservations required, tel. 956-168-628, www.bodegastradicion.es.

Bodegas Rey Fernando de Castilla

Founded in the 1960s by a family with 200 years of winemaking experience, this *bodega* has become a powerhouse, focusing on producing amazing sherry, brandies, and vinegars. Of note are their Palo Cortado and Pedro Ximénez varieties.

Cost and Hours: €15 for tour and tasting; English tours available Mon-Fri at 12:30; reservations required; Jardinillo 7, tel. 956-182-454, www.fernandodecastilla.com.

Sandeman

Just around the corner from the equestrian school is the venerable Sandeman winery, founded in 1790 and the longtime drink of English royalty. This tour is the aficionado's choice for its knowledgeable guides and their quality explanations of the process. Each stage is explained in detail, with visual examples of *flor* (the yeast crust) in backlit barrels, graphs of how different blends are made, and a quick walk-through of the bottling plant. The finale is a chance to taste three varieties.

Cost and Hours: €8 for regular sherries, €15 for rare sherries, €7.50 adds tapas to the tasting, tour/tasting lasts 1-1.5 hours; English tours Mon, Wed, and Fri at 11:30, 12:30, and 13:30 plus April-Oct also at 14:30; Tue and Thu at 10:30, 12:00, 13:00, and 14:15; Sat by appointment only, closed Sun; fewer tours in winter; reservations not required, tel. 675-647-177, www.sandeman.com.

Tío Pepe González Byass

The makers of the famous Tío Pepe offer a tourist-friendly tour, with more pretense and less actual sherry-making on display (that's done in a new, enormous plant outside town). But the grand circle of sherry casks signed by a *Who's Who* of sherry drinkers is worthwhile. Taste two sherries at the end of the 1.5-hour tour.

Cost and Hours: €15 for tour/tasting, €18 for light tapas lunch with tour; tours run Mon-Sat at 12:00, 13:00, 14:00, and 17:15; Sun at 12:00, 13:00, and 14:00; Manuel María González 12, tel. 956-357-016, www.bodegastiopepe.com. Drivers can park in the underground lot at the skippable Alcázar (€2.10/hour).

Other Sherry Bodegas

You'll come across many other sherry bodegas in town, including **Fundador Pedro Domecq**, located near the cathedral. This bodega is the oldest in Jerez, and the birthplace of the city's brandy. Tastings here are generous (€8, Mon-Fri at 12:00, 14:00, and 16:00; Sat at 12:00; tapas offered for about €4 each, Calle San Ildefonso 3, tel. 956-151-500, www.bodegasfundador.com).

Jerez Connections

Jerez's bus station is shared by six bus companies, each with its own schedule. The big ones serving most southern Spain destinations are Los Amarillos (tel. 902-210-317, www.losamarillos.es), Comes (tel. 956-291-168, www.tgcomes.es), and Autocares Valenzuela (tel. 956-702-609, www.grupovalenzuela.com). Shop around for the best departure time and most direct route. While here, clarify routes for any further bus travel you may be doing in Andalucía—especially if you're going through Arcos de la Frontera, where the ticket office is often closed. Also try the privately run www.movelia.es for bus schedules and routes.

From Jerez by Bus to: Tarifa (1/day on Algeciras route, 2 hours, more frequent with transfer in Cádiz, Comes), **Algeciras** (2/day, 2.5 hours, Comes; 6/day, fewer on weekends, 1.5 hours, Autocares Valenzuela), **Arcos** (hourly, 40 minutes), **Ronda** (2/day, 2.5-3 hours), **La Línea/Gibraltar** (1/day, 2.5 hours), **Sevilla** (hourly, 1-1.5 hours), **Granada** (1/day, 4.5 hours).

By Train to: Sevilla (hourly, 1 hour), **Madrid** (3-4/day direct, 4 hours; nearly hourly with change in Sevilla, 4 hours), **Barcelona** (nearly hourly, 7-8 hours, all with change in Sevilla and/or Madrid). Train info: tel. 902-320-320, www.renfe.com.

Near the Hill Towns

If you're driving between Arcos and Tarifa, here are several sights to explore.

YEGUADA DE LA CARTUJA

This breeding farm, which raises Hispanic Arab horses according to traditions dating back to the 15th century, offers a 2.5-hour guided visit and show on Saturday at 11:00 (€22 for best seats in *tribuna* section, €16 for seats in the stands, Finca Fuente del Suero, Carretera Medina-El Portal, km 6.5, Jerez de la Frontera, tel. 956-162-809, www.yeguadacartuja.com). From Jerez, take the road to Medina Sidonia, then turn right in the direction of El Portal—you'll see a cement factory on your right. Drive for five minutes until you see the farm. A taxi from Jerez will cost about €15 one-way.

MEDINA SIDONIA

This town is as whitewashed as can be, surrounding its church and hill, which is topped with castle ruins. I never drive through here without a coffee break and a quick stroll. Signs to *centro urbano* route you through the middle to Plaza de España (lazy cafés, bakery, plenty of free parking just beyond the square out the gate). If it's lunchtime, consider buying a picnic, as all the necessary shops are nearby and the plaza benches afford a solid workaday view of a perfectly untouristy Andalusian town. According to its own TI, the town is "much appreciated for its vast gastronomy." Small lanes lead from the main square up to Plaza Iglesia Mayor, where you'll find the church and TI (tel. 956-412-404, www.medinasidonia. com). At the church, an attendant will show you around for a tip. Even without giving a tip, you can climb yet another belfry for yet another vast Andalusian view. The castle ruins just aren't worth the trouble.

VEJER DE LA FRONTERA

Vejer, south of Jerez and just 30 miles north of Tarifa, will lure all but the very jaded off the highway. Vejer's strong Moorish roots give it a distinct Moroccan (or Greek Island) flavor—you know, black-clad women whitewashing their homes, and lanes that can't decide if they're roads or stairways. The town has no real sights—other than its remarkable views—and very little tourism, making it a pleasant stop. The TI is at Calle de los Remedios 2 (tel. 956-451-736, www.turismovejer.es).

The coast near Vejer has a lonely feel, but its pretty, windswept beaches are popular with windsurfers and sand flies. The Battle of Trafalgar was fought just off Cabo de Trafalgar (only a nondescript lighthouse today). I drove the circle so you don't have to.

Sleeping in Vejer: A newcomer on Andalucía's tourist map, the old town of Vejer has just a few hotels. **$$ Hotel La Botica de Vejer** provides 13 comfortable rooms in what was once a local apothecary. Homey decor and view patios add to the charm (Calle Canalejas 13, near Plaza de España, tel. 956-450-225, www. laboticadevejer.com). **$$ Hotel Convento San Francisco** is a poor-man's parador with spacious rooms in a refurbished convent (Calle Plazuela, tel. 956-451-001, www.tugasa.com), while **¢ Hostal La Posada** is family-run place in a modern apartment flat (Calle de los Remedios 21, tel. 956-450-258, www.hostal-laposada.com, no English spoken).

ROUTE TIPS FOR DRIVERS

The road-numbering system from the coast into Sevilla was changed a few years back—don't rely on an old driving map.

Sevilla to Arcos (55 miles): The remote hill towns of Andalucía are a joy to tour by car with Michelin map 578 or any other good map. Drivers can follow signs to *Cádiz* on the fast toll expressway (blue signs, E-5, AP-4); the toll-free N-IV is curvy and dangerous. About halfway to Jerez, at Las Cabezas de San Juan, take A-371 to Villamartín. From there, circle scenically (and clockwise) through the thick of the Pueblos Blancos—Zahara and Grazalema—to Arcos.

It's about two hours from Sevilla to Zahara. You'll find decent but winding roads and sparse traffic. It gets worse (but very scenic) if you take the tortuous series of switchbacks over the 4,500-foot summit of Puerto de Las Palomas (Pigeons Pass, climb to the viewpoint) on the direct but difficult road (CA-9104) from Zahara to Grazalema (you'll see several hiking trailheads into Sierra de Grazalema Natural Park).

Another scenic option through the park from Grazalema to Arcos is the road (A-372) that goes up over Puerto del Boyar (Boyar Pass), past the pretty little valley town of Benamahoma, and down to El Bosque.

To skirt the super-twisty roads within the park while passing through a few more hill towns, the road from Ronda to El Gastor, Setenil (cave houses and great olive oil), and Olvera is another picturesque alternative.

Arcos to Tarifa (80 miles): If you're going to Tarifa, take the tiny A-389 road at the Jerez edge of Arcos toward Paterna and Medina Sidonia, where you'll pick up A-381 to Algeciras, then on to Tarifa. Another option is to continue through Medina Sidonia to Vejer on A-396, from where you can cut south to Tarifa.

Costa del Sol to Ronda and Beyond: Drivers coming up from the coast catch A-397 at San Pedro de Alcántara and climb about 20 miles into the mountains. Many trucks use this route as well, so the going may be slow if following a convoy. The much longer, winding A-377/A-369 (west of Estepona) offers a scenic alternative that takes you through gorgeous countryside and a series of whitewashed villages. But note that the A-377 stretch of this road (from the coast to Gaucín), while perfectly drivable, is in rough shape—expect to go slowly.

SPAIN'S SOUTH COAST

Nerja • Gibraltar • Tarifa

Much of Spain's south coast is so bad, it's interesting. To northern Europeans, the sun is a drug, and this is their needle. Anything resembling a quaint fishing village has been bikini-strangled and Nivea-creamed. Oblivious to the concrete, pollution, ridiculous prices, and traffic jams, tourists lie on the beach like game hens on skewers—cooking, rolling, and sweating under the sun. It's a fascinating study in human nature.

The most famous stretch of coast is the Costa del Sol, where human lemmings make the scene and coastal waters are so polluted that hotels are required to provide swimming pools. And where Europe's most popular beach isn't crowded by high-rise hotels, most of it's in a freeway chokehold. But the Costa del Sol suffered in the recent economic crisis: Real estate, construction, and tourism had powered the economy, and the effects of their decline are still apparent. Crime and racial tension have risen, as many once-busy individuals are now without work.

But the south coast holds a few gems. If you want a place to stay and play in the sun, unroll your beach towel at Nerja, the most appealing resort town on the coast.

And remember that you're surprisingly close to jolly olde England: the land of tea and scones, fish-and-chips, pubs, and bobbies awaits you—in Gibraltar. Although a British territory, Gibraltar has a unique cultural mix that makes it far more interesting than the anonymous resorts that line the coast.

Beyond "The Rock," the whitewashed port of Tarifa—the least-developed piece of Spain's generally overdeveloped southern coast—is a workaday town with a historic center, broad beaches,

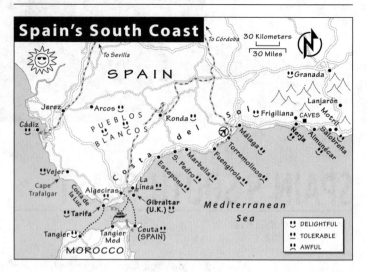

Spain's South Coast

and good hotels and restaurants. Most important, Tarifa is the perfect springboard for a quick trip to Tangier, Morocco.

These three places alone—Nerja, Gibraltar, and Tarifa—make Spain's south coast worth a trip.

PLANNING YOUR TIME

My negative opinions on the "Costa del Turismo" are valid for peak season (mid-July–mid-Sept). If you're there during a quieter time and you like the ambience of a beach resort, it can be a pleasant stop. Off-season it can be neutron-bomb quiet with many hotels and restaurants closed until their clients return for the sun.

The whole 150 miles of coastline takes six hours by bus or three hours to drive with no traffic jams. You can resort-hop by bus across the entire Costa del Sol and reach Nerja for dinner. If you want to party on the beach, it can take as much time as it would to get to Mazatlán.

To day-trip to Tangier, Morocco, head for Tarifa.

Nerja

While cashing in on the fun-in-the-sun culture, Nerja has actually kept much of its quiet Old World charm. It has good beaches, a fun evening paseo (strolling scene) that culminates at the Balcony of Europe viewpoint, enough pastry shops and nightlife to keep you fed and entertained, and locals who get more excited about their many festivals than the tourists do.

Although Nerja's population swells from about 22,000 in

winter to about 90,000 in the summer, it's more of a year-round destination and a real town than many other resorts. Thanks to cheap airfares to Costa del Sol destinations and the completion of the express-way, real estate boomed here in the last decade (property values

doubled in six years). The bubble collapsed to some extent with the 2008 financial crisis, but Nerja has remained hardier than other parts of the Costa del Sol. New restaurants and hotels open here all the time.

Nerja is more diverse than many of the rival resorts—in addition to British accents, you'll overhear French, German, Dutch, and Scandinavian languages being spoken on the beaches. Spaniards also have a long tradition of retiring and vacationing here. Pensioners from northern Spain move here—enjoying long life spans, thanks in part to the low blood pressure that comes from a diet of fish and wine. While they could afford to travel elsewhere, in summer, to escape the brutal heat of inland Spain, many Spanish parents take turns with their kids in family condos on the south coast. Whoever stays home to work gets to "be Rodriguez" *(estar de Rodríguez),* an idiom whose closest English equivalent is "when the cat's away, the mice will play."

Orientation to Nerja

The tourist center of Nerja is right along the water and crowds close to its famous bluff, the Balcony of Europe (Balcón de Europa). Fine strings of beaches flank the bluff, stretching in either direction. The old town is just inland from the Balcony, while the more modern section slopes up and away from the water.

Tourist Information: The helpful English-speaking TI has bus schedules, tips on beaches and side-trips, and brochures for nearby destinations, such as the Caves of Nerja, Frigiliana, Málaga, and Ronda (generally Mon-Sat 10:00-14:00 & 17:00-20:30, Sun 10:00-13:45; longer evening hours in summer, mornings only off-season; 100 yards from the Balcony of Europe and half a block inland from the big church, tel. 952-521-531, www.nerja.es). Their *Route on Walks* booklet describes good local walks.

ARRIVAL IN NERJA

By Bus: The Nerja bus station is just a bus stop with an info kiosk on Avenida de Pescia (Mon-Tue 6:00-20:15, Wed-Sun 7:00-12:15 & 14:45-19:00, schedules posted, Alsa tel. 902-422-242, www.

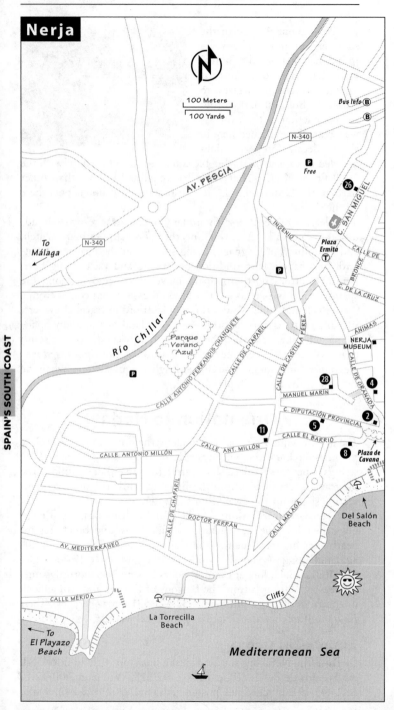

Nerja

100 Meters
100 Yards

Bus Info **B**

B

N-340

P Free

26

AV. PESCIA

C. INGENIO

C. SAN MIGUEL

CALLE DE

P

Plaza Ermita **T**

C. BRONCE

To Málaga N-340

C. DE LA CRUZ

P

Río Chillar

Parque Verano Azul

ÁNIMAS

CALLE DE CASTILLA PÉREZ

NERJA MUSEUM

CALLE ANTONIO FERRANDIS CHANQUETE

CALLE DE CHAPARIL

28

CALLE DE GRANADA

4

MANUEL MARÍN

C. DIPUTACIÓN PROVINCIAL

2

P

11

CALLE ANT. MILLÓN

5

CALLE EL BARRIO

8

Plaza de Cavana

CALLE ANTONIO MILLÓN

CALLE DE CHAPARIL

DOCTOR FERRÁN

CALLE MÁLAGA

Del Salón Beach

AV. MEDITERRÁNEO

CALLE MÉRIDA

Cliffs

La Torrecilla Beach

To El Playazo Beach

Mediterranean Sea

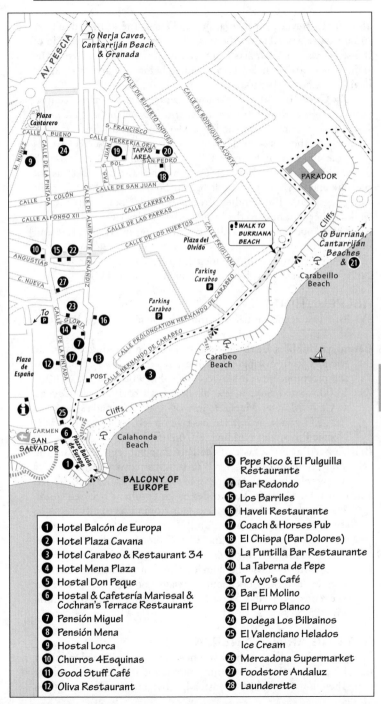

1 Hotel Balcón de Europa
2 Hotel Plaza Cavana
3 Hotel Carabeo & Restaurant 34
4 Hotel Mena Plaza
5 Hostal Don Peque
6 Hostal & Cafetería Marissal & Cochran's Terrace Restaurant
7 Pensión Miguel
8 Pensión Mena
9 Hostal Lorca
10 Churros 4Esquinas
11 Good Stuff Café
12 Oliva Restaurant
13 Pepe Rico & El Pulguilla Restaurante
14 Bar Redondo
15 Los Barriles
16 Haveli Restaurante
17 Coach & Horses Pub
18 El Chispa (Bar Dolores)
19 La Puntilla Bar Restaurante
20 La Taberna de Pepe
21 To Ayo's Café
22 Bar El Molino
23 El Burro Blanco
24 Bodega Los Bilbainos
25 El Valenciano Helados Ice Cream
26 Mercadona Supermarket
27 Foodstore Andaluz
28 Launderette

SPAIN'S SOUTH COAST

alsa.es). To travel from Nerja, buy tickets at the kiosk—don't assume they're available on the bus. If uncertain, ask which side of the street your bus departs from. Because many buses leave at the same times, arrive at least 15 minutes before departure to avoid having to elbow other tourists.

By Car: To find the old-town center and the most central parking, follow *Balcón de Europa, Centro Urbano,* or *Centro Ciudad* signs, and then pull into the big underground municipal parking lot beneath the Plaza de España (which deposits you 200 yards from the Balcony of Europe; €2.10/hour, €22.25/24 hours, cash only). The enormous above-ground Parking Carabeo, just east of the Balcony, is slightly cheaper (€1.80/hour, €18/24 hours, credit cards accepted). The handiest free parking is about a 10-minute walk farther out, next to the bridge over the dry riverbed (near the town bus stop, just off N-340). Street parking in Nerja is free and unlimited, but it's very tight. If you do find a space, read signs carefully—on certain days of the month you're required to move your car. It's best to ask your hotelier if your street spot is OK.

HELPFUL HINTS

Wi-Fi: Most accommodations and many cafés in Nerja have free Wi-Fi.

Laundry: Bubbles Burbujas is a full-service launderette run by friendly Jo from England (same-day service if you drop off in the morning, no self-service, Mon-Fri 9:00-17:00, Sat 9:00-13:00, closed Sun; a few blocks north of Plaza de Cavana at Calle Manuel Marín 1, just off Calle Granada—look for Pasaje Granada pedestrian passage on left, just past the Irish-Nordic Properties building, tel. 665-539-256).

British Media: For a taste of the British expat scene, pick up the monthly magazines *Street Wise* (www.streetwise.es) or *Soltalk* (www.soltalk.com), or tune in to Coastline Radio at 97.6 FM.

Local Guide: Carmen Fernández is an excellent licensed guide whose regional knowledge extends from tailored cityscapes to stunning natural areas around Nerja, Frigiliana, Antequera, and Málaga. (€90/3 hours, €125/5 hours, mobile 610-038-437, mfeyus@gmail.com).

Massage: Tiny yet muscular **Marie,** who moved here from France, does an excellent one-hour massage for €40 (€10 more on weekends; Amarilys Masaje, Calle Castilla Pérez 10, mobile 667-825-828).

GETTING AROUND NERJA

You can easily **walk** anywhere you need to go. If you need to take a **taxi,** it's pricey—the in-town minimum is about €7, even for a short trip. They don't use meters—instead, most journeys have a set fee

Costa del Sol History

Many Costa del Sol towns come in pairs: the famous beach town with little history, and its smaller yet much more historic partner established a few miles inland—safely out of reach of the Barbary pirate raids that plagued this coastline for centuries. Nerja is a good example of this pattern. Whereas it has almost no history and was just an insignificant fishing village until tourism hit, its more historic sister, Frigiliana, hides out in the nearby hills. The Barbary pirate raids were a constant threat. In fact, the Spanish slang for "the coast is clear" is *"no hay moros en la costa"* (there are no Moors on the coast).

Nerja was overlooked by the tourism scene until about 1980, when the phenomenal Spanish TV show *Verano Azul (Blue Summer)* was set here. This post-Franco program featured the until-then off-limits topics of sexual intimacy, marital problems, adolescence, and so on in a beach-town scene (imagine combining *All in the Family, Baywatch,* and *The Hills*). To this day, when Spaniards hear the word "Nerja," they think of this TV hit.

Despite the fame, development didn't really hit until about 2000, when the expressway finally and conveniently connected Nerja with the rest of Spain. Thankfully, a building code prohibits any new buildings higher than three stories in the old town.

(for example, €8 to Burriana Beach, €12 to Frigiliana, tel. 952-524-519 or 952-520-537).

To clip-clop in a **horse-drawn buggy** through town, it's €35 for about 25 minutes (you'll usually find these at the Plaza de los Cangrejos above Playa la Torrecilla).

The hop-on/hop-off **Cueva Tren tourist train** takes you to four stops: Nerja Museum, Nerja Caves, Maro Square, and Parque Verano Azul (€15, valid all day, includes entry to museum and caves, buy tickets at the museum and look for signs to catch it at a stop around the corner; 1-2/hour, departs at :30 all year and also at :00 in high season).

Sights in Nerja

▲▲Balcony of Europe (Balcón de Europa)

The bluff, jutting happily into the sea, is completely pedestrianized. It's the center of Nerja's paseo and a magnet for street performers. The mimes, music, and puppets can draw bigger crowds than the Balcony itself, which overlooks the Mediterranean, miles of coastline, and little coves and caves below. A castle, and later a fort, occupied this spot from the ninth century until the earthquake of 1884. Now it's a people-friendly view terrace. Walk out to the very tip, and soak up the sun and the sound of the pounding surf.

The demolished Nerja castle was part of a 16th-century lookout system. After the Christian Reconquista in 1492 drove Muslim Moors into exile, pirate action from Muslim countries in North Africa picked up. Lookout towers were stationed within sight of one another all along the coast. Warnings were sent whenever pirates threatened (smoke by day, flames by night). Look to the east—if you look closely, you can see three towers crowning bluffs in the distance.

Later, an English-Spanish fort, built here in the early 1800s to defend against Napoleon, protected the harbor with the help of seven cannons. When the 1884 earthquake destroyed the castle and fort, it sent the cannons into the sea. A century later, two were salvaged, cleaned up, and placed here, pointing east and west. Study the beautifully aged metal work.

Nearby, a cute statue of King Alfonso XII reminds locals of this popular sovereign—the great-great-grandfather of today's King Felipe VI—who came here after the devastating earthquake (a huge number of locals died). He mobilized the local rich to dig out the community and put things back together. Standing on this promontory amid the ruins of the earthquake-devastated castle, he marveled at the view and coined its now-famous name, Balcón de Europa.

Walk beneath the Balcony for views of the scant remains (bricks and stones) of the ninth-century Moorish castle. Locals claim an underground passage connected the Moorish fortress with the mosque that stood where the Church of San Salvador stands today.

Church of San Salvador

Just a block inland from the Balcony, this church was likely built upon the ruins of a mosque (c. 1600). It is only open for Mass, but you can visit it briefly before the daily 19:00 service starts. Its wooden ceiling is Mudejar—made by Moorish artisans working in Christian times. The woodworking technique is similar to that featured in the Alhambra in Granada. The modern fresco of the Annunciation (in the rear of the nave) is by Paco Hernandez, the top local artist of this generation. In front, on the right, is a niche featuring Jesus with San Isidoro (as a little boy). Isidoro is the patron saint of Madrid, Nerja, and farmers (sugarcane farming was the leading industry here before tourism hit). From the porch of the church, look inland to see City Hall, marked by four flags (Andalucía's is green for olive trees and white for the color of the houses in this part of Spain).

Nerja Museum (Museo de Nerja)

This mildly interesting and slightly disjointed museum is a good option on a rainy day or if you've just had too much sun. It's run in association with the Nerja Caves. Exhibits focus on the history of Nerja and the surrounding region, from prehistoric to modern times. Each of its four floors contains interactive exhibits and displays, including prehistoric tools, weapons, and a skeleton found within the Nerja Caves.

Cost and Hours: €4, €15 combo-ticket includes Nerja Caves and the Cueva Tren tourist train; open daily 9:00-16:00, July-Aug until 18:30; Plaza de España 4, tel. 952-527-224, www.cuevadenerja.es.

Town Strolls

Nerja was essentially destroyed after the 1884 earthquake—and at the time there was little more here beyond the castle anyway—so there's not much to see in the town itself. However, a few of its main streets are worth a ramble. From the Balcony of Europe head inland. Consider first grabbing some ice cream at El Valenciano Helados, a local favorite run by a Valencia family. Ignore their next-door competitors who "have more flavors" and try the refreshing *chufa*-nut Valencian specialty called *horchata*.

A block farther inland, the old town's three main streets come together. The oldest and most picturesque street, Calle Hernando de Carabeo, heads off to your right (notice how buildings around here are wired on the outside). On the left, Calle Pintada heads inland. Its name means "the painted street," as it was spiffed up in 1885 for the king's visit. Today it's the town's best shopping street, especially the stretch below Calle de la Gloria. And between Calles Carabeo and Pintada runs Calle Almirante Ferrándiz, Nerja's restaurant row, which is particularly lively in the evenings.

BEACHES

The single best thing to do on a sunny day in Nerja is to hit the beach: swim, sunbathe, sip a drink, go for a hearty hike along the rocky coves...or all of the above.

Many of Nerja's beaches are well-equipped with bars and restaurants, free showers, and rentable lounge chairs and umbrellas (about €4/person for chair and umbrella, same cost for 10 minutes or all day). Nearby restaurants rent umbrellas, and you're welcome to take drinks and snacks out to your spot. Spanish law requires all beaches to be open to the public (except the one in Rota, which is reserved for American soldiers).  While there are some nude beaches (such as Cantarriján, described later) keep in mind that in Europe, any beach can be topless. During the summer, Spanish sun worshippers pack the beach from about 11:00 until around 13:30, when they move into the beach restaurants for relief from the brutal rays. Watch out for red flags on the beach, which indicate when the seas are too rough for safe swimming (blue = safe, orange = caution, red = swimming prohibited). Don't take valuables to the beach, as thieves have fast fingers.

Beaches lie west and east of the Balcony of Europe. For each area, I've listed beaches from nearest to farthest. Even if you're not swimming or sunbathing, walking along these beaches (and the trails that connect them, if open) is a delightful pastime.

West of the Balcony of Europe
A pleasant promenade and trails connect these beaches.

Del Salón Beach (Playa del Salón)
The sandiest (and most crowded) beach in Nerja is down the walkway to the right of Cafetería Marissal, just west of the Balcony of Europe (to the right as you look out to sea). For great drinks with a view, stop by the recommended Cochran's Terrace on the way down. Continuing farther west, you'll reach another sandy beach, **Playa la Torrecilla,** at the end of Calle Málaga.

El Playazo ("Big Beach")
A short hike on a promenade west of Playa la Torrecilla, this beach is preferred by locals, as it's less developed than the more central ones, offering a couple of miles of wide-open spaces that allow for fine walks and a chance to "breathe in the beach."

East of the Balcony of Europe
One of Nerja's most appealing draws has been the walkway called the Paseo de los Carabineros, which scampers up and down cliffs, just above the pebbles and sand, to connect the enticing beaches east of the Balcony. Unfortunately, due to erosion and a lack of funds (and municipal motivation), the path has been closed for the past few years. That's why you have to walk through the modern

town above the coast to reach the beaches east of the Balcony of Europe.

To discourage people from venturing along the Paseo de los Carabineros, city officials have erected concrete barriers in a few places along the walkway, removed guardrails (so in some cases you're walking precariously along the cliffs), and allowed the path to become overgrown with plants. While it's possible to follow this pathway at your own risk, it's quite treacherous—and not recommended.

Calahonda Beach (Playa Calahonda)

Directly beneath the Balcony of Europe (to the left as you face the sea) is one of Nerja's most characteristic little patches of sun. This pebbly beach is full of fun pathways, crags, and crannies. To get to the beach from the Balcony, simply head down through the arch across from the El Valenciano Helados ice-cream stand...you'll be on the beach in seconds.

Carabeo and Carabeillo Beaches (Playa Carabeo/Playa Carabeillo)

Tiny and barely developed, these two beaches are wedged into wee coves between the bustling Calahonda and Burriana beaches. For many, their lack of big restaurants and services is a plus. To reach them, walk along Calle Hernando de Carabeo. The stairs down to Carabeo Beach are at a little viewpoint on the right (with a big wall map of the area). A bit farther along, a larger view plaza has stairs down to Carabeillo.

Burriana Beach (Playa de Burriana)

Nerja's leading beach is a 20-minute walk east from the Balcony of Europe. Big, bustling, crowded, and fun, it's understandably a top

attraction. Burriana is ideal for families, with paddleboats, playgrounds, volleyball courts, and other entertainment options. The beach is also lined with a wide range of cafés and restaurants, including the recommended Ayo's, whose paella feast is a destination in itself.

Getting There: It's an easy walk or an €8 taxi ride. To walk, follow Calle Hernando de Carabeo to the viewpoint plaza above Carabeillo Beach. At the roundabout, go up the first street to the right (you'll see a no-entry sign for cars), jog left (up Calle Cómpeta) alongside Nerja's boxy parador, then walk around the parador, following the signs for *Playa Burriana*. The path will curl right, then twist down a switchbacked path to the beach.

Cantarriján Beach (Playa del Cantarriján)

The only beach listed here not within easy walking distance of Nerja, this is the place if you're craving a more desolate beach (and have a car). Drive about 4.5 miles (15 minutes) east (toward Herradura) to the Cerro Gordo exit, and follow *Playa Cantarriján* signs (paved road, just before the tunnel). Park at the viewpoint and hike 30 minutes down to the beach (or, in mid-June-Sept, ride the shuttle bus down). Down below, rocks and two restaurants separate two pristine beaches—one for people with bathing suits (or not); the other, more secluded, more strictly for nudists. As this beach is in a natural park and requires a long hike, it provides a fine—and rare—chance to experience the Costa del Sol in some isolation.

SIGHTS NEAR NERJA

▲Nerja Caves (Cueva de Nerja)

These caves (2.5 miles east of Nerja), with an impressive array of stalactites and stalagmites, are a classic roadside attraction. The huge caverns, filled with backlit formations, are a big hit with cruise-ship groups and Spanish families. The visit involves a 45-minute ramble deep into the mountain, up and down 400 dark stairs. At the end you reach the Hall of the Cataclysm, where you'll circle the world's largest stalactite column (certified by the *Guinness Book of World Records*). Someone figured out that it took one trillion drops to make the column.

The free exhibit in the Centro de Interpretación explains the cave's history and geology (in house next to bus parking; exhibit in Spanish, but includes free English brochure).

Cost and Hours: €10, €15 combo-ticket also covers Nerja Museum and the Cueva Tren tourist train—buy at Nerja Museum; daily 9:00-16:00, July-Aug until 18:30, timed entry on the hour and half-hour, smart to book online in high season, last entry one hour before closing; easy parking-€1/day, tel. 952-529-520, www.cuevadenerja.es.

Concerts: During the festival held here the third week of July, the caves provide a cool venue for hot flamenco and classical concerts (tickets sell out long in advance).

Services: The restaurant offers a view and three-course fixed-price meals, and the picnic spot (behind the ticket office) has pine trees, benches, and a kids' play area.

Getting There: To reach the caves, use the hourly Cueva Tren, or catch a bus across the street from Nerja's main bus stop (€1.16, roughly 1/hour, 10-minute ride—get schedule from TI). A taxi costs €10 one-way. Drivers will find the caves well-signed (exit 295 on A-7)—just follow the *Cueva de Nerja* signs right to the parking lot.

Frigiliana

The picturesque whitewashed village of Frigiliana (free-hee-lee-AH-nah), only four miles inland from Nerja, is easily reached by bus (€1, 10/day weekdays, 8/day Sat, none on Sun, 15 minutes) or taxi (€12 one-way). While it doesn't match up to the striking white hill towns listed in the preceding chapter, its proximity to Nerja makes it an enticing side-trip if this is the nearest you'll get to hill towns on your trip.

The bus stop is in the middle of town, on Plaza del Ingenio. This is also the point that separates the new town from the old town (the steep old Moorish quarter climbing the hill up ahead). The **TI** is a 100-yard walk uphill, in the new town (tel. 952-534-261, www.frigiliana.es). Pick up a map and the translations of the tile you'll see displayed around town. The TI shares a building with the **archaeological museum,** with artifacts unearthed near Frigiliana; their prized piece is the fifth-century B.C. skull of a 10-year-old child.

Focus your visit on the **old town.** Begin by climbing up to the terrace in front of the factory *(ingenio)*—the blocky, un-whitewashed, double-smokestack building that dominates the town. Dating from the 16th century, this still produces sugarcane honey. From the end of the terrace, hike up the steep street, bearing right at the fork up Calle Hernando el Darra. At #10 (on the right), notice the tile in the wall—the first in a series of a dozen around town that describe, in poetic Spanish, the story of the 1568 Battle of Peñón. At the next fork, bear right (uphill) on Calle Amargura and walk steeply uphill, enjoying the flowerpot-lined lane. Notice the distinctive traditional door-knockers, shaped like a woman's hand. More common in Morocco, these are known as the "hand of Fatima"—the daughter of the Prophet Muhammad—and are intended to ward off evil.

After turning the corner, take the left/downhill road at the next fork, than head right up Calle Sta. Teresa de Ávila. Then head left down the steep, stepped Calle del Garral. You'll pop out just below the main church. Before going there, detour a few steps to the right, then head left to **Plaza de la Fuente Vieja**—home of a 17th-century fountain that's one of the town's trademarks. Then head back up the way you came to find your way to the inviting café-lined plaza in front of the **Church of San Antonio of Padua**

SPAIN'S SOUTH COAST

(with a stark interior). From here, you can follow the main drag back to where you entered town, or enjoy exploring Frigiliana's back lanes.

Hiking

Europeans visiting the region for a longer stay generally use Nerja as a base from which to hike. The TI can describe a variety of hikes (ask for the *Route on Walks* booklet). One of the most popular hikes is a refreshing walk up a river (at first through a dry riverbed, and later up to your shins in water; 7.5 miles one-way, 2-3 hours total). Another, more demanding hike takes you to the 5,000-foot summit of El Cielo for the most memorable king-of-the-mountain feeling this region offers.

Nightlife in Nerja

Bar El Molino offers live Spanish folk singing nightly in a rustic cavern that's actually an old mill—the musicians perform where the mules once trod. It's touristy but fun (starts at 22:00 but pretty dead before 23:00, no cover—just buy a drink, Calle San José 4). The local sweet white wine, *vino del terreno*—made up the hill in Frigiliana—is popular here (€3/glass).

El Burro Blanco is a touristy flamenco bar that's enjoyable and intimate, with shows nightly from 22:30. Keeping expectations pretty low, they advertise "The Best Flamenco Show in Nerja" (no cover—just buy a drink, live music Fri-Sat after flamenco, fewer shows off-season, on corner of Calle Pintada and Calle de la Gloria).

Bodega Los Bilbainos is a classic dreary old dive—a favorite with local men and communists (tapas and drinks, Calle Alejandro Bueno 8).

For more trendy and noisy nightlife, check out the bars and dance clubs on Antonio Millón and Plaza Tutti Frutti.

Sleeping in Nerja

The entire Costa del Sol is crowded during August and Easter Week, when prices are at their highest. Reserve in advance for peak season—basically mid-July through mid-September—which is prime time for Spanish families to hit the beaches. Any other time of year, you'll find that Nerja has plenty of comfy, easygoing low-rise resort-type hotels and rooms.

Compared to the pricier hotels, the better *hostales* are an excellent value. Hostal Don Peque, Pensión Miguel, and Pensión Mena are all within a few blocks of the Balcony of Europe.

CLOSE TO THE BALCONY OF EUROPE

$$$$ Hotel Balcón de Europa is the most central place in town. It's right on the water and the square, with the prestigious address Balcón de Europa 1. It has 110 rooms with modern style, plus all the comforts—including a pool and an elevator down to the beach. It's popular with groups. All the suites have sea-view balconies, and most regular rooms also come with views (some view rooms, air-con, elevator, gym, sauna, pay parking, tel. 952-520-800, www.hotelbalconeuropa.com, reservas@hotelbalconeuropa.com).

$$$ Hotel Plaza Cavana, with 39 rooms, overlooks a plaza lily-padded with cafés. It feels a bit institutional, but if you'd like a central location, marble floors, modern furnishings, an elevator, and a small unheated rooftop swimming pool, dive in (RS%, breakfast included for Rick Steves readers, some view rooms, family rooms, air-con, mini fridge, elevator, pay parking, 2 blocks from Balcony of Europe at Plaza de Cavana 10, tel. 952-524-000, www.hotelplazacavana.com, info@hotelplazacavana.com).

$$ Hotel Carabeo, a boutique-hotel splurge, has seven classy rooms on the cliff east of downtown—less than a 10-minute walk away, but removed from the bustle of the Balcony of Europe (some view rooms, includes continental breakfast, air-con, Calle Hernando de Carabeo 34, tel. 952-525-444, www.hotelcarabeo.com, info@hotelcarabeo.com). This is also home to the recommended Restaurant 34.

$$ Hotel Mena Plaza is clean, bright, and friendly, offering 34 rooms on Plaza de España right by the Nerja Museum. Some rooms have views and wide balconies (family room, air-con, elevator, pay parking, pool, rooftop terrace, tel. 952-520-965, www.hotelmenaplaza.es, info@hotelmenaplaza.es).

$$ Hostal Don Peque, an easy couple of blocks' walk from the Balcony of Europe, has 10 bright, colorful, and cheery rooms (eight with balconies—a few with sea views). Owners Roberto and Clara moved here from France and have infused the place with their personalities. They lend beach equipment, and their bar-terrace with rooftops-and-sea views is enticing (family room, breakfast only in high season; air-con, thin walls, Calle Diputación 13, tel. 952-521-318, www.hostaldonpeque.com, info@hostaldonpeque.com).

$ Hostal Marissal has an unbeatable location next door to the fancy Balcón de Europa hotel, and 23 modern, spacious rooms with old-fashioned furniture. Some rooms have small view balconies overlooking the Balcony of Europe action. Their cafeteria and bar, run by helpful staff, make the Marissal even more welcoming (family room, some view rooms, apartment, double-paned windows, air-con, elevator, Balcón de Europa 3, reception at Cafetería Marissal—staffed mornings only in off-season but they'll send you

SPAIN'S SOUTH COAST

a code to access your room, tel. 952-520-199, www.hostalmarissal. com, reservas@hostalmarissal.com).

$ Pensión Miguel offers nine sunny and airy rooms in the heart of "Restaurant Row" (some street noise in front rooms). Breakfast is served on the pretty green terrace with mountain views. The owners—British expats Ian and Jane—are long-time Nerja devotees who will help make your stay a delight (family suite, no air-con but fans and fridges, laundry service, beach equipment, Calle Almirante Ferrándiz 31, tel. 952-521-523, mobile 696-799-218, www.pensionmiguel.net, pensionmiguel@gmail.com).

¢ Pensión Mena rents 11 nice rooms—four with sea-view terraces—and offers a quiet, breezy garden (family room, Calle el Barrio 15, tel. 952-520-541, www.hostalmena.es, info@hostalmena. es, María). The reception has limited hours (daily 9:30-13:30 & 17:00-20:30); if they're closed when you arrive to check in, report to their sister hotel, Hotel Mena Plaza, a few blocks away at Plaza de España 2.

IN A RESIDENTIAL NEIGHBORHOOD

$ Hostal Lorca is located in a quiet residential area a five-minute walk from the center, three blocks from the bus stop, and close to a small, handy grocery store. Run by a friendly, energetic Dutch couple, Femma and Rick, this *hostal* has nine modern, comfortable rooms and an inviting backyard with a terrace and a small pool. You can use the microwave and take drinks (on the honor system) from the well-stocked fridge. This quiet, homey place is a winner (no air-con but fans, look for a house with flags at Calle Méndez Núñez 20, tel. 952-523-426, www.hostallorca.com, info@ hostallorca.com).

Eating in Nerja

There are three Nerjas: the private domain of the giant beachside hotels; the central zone, packed with fun-loving (and often tipsy) expats and tourists eating and drinking from trilingual menus; and the back streets, where local life goes on as if there were no tourists. The whole old town (around the Balcony of Europe) is busy with lively restaurants. Wander around and see who's eating best.

To pick up picnic supplies, head to the **Mercadona** supermarket (Mon-Sat 9:00-21:00, closed Sun, inland from Plaza Ermita on Calle San Miguel). For an interesting selection of imported foods, check out **Foodstore Andaluz**, a Dutch-run grocery that stocks especially good chocolates and sweets (daily 10:00-14:30 & 17:00-19:30, Calle Pintada 46, mobile 681-327-841).

Breakfast: Some hotels here overcharge for breakfast. Don't hesitate to go elsewhere, as many places serve breakfast for more reasonable prices. For a cheap breakfast with a front-row view of the promenade action on the Balcony of Europe, head to **$$ Cafetería Marissal** (in the recommended *hostal* of the same name) and grab a wicker seat under the palm trees (options include English breakfasts, daily from 9:00). Another option is at **$ Churros 4Esquinas** where the chef fries up hot churros to dip into a hot pudding-like chocolate drink (daily 7:00-23:00, churros from 7:00-12:30 & 17:00-20:30, Calle Pintada 57, on the corner of Calle Angustias, mobile 626-126-564). If you're up for a short hike before breakfast, consider the recommended **$ Ayo's** on Burriana Beach. And sample an expat Dutch couple's take on the Great British Bake Off at the **$ Good Stuff Café,** where Adam makes savory quiches and pies, and Irene makes scones, brownies, carrot cake, banana bread, and Victoria sponge cake (Mon-Fri 9:00-20:00, Sat until 18:00, closed Sun and August; Calle Castilla Perez 4, mobile 606-512-586).

NEAR THE BALCONY OF EUROPE

$$ Cochran's Terrace serves mediocre meals in a wonderful seaview setting, overlooking Del Salón Beach (daily 12:00-15:30 & 19:00-23:00, also offers breakfast from 8:30, drinks all day, shorter hours off-season, just behind Hostal Marissal).

$$$ Restaurant 34, in Hotel Carabeo, manages white-tablecloth elegance in an eclectic, relaxed atmosphere that successfully mixes antiques with modern accents. More tables sprawl outside, along the swimming pool and toward sweeping sea views (call ahead to reserve a sea-view table). They offer inexpensive *raciones*— and a free tapa if you buy a drink in the bar (Tue-Sun 12:30-15:30 & 19:00-late, closed Mon, Calle Hernando de Carabeo 34, tel. 952-525-444).

ALONG RESTAURANT ROW

Strolling up Calle Almirante Ferrándiz (which some locals call "Cristo" at its far end), you'll find a good variety of eateries, albeit filled with tourists. On the upside, the presence of expats means you'll find places serving food earlier in the evening than the Spanish norm.

$$$ Oliva has white-tablecloth ambience if you're in the mood for a splurge. It's tucked away through a courtyard off the Calle Pintada, offering a gourmet twist of international fusion cuisine made from local products (daily 13:00-16:00 & 19:00-23:00, Calle Pintada 7, tel. 952-522-988).

$$$ Pepe Rico is romantic (in a schlocky adult-contemporary way) along this street, with a big terrace and a cozy dining room (Mon-Sat 12:30-15:00 & 19:00-23:00, closed Sun, Calle Almirante Ferrándiz 28, tel. 952-520-247).

$$ Bar Redondo, popular with locals and visitors alike, is a colorfully tiled *taparía* and watering hole. Bartenders work from within the completely round, marble-topped bar; if you can't find room there, grab a spot at a wine-barrel table on the street. Belly up to the bar with a drink and pick your free tapa from 25 options; don't miss the tasty *habas con jamón* (daily 12:30-24:00, Calle de la Gloria 10, tel. 952-523-344).

$$ El Pulguilla is a great, high-energy place for Spanish cuisine, fish, and tapas. Its two distinct zones (tapas bar up front and more-formal restaurant out back) are both jammed with enthusiastic locals and tourists. The lively no-nonsense stainless-steel tapas bar doubles as a local pick-up joint later in the evening. Drinks come with a free small plate of clams, mussels, shrimp, chorizo sausage, or seafood salad. For a sit-down meal, head back to the gigantic terrace. Though not listed on the menu, half-portions *(media-raciones)* are available for many items, allowing you to easily sample different dishes (Tue-Sun 12:30-16:30 & 19:00-24:00, closed Mon, Calle Almirante Ferrándiz 26, tel. 952-521-384).

$$ Los Barriles is a family-run bar where Rafa, Carmen, and their son serve up drinks and a short, simple menu of *raciones,* including a fiery chorizo sausage. Your best bet is to order a drink and wait for the tapa that comes with it. Locals flock here and tourists are treated like locals (long hours, closed Sunday, Calle San José 28).

$$ Haveli, run by Amit and his Swedish wife, Eva, serves good Indian cuisine in an informal atmosphere. For more than two decades, it's been a hit with Brits, who know their Indian food (daily 19:00-24:00, closed Wed off-season, upstairs at Calle Almirante Ferrándiz 44, tel. 952-524-297).

$$ Coach and Horses is a British pub run by no-nonsense expat Catherine. Although she serves the only real Irish steaks in town, she also caters to vegetarians, with daily specials that go beyond the usual omelet. This is where to find bangers and mash (daily 10:30-15:00 & 18:30-late, closed Mon off-season, Calle Almirante Ferrándiz 19, tel. 952-520-071).

TAPAS BARS ON OR NEAR CALLE HERRERA ORIA

A 10-minute gentle uphill hike from the water takes you into the residential thick of things, where the sea views come thumbtacked to the walls, prices are lower, and locals fill the tables. The first three are tapas bars within a few blocks of one another. Each is a colorful local hangout with different energy levels on different nights. Survey all three before choosing one, or have a drink and tapa at each. These places are generally open all day for tapas and drinks, and serve table-service meals during normal dining hours. If you prefer a restaurant setting to a bar, try La Taberna de Pepe.

Remember that in Nerja, tapas are snack-size portions, generally not for sale but free with each drink. To turn them into more of a meal, ask for the menu and order a full-size *ración*, or half-size *media-ración*. The half-portions are generally bigger than you'd expect.

$$ El Chispa (a.k.a. Bar Dolores) is big on seafood, which locals enjoy on an informal terrace. Their *tomate ajo* (garlic tomato) is tasty, and their piping-hot *berenjena* (fried and salted eggplant) is worth considering—try it topped with molasses-like sugarcane syrup. They serve huge portions—*media-raciones* are enough for two (daily, Calle San Pedro 12, tel. 952-523-697).

$$ La Puntilla Bar Restaurante is a boisterous little place, with rickety plastic furniture spilling out onto the cobbles on hot summer nights (show this book and get a free *digestivo*, daily 12:00-24:00, a block in front of Los Cuñaos at Calle Bolivia 1, tel. 952-528-951).

$$ La Taberna de Pepe is more of a sit-down restaurant, though it does have a small bar with tapas. The tight, cozy (almost cluttered) eight-table interior is decorated with old farm tools and crammed with happy eaters choosing from a short menu of well-executed seafood. It feels classier than the tapas bars listed above, but isn't pretentious (Fri-Wed 12:15-16:00 & 19:00-24:00, closed Thu, Calle Herrera Oria 30, tel. 952-522-195).

PAELLA FEAST ON BURRIANA BEACH

$ Ayo's is famous for its character of an owner and its €7 beachside all-you-can-eat paella feast at lunchtime. For 30 years, Ayo—a lovable ponytailed bohemian who promises to be here until he dies—has been feeding locals. Ayo is a very big personality—one of the five kids who discovered the Nerja Caves, formerly a well-known athlete, and now someone who makes it a point to hire hard-to-employ people as a community service. The paella fires get stoked up at about noon and continue through mid-to-late afternoon. Grab one of a hundred tables under the canopy next to the rustic open-fire cooking zone, and enjoy the beach setting in the shade with a jug of sangria. It's a 20-minute walk from the Balcony of Europe, at the east end of Burriana Beach—look for Ayo's rooftop pyramid (open daily "sun to sun," paella served only in the afternoon, cash only, Playa de Burriana, tel. 952-522-289).

Breakfast at Ayo's: Consider arriving at Ayo's at 9:00. Locals order the *tostada con aceite de oliva* (toast with olive oil and salt). Ayo also serves toasted ham-and-cheese sandwiches and good coffee.

Nerja Connections

While there are some handy direct bus connections from Nerja to major destinations, many others require a transfer in the town of **Málaga.** The closest train station to Nerja is in Málaga. Fortunately, connections between Nerja and Málaga are easy, and the train and bus stations in Málaga are right next to each other.

NERJA

Almost all buses from Nerja are operated by Alsa (tel. 902-422-242, www.alsa.es), except the local bus to Frigiliana, which is run by Autocares Nerja (tel. 952-520-984). Remember to double-check the codes on bus schedules—for example, 12:00*S* means 12:00 daily except Saturday.

From Nerja by Bus to: Málaga (1-2/hour, 1.5 hour *directo*, 2 hours *ruta*), **Nerja Caves** (1/hour, 10 minutes), **Frigiliana** (10/day weekdays, 8/day on Sat, none on Sun, 15 minutes), **Granada** (6/day, 2.5 hours), **Córdoba** (2/day, 4-5.5 hours), **Sevilla** (2/day, 5 hours). To reach **Ronda, Gibraltar,** or **Tarifa,** you'll transfer in Málaga.

To Málaga Airport (about 40 miles west): First catch the bus to Málaga (see above). To reach the airport from Málaga, take a local bus (about 2/hour, 30 minutes, €2, buy ticket on board) or train (2/hour, 30 minutes, €2.20; Málaga's train station is a quick five-minute walk across the street from the bus station). If you'd rather take a taxi from Nerja to the airport, figure on paying about €65, or ask your Nerja hotelier about airport shuttle transfers (airport code: AGP, tel. 952-048-804).

MÁLAGA

Málaga's busy airport is the gateway to the Costa del Sol, and taking a long layover in this seaside city may be worth your while. It has spruced itself up in recent years and deserves at the very least a lengthy stroll and visits to the two impressive museums.

Tourist Information: Find the TI (Mon-Sat 10:00-20:00, Sun until 13:00) and information desk in the center of the train station (in front of tracks 1-8).

Arrival in Málaga: The bus and train stations—a block apart at the western edge of the town center—both have pickpockets and lockers. You'll want to store your bags in the more-modern lockers at the train station.

Sights in Málaga: Either take a taxi (about €7, 10 minutes) to the *casco viejo* (old town), or go through the taxi line to public bus C2 (€1.30, 20 minutes), and get off at the fourth stop where there's a long tree-lined plaza with florist stalls—just blocks from the cathedral. From there wander into the old town's pedestrian-

Britain's Home Away from Home

Particularly in the resorts around Málaga, many of the foreigners who settle in for long holidays are British—you'll find beans on your breakfast plate and Adele for Muzak. Spanish visitors complain that some restaurants have only English menus, and indeed, the typical expats here actually try *not* to integrate. I've heard locals say of the British, "If they could, they'd take the sun back home with them—but they can't, so they stay here." The Brits enjoy their English TV and radio stations, and many barely learn a word of Spanish. (Special school buses take their children to private English-language schools that connect with Britain's higher-education system.) For an insight into this British community, read the free local expat magazines.

ized zone, which is easy to navigate thanks to signposts on almost every corner indicating tourist sights.

The **Museo Picasso Málaga** holds over 200 paintings, sculptures, and ceramics spanning the artist's life and artistic styles. Pablo Picasso was born in Málaga and first discussed establishing a museum here in 1953. It finally opened 50 years later, thanks to a donation by the artist's daughter-in-law and grandson (€10, audioguide included; daily July-Aug 10:00-20:00, March-June & Sept-Oct until 19:00, Nov-Feb until 18:00; Calle San Agustín 8, a block away from the cathedral entrance; tel. 902-443-377, www.museopicassomalaga.org).

For a look at Spanish art just prior to Picasso, visit the **Museo Carmen Thyssen Málaga,** which features 19th-century paintings with mostly Andalusian themes from the collection of Carmen Cervera. (A former Miss Spain, she's the widow of industrial tycoon Hans Heinrich von Thyssen-Bornemisza, whose famous art collection is housed in Madrid.) There are more than 250 works by Sorolla, Fortuny, Zuloaga, Zurbarán, and other Spanish artists exhibited in the restored 16th-century Palace of Villalón (€6, Tue-Sun 10:00-20:00, closed Mon; audioguide-€1.50, Plaza Carmen Thyssen/Calle Compañía 10; tel. 902-303-131, www.carmenthyssenmalaga.org).

Málaga Connections: Málaga's big, airy U-shaped **bus station,** on Paseo de los Tilos, has long rows of counters for the various bus companies. In the center of the building is a helpful info desk that can print out schedules for any destination and point you to the right ticket window (daily 7:00-22:00, tel. 952-350-061, www.estabus.emtsam.es). Flanking the information desk on either side are old-fashioned pay lockers (buy a token—*una ficha*—from the automat, access closed overnight). The station also has several basic eateries, newsstands, and WCs.

The slick, modern **train station** is just a five-minute walk away: exit at the far corner of the bus station, cross the street, and enter the big shopping mall (with a food court upstairs) labeled *Estación María Zambrano*—walk a few minutes through the mall to the train station. Modern lockers are by the entrance to tracks 10-11 (security checkpoint), and car-rental offices are by the entrance to tracks 1-9 (Hertz, Avis, Europcar, and National/Atesa). A TI kiosk is in the main hall, just before the shopping mall. To reach the bus station (five minutes away on foot), enter the mall by the TI kiosk and follow signs to *estación de autobuses*.

From Málaga by Bus to: Nerja (1-2/hour, 1.5 hour *directo*, 2 hours *ruta;* final destination may be Almería; Alsa), **Ronda** (*directo* buses by Los Amarillos: 10/day Mon-Fri, 6/day Sat-Sun, 2 hours; avoid the *ruta* buses by Portillo: 2/day, 5 hours), **Algeciras** (hourly, 2 hours *directo*, 3 hours *ruta*, Portillo), **La Línea de Concepción/ Gibraltar** (5/day, 3 hours, Portillo), **Tarifa** (2/day, 2.5-4 hours, Portillo), **Sevilla** (6/day direct plus 2/day from Málaga's airport, 2.5-4 hours, Alsa), **Granada** (hourly, 1.5-2 hours, Alsa), **Córdoba** (4/day, 3 hours *directo*, Alsa), **Madrid** (5/day, 6 hours, Interbus), **Marbella** (hourly, 1 hour *directo*, 1.25 hours *ruta*, Portillo). Bus info: Alsa (tel. 902-422-242, www.alsa.es), Los Amarillos (tel. 902-210-317, www.losamarillos.es), Interbus (tel. 902-646-428, http://mma.interbus.es), Portillo (tel. 902-450-550, http://portillo.avanzabus.com).

From Málaga by Train to: Ronda (1/day, 2 hours, 1 more with transfer in Bobadilla), **Algeciras** (1/day, 4.5 hours, transfer in Bobadilla—same as Ronda train, above), **Madrid** (9/day, 2.5-3 hours on AVE), **Córdoba** (best option: 6/day on Avant, 1 hour; more expensive but no faster on AVE: 10/day, 1 hour), **Granada** (6/day, 2.5 hours, 1 transfer—bus is better), **Sevilla** (6/day, 2 hours on Avant; 5/day, 2.5-3 hours on slower regional trains), **Jerez** (9/ day, 3.5-4 hours, with transfer), **Barcelona** (3/day direct on AVE, 6 hours; more with transfer). Train info: tel. 902-320-320, www.renfe.com.

Between Nerja and Gibraltar

Buses take five hours to make the Nerja-Gibraltar trip, including a transfer in Málaga, where you may have to change bus companies. Along the way, buses stop at each of the following towns.

FUENGIROLA AND TORREMOLINOS

The most built-up part of the region, where those most determined to be envied settle down, is a bizarre world of Scandinavian package tours, flashing lights, pink flamenco, multilingual menus, and all-night happiness. Fuengirola is like a Spanish Mazatlán with a few older, less-pretentious budget hotels between the main drag and the beach. The water here is clean and the nightlife fun and easy. James Michener's idyllic Torremolinos has been strip-malled and parking-metered.

MARBELLA

This is the most polished and posh town on the Costa del Sol. High-priced boutiques, immaculate streets set with intricate pebble designs, and beautifully landscaped squares testify to Marbella's arrival on the world-class-resort scene. Have a *café con leche* on the beautiful Plaza de Naranjos in the old city's pedestrian section. Wander down to modern Marbella and the high-rise beachfront apartment buildings to walk along the wide promenade lined with restaurants. Check out the beach scene. Marbella is an easy stop on the Algeciras-Málaga bus route (as you exit the bus station, take a left to reach the center of town). You can also catch a handy direct bus here from the Málaga airport (roughly every 1-2 hours, fewer off-season, 45 minutes, http://portillo.avanzabus.com).

SAN PEDRO DE ALCÁNTARA

This town's relatively undeveloped sandy beach is popular with young travelers. San Pedro's neighbor, Puerto Banús, is "where the world casts anchor." This luxurious, Monaco-esque jet-set port, complete with casino, is a strange mix of Rolls-Royces, yuppies, boutiques, rich Arabs, and budget browsers.

Gibraltar

One of the last bits of the empire upon which the sun never set, Gibraltar is an unusual mix of Anglican propriety, "God Save the Queen" tattoos, English bookstores, military memories, and tour-ist shops. It's understandably famous for its dramatic Rock of Gibraltar, which rockets improbably into the air from an otherwise flat terrain, dwarf-ing everything around it. If the Rock didn't exist, some clever military tac-tician would have tried to build it to keep an eye on the Strait of Gibraltar.

Britain has controlled this highly strategic spit of land since they took it by force in 1704, in the War of Spanish Succession. In 1779, while Britain was preoccupied with its troublesome overseas colonies, Spain (later allied with France) declared war and tried to retake Gibraltar; a series of 14 sieges became a way of life, and the already-imposing natural features of the Rock were used for defensive purposes. During World War II, the Rock was further fortified and dug through with more and more strategic tunnels. In the mid- to late-20th century, during the Franco period, tensions ran high—and Britain's grasp on the Rock was tenuous.

Strolling Gibraltar, you can see that it was designed as a mod-ern military town (which means it's not particularly charming). But over the past 20 years the economy has gone from one dominated by the military to one based on tourism (as, it seems, happens to many empires). On summer days and weekends, the tiny colony is inundated by holiday-goers, primarily the Spanish (who come here for tax-free cigarettes and booze) and British (who want a change in weather but not in culture). As more and more glitzy high-rise resorts squeeze between the stout fortresses and ramparts—as if trying to create a mini-Monaco—there's a sense that this is a town in transition.

Though it may be hard to imagine a community of 30,000 that feels like its own nation, real Gibraltarians, as you'll learn when you visit, are a proud bunch. They were evacuated during World War II, and it's said that after their return, a national spirit was forged. If you doubt that, be here on Gibraltar's national holiday—September 10—when everyone's decked out in red and white, the national colors.

Gibraltarians have a mixed and interesting heritage. Span-iards call them Llanitos (yah-NEE-tohs), meaning "flat" in Span-ish, though the residents live on a rock. The locals—a fun-loving

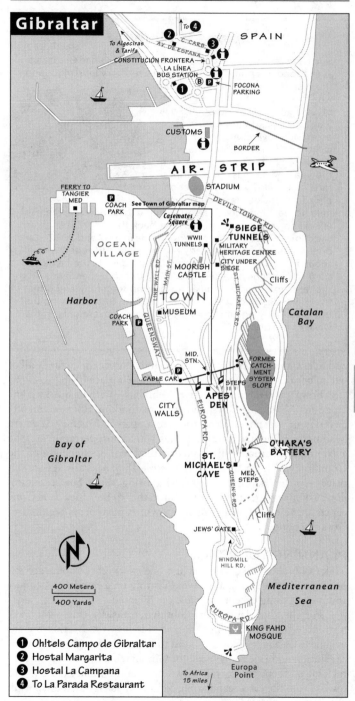

Gibraltar

SPAIN

To Algeciras & Tarifa

AV. DE ESPANA

C. CARR.

To ❹

❷

❸

CONSTITUCIÓN FRONTERA

LA LÍNEA BUS STATION

❶

Ⓑ Ⓟ

FOCONA PARKING

CUSTOMS

BORDER

AIR-STRIP

STADIUM

FERRY TO TANGIER MED

Ⓟ COACH PARK

See Town of Gibraltar map

DEVILS TOWER RD.

Casemates Square

OCEAN VILLAGE

WWII TUNNELS

MOORISH CASTLE

TOWN

MUSEUM

LINE WALL RD.

MAIN ST.

SIEGE TUNNELS

MILITARY HERITAGE CENTRE

CITY UNDER SIEGE

Cliffs

Catalan Bay

ST. MICHAEL'S RD.

Harbor

COACH PARK Ⓟ

QUEENSWAY

MID. STN.

CABLE CAR

Ⓟ

FORMER CATCHMENT SYSTEM SLOPE

STEPS

APES' DEN

EUROPA RD.

CITY WALLS

O'HARA'S BATTERY

Bay of Gibraltar

ST. MICHAEL'S CAVE

MED. STEPS

QUEEN'S RD.

Cliffs

JEWS' GATE

N

400 Meters

400 Yards

WINDMILL HILL RD.

Mediterranean Sea

EUROPA RD.

KING FAHD MOSQUE

To Africa 15 miles

Europa Point

❶ Oh!tels Campo de Gibraltar
❷ Hostal Margarita
❸ Hostal La Campana
❹ To La Parada Restaurant

Spain vs. Gibraltar

Spain has been annoyed about Gibraltar ever since Great Britain nabbed this prime 2.5-square-mile territory in 1704 (during the War of Spanish Succession) and was granted it through the Treaty of Utrecht in 1713. Although Spain long ago abandoned efforts to re-assert its sovereignty by force, it still tries to make Gibraltarians see the error of their British ways. Over the years Spain has limited Gibraltar's air and sea connections, choked traffic at the three-quarter-mile border, and even messed with the local phone system in efforts to convince Britain to give back the Rock. Still, given the choice—which they got in referenda in 1967 and 2002—Gibraltar's residents steadfastly remain Queen Elizabeth's loyal subjects, voting overwhelmingly (99 percent in the last election) to continue as a self-governing British dependency. Gibraltar's governor is popular for dealing forcefully and effectively with Spain on these issues. But with Britain leaving the EU, Spain may again challenge Gibraltar's sovereignty in the wake of the Brexit.

and tolerant mix of British, Spanish, and Moroccan, virtually all of whom speak the Queen's English—call their place "Gib."

From a traveler's perspective, Gibraltar—with its quirky combination of Brits, monkeys, and that breathtaking Rock—is an off-beat detour that adds some variety to a Spanish itinerary. If you're heading to Gibraltar from Spain (as you almost certainly are), be aware most Spaniards still aren't thrilled with this enclave of the Commonwealth on their sunny shores. They basically ignore the place—so, for example, if you're inquiring about bus schedules, don't ask how to get to Gibraltar, but rather to La Línea de la Concepción, the neighboring Spanish town. A passport is required to cross the border.

PLANNING YOUR TIME

Make Gibraltar a day trip (or just one overnight); rooms are expensive compared to Spain. Avoid visiting on a Sunday, when just about everything except the cable car is closed.

For the best day trip to Gibraltar, consider this plan: walk across the border, catch bus #5, and ride it to the Market Square stop near Casemates Square. From there, catch bus #2 to the cable-car station and ride to the peak for Gibraltar's ultimate top-of-the-rock view. Then, either walk down or take the cable car back into town. From the cable-car station, follow my self-guided town walk all the way back to Casemates Square. Spend your remaining free time in town before returning to Spain. Note that, with all the old walls and fortresses, Gibraltar can be tricky to navigate. Ask for directions: Locals speak English.

Tourists who stay overnight find Gibraltar a peaceful place in the evening, when the town can just be itself. No one's in a hurry. Families stroll, kids play, seniors window-shop, and everyone chats...but the food is still pretty bad.

There's no reason to take a ferry from Gibraltar to visit Morocco—for many reasons, it's a better side-trip from Tarifa.

Orientation to Gibraltar

Gibraltar is a narrow peninsula (three miles by one mile) jutting into the Mediterranean. Virtually the entire peninsula is dominated by the steep-faced Rock itself. The locals live down below in the long, skinny town at the western base of the mountain (much of it on reclaimed land).

For information on all the little differences between Gibraltar and Spain—from area codes to electricity—see "Helpful Hints," later.

Tourist Information: Gibraltar's helpful TI is at Casemates Square, the grand square at the Spain end of town. Pick up a free map and—if it's windy—confirm that the cable car is running (Mon-Fri 9:00-17:30, Sat 10:00-15:00, Sun 10:00-13:00, tel. 74982, www.visitgibraltar.gi). At the border, there's a TI window in the customs building (Mon-Fri 9:00-16:30, closed Sat-Sun).

ARRIVAL IN GIBRALTAR

No matter how you arrive, you'll need your passport to cross the border. These directions will get you as far as the border; from there, see "Getting from the Border into Town."

By Bus: Spain's La Línea de la Concepción bus station is a five-minute walk from the Gibraltar border. To reach the border, exit the station and bear left toward the Rock (you can't miss it). If you need to store your bags, you can do so at the Gibraltar Airport (see "Helpful Hints," later).

By Car: You don't need a car in Gibraltar. It's simpler to park in La Línea and just walk across the border.

Freeway signs in Spain say *Algeciras* and *La Línea*, often pretending that Gibraltar doesn't exist until you're very close. After taking the La Línea-Gibraltar exit off the main Costa del Sol road, your best bet is to follow signs for *Aduana de Gibraltar* (Gibraltar customs). La Línea's main square—Plaza de la Constitución—covers a huge underground municipal parking lot; just look for the blue *"P"* signs (€18.20/day). The Focona underground lot is also handy (€2.40/hour, €16.50/day, on Avenida 20 de Abril, near the bus station). You'll also find blue-lined parking spots in this area (€1.25/hour from meter, 6-hour limit 9:00-20:00, free before and after that, bring coins, leave ticket on dashboard). From the square, it's a five-minute stroll to the border, where you can catch a bus or taxi into town (see "Getting from the Border into Town," below).

If you do drive into Gibraltar, customs checks at the border create a bottleneck. There's often a 30-minute wait during the morning rush hour into Gibraltar and during the evening rush hour back out. Once in Gibraltar, drive along the harbor side of the ramparts (on Queensway—but you'll see no street name). There are big parking lots here and at the cable-car terminal. Parking is generally free—if you can find a spot (it's tight during weekday working hours). By the way, while you'll still find English-style roundabouts, cars here stopped driving on the British side of the road in the 1920s.

Getting from the Border into Town

The "frontier" (as the border is called) is a chaotic hubbub of travel agencies, confused tourists, crafty pickpockets, and duty-free shops (you may see people standing in long lines, waiting to buy cheap cigarettes). The guards barely even look up as you flash your passport. Before exiting the customs building, pick up a map at the TI window on your left (Mon-Fri 9:00-16:30, closed Sat-Sun). Note that as soon as you cross the border, the currency changes from euros to pounds (see "Helpful Hints," next).

To reach downtown, you can walk (20 minutes), catch a bus, or take a taxi. To get into town by **foot,** walk straight across the runway (look left, right, and up), then head down Winston Churchill Avenue. Angle right at the second roundabout, then walk along the fortified Line Wall Road to Casemates Square.

From the border, you can ride **bus #5** (regular or London-style double-decker, runs every 15 minutes) three stops to Market Square (just outside Casemates Square, with the TI), or stay on to Cathedral Square, at the center of town. From Market Square, Gibraltar city buses head to various points on the peninsula—a useful route for most tourists is bus #2, which goes to the cable-car station and Europa Point (Gibraltar's southernmost point). The privately run border buses and the city buses have slightly different tickets at the same prices, and they are not transferable between the two systems (€2/£1.50 one-way, €3/£2.25 round-trip; €3/£2.25 all-day

"Hoppa" ticket on city buses; drivers accept either currency and give change).

A **taxi** from the border is pricey (€9/£6 to the cable-car station). If you plan to join a taxi tour up to the Rock, note that you can book one right at the border.

HELPFUL HINTS

Gibraltar Isn't Spain: Gibraltar, a British colony, uses different coins, currency (see below), stamps, and phone cards than those used in Spain. Note that British holidays such as the Queen's (official) birthday (on a Saturday in June) and Bank Holidays are observed, along with local holidays such as Gibraltar's National Day (Sept 10).

Use Pounds, not Euros: Gibraltar uses the British pound sterling (£1 = about $1.30). A pound is broken into 100 pence (abbreviated p). Like other parts of the UK (such as Scotland, Wales, and Northern Ireland), Gibraltar mints its own Gibraltar-specific banknotes and coins featuring local landmarks, people, and historical events—offering a colorful history lesson. Gibraltar's pounds are interchangeable with other British pounds only in Gibraltar, so try to use up your Gibraltar bills before you leave.

Merchants in Gibraltar also accept euros...but at about a 20 percent extra cost to you. Gibraltar is expensive even at fair exchange rates. You'll save money by hitting up an ATM and taking out what you'll need (look along Main Street). Before you leave, stop at an exchange desk and change back what you don't spend (at about a 5 percent loss), since Gibraltar currency is hard to change in Spain.

On a quick trip, or if you'll be making few purchases, don't bother drawing out cash; you can buy things with your credit card and use euros when you have to. Be aware that if you pay for anything in euros, you may get pounds back in change.

Hours: This may be the United Kingdom, but Gibraltar follows a siesta schedule, with some businesses closing from 13:00 to 15:00 on weekdays, and shutting down at 14:00 on Saturdays until Monday morning.

Electricity: If you have electrical gadgets, note that Gibraltar uses the British three-pronged plugs (not the European two-pronged ones). Your hotel may be able to loan you an adapter.

Phoning: To telephone Gibraltar from anywhere in Europe, dial 00-350-200 and the five-digit local number. To call Gibraltar from the US or Canada, dial 011-350-200-local number.

Baggage Storage: You can't store your luggage at the bus station, but there is a bag check at the Gibraltar Airport, which is right across the border (go to airport information desk in departures hall).

John Mackintosh Cultural Centre: This is your classic British effort to provide a cozy community center. Without a hint of tourism, the upstairs library welcomes drop-ins to enjoy local newspapers and publications, and to check their email (Mon-Fri 9:30-19:30, closed Sat-Sun, free Wi-Fi, 308 Main Street, tel. 75669).

Activities: The **King's Bastion Leisure Centre** fills an old fortification (the namesake bastion) with a modern entertainment complex just outside Cathedral Square. On the ground floor is a huge bowling alley; upstairs are an ice-skating rink and a three-screen cinema (www.leisurecinemas.com). Rounding out the complex are bars, restaurants, discos, and lounges (daily 10:00-24:00, air-con, free Wi-Fi, tel. 44777, www.kingsbastion.gov.gi).

Monkey Alert: The monkeys, which congregate at the Apes' Den on the Rock, have gotten more aggressive over the years, spoiled by being fed by tourists. Keep your distance and don't feed them.

Side-Trip to Tangier, Morocco: While a very sporadic ferry does run from Gibraltar directly to Tangier, it's designed for Moroccan workers (returning home to Tangier for the weekend) and doesn't work for a same-day round-trip. Instead, go via Tarifa (best choice, with direct connections to downtown Tangier). Service exists from Algeciras (closer to Gibraltar) but ferries drop you at a port 25 miles from downtown Tangier. Various travel agencies in town sell package tours that include a bus transfer to the boat in Algeciras, but these should be a last resort.

Gibraltar Walk

Gibraltar town is long and skinny, with one main street (called Main Street). Stroll the length of it from the cable-car station to Casemates Square, following this little self-guided walk. A good British pub and a room-temperature pint of beer await you at the end.

From the cable-car terminal, turn right (as you face the harbor) and head into town. Soon you'll come to the **Trafalgar cemetery,** a reminder of the colony's English military heritage; two of the seamen who died of wounds after the 1805 Battle of Trafalgar are buried here, and those who perished during the battle were consigned to the sea. (Of course, Lord Nelson was taken to London and buried in St. Paul's Cathedral.) Next you'll arrive at the **Charles V wall**—a reminder of Gibraltar's Spanish military

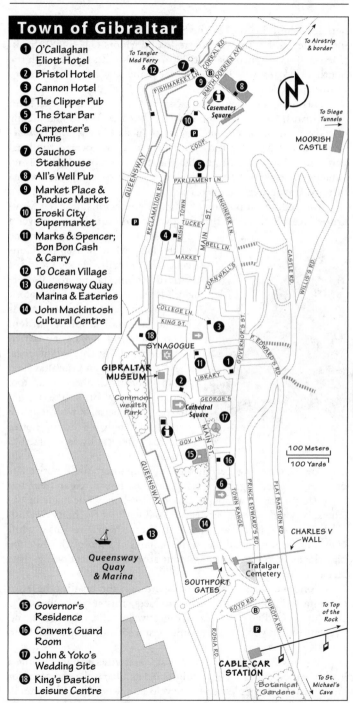

Town of Gibraltar

1. O'Callaghan Eliott Hotel
2. Bristol Hotel
3. Cannon Hotel
4. The Clipper Pub
5. The Star Bar
6. Carpenter's Arms
7. Gauchos Steakhouse
8. All's Well Pub
9. Market Place & Produce Market
10. Eroski City Supermarket
11. Marks & Spencer; Bon Bon Cash & Carry
12. To Ocean Village
13. Queensway Quay Marina & Eateries
14. John Mackintosh Cultural Centre
15. Governor's Residence
16. Convent Guard Room
17. John & Yoko's Wedding Site
18. King's Bastion Leisure Centre

SPAIN'S SOUTH COAST

heritage—built in 1540 by the Spanish to defend against maraud-ing pirates. Gibraltar was controlled by Moors (711-1462), Spain (1462-1704), and then the British (since 1704). Passing through the Southport Gates, you'll see one of the many blue-and-white history plaques posted about town.

Heading into town, you pass the tax office, then the **John Mackintosh Cultural Centre,** which has free Wi-Fi and a copy of today's *Gibraltar Chronicle* upstairs in its library. The *Chronicle* comes out Monday through Friday and has covered the local news since 1801. The Methodist church (which puts on a rousing karaoke-style service on Sunday afternoons) sponsors the recom-mended **Carpenter's Arms** tearoom.

The pedestrian portion of Main Street begins near the **Governor's Residence.** The British governor of Gibraltar took over a

Franciscan convent, hence the name of the local white house: The Con-vent. The formally classic **Convent Guard Room,** facing the Gover-nor's Residence, is good for photos.

Gibraltar's courthouse stands behind a **small tropical garden,** where John and Yoko got married back in 1969 (as the ballad goes, they "got married in Gibraltar near Spain"). Sean Connery did, too. Actually, many Brits like to get married here because weddings are cheap, fast (only 48 hours' notice required), and legally recognized as British.

Main Street now becomes a **shopping drag.** You'll notice lots of colorful price tags advertising tax-free booze, cigarettes, and sugar (highly taxed in Spain). Lladró porcelain, while made in Va-lencia, is popular here (because it's sold without the hefty Spanish VAT—Value-Added Tax). The Catholic cathedral retains a whiff of Arabia (as it was built upon the remains of a mosque), while the big **Marks & Spencer department store** helps vacationing Brits feel at home.

Continue several more blocks through the bustling heart of Gibraltar. If you enjoy British products, this is your chance to stock up on Cadbury chocolates, digestive biscuits, wine gums, and Weetabix—but you'll pay a premium, since it's all "imported" from the UK.

The town (and this walk) ends at **Casemates Square.** While a lowbrow food circus today, it originated as a barracks and place for ammunition storage. When Franco closed the border with Spain in

1969, Gibraltar suffered a labor shortage, as Spanish guest workers could no longer commute into Gibraltar. The colony countered by inviting Moroccan workers to take their place—ending a nearly 500-year Moroccan absence, which began when the Moors fled in 1462. As a result, today's Moroccan community dates only from the 1970s. Whereas the previous Spanish labor force simply commuted into work, the Moroccans needed apartments, so Gibraltar converted the Casemates barracks for that purpose. Cheap Spanish labor has crept back in, causing many locals to resent store clerks who can't speak proper English.

At the far end of Casemates Square is the **Gibraltar Crystal shop** which makes its own glass right there (you can watch). They claim it's the only thing actually "made in Gibraltar." But just upstairs, on the upper floor of the barracks, you'll find a string of local crafts shops.

If you go through the triple arches at the end of the square (behind the TI), you'll reach the covered **produce market** and food stalls. Across the busy road a few minutes' walk farther is the well-marked entrance to the **Ocean Village** boardwalk and entertainment complex (described later, under "Eating in and near Gibraltar").

Sights in Gibraltar

IN TOWN
▲Gibraltar Museum

Built atop a Moorish bath, this museum tells the story of a chunk of land that has been fought over for centuries. Start with the cheerleading 15-minute video overview of the story of the Rock—a worthwhile prep for the artifacts (such as ancient Roman anchors made of lead) you'll see in the museum. Then wander through the remains of the 14th-century Moorish baths. Upstairs you'll see military memorabilia, a 15-foot-long model of the Rock (compare it with your map to see all the changes), wonderful century-old photos of old Gibraltar, paintings by local artists, and, in a cave-like room off the art gallery, a collection of prehistoric remains and artifacts. The famous skull of a Neanderthal woman found in Forbes' Quarry is a copy (the original is in the British Museum in London). Found in Gibraltar in 1848, this was the first Neanderthal skull ever discovered. No one realized its significance until a similar skull found years later in Germany's Neanderthal Valley was correctly identified—stealing the name, claim, and fame from Gibraltar.

Cost and Hours: £2, Mon-Fri 10:00-18:00, Sat until 14:00, closed Sun, on Bomb House Lane near the cathedral, www.gibmuseum.gi.

ON THE ROCK OF GIBRALTAR

The actual Rock of Gibraltar is the colony's best sight. Its attractions include the stupendous view from the very top, temperamental apes, a hokey cave (St. Michael's), and the impressive Siege Tunnels drilled through the rock face for military purposes. Frankly, the sights that charge admission aren't that exciting; the Rock's attractions—enjoying views from the top and seeing the monkeys—are practically free. Hikers can ride the lift up and take a long, steep, scenic walk down, connecting the various sights by strolling along paved military lanes.

Cost: £0.50 fee to enter the grounds of the Rock, technically called the Upper Rock Nature Reserve—that's just to walk around and take in the views and see the monkeys. A £10 nature reserve ticket is required to visit any or all of these major sights within the reserve: St. Michael's Cave, Siege Tunnels, Moorish Castle, Military Heritage Centre, and City Under Siege exhibit (includes the £0.50 nature reserve entrance fee). If you take a taxi tour, entry to the nature reserve and sights is included; if you ride the cable car, the nature reserve grounds entry fee is included, but you'll have to buy the £10 ticket to go in the sights. (Both options are explained below.)

Hours: Daily 9:30-19:15, until 18:15 late Oct-late March.

Additional Sights at the Rock: Two attractions at the Rock are not part of the official £10 nature reserve ticket, and have their own separate tickets and hours: O'Hara's Battery and the World War II Tunnels (both described later).

Visiting the Rock: You have two options for touring the Rock—take a taxi tour or ride the cable car. The **taxi tour** includes entry to St. Michael's Cave and the Siege Tunnels, a couple of extra stops, and running commentary from your licensed cabbie/guide. Because the cable car doesn't get you very close to the cave and tunnels (and doesn't cover cave and tunnel admission), take the taxi tour if you'll be visiting these sights and don't want to walk. On the other hand, the **cable car** takes you to the very top of the Rock (which the taxi tours don't). You can still see the sights, but you'll have to pay for an entry ticket and connect them by foot (not a bad thing—it's a pleasant walk down).

There's no reason to take a big-bus tour (advertised and sold all over town) considering how fun and easy the taxi tours are. Private cars are not allowed high on the Rock.

By Taxi Tour: Minivans driven by cabbies trained and licensed to lead these 1.5-hour trips are standing by at the border and at various points in town (including Cathedral Square,

John Mackintosh Square, Casemates Square, Trafalgar Cemetery, and near the cable-car station). They charge £20/person (4-person minimum, or £65 for only 2 people in one taxi, includes nature reserve and sights ticket, tel. 70027). Taxi tours and big buses do the same 1.5-hour loop tour with four stops: a Mediterranean viewpoint (called the Pillar of Hercules), St. Michael's Cave (15-minute visit), a viewpoint near the top of the Rock where you can get up close to the monkeys, and the Siege Tunnels (20-minute visit). Buddy up with other travelers and share the cost.

By Cable Car to the Summit: A ticket for just the cable car is £10.75 one-way and £12.75 round-trip. The £20.25 nature reserve ticket (combining a one-way cable-car ride and the £10 ticket to the sights) doesn't save any money over buying the tickets separately (credit cards accepted). You'll probably want to skip the round-trip option, as I recommend walking downhill to the sights rather than taking the cable car down. Check to make sure the cable car is running and then buy your tickets online at http://gibraltarinfo.gi/en/tickets/; the prepaid line will save you time.

The cable car runs every 10-15 minutes, or continuously in busy times (daily from 9:30; April-Oct last ascent at 19:15, last descent at 19:45; Nov-March last ascent at 17:15, last descent at 17:45). Lines can be long if a cruise ship is in town. The cable car won't run if it's windy or rainy; if the weather is questionable, ask at the TI before heading to the station. The cable-car ride includes a handheld videoguide that explains what you're seeing from the spectacular viewpoints (pick it up at the well-marked booth when you disembark at the top—must leave ID as a deposit—and return it before leaving the summit). In winter (Nov-March), the cable car stops halfway down for those who want to get out, gawk at the monkeys, and take a later car down—but you'll probably see monkeys at the top anyway.

To take in all the sights, you'll want to **hike down** instead of taking the cable car back (be sure to specify that you want a one-way ticket up). Simply hiking down without visiting the sights is enjoyable, too. Approximate hiking times: from the top of the cable car to St. Michael's Cave—25 minutes; from the cave to the Apes' Den—20 minutes; from the Apes' Den to the Siege Tunnels—30 minutes; from the tunnels back into town, passing the Moorish Castle—20 minutes. Total walking time, from top to bottom: about 1.5 hours (on paved roads with almost no traffic), not including sightseeing. For hikers, I've connected the dots with directions later.

▲▲▲**The Summit of the Rock**

The cable car takes you to the real highlight of Gibraltar: the summit of the spectacular Rock itself. (Taxi tours don't go here; they

SPAIN'S SOUTH COAST

stop on a ridge below the summit, where you enjoy a commanding view—but one that's nowhere near as good as this one.) The limestone massif, or large rock mass, is nearly a mile long, rising 1,400 feet with very sheer faces. According to legend, this was one of the Pillars of Hercules (paired with Djebel Musa, another mountain across the strait in Morocco), marking the edge of the known world in ancient times. Local guides say that these pillars are the only places on the planet where you can see two seas and two continents at the same time.

In A.D. 711, the Muslim chieftain Tarik ibn Ziyad crossed over from Africa and landed on the Rock, beginning the Moorish conquest of Spain and naming the Rock after himself—Djebel-Tarik ("Rock of Tarik"), which became "Gibraltar."

At the top of the Rock (the cable-car terminal) are a view terrace and a café. From here you can explore old ramparts and drool at the 360-degree view of Morocco (including the Rif Mountains and Djebel Musa), the Strait of Gibraltar, the bay stretching west toward Algeciras, and the twinkling Costa del Sol arcing eastward. The views are especially crisp on brisk off-season days. Below you (to the east) stretches a vast, vegetation-covered slope—part of a giant catchment system built by the British in the early 20th century to collect rainwater for use by the military garrison and residents. Broad sheets once covered this slope, catching the rain, and sending it through channels to reservoirs carved inside the rock. (Gibraltar's water is now provided through a desalination system.)
• *Up at the summit, you'll likely see some of the famed...*

▲▲Apes of Gibraltar

The Rock is home to about 200 "apes" (actually, tailless Barbary macaques—a type of monkey). Taxi tours stop at the Apes' Den, but if you're on your own, you'll probably see them at the top and at various points on the walk back down (basically, the monkeys cluster anywhere that tourists do—hoping to get food). The males are bigger, females have beards, and newborns are black. They live about 15 to 20 years. Legend has it that as long as the monkeys remain here, so will the Brits. (According to a plausible local legend, when word

came a few decades back that the ape population was waning, Winston Churchill made a point to import reinforcements.) Keep your distance from the monkeys. Guides say that for safety reasons, "They can touch you, but you can't touch them." And while guides may feed them, you shouldn't—it disrupts their diet and encourages aggressive behavior, not to mention it's illegal and there's a £500 fine. Taxi drivers have been known to feed them, but have recently been warned to stop. Beware of the monkeys' kleptomaniac tendencies; they'll ignore the peanut in your hand and claw after the full bag in your pocket. Because the monkeys associate plastic bags with food, keep your bag close to your body: Tourists who wander by absentmindedly, loosely clutching a bag, are apt to have it stolen by a purse-snatching simian.

• *If you're hiking down, you'll find that your options are clearly marked at most forks. I'll narrate the longest route down, which passes all the sights en route.*

From the top cable-car station, exit and head downhill on the well-paved path (toward Africa). You'll pass the viewpoint for taxi tours (with monkeys hanging around, waiting for tour groups to come feed them), pass under a ruined observation tower, and eventually reach a wide part of the road. Most visitors will want to continue to St. Michael's Cave (skip down to that section), but you also have an opportunity to hike (or ride a shuttle bus) steeply up to...

O'Hara's Battery

At 1,400 feet, this is the actual highest point on the Rock. A massive 9.2-inch gun sits on the summit, where a Moorish lookout post once stood. The battery was built after World War I, and the last test shot was fired in 1974. Locals are glad it's been mothballed—during test firings, they had to open their windows, which might otherwise have shattered from the pressurized air blasted from this gun. The battery was recently opened to the public; you can go inside to see not only the gun, but also the powerful engines underneath that were used to move and aim it. The iron rings you see every 30 yards or so along the military lanes around the Rock once anchored pulleys used to haul up guns like the huge one at O'Hara's Battery.

Cost and Hours: £3, not covered by £10 nature reserve ticket, shuttle runs up every 20 minutes when open, Mon-Fri 10:00-17:00, closed Sat-Sun.

• *From the crossroads below O'Hara's Battery, taking the right (downhill) fork leads you down to a restaurant and shop, then the entrance to...*

▲St. Michael's Cave

Studded with stalagmites and stalactites, eerily lit, and echoing with classical music, this cave is dramatic, corny, and slippery when wet. Considered a one-star sight since Neolithic times, these caves were alluded to in ancient Greek legends—when the caves were believed to be the Gates of Hades (or the entrance of a tunnel to Africa). All taxi tours stop here (entry included in cost of taxi tour). This sight requires a long walk for cable-car riders (who must have the £10 nature reserve ticket to enter; same hours as other nature reserve sights). Walking through takes about 15 minutes; you'll pop out at the gift shop.

• *From here, most will head down to the Apes' Den (see next paragraph), but serious hikers have the opportunity to curl around to* **Jews' Gate** *at the tip of the Rock, then circle around the back of the Rock on the strenuous* **Mediterranean Steps** *(leading back up to O'Hara's Battery). To do this, turn sharply left after St. Michael's Cave and head for Jews' Gate. Since it's on the opposite side from the town, it's the closest thing in Gibraltar to "wilderness." If this challenging 1.5-to-2-hour hike sounds enjoyable, ask for details at the TI.*

The more standard route is to continue downhill. At the three-way fork, you can take either the middle fork (more level) or the left fork (hillier, but you'll see monkeys at the Apes' Den) to the Siege Tunnels. The **Apes' Den,** *at the middle station for the cable car, is a scenic terrace where monkeys tend to gather, and where taxi tours stop for photo ops.*

Continue on either fork (they converge), following signs for Siege Tunnels, for about 30 more minutes. Eventually you'll reach a terrace with three flags (from highest to lowest: United Kingdom, Gibraltar, EU) and a fantastic view of Gibraltar's airport, "frontier" with Spain, and the Spanish city of La Línea de la Concepción. From here, the Military Heritage Centre is beneath your feet (described later), and it's a short but steep hike up to the...

▲Siege Tunnels

Also called the Upper Galleries, these chilly tunnels were blasted out of the rock by the Brits during the Great Siege by Spanish and French forces (1779-1783). The clever British, safe inside the Rock, wanted to chip and dig to a highly strategic outcrop called "The Notch," ideal for mounting a big gun. After blasting out some ventilation holes for the miners, they had an even better idea: Use gunpowder to carve out a whole network of tunnels with shafts that

would be ideal for aiming artillery. Eventually they excavated St. George's Hall, a huge cavern that housed seven guns. These were the first tunnels inside the Rock; more than a century and a half later, during World War II, 30 more miles of tunnels were blasted out. Hokey but fun dioramas help recapture a time when Brits were known more for conquests than for crumpets. All taxi tours stop here (entry included in cost of taxi tour); hikers must have the £10 nature reserve ticket to enter (same hours as other nature reserve sights).

• *Hiding out in the bunker below the three flags (go down the stairs and open the heavy metal door—it's unlocked) is the...*

Military Heritage Centre

This small, one-room collection features old military photographs from Gibraltar. The second room features a poignant memorial to the people who "have made the supreme sacrifice in defence of Gibraltar" (covered by nature reserve ticket—but tickets rarely checked, same hours as other nature reserve sights).

• *From here, the road switchbacks down into town. At each bend in the road you'll find one of the next three sights.*

City Under Siege

This hokey exhibit is worth a quick walk-through if you've been fascinated by all this Gibraltar military history. Displayed in some of the first British structures built on Gibraltar soil, it re-creates the days of the Great Siege, which lasted for more than three and a half years (1779-1783)—one of 14 sieges that attempted but failed to drive the Brits off the Rock. With evocative descriptions, some original "graffiti" scratched into the wall by besieged Gibraltarians, and some borderline-hokey dioramas, the exhibit explains what it was like to live on the Rock, cut off from the outside world, during those challenging times (covered by nature reserve ticket—but tickets rarely checked, same hours as other nature reserve sights).

World War II Tunnels

This privately run operation takes you on a tour through some of the tunnels carved out of the Rock during a much later conflict than the others described here. You'll emerge back up at the Military Heritage Centre.

Cost and Hours: £8, not covered by £10 nature reserve ticket; must show proof of £0.50 nature reserve fee payment; daily 10:00-16:30.

Moorish Castle

Actually more a tower than a castle, this recently restored building is basically an empty shell. (In the interest of political correctness, the tourist board recently tried to change the name to "Medieval Castle"...but it *is* Moorish, so the name didn't stick.) It was constructed on top of the original castle built in A.D. 711 by the Moor Tarik ibn Ziyad, who gave his name to Gibraltar.

• *The tower marks the end of the Upper Rock Nature Reserve. Heading downhill, you begin to enter the upper part of modern Gibraltar. While you could keep on twisting down the road, keep an eye out for staircase shortcuts into town (most direct are the well-marked Castle Steps).*

Nightlife in Gibraltar

Compared to the late-night bustle of Spain, where you'll see young parents out strolling with their toddlers at midnight, Gibraltar is extremely quiet after-hours. Main Street is completely dead (with the exception of a few lively pubs, mostly a block or two off the main drag). Head instead to the **Ocean Village** complex, a five-minute walk from Casemates Square, where the boardwalk is lined with bars, restaurants, and a casino. Another waterfront locale—a bit more sedate—is the **Queensway Quay Marina.** (Both areas are described later, under "Eating in and near Gibraltar.") Kids love the **King's Bastion Leisure Centre** (described earlier, under "Helpful Hints").

Some pubs, lounges, and discos—especially on Casemates Square—offer live music (look around for signs, or ask at the TI). **O'Callaghan Eliott Hotel** hosts free live jazz on Thursday and Saturday evenings.

Sleeping in and near Gibraltar

Gibraltar is not a good value for accommodations. There are only a handful of hotels and (disappointingly) no British-style B&Bs. As a general rule, the beds are either bad or overpriced. Remember, you'll pay a 20 percent premium if paying with euros—pay with pounds or by credit card. I've ranked them as **$** Budget: £40-70; **$$** Moderate: £70-100; **$$$** Pricier: £100-135; and **$$$$** Splurge: Over £135.

As an alternative, consider staying at one of my recommended accommodations in La Línea de la Concepción, across the border from Gibraltar in Spain, where hotels are a much better value.

IN GIBRALTAR TOWN

$$$$ O'Callaghan Eliott Hotel, with four stars, boasts a rooftop pool with a view, a fine restaurant, bar, terrace, inviting sit-a-bit public spaces, and 122 modern, stylish business-class rooms—all with balconies (air-con, elevator, pay parking, centrally located at Governor's Parade 2, up Library Street from main drag, tel. 70500, www.ocallaghanhotels.com, eliott@ocallaghanhotels.com).

$$ Bristol Hotel offers 60 basic, slightly worn English rooms in the heart of Gibraltar (air-con, elevator, swimming pool; limited free parking—first come, first served; Cathedral Square 10, tel. 76800, www.bristolhotel.gi, reservations@bristolhotel.gi).

$ Cannon Hotel is a well-located, run-down dive with the only cheap hotel rooms in town. Its 16 rooms (most with wobbly cots and no private bathrooms) look treacherously down on a little patio (family rooms, includes full English breakfast, behind cathe-

dral at Cannon Lane 9, tel. 51711, www.cannonhotel.gi, cannon@
sapphirenet.gi).

ACROSS THE BORDER, IN LA LÍNEA

Staying in Spain—in the border town of La Línea de la Concepción—offers an affordable, albeit less glamorous, alternative to
sleeping in Gibraltar. The streets north of the bus station are lined
with inexpensive *hostales* and restaurants. These options are just a
few blocks from the La Línea bus station and an easy 15-minute
walk to the border—get directions when you book. All but Oh!tels
Campo are basic, family-run *hostales*, offering simple, no-frills
rooms at a good price for a mix of tourists and refinery and port
laborers.

$$$ Oh!tels Campo de Gibraltar is a huge blocky building,
with 227 cookie-cutter rooms spread over seven floors. It's a big,
friendly business-class hotel that is just blocks from the border,
around the corner from the bus station. It's also easy to access by
car as it's on the main road coming into town. Stay here if you rent-
ed a car to avoid lining up to cross the border. Ask for a room on
the top floors with expansive views of the Rock (air-con, elevator,
pool, large patio, underground pay parking, at the intersection of
Avenida Príncipe de Asturias and Avenida del Ejército,
tel. 956-178-213, www.ohtelscampodegibraltar.es, recepcion.
campodegibraltar@ohtels.es).

$ Hostal Margarita is a bit farther from the border, but its
fresh, modern rooms are a step above the other *hostales* in the area
(air-con, elevator, limited pay parking, Avenida de España 38, tel.
856-225-211, www.hostalmargarita.com, info@hostalmargarita.
com).

¢ Hostal La Campana has 17 rooms at budget prices. Run by
Ivan and his dad Andreas, this place is simple, clean, and friendly,
but lacks indoor public areas except for its breakfast room (air-
con, elevator, limited free street parking, pay parking in nearby
underground garage, just off Plaza de la Constitución at Calle
Carboneros 3, tel. 956-173-059, www.hostalcampana.es, info@
hostalcampana.es).

Eating in and near Gibraltar

IN GIBRALTAR TOWN

Take a break from *jamón* and sample some English pub grub: fish-
and-chips, meat pies, jacket potatoes (baked potatoes with fillings),
or a good old greasy English breakfast. English-style beers in-
clude chilled lagers and room-temperature ales, bitters, and stouts.
In general, the farther you venture away from Main Street, the
cheaper and more local the places become. Since budget-priced

English food isn't exactly high cuisine, the best plan may be to stroll the streets and look for the pub with the ambience you like best (various options: lots of chatting, sports fans riveted to a football match, noisy casino machines, or whatever). I've listed a few of my favorites next. Or venture to one of Gibraltar's more upscale recent developments at either end of the old town: Ocean Village or Queensway Quay.

Downtown, near Main Street

$ The Clipper pub offers filling meals—including some salads and all-day breakfast—and Murphy's stout on tap (Mon-Sat 9:30-22:00, Sun 10:30-22:00, on Irish Town Lane, tel. 79791).

$$ The Star Bar, which claims that it's "Gibraltar's Oldest Bar," is on a quiet side street with an unpubby, modern interior (daily 8:00-22:00, on Parliament Lane off Main Street, across from Corner House Restaurant, tel. 75924).

$ Carpenter's Arms is a fast, cheap-and-cheery café run by the Methodist church with a missionary's smile. It's upstairs in the Methodist church on Main Street (Mon-Fri 9:30-14:00, closed Sat-Sun and Aug, volunteer-run, 100 yards past the Governor's Residence at 297 Main Street).

$$$ Gauchos is a classy, atmospheric steakhouse actually inside the wall, just outside Casemates Square (daily 12:00-16:00 & 19:00-23:00, Waterport Casemates, tel. 59700).

Casemates Square Food Circus: The big square at the entrance of Gibraltar contains a variety of restaurants, ranging from fast food (fish-and-chips joint, Burger King, and Pizza Hut) to inviting pubs spilling out onto the square. The **$$ All's Well** pub serves everything from Moroccan tagine to fish-and-chips, and offers pleasant tables with umbrellas under leafy trees (daily 10:00-19:00, tel. 72987). Fruit stands and cheap takeout food stalls bustle just outside the entry to the square at the **Market Place** (Mon-Sat 9:00-14:00, closed Sun).

Groceries: Eroski City, the Spanish supermarket chain, sits at the corner of Casemates Square and Winston Churchill Avenue (Sun-Fri 8:00-20:00, closed Sat). The **Bon Bon Cash & Carry** minimarket is on the main drag, off Cathedral Square (daily 9:30-19:00, Main Street 239). Nearby, **Marks & Spencer** has a small food market on the ground floor, with fresh-baked pastries and lots of UK snacks (Mon-Thu 9:00-19:00, Fri 11:00-18:00, Sat 9:30-17:00, closed Sun).

Ocean Village

This development is the best place to get a look at the bold new face of Gibraltar. Formerly a dumpy port, it's been turned into a swanky

marina fronted by glassy high-rise condo buildings. The boardwalk arcing around the marina is packed with shops, restaurants, and bars— Indian, Mexican, sports bar, pizza parlor, Irish pub, fast food, wine bar, and more. Anchoring everything is Gibraltar's casino. While the whole thing can feel a bit corporate, it offers an enjoyable 21st-century contrast to the "English village" vibe of Main Street (which can be extremely sleepy after-hours).

Queensway Quay Marina

To dine in yacht-club ambience, stroll the marina and choose from a string of restaurants serving the boat-owning crowd. When the sun sets, the quay-side tables at each of these places are prime dining real estate. **$$$ Waterfront Restaurant** serves up Indian and classic British fare in its lounge-lizard interior and at great marina-side tables outside (daily 9:00-24:00, last orders at 22:45, tel. 45666). Other options include Indian, Italian, trendy lounges, and (oh, yeah) Spanish.

IN LA LÍNEA

The pedestrian street Calle Real, several blocks north of the La Línea bus station, is lined with inexpensive cafeterias, restaurants, and tapas bars. La Línea doesn't offer anything particularly out of the ordinary, but you could try the local indoor/outdoor ambience of **La Parada** for *pescadito frito*—typical Andalusian batter-fried fish (Calle Duque de Tetuán 2, Plaza de la Iglesia, tel. 856-121-696).

Gibraltar Connections

BY BUS

The nearest bus station to Gibraltar is in La Línea de la Concepción in Spain, five minutes from the border (tel. 956-291-168 or 956-172-396). The nearest train station is at Algeciras, which is the region's main transportation hub.

From La Línea de la Concepción by Bus to: **Algeciras** (8/day, less on weekends, 45 minutes), **Tarifa** (2/day direct to Cádiz, 1 hour; more possible with change in Algeciras, 1.5 hours), **Málaga** (4/day, 3 hours), **Ronda** (no direct bus, transfer in Algeciras; Algeciras to Ronda: 1/day, 3 hours), **Granada** (3/day, 6-7 hours, change in Algeciras), **Sevilla** (5/day, 4-4.5 hours), **Córdoba** (1/day, 5 hours), **Madrid** (1/day, 8 hours).

BY PLANE

From Gibraltar, you can fly to various points in Britain: British Airways flies to London Heathrow (www.ba.com); EasyJet connects to London Gatwick and Liverpool (www.easyjet.com); and Monarch Airlines goes to London Luton and Manchester (www.monarch.co.uk). The airport is easy to reach; after all, you can't enter town without crossing its runway, one way or another (airport code: GIB, www.gibraltarairport.gi).

Tarifa

Mainland Europe's southernmost town is whitewashed and Arab-feeling, with a lovely beach, an old castle, restaurants swimming in fresh seafood, inexpensive places to sleep, enough windsurfers to sink a ship, and best of all, hassle-free boats to Morocco. Though Tarifa is pleasant, the main reason to come here is to use it as a springboard to Tangier, Morocco—a remarkable city worth ▲▲.

As I stood on Tarifa's town promenade under the castle, looking across the Strait of Gibraltar at the almost-touchable Morocco, my only regret was that I didn't have this book to steer me clear of gritty Algeciras on earlier trips. Tarifa, with 35-minute boat transfers to Tangier departing about every hour, is the best jumping-off point for a Moroccan side-trip, as its ferry route goes directly to Tangier's city-center Medina Port. (The other routes, from Algeciras or Gibraltar, take you to the Tangier MED Port, 25 miles east of Tangier city.) For details on taking the ferry to Tangier from Tarifa—or joining an easy belly-dancing-and-shopping excursion-type tour—see the Tangier chapter.

Don't expect blockbuster sights or a Riviera-style beach resort. Tarifa is a town where you just feel good to be on vacation. Its atmospheric old town and long, broad stretch of wild Atlantic beachfront more than compensate for the more functional parts of this port city. The town is a hip and breezy mecca among windsurfers, drawn here by the strong winds created by the bottleneck at the Strait of Gibraltar. Tarifa is mobbed with young German and French adventure seekers in July and August (but can be quiet off-season). This crowd from all over Europe (and beyond) makes Tarifa one of Spain's trendiest-feeling towns. It has far more artsy, modern hotels than most Spanish towns its size, a smattering of fine boutique shopping, and restaurant offerings that are atypically eclectic for normally same-Jane Spain—you'll see vegetarian and organic, Italian and Indian, gourmet burgers and tea houses, and on each corner, it seems, there's a stylish bar-lounge with techno music, mood lighting, and youthful Europeans just hanging out.

Orientation to Tarifa

The old town, surrounded by a wall, slopes gently up from the water's edge (and the port to Tangier). The modern section stretches farther inland from Tarifa's fortified gate.

Tourist Information: The TI is on Paseo de la Alameda (Mon-Fri 10:00-13:30 & 16:00-18:00, Sat-Sun 10:00-13:30; hours may be longer in summer and shorter on slow or bad-weather days, tel. 956-680-993, www.aytotarifa.com, turismo@aytotarifa.com).

Experiencia Tarifa: This organization, run by can-do Quino of the recommended Hostal Alborada, produces a good free magazine and town map featuring hotels, restaurants, and a wide array of activities (also online at www.experienciatarifa.com).

ARRIVAL IN TARIFA

By Bus: The bus station is on Calle Batalla del Salado, about a five-minute walk from the old town. (The TI also has bus schedules.) Buy tickets directly from the driver if the station is closed (Mon-Thu 7:30-12:30 & 14:15-18:00, Fri 8:30-12:30 & 14:15-16:45, Sun 14:00-20:00, closed Sat, bus station tel. 956-807-059, Comes bus company tel. 902-199-208, www.tgcomes.es). To reach the old town, walk away from the wind turbines perched on the mountain ridge.

By Car: If you're staying in the center of town, follow signs for *Alameda* or *Puerto,* and continue along Avenida de Andalucía to Tarifa's one traffic light. Take the next left after the light, down Avenida de la Constitución, to find the TI, ferry ticket offices, and the port. You can pay to park on the street here (€1/hour, get parking ticket from machine) or look for free street parking just beyond the port customs building (on the harbor, at the base of the castle). During the busiest summer months (July-Aug), these street spaces fill up, in which case you'll need to use a pay lot or park farther out, in the new town (for more on parking, see "Helpful Hints," next).

HELPFUL HINTS

Wi-Fi: Hotels, cafés, and restaurants in the heart of the old town and even along the beach offer Wi-Fi access for customers.

Laundry: Top Clean Tarifa will wash, dry, and fold your clothes (full service only, same-day service if you drop off early in the morning, Mon-Fri 10:00-14:00 & 18:00-22:00, Sat 10:00-14:00, closed Sun, Avenida de Andalucía 24, tel. 956-680-303).

Tickets and Tours to Morocco: Two ferry companies—FRS and InterShipping—make the crossing between Tarifa and Tangier. You can buy tickets for either boat at the port. FRS also has a couple of offices in town. If taking a tour to Tangier, you can book through a ferry company, your hotel, or one of several travel agencies in Tarifa.

Long-Term Parking: Tangier day-trippers looking to leave their cars for the day or overnight can try one of these three long-term lots—on Calle San Sebastián, just off Avenida de Andalucía (€14.50/24 hours, long-stay discounts, secured garage); east of the old-town wall (guarded lot just behind the church, €12.50/24 hours); or the expensive port facility (€28/24 hours).

You can also park for free. Many drivers leave their cars for a few days on the street, especially in free spaces lining the road alongside the port customs building (under the castle). Free street parking is becoming rare in the new town, but look either just north of the old-town walls or near the beach; the little Glorieta de León square, just west of the castle and right near a police station, has a number of free spaces. For any street parking, observe the curb color: Blue lines indicate paid parking, and yellow lines are no-parking areas. If there's no color, it's free.

Excursions: Girasol Adventure offers mountain-bike rentals (€15/day with helmet), guided bike tours, national-park hikes, rock-climbing classes, tennis lessons, and, when you're all done...a massage (€30-60). They also offer tours of Tarifa and Bolonia. Activities generally last a half-day and cost around €25-50. Ask Sabine or Chris for details (Mon-Fri 10:00-14:00 & 18:30-20:30, Sat-Sun 11:00-14:00, Calle Colón 12, tel. 956-627-037, www.girasol-adventure.com).

Sights in Tarifa

Church of St. Matthew (Iglesia de San Mateo)

Tarifa's most important church, facing its main drag, is richly decorated for being in such a small town. Most nights, it seems life squirts from the church out the front door and into the fun-loving Calle Sancho IV El Bravo.

Cost and Hours: Free, daily 8:30-13:00 & 17:30-21:00; English-language leaflets may be inside on the right.

Visiting the Church: Find the fragment of an **ancient tombstone**—a tiny square (eye-level, about the size of this book) in the wall on the right—next to a chapel with a small iron gate (the third one off the right nave). Probably the most important historical item in town, this stone fragment proves there was a functioning church here during Visigothic times, before the Moorish conquest. The tombstone reads, in a kind of Latin Spanish (try reading it), "Flaviano lived as a Christian for 50 years, a little more or less. In death he received forgiveness as a servant of God on March 30, 674. May he rest in peace." If that gets you in the mood to light a candle, switch on an electric "candle" by dropping in a coin. (It works.)

Head back out into the main nave, and face the high altar. A relief of **St. James the Moor-Slayer** (missing his sword) is on the right wall of the main central altar. Since the days of the Reconquista, James has been Spain's patron saint.

The left side of the nave harbors several **statues**—showing typically over-the-top Baroque emotion—that are paraded through town during Holy Week. The **Captive Christ** (with hands bound) evokes a time when Christians were held captive by Moors. The door on the left side of the nave is the **"door of pardons."** For a long time Tarifa was a dangerous place—on the edge of the Reconquista. To encourage people to live here, the Church offered a second helping of forgiveness to anyone who lived in Tarifa for a year. One year and one day after moving to Tarifa, they would have the privilege of passing through this special "door of pardons," and a Mass of thanksgiving would be held in that person's honor.

Castle of Guzmán el Bueno (Castillo de Guzmán el Bueno)

This castle, little more than a concrete hulk in a vacant lot, is interesting only for the harbor views from its ramparts (the interior is undergoing a lengthy restoration and will most likely be closed for

several years). It was named after a 13th-century Christian general who gained fame in a sad show of courage while fighting the Moors. Holding Guzmán's son hostage, the Moors demanded he surrender the castle or they'd kill the boy. Guzmán refused, even throwing his own knife down from the ramparts. It was used on

Tarifa

To **18** via Beach

BULLRING

Accommodations
1. Hotel La Mirada
2. Hostal Alborada
3. La Sacristía
4. Hotel Misiana
5. Dar Cilla Guesthouse & Apartments
6. Casa Blanco
7. La Casa Amarilla
8. Hostal La Calzada
9. Hostal Alameda
10. Hostal Africa
11. Pensión Correo
12. Hostal Villanueva

Eateries
13. El Puerto Restaurante
14. Ristorante La Trattoria
15. Restaurante Morilla
16. La Oca da Sergio
17. Mandrágora
18. To Restaurante Souk & Surla
19. Bar El Francés
20. Café Bar Los Melli & Bar El Pasillo
21. El Otro Melli
22. La Posada
23. Café Central & FIRMM
24. Casino Tarifeño
25. Mesón El Picoteo
26. Confitería La Tarifeña
27. Churrería La Palmera
28. Chilimoso Restaurante

Beach

Atlantic Ocean

To Isla de las Palomas

GLORIETA DE LEON

AV. DE LAS FUERZAS ARMADAS

SPAIN'S SOUTH COAST

his son's throat. Ultimately, the Moors withdrew to Africa, and Guzmán was a hero. *Bueno.*

Cost and Hours: €4; Tue-Sun 11:30-17:00, closed Mon, longer but unpredictable hours some summer evenings; last entry 45 minutes before closing.

Nearby Views: If you skip the castle, you'll get equally good views from the plaza just left of the Town Hall. Following *ayunta-*

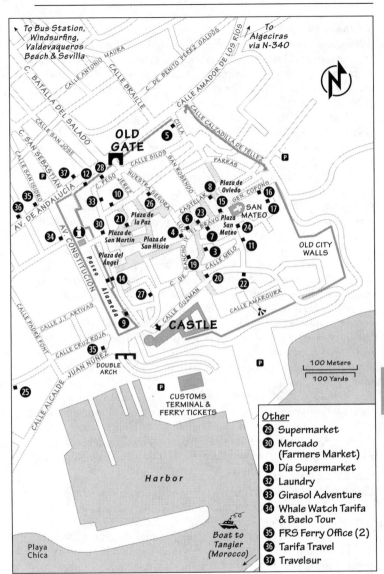

miento signs, go up the stairs to the ceramic frog fountain in front of the Casa Consistorial, and continue left.

Bullfighting

Tarifa has a third-rate bullring where novices botch fights on occasional Saturdays through the summer. Professional bullfights take place during special events in August and September. The ring is a short walk from town. You'll see posters everywhere.

▲Whale-Watching

Several companies in Tarifa offer daily whale- and dolphin-watching excursions. Over the past four decades, people in this area went from eating whales to protecting them and sharing them with 20,000 visitors a year. The Spanish side of the Strait of Gibraltar is protected as part of El Estrecho Natural Park.

For any of the tours, it's wise (but not always necessary) to reserve one to three days in advance. You'll get a multilingual tour and a two-hour boat trip. Sightings occur on nearly every trip: Dolphins and pilot whales frolic here any time of year (they like the food), sperm whales visit from March through July, and orcas pass through in July and August. In bad weather, trips may be canceled or boats may leave instead from Algeciras (in which case, drivers follow in a convoy, people without cars usually get rides from staff, and you'll stand a lesser chance of seeing whales).

The best company is the Swiss nonprofit **FIRMM** (Foundation for Information and Research on Marine Mammals), which gives a 30-minute educational talk before departure. To reserve, it's best to call ahead or stop by one of their two offices (€30-45/person, 1-5 trips/day April-Oct, sometimes also Nov, one office around the corner from Café Central at Pedro Cortés 4, second office inside the ferry port, offices open 9:00-21:00, tel. 956-627-008, mobile 619-459-441, www.firmm.org, mail@firmm.org). If you don't see any whales or dolphins on your tour, you can join another trip for free.

Whale Watch Tarifa is another good option. In addition to a two-hour whale-watching trip (€35), they offer a three-hour orca trip in July and August (€50, Avenida de la Constitución 6, tel. 956-627-013, mobile 639-476-544, www.whalewatchtarifa.net, whalewatchtarifa@whalewatchtarifa.net, run by Lourdes).

Isla de las Palomas

Extending out between Tarifa's port and beaches, this island connected by a spit is the actual "southernmost point in mainland Europe." Walk along the causeway, with Atlantic Ocean beaches stretching to your right and a bustling Mediterranean port to your left. Head to the tip, which was fortified in the 19th century to balance the military might of Britain's nearby Rock of Gibraltar. The actual tip, still owned by the Ministry of Defense, is closed to the public, but a sign at the gate still gives you that giddy "edge of the world" feeling.

▲▲Beach Scene

Tarifa's vast, sandy, and untamed beach stretches west from Isla de las Palomas for about five miles. You can walk much of its length on the Paseo Marítimo, a wide, paved walkway that fronts the sand and surf. Beach cafés and benches along the way make good

resting or picnicking stops. Pick up the paseo where the causeway leads out to Isla de las Palomas, near Playa Chica. You'll join dog walkers, runners, and neighbors comparing notes about last night's rainstorm (they get some doozies here). Keep in mind that this is the Atlantic—the waves can be wild and the wind strong (if you're looking for calm, secluded coves, spend your beach time in Nerja instead). On windy summer days, the sea is littered with sprinting windsurfers, while kitesurfers' kites flutter in the sky. Paddleboarding is also popular.

Those with a car can explore farther (following the N-340 road toward Cádiz). It's a fascinating scene: A long string of funky beach resorts is packed with vans and fun-mobiles from northern Europe under mountain ridges lined with modern energy-generating windmills. The various resorts each have a sandy access road, parking, a cabana-type hamlet with rental gear, beachwear shops, a bar, and a hip, healthy restaurant. I like Valdevaqueros beach (five miles from Tarifa), with a wonderful thatched restaurant serving hearty salads, paella, and burgers. Camping Torre de la Peña also has some fun beach eateries.

In July and August, inexpensive buses do a circuit of nearby campgrounds, all on the waterfront (€2, departures about every 1-2 hours, confirm times with TI). Trying to get a parking spot in August can take the joy out of this experience.

Nightlife in Tarifa

You'll find plenty of enjoyable nightspots—the entire town seems designed to cater to a young, international crowd of windsurfers and other adventure travelers. Just stroll the streets of the old town and dip into whichever trendy lounge catches your eye. For something more sedate, the evening paseo fills the park-like boulevard called Paseo de la Alameda (just outside the old-town wall); the Almedina bar hosts flamenco shows every Thursday (at the south end of town, just below Plaza de Santa María); and the theater next to the TI sometimes has musical performances (ask at the TI or look for posters).

Sleeping in Tarifa

Room rates vary with the season: lowest in winter and highest during Easter and from mid-June through September. Many hotels are closed in winter months and reopen the first week of March.

OUTSIDE THE CITY WALL

These hotels are about five blocks from the old town, close to the main drag, Batalla del Salado, in the plain, modern part of town. While in a drab area, they are well-run oases that are close to the beach and the bus station, with free and easy street parking.

$$ Hotel La Mirada, which feels sleek and stark, has 25 mod and renovated rooms—most with sea views at no extra cost. While the place lacks personality, it's well-priced and comfortable, with expansive sea views from it's large roof terrace with inviting lounge chairs (elevator, Calle San Sebastián 41, tel. 956-684-427, www. hotel-lamirada.com, reservas@hotel-lamirada.com, Antonio and Salvador).

$ Hostal Alborada is a squeaky-clean, family-run 37-room place with two attractive courtyards and modern conveniences. Father Rafael—along with sons Quino (who speaks English and is generous with travel tips), Fali, and Carlos—are happy to help make your Morocco tour or ferry reservation, or arrange any other activities you're interested in. If they're not too busy, they'll even give you a free lift to the port (RS%, air-con, pay laundry, Calle San José 40, tel. 956-681-140, www.hotelalborada.com, info@hotelalborada.com).

INSIDE OR NEXT TO THE CITY WALL

The first three listings are funky, stylish boutique hotels in the heart of town—*muy* trendy and a bit full of themselves.

$$$ La Sacristía, formerly a Moorish stable, now houses travelers who want stylish surroundings. It offers 10 fine and uniquely decorated rooms, mingling eclectic elements of chic Spanish and Asian style. They offer spa treatments, custom tours of the area, and occasional special events—join the party since you won't sleep (sometimes includes breakfast, air-con, massage room, sauna, small roof terrace, very central at San Donato 8, tel. 956-681-759, www. lasacristia.net, tarifa@lasacristia.net).

$$$ Hotel Misiana has 15 comfortable, recently remodeled, spacious rooms above a bar-lounge. Their designer gave the place a mod pastel boutique-ish ambience. To avoid noise from the lounge below, which is open until 3:00 in the morning, request a room on a higher floor (minimum stays of 2-4 nights in high season, double-paned windows, elevator, 100 yards directly in front of the church at Calle Sancho IV El Bravo 16, tel. 956-627-083, www.misiana. com, info@misiana.com).

$$$ Dar Cilla Guesthouse & Apartments is a Moroccan-influenced *riad* (or guesthouse), built into the town wall and remodeled into eight chic apartments surrounding a communal courtyard. Each apartment has a kitchen and is decorated in modern Moroccan style, with earth-tone walls, terracotta-tiled floors, and Moroccan rugs (family rooms; 2-, 4- and 7-night minimums; bigger rooms have air-con, large roof terrace with remarkable bird's-eye view over the old town to the sea, just east of the old-town gate at Calle Cilla 7, tel. 653-467-025, www.darcilla.com, info@darcilla.com).

$$ Casa Blanco, where minimalist meets Moroccan, is the newest reasonably priced designer hotel on the block. Each of its seven rooms (with double beds only—no twins) is decorated (and priced) differently. The place is decked out with practical amenities (minifridge and stovetop) as well as romantic touches—loft beds, walk-in showers, and subtle lighting (small roof terrace, reception open 9:00-14:00 only, off main square at Calle Nuestra Señora de la Luz 2, mobile 622-330-349, www.hotelcasablanco.com, info@hotelcasablanco.com).

$$ La Casa Amarilla ("The Yellow House") offers 10 posh apartments with tiny kitchens, plus three smaller studios with modern decor (family rooms, reception is across the street from Café Central at La Bodega de la Casa Amarilla, Calle Sancho IV El Bravo 9, tel. 956-681-993, www.tarifastay.com, lacasaamarilla@tarifastay.com).

$$ Hostal La Calzada has eight airy, well-appointed rooms right in the lively old-town thick of things, though the management is rarely around (closed Dec-March, air-con, 20 yards from church at Calle Justino Pertinez 7, tel. 956-681-492, www.hostallacalzada.com, info@hostallacalzada.com).

$ Hostal Alameda, overlooking a square where the local children play, glistens with pristine marble floors and dark red decor. The main building has 11 bright rooms and the annex has 16 more modern rooms; both face the same delightful square (air-con, Paseo de la Alameda 4, tel. 956-681-181, www.hostalalameda.com, reservas@hostalalameda.com, Antonio).

$ Hostal Africa, with 13 bright rooms and an inviting roof terrace, is buried on a very quiet street in the center of town. Its dreamy blue-and-white color scheme and stripped-down feel give it a Moorish ambience (laundry service, storage for boards and bikes, Calle María Antonia Toledo 12, tel. 956-680-220, mobile 606-914-294, www.hostalafrica.com, info@hostalafrica.com, charming Eva and Miguel keep the reception desk open 9:00-24:00).

$ Pensión Correo rents nine simple rooms (two sharing one bathroom, one available with kitchen during high season) at a fair value. Room 8 has a private roof terrace, and rooms 6 and 7 have gorgeous views of the town (reception 9:00-22:00, family room, Coronel Moscardo 8, tel. 956-680-206, www.pensioncorreo.com, welcome@pensioncorreo.com).

¢ Hostal Villanueva offers 17 remodeled rooms at budget prices. It's simple, clean, and friendly. It lacks indoor public areas, but has an inviting terrace overlooking the old town on a busy street. Reconfirm your reservation by phone the day before you arrive (just west of the old-town gate at Avenida de Andalucía 11, access from outside the wall, tel. 956-684-149, hostalvillanueva@ hotmail.com).

Eating in Tarifa

I've grouped my recommendations below into two categories: Sit down to a real restaurant meal, or enjoy a couple of the many characteristic tapas bars in the old town.

RESTAURANTS
Near the Port

$$$ El Puerto, in an untouristy area near the causeway out to Isla de las Palomas, has a great reputation for its pricey but very fresh seafood. Locals swear that it's a notch or two above the seafood places in town (Thu-Mon 12:00-16:00 & 20:00-24:00, Tue-Wed 12:00-16:00 only, Avenida Fuerzas Armadas 13, tel. 956-681-914).

$$$ Ristorante La Trattoria, on the Alameda, is a good Italian option, with cloth-napkin class, friendly staff, and ingredients from Italy. Sit inside, near the wood-fired oven, or out along the main strolling street (daily 13:00-16:00 & 19:30-23:00, closed Wed off-season; Paseo de la Alameda, tel. 956-682-225).

Near the Church

$$ Restaurante Morilla, facing the church, is on the town's prime piece of people-watching real estate. This is a real restaurant (tapas sold only at the stand-up bar and sometimes at a few tables), with good indoor and outdoor seating. It serves tasty local-style fish, grilled or baked—your server will tell you about today's fish; it's sold by weight, so confirm the price carefully (daily 9:00-24:00, Calle Sancho IV El Bravo, tel. 956-681-757).

$$ La Oca da Sergio, cozy and fun, is one of the numerous pizza-and-pasta joints supported by the large expat Italian community. Sergio prides himself on importing authentic Italian ingredients (indoor and outdoor seating; daily 13:00-16:00 & 20:00-24:00, closed Tue off-season; around the left side of the church and straight back, just before the Moorish-style old-folks' home at Calle General Copons 6; tel. 956-681-249, mobile 615-686-571).

$$$ Mandrágora serves a stylish fusion of Moroccan, Mediterranean, and Asian flavors: lamb shanks with plums and almonds, classic tagines and couscous, generous salads, and the best-anywhere *berenjenas* (eggplant drizzled with honey). It's a white-tablecloth place, but your servers will be wearing jeans (dinner from

18:30 Mon-Sat, closed Sun, tucked just behind the church at Calle Independencia 3, tel. 956-681-291).

In the New Town

These two restaurants are in a residential area just above the beach, about a 15-minute walk along the Paseo Marítimo (or an easy car or taxi ride) from the old town. They're worth a detour for their great food, and for the chance to see an area away from the main tourist zone (though the sushi bar is near the beach and is no stranger to tourists). As you walk the promenade, keep going until you pass a bright-blue apartment complex, then turn right into the passageway at Restaurant Chill. You'll find Surla just ahead on the left (in a corner of the large beige building). Souk is straight ahead, across the street and up two flights of stairs. To drive there, head up Calle San Sebastián, which turns into Calle Pintor Pérez Villalta. You'll see the Surla building on the left.

$$ Restaurante Souk serves a tasty mix of Moroccan, Indian, and Thai cuisine in a dark, exotic, romantic, purely Moroccan ambience. The ground floor (where you enter) is a bar and atmospheric teahouse, while the dining room is downstairs (daily 20:00-24:00, closed Tue off-season; good wine list, Mar Tirreno 46, tel. 956-627-065, friendly Claudia).

$$ Surla, a hipster surfer bar, serves up breakfast, lunch, and dinner, including wonderfully executed sushi, along with good coffee and free Wi-Fi. Situated just a few steps above the beachfront walkway, it's at the center of a sprawling zone of après-surf hangouts. They also offer delivery (€16-21 shareable sushi platters, daily 9:00-24:00, Tue-Wed until 20:00, closed Wed off-season, Calle Pintor Pérez Villalta 1—look for the surfboard nailed to the corner of the building, tel. 956-685-175).

TAPAS

$$ Bar El Francés is a thriving place where "Frenchies" (as the bar's name implies) Marcial and Alexandra serve tasty little plates of tapas. This spot is popular for its fine *raciones* (€6-14) and tapas (€1.50-2)—especially octopus *(pulpo a la brasa),* fish in brandy sauce *(pescado en salsa al cognac),* and garlic-grilled tuna *(atún a la plancha).* It's standing-and-stools only inside, but the umbrella-shaded terrace outside has plenty of tables and is an understandably popular spot to enjoy a casual meal (no tapas on terrace; order off regular menu). Show this book and Marcial will be happy to bring you a free glass of sherry (open Fri-Wed long hours June-Aug; closed Thu; closed Dec-Feb; Calle Sancho IV El Bravo 21A—from Café Central, follow cars 100 yards to first corner on left; mobile 685-857-005).

$$ Café Bar Los Melli is a local favorite for feasts on barrel tables set outside. This family-friendly place, run by Ramón and Juani, is a hit with locals and offers a good chorizo sandwich and *patatas bravas*—potatoes with a hot tomato sauce served on a wooden board (Thu-Tue 20:00-24:00, Sat-Sun also 13:00-16:00, closed Wed; across from Bar El Francés—duck down the little lane next to the Radio Alvarez sign and it will be on your left; mobile 605-866-444). **$$ Bar El Pasillo,** next to Los Melli, also serves tapas (closed midday and Mon-Tue). **$$ El Otro Melli,** run by Ramón's brother José, is a few blocks away on Plaza de San Martín.

$$ La Posada, a local-feeling place a block beyond the main tourist zone (and just up the street from Los Melli), takes pride in its fresh ingredients. It has a small dining room, a nondescript bar with a giant stone beer tap that's a replica of the city's first communal faucet, and tables out front near the real thing (July-Aug daily 13:00-16:30 & 20:00-24:00; Sept-June Wed-Mon 20:00-24:00 and Sat-Sun 13:00-16:30, closed Tue; Calle Guzman el Bueno 3A, mobile 636-929-449).

$$ Café Central is *the* happening place nearly any time of day—it's the perch for all the cool tourists. With a decidedly international vibe, it's less authentically Spanish than the others I've listed. The bustling ambience and appealing setting in front of the church are better than the food, but they do have breakfast with eggs, good salads, and impressive healthy fruit drinks when fruit is in season (daily 8:30-24:00, off Plaza San Mateo, near church, tel. 956-682-877).

$$ Casino Tarifeño is just to the sea side of the church. It's an old-boys' social club "for members only," but offers a musty Andalusian welcome to visiting tourists, including women. Wander through. It has a low-key bar with tapas, a TV room, a card room, and a lounge. There's no menu, but prices are standard. Just point and say the size you want: tapa, *media-ración,* or *ración.* A far cry from some of the trendy options around town, this is a local institution (daily 12:00-24:00).

$$ Mesón El Picoteo is a small, characteristic bar popular with locals and tourists alike for its good tapas and *montaditos.* Eat in the casual, woody interior or at one of the barrel tables out front (long hours daily, a few blocks west of the old town on Calle Mariano Vinuesa, tel. 956-681-128).

OTHER EATING OPTIONS

Breakfast or Dessert: $ Confitería La Tarifeña serves super pastries and flan-like *tocino de cielo* (daily 9:00-21:00, at the top of Calle Nuestra Señora de la Luz, near the main old-town gate).

$ Churrería La Palmera serves breakfast before most hotels and cafés have even turned on the lights—early enough for you to get your coffee fix, and/or bulk up on *churros* and chocolate, before hopping the first ferry to Tangier (daily 6:00-13:00, Calle Sanchez IV El Bravo 34).

Vegetarian: Literally a small hole in the old town wall, **$ Chilimoso** serves fresh and healthy vegetarian options, homemade desserts, and a variety of teas. It's a rare find in meat-loving Spain. Eat at one of the few indoor tables, or get it to-go and find a bench on the nearby Paseo de la Alameda (daily 12:30-15:30 & 19:30-23:00, just west of the old-town gate on Calle del Peso).

Windsurfer Bars: If you have a car, head to the string of beaches. Many have bars and fun-loving thatched restaurants that keep the wet-suit gang fed and watered.

Picnics: Stop by the *mercado municipal* (farmers market, Mon-Sat 8:00-14:00, closed Sun, in old town, inside gate nearest TI), any grocery, or the **superSol** supermarket (Mon-Sat 9:30-21:30, closed Sun, at Callao and San José), or the **Día** supermarket (daily, Calle San Sebastián 30) both near the hotels in the new town.

Tarifa Connections

TARIFA

From Tarifa by Bus to: La Línea/Gibraltar (6/day direct, 1 hour, starting around 12:00; more possible with change in Algeciras, 1.5 hours), **Algeciras** (14/day, fewer on weekends, 45 minutes, Comes), **Jerez** (1/day, 2 hours, more frequent with transfer in Cádiz), **Sevilla** (4/day, 2.5-3 hours), and **Málaga** (3/day, 2.5-4 hours, Comes and Portillo). Bus info: Comes (tel. 956-291-168, www.tgcomes.es), Portillo (tel. 902-450-550, http://portillo.avanzabus.com).

Ferries from Tarifa to Tangier, Morocco: Two boat companies make the 35-minute journey to Tangier's city-center Medina Port about every hour.

ALGECIRAS

Algeciras (ahl-*h*eh-THEE-rahs) is only worth leaving. It's useful to the traveler mainly as a transportation hub, with trains and buses to destinations in southern and central Spain (it also has a ferry to Tangier, but it takes you to the Tangier MED port about 25 miles from Tangier city—going from Tarifa is much better). If you're headed for Gibraltar or Tarifa by public transport, you'll almost certainly change in Algeciras at some point.

Everything of interest is on Juan de la Cierva, which heads inland from the port. The **TI** is about a block in (tel. 956-784-131), followed by the side-by-side **train station** (opposite Hotel Octavio) and **bus station** three more blocks later.

Trains: If arriving at the train station, head out the front door: the bus station is ahead and on the right; the TI is another three blocks (becomes Juan de la Cierva when the road jogs), also on the right; and the port is just beyond.

From Algeciras by Train to: Madrid (4/day, half transfer in Antequera, 5.5-6 hours, arrives at Atocha), **Ronda** (5-6/day, 1.5-2 hours), **Granada** (3/day, 4-5 hours), **Sevilla** (3/day, 5-6 hours, transfer at Antequera or Bobadilla, bus is better), **Córdoba** (2/day direct on Altaria, 3 hours; more with transfer in Antequera or Bobadilla, 4 hours), **Málaga** (3-4/day, 4 hours, transfer in Bobadilla; bus is faster). With the exception of the route to Madrid, these are particularly scenic trips; the best (though slow) is the mountainous journey to Málaga via Bobadilla.

Buses: Algeciras is served by three bus companies (Comes, Portillo, and Autocares Valenzuela), all located in the same terminal (called San Bernardo Estación de Autobuses) next to Hotel Octavio and directly across from the train station. The companies generally serve different destinations, but there is some overlap. Compare schedules and rates to find the most convenient bus for you. By the ticket counter you'll find an easy red letter board that lists departures *(salidas)* and arrivals *(llegadas)*. Lockers are near the platforms—purchase a token at the machines.

From Algeciras by Bus: Comes (tel. 956-291-168, www.tgcomes.es) runs buses to **La Línea/Gibraltar** (2/hour, fewer on weekends, 45 minutes), **Tarifa** (12/day, fewer on weekends, 45 minutes), **Ronda** (1/day, 3.5 hours), **Sevilla** (4/day, 3-4 hours), **Jerez** (2/day 2.5 hours), **Nerja** (1/day, 3.5 hours), and **Madrid** (5/day, 8 hours).

Portillo (tel. 956-654-304, http://portillo.avanzabus.com) offers buses to **Málaga** (hourly, 2 hours *directo*, 3 hours *ruta*), **Málaga Airport** (2/day, 2 hours), and **Granada** (3/day *directo*, 4 hours; 1/day *ruta*, 5.5 hours).

Autocares Valenzuela (tel. 956-702-609, www.grupovalenzuela.com) runs the most frequent direct buses to **Sevilla** (8/day, fewer on weekends, 2.5-3 hours) and **Jerez** (6/day, fewer on weekends, 1.5 hours).

Ferries from Algeciras to Tangier, Morocco: Although it's possible to sail from Algeciras to Tangier, the ferry takes you to the Tangier MED Port, which is 25 miles east of Tangier city and a hassle. You're better off taking a ferry from Tarifa: They sail directly to the port in Tangier. If you must sail from Algeciras, buy your ticket at the port (skip the divey-looking travel agencies littering the town). Official offices of the boat companies are inside the main port building, directly behind the helpful little English-speaking info kiosk (8-22 ferries/day, port open daily 6:45-21:45, tel. 956-585-463).

ROUTE TIPS FOR DRIVERS

Tarifa to Gibraltar (45 minutes): This short drive takes you past a silvery-white forest of windmills, from peaceful Tarifa past Algeciras to La Línea (the Spanish town bordering Gibraltar). Passing Algeciras, continue in the direction of Estepona. At San Roque, take the La Línea-Gibraltar exit.

Gibraltar to Nerja (130 miles): Barring traffic problems, the trip along the Costa del Sol is smooth and easy by car—much of it on a new highway. Just follow the coastal highway east. After Málaga, follow signs to *Almería* and *Motril*.

Nerja to Granada (80 miles, 1.5 hours, 100 views): Drive along the coast to Motril, catching the slower N-323 or the quicker A-44 north for about 40 miles to Granada. While scenic side-trips may beckon, don't arrive late in Granada without a confirmed hotel reservation.

MOROCCO

Al-Maghreb

A young country with an old history, Morocco is a photographer's delight and a budget traveler's dream. It's cheap, exotic, and easier and more appealing than ever. Along with a rich culture, Morocco offers plenty of contrast—from beach resorts to bustling desert markets, from jagged mountains to sleepy, mud-brick oasis towns. And there's been a distinct new energy since King Mohammed VI took the throne in 1999.

Morocco ("Marruecos" in Spanish; "Al-Maghreb" in Arabic) also provides a good dose of culture shock—both bad and good. It makes Spain seem meek and mild. You'll encounter oppressive friendliness, pushy hustlers, brutal heat, the Arabic language, the Islamic faith, ancient cities, and aggressive beggars.

While Morocco is clearly a place apart from Mediterranean Europe, it doesn't really seem like Africa either. It's a mix, reflecting its strategic position between the two continents. Situated on the Strait of Gibraltar, Morocco has been flooded by waves of invasions over the centuries. The Berbers, the native population, have had to contend with the Phoenicians, Carthaginians, Romans, Vandals, and more.

The Arabs brought Islam to Morocco in the seventh century A.D. and stuck around, battling the Berbers in various civil wars. A series of Berber and Arab dynasties rose and fell; the Berbers won out and still run the country today.

From the 15th century on, European countries carved up much of Africa. By the early 20th century, most of Morocco was under French control, and strategic Tangier was jointly ruled by multiple European powers as an international zone. The country wasn't granted independence until 1956. In the late 1970s, Morocco itself became an invading country, grabbing Spain's Western Sahara territory

Morocco

SPAIN

MOROCCO
AFRICA

Mediterranean Sea

Algeciras
Tarifa
GIBRALTAR (U.K.)
Tangier
Ceuta (SPAIN)
Tangier MED
Tétouan
Asilah
Larache
Chefchaouen
Sidi Kacem
Rif Mtns.
Kenitra
Rabat
Meknes
Fès
Ifrane
Casablanca
Azrou
Oued Zem
Atlas Mtns.
Safi
Beni Mellal
Er-Rachidia
Marrakech
Tinerhir
Erfoud
Essaouira
Rissani
Ouarzazate
Merzouga
Agadir
Zagora
Sahara Desert
Oujda
ALGERIA
Bouarfa

Atlantic Ocean

100 Miles
200 Kilometers

To Timbuktu

NOTE: Bus lines parallel all rail lines

Rail — Bus

and causing the relatively few inhabitants there to clamor for independence. Western Sahara's claim still has not been settled by the United Nations.

Unfortunately, most of the English-speaking Moroccans the typical tourist meets are vendors, hustling to make a buck. Many visitors develop some intestinal problems by the end of their visit. Most women traveling alone are harassed on the streets by annoyingly persistent but generally harmless men. And in terms of efficiency, Morocco makes Spain look like Sweden. When you cruise south across the Strait of Gibraltar, leave your busy itineraries and split-second timing behind. Morocco must be taken on its own terms. In Morocco things go smoothly only *"Inshallah"*—if God so wills.

Politics and Safety: As throughout the Arab world, Morocco has had its share of political unrest in recent years. Widespread but mostly peaceful protests in 2011, influenced by the Arab Spring, called for greater democracy and economic reforms. A new constitution, adopted later that year, gave more power to the legislative branch and the prime minister—the ostensible head of government (although critics say King Mohammed VI retained the actual authority).

Morocco is also struggling to reconcile tensions between Is-

Islam 101

Islam has more than a billion adherents worldwide, and traveling in an Islamic country is an opportunity to better understand the religion. This admittedly basic and simplistic outline (written by a non-Muslim) is meant to help travelers from the Christian West understand a very rich but often misunderstood culture.

Muslims, like Christians and Jews, are monotheistic. They call God "Allah." The most important person in the Islamic faith is the prophet Muhammad, who lived in the sixth and seventh centuries A.D. The holy book of Islam is the Quran, believed by Muslims to be the word of Allah as revealed to Muhammad.

The "five pillars" of Islam are the core tenets of the faith. Followers of Islam should:

1. Say and believe, "There is only one God, and Muhammad is his prophet."
2. Pray five times a day, facing Mecca. Modern Muslims explain that it's important for this ritual to include washing, exercising, stretching, and thinking of God.
3. Give to the poor (one-fortieth of your wealth, if you are not in debt).
4. Fast during daylight hours through the month of Ramadan. Fasting is a great social equalizer and helps everyone to feel the hunger of the poor.
5. Make a pilgrimage to Mecca. Muslims who can afford it, and who are physically able, are required to travel to the sacred sites in Mecca and Medina at least once in their lifetimes.

Just as it helps to know about spires, feudalism, and the saints to comprehend European sightseeing, a few basics on Islam help make your sightseeing in Morocco more meaningful.

MOROCCO

lamist and secular factions within its government and in the region. Bombings attributed to Islamic fundamentalists killed 45 people in Casablanca in 2003 and 17 in Marrakech in 2011, and were met with widespread condemnation by the Moroccan people.

Americans pondering a visit may wonder how they'll be received in this Muslim nation. Al Jazeera blares from televisions in all the bars, but I've seen no angry graffiti or posters and felt no animosity toward American individuals there (even on a visit literally days after US forces killed Osama bin Laden). And it's culturally enriching for Westerners to experience Morocco—a Muslim monarchy with many women still in traditional dress and roles, succeeding on its own terms without embracing modern Western "norms."

If you're still concerned, check the state department's website for travel advisories: www.travel.state.gov.

Hustler Alert: Moroccans may be some of Africa's wealthiest people, but you are still incredibly rich to them. This imbalance  causes predictable problems. Wear your money belt. Assume con artists are cleverer than you. Haggle when appropriate; prices skyrocket for tourists. You'll attract hustlers like flies at every famous tourist site or whenever you pull out your guidebook or a map. In the worst-case scenario, they'll lie to you, get you lost, blackmail you, and pester the heck out of you. Never leave your car or baggage where you can't get back to it without someone else's "help." Anything you buy in a guide's company gets him a 20 percent commission. Normally, locals, shopkeepers, and police will come to your rescue if the hustlers' heat becomes unbearable. Consider hiring a guide, since it's helpful to have a translator, and once you're "taken," the rest seem to leave you alone.

Marijuana Alert: In Morocco, marijuana *(kif)* is as illegal as it is popular, a fact that many Westerners in local jails would love to remind you of. As a general rule, just walk right by those hand-carved pipes in the marketplace. Some dealers who sell it cheap make their profit after you get arrested. Cars and buses are stopped and checked by police routinely throughout Morocco—especially in the north and in the Chefchaouen region, which is Morocco's *kif* capital.

Health: Morocco is much more hazardous to your health than Spain. Eat in clean—not cheap—places. Peel fruit, eat only cooked vegetables, and drink reliably bottled water (Sidi Ali or Sidi Harazem). When you do get diarrhea—and you should plan on it—adjust your diet (small and bland meals, no milk or grease) or fast for a day, but make sure you replenish lost fluids. Relax: Most diarrhea is not serious, just an adjustment that will run its course.

Closed Days and Ramadan: Friday is the Muslim day of rest, when most of the country (except Tangier) closes down. During the major month-long religious holiday of Ramadan (May 16-June 14 in 2018), Muslims focus on prayer and reflection. Following Islamic doctrine, they refrain during daylight hours from eating, drinking (including water), smoking, and having sex. On the final day of Ramadan, Muslims celebrate Eid (an all-day feast and gift-

MOROCCO

giving party, similar to Christmas), and travelers may find some less-touristy stores and restaurants closed.

Money: Euros work here (as do dollars and pounds). If you're on a five-hour tour, bring along lots of €1 and €0.50 coins for tips, small purchases, and camel rides. But if you plan to do anything independently, change some money into Moroccan dirhams or find an ATM upon arrival (10 dh = about $1).

Information: Travel information, English or otherwise, is rare here. For an extended trip, bring a supplemental guidebook: Lonely Planet and Rough Guide both publish good ones, available at home and in Spain. Once in Morocco, buy the best map you can find. If you need to ask someone for help, it's helpful to have towns, roads, and place names written in Arabic. A good English guidebook available locally is *Tangier and Its Surroundings* by Juan Ramón Roca.

Language: With its unique history of having been controlled by so many different foreign and domestic rulers, Tangier is a babel of languages. Most locals speak Arabic first and French second (all Moroccans must learn it in schools); sensing that you're a foreigner, they'll most likely address you in French. Spanish ranks third, and English a distant fourth. The Arabic squiggle-script, its many difficult sounds, and the fact that French is Morocco's second language combine to make communication tricky for English-speaking travelers. A little French goes a long way, but learn a few words in Arabic. Have your first local friend help you with the pronunciation:

English	Arabic
Hello ("Peace be with you")	*Salaam alaikum* (sah-LAHM ah-LAY-koom)
Hello (response: "Peace also be with you")	*Wa alaikum salaam* (wah ah-LAY-koom sah-LAHM)
Please	*Min fadlik* (meen FAHD-leek)
Thank you	*Shokran* (SHOH-kron)
Excuse me	*Ismahli* (ees-SMAH-lee)
Yes	*Yeh* (EE-yeh)
No	*Lah* (lah)
Give me five (kids enjoy this...not above but straight ahead)	*Ham sah* (hahm sah)
OK	*Wah hah* (wah hah)
Very good	*Miz yen biz ef* (meez EE-yehn beez ehf)
Goodbye	*Maa salama* (mah sah-LEM-ah)

Moroccans have a touchy-feely culture. Expect lots of hugs if you make an effort to communicate. When greeting someone, a handshake is customary, followed by placing your right hand over your heart. Listen carefully and write new words phoneti-

MOROCCO

cally. Bring an Arabic phrase book. It helps to know that *souk* means a particular market (such as for leather, yarn, or metal-work), while a *kasbah* is loosely defined as a fortress (or a town within old fortress walls). In markets, I sing, "la la la la la" to my opponents. *Lah shokran* means "No, thank you."

TANGIER

Tanja

Go to Africa. As you step off the boat, you realize that the crossing (less than an hour) has taken you farther culturally than did the trip from the US to Spain. Morocco needs no museums; its sights are living in the streets. For decades, its once-grand coastal city of Tangier deserved its reputation as the "Tijuana of Africa." But that has changed. King Mohammad VI is enthusiastic about Tangier, and there's a fresh can-do spirit in the air. The town is as Moroccan as ever...yet more enjoyable and less stressful.

MOROCCO IN A DAY?

Though Morocco certainly deserves more than a day, many visitors touring Spain see it in a side-trip. And, though such a short sprint through Tangier is only a tease, it's far more interesting than another day in Spain. A day in Tangier gives you a good introduction to Morocco, a legitimate taste of North Africa, and an authentic slice of Islam. All you need is a passport (no visa or shots required) and around €65 for a tour package or the round-trip ferry crossing.

Your big decisions are when to sail; whether to go on your own or with a ferry/guided tour day-trip package; and how long to stay (day-trip or overnight). Of these, the most important question is:

With a Tour or on My Own? Because the ferry company expects you to do a lot of shopping (providing them with kickbacks), it's actually about the same cost to join a one-day tour as it is to buy a round-trip ferry ticket. Do you want the safety and comfort of having Morocco handed to you on a user-friendly platter? Or do you want the independence to see what you want to see, with fewer cultural clichés and less forced shopping? There are pros and cons to each approach, depending on your travel style.

On a **package tour,** visitors are met by a guide, taken on a bus tour and a walk through the old-town market, offered a couple of crass Kodak moments with snake charmers and desert dancers, and given lunch with live music and belly dancing. Then they visit a big shop and are hustled back down to their boat where—five hours after they landed—they return to the First World thankful they don't have diarrhea.

The alternative is to take the ferry and see Morocco **on your own.** Morocco is cheap and relatively safe. Independent adventurers get to see all the sights and avoid all the kitsch. You can catch a morning boat and spend the entire day, returning that evening; extend with an overnight in Tangier; or even head deeper into Morocco (if you do that, you'll need another guidebook).

My preferred approach is a **hybrid:** Go to Morocco "on your own," but arrange in advance to meet a local guide to ease your culture shock and accompany you to your choice of sights. While this costs a bit more than joining a package tour, ultimately the cost difference (roughly €10-20 more per person) is pretty negligible, considering the dramatically increased cultural intimacy.

Time Difference: Morocco is on Greenwich Mean Time (like Great Britain), so it's one hour behind Spain. It observes Daylight Saving Time at the same time as Europe (Morocco "springs forward" in late March and "falls back" in late October), except during the month of Ramadan—May 15-June 14 in 2018. During Ramadan, Morocco is two hours behind Spain (which means the daylight fasting hours end earlier in the evening).

In general, ferry and other schedules use the local time (if your boat leaves Tangier "at 17:00," that means 5:00 p.m. Moroccan time—not Spanish time). Be sure to change your watch when you get off the boat.

Terminology: Note that the Spanish refer to Morocco as "Marruecos" (mar-WAY-kohs) and Tangier as "Tánger" (TAHN-*h*air).

Going on Your Own, by Ferry from Tarifa

While the trip to Tangier can be made from various ports, only the ferry from Tarifa takes you to Tangier's city-center port, the Tangier Medina Port (Spaniards call it the *Puerto Viejo,* "Old Port"). The port is in the midst of a massive renovation and beautification project expected to last through 2018 or later. (The project keeps advancing, but locals tend to be overly optimistic about the finish date.) The improvements will stick the fishermen on one side, renovate the beach, extend the pier to accommodate large cruise ships, and create a marina for yachts, while more directly connecting the port with the old town.

Note that ferries also travel from Algeciras and Gibraltar to

Morocco, but they arrive at the Tangier MED Port, 25 miles from downtown (connected to the Tangier Medina Port by a free one-hour shuttle bus). But the most logical route for the typical traveler is the one I'll describe here—sailing from Tarifa to Tangier's city-center Medina Port.

Ferry Schedule and Tickets: Two companies make the 35-minute crossing from Tarifa, Spain to Tangier, Morocco, with a ferry departing about every hour from 8:00 to 22:00. **FRS** ferries depart Tarifa on odd hours (9:00, 11:00, and so on; tel. 956-681-830, www.frs.es) and **InterShipping** ferries leave Tarifa most even hours (8:00,

10:00, and so on—but confirm schedule; tel. 956-684-729, www.intershipping.es). Returns are just the opposite: FRS departs Tangier on even hours and InterShipping on odd hours. Both companies have ticket offices at the Tarifa ferry terminal. Prices are roughly €37 one-way and €67 round-trip. Return boats from Tangier to Tarifa run from about 7:00 to 21:00.

Tickets are easy to get: you can buy them online (exchange your online voucher for a ticket at the port), at the port, through your hotel in Tarifa, or from a Tarifa travel agency (you may be asked for your passport when you buy your ticket). You can also get FRS tickets at their offices in Tarifa: one is just outside the old-town wall, at the corner of Avenida de Andalucía and Avenida de la Constitución (closed Sun, tel. 956-681-830); the other location is near the port on Calle Alcalde Juan Núñez 2 (open daily). You can almost always just buy a ticket and walk on, though in the busiest summer months (July-Aug), the popular 8:00 and 9:00 departures can fill up. Boats are most crowded in July, August, and during the month of Ramadan. A few cross-

ings a year are canceled because of storms or wind, mostly in winter.

Ferry Crossing: The ferry from Tarifa is a fast Nordic hydrofoil that theoretically takes 35 minutes to cross. It often leaves late, but you'll still want to arrive early to give yourself time to clear customs (making the whole trip take closer to an hour). You'll go through Spanish customs at the port and Moroccan customs on the ferry. Whether taking a tour or traveling on your own, you *must* get a stamp (only available on board) from the Moroccan immigration officer: After you leave Tarifa, find the Moroccan customs officer on the boat (usually in a corner booth that's been turned into an impromptu office), line up early, and get your passport and entry paper—which they keep—stamped. The ferry is equipped with WCs, a shop, and a snack bar. Tarifa's modern little terminal has a cafeteria and WCs.

Hiring a Guide: If you forgo a package tour, I recommend hiring a local guide to show you around Tangier.

Returning to Tarifa: It's smart to return to the port about 30 minutes before your ferry departs. For the return trip, you must complete a yellow passport-control form and get an exit stamp at the Tangier ferry terminal before you board.

Taking a Package Tour

Taking a package tour is easier but less rewarding than doing it on your own or with a private local guide. A typical day-trip tour includes a round-trip crossing and a guide who meets your big group at a prearranged point in Tangier, then hustles you through the hustlers and onto your tour bus. Several guides await the arrival of each ferry in Tangier and assemble their groups. (Tourists wear stickers identifying which tour they're with.) All offer essentially the same five-hour Tangier experience: a city bus tour, a drive through the ritzy palace neighborhood, a walk through the medina (old town), and an overly thorough look at a sales-starved carpet shop (where prices include a 20  percent commission for your guide and tour company; some carpet shops are actually owned by the ferry company). Longer tours may include a trip to the desolate Atlantic Coast for some rugged African scenery, and the famous ride-a-camel stop (five-minute camel ride for a couple of euros). Any tour wraps up with lunch in a palatial Moroccan setting with live music (and non-Moroccan belly dancing), topped off by a final walk back to your boat through a gauntlet of desperate merchants.

Sound cheesy? It is. But no amount of packaging can gloss over this exotic and different culture. This kind of cultural voyeurism is almost embarrassing, but it's nonstop action.

You rarely need to book a tour more than a day in advance, even during peak season. Tours generally cost about €55-65 (less than a round-trip ferry ticket alone; they are counting on you buying). Prices are roughly the same no matter where you buy. While some agencies run their own tours, others simply sell tickets on excursions operated by FRS or InterShipping. Ultimately, it's the luck of the draw as to which guide you're assigned. Don't worry about which tour company you select. (They're all equally bad.)

Tours leave Tarifa on a variable schedule throughout the day: For example, one tour may depart at 9:00 and return at 15:00, the next could run 11:00-19:00 (offering a longer experience), and the next 13:00-19:00. If you're an independent type on a one-day tour, you could stay with your group until you return to the ferry dock, and then just slip back into town on your own, thinking, "Freedom!" You're welcome to use your return ferry ticket on a later boat. (Note that tickets are *not* interchangeable between the two ferry companies.)

If you want a longer visit, it's cheap to book a package through the ferry company that includes a one-night stay in a Tangier hotel. There are also two-day options with frills (all meals and excursions outside the city) or no-frills (no guiding or meals—€50-60 for a basic overnight, €10-12 extra in peak season; two-day options range from €70-110).

Booking a Package Tour: If you're taking one of these tours, you may as well book directly with the **ferry company** (see contact information earlier, under "Ferry Schedule and Tickets," or visit their offices at the port in Tarifa), or through your **hotel** (you'll pay the same; if you know you want to visit Morocco with a tour, ask your hotel to book it when you reserve). There's not much reason to book with a **travel agency,** but offices all over southern Spain and in Tarifa sell ferry tickets and seats on tours. In Tarifa, Luís and Antonio at Baelo Tour offer Rick Steves readers a 10 percent discount; they also have baggage storage (daily in summer 7:00-21:00, across from TI at Avenida de la Constitución 5, tel. 956-681-242); other Tarifa-based agencies are Tarifa Travel and Travelsur (both on Avenida de Andalucía, above the old-town walls).

Tangier

Artists, writers, and musicians have always loved Tangier. Delacroix and Matisse were drawn by its evocative light. The Beat generation, led by William S. Burroughs and Jack Kerouac, sought the city's multicultural, otherworldly feel. Paul Bowles found his sheltering sky here. From the 1920s through the 1950s, Tangier was an "international city," too strategic to give to any one nation, and jointly governed by as many as nine different powers, including France, Spain, Britain, Italy, Belgium, the Netherlands...and Morocco. The city was a tax-free zone (since there was no single authority to collect taxes), which created a booming free-for-all atmosphere, attracting playboy millionaires, bon vivants, globetrotting scoundrels, con artists, and expat romantics. Tangier enjoyed a cosmopolitan Golden Age that, in many ways, shaped the city visitors see today.

Tangier is always defying expectations. Ruled by Spain in the 19th century and France in the 20th, it's a rare place where signs are in three languages...and English doesn't make the cut. In this Muslim city, you'll find a synagogue, Catholic and Anglican churches, and the town's largest mosque in close proximity.

Because of its "international zone" status, Morocco's previous king effectively disowned the city, denying it national funds

for improvements. Over time, neglected Tangier became the armpit of Morocco. But when the new king—Mohammed VI—was crowned in 1999, the first city he visited was Tangier. His vision has been to restore Tangier to its former glory.

While the city (with a population of 950,000 and growing quickly) has a long way to go, restorations are taking place on a grand scale: the beach has been painstakingly cleaned, the Kasbah is getting spruced up, pedestrian promenades are popping up, and gardens bloom with lush new greenery. A futuristic soccer stadium opened in 2011, and the city-center port is being converted into a huge, slick leisure-craft complex that will handle cruise megaships, yachts, and ferries from Tarifa.

I'm uplifted by the new Tangier—it's affluent and modern without having abandoned its roots. Many visitors are impressed by the warmth of the Moroccan people. Notice how they touch their right hand to their heart after shaking hands or saying, "thank you"—a kind gesture meant to emphasize sincerity. (In Islam, the right hand is seen as pure, while the left hand is impure. Moroc-

TANGIER

cans who eat with their hands—as many civilized people do in this part of the world—always eat with their right hand; the left hand is for washing.)

A visit to Morocco—so close to Europe, yet embracing the Arabic language and script and Muslim faith—lets a Westerner marinated in anti-Muslim propaganda see what Islam aspires to be and can be...and realize it is not a threat.

PLANNING YOUR TIME

If you're not on a package tour, arrange for a guide to meet you at the ferry dock, hire a guide upon arrival, or head on your own to the big square called the Grand Socco to get oriented (you could walk, but it's easier to catch a Petit Taxi from the port to the Grand Socco). Get your bearings with my Grand Socco spin-tour, then delve into the old town (the lower medina, with the Petit Socco, market, and American Legation Museum; and the upper medina's Kasbah, with its museum and residential lanes). With more time, take a taxi to sightsee along the beach and then along Avenue Mohammed VI, through the urban new town, and back to the port. You'll rarely see other tourists outside the tour-group circuit.

Orientation to Tangier

Like almost every city in Morocco, Tangier is split in two: old and new. From the ferry dock you'll see the old town (medina)—encircled by its medieval wall. The old town has the markets, the Kasbah (with its palace and the mosque of the Kasbah—marked by the higher of the two minarets you see), cheap hotels, characteristic guesthouses, homes both decrepit and recently renovated, and 2,000 wannabe guides. The twisty, hilly streets of the old town are caged within a wall accessible by keyhole gates. The larger minaret (on the left) belongs to the modern Mohammed V mosque—the biggest one in town.

The new town, with the TI and modern international-style hotels, sprawls past the port zone to your left. The big square, Grand Socco, is the hinge between the old and new parts of town.

Note that while tourists (and this guidebook) refer to the twisty old town as "the medina," locals consider both the old and new parts of the city center to be medinas.

Tangier is the third-largest city in Morocco, and many visitors assume they'll get lost here. While the city could use more street signs,

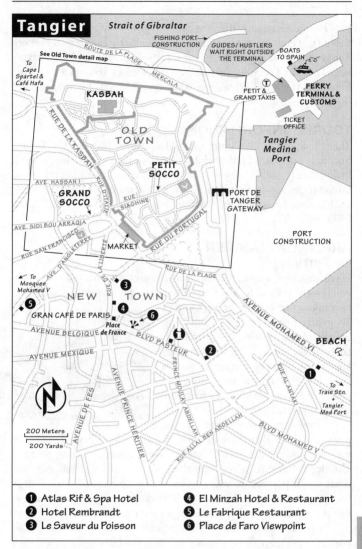

Tangier

Strait of Gibraltar

FISHING PORT
CONSTRUCTION
GUIDES/ HUSTLERS
WAIT RIGHT OUTSIDE
THE TERMINAL
BOATS
TO SPAIN

ROUTE DE LA PLAGE

MERCALA

See Old Town detail map

To
Cape
Spartel &
Café Hafa

PETIT &
GRAND TAXIS

FERRY
TERMINAL &
CUSTOMS

TICKET
OFFICE

KASBAH

RUE DE LA KASBAH

OLD
TOWN

*Tangier
Medina
Port*

AVE. HASSAN I

RUE D'ITALIE

PETIT
SOCCO

GRAND
SOCCO

RUE
SIAGHINE

PORT DE
TANGER
GATEWAY

AVE. SIDI BOU ARRAQIA

RUE DU PORTUGAL

PORT
CONSTRUCTION

RUE SAN FRANCISCO

AVE. D'ANGLETERRE

MARKET

To
Mosquée
Mohamed V

RUE DE LA LIBERTÉ

RUE DE LA PLAGE

NEW

TOWN

③

⑤

GRAN CAFÉ DE PARIS

RUE DU PRINCE

④

⑥

AVENUE MOHAMED VI

BEACH

AVENUE BELGIQUE

*Place
de France*

BLVD PASTEUR

①

AVENUE MEXIQUE

②

PRINCE MOULAY ABDELLAH

①

To
Train Stn.
+
Tangier
Med Port

AVENUE DE FÈS

AVENUE PRINCE HÉRITIER

RUE AL-ANDAK

RUE ALLAL BEN ABDELLAH

BLVD MOHAMED V

200 Meters
200 Yards

① Atlas Rif & Spa Hotel
② Hotel Rembrandt
③ Le Saveur du Poisson
④ El Minzah Hotel & Restaurant
⑤ Le Fabrique Restaurant
⑥ Place de Faro Viewpoint

it's laid out simply, and maps are posted at the major gates. In the maze-like medina, efforts are being made to post street names on ceramic plaques on the corners of buildings, as well as signs directing you to sights in the Kasbah. Nevertheless, you are bound to get turned around. Nothing listed under "Sights in Tangier" is more than a 20-minute walk from the port, which is always downhill. Petit Taxis (described later, under "Getting Around Tangier") are a remarkably cheap godsend for the hot and tired tourist. Use them liberally.

Because so many different colonial powers have had a finger in this city, it goes by many names: In English, it's Tangier; in French, Tanger (tahn-zhay); in Arabic, it's Tanja (TAHN-zhah); in Spanish, Tánger (TAHN-hair); and so on. Unless you speak Arabic, French is the handiest second language, followed by Spanish and (finally) English.

TOURIST INFORMATION

The TI, about a 15-minute gradual uphill walk from the Grand Socco, is not particularly helpful (English is in short supply, but a little French goes a long way). But at least you can pick up a free town brochure—in French only—with a town map (Mon-Fri 8:30-16:30, closed Sat-Sun, in new town at Boulevard Pasteur 29, tel. 0539-948-050).

ARRIVAL IN TANGIER
By Ferry

If you're taking a tour, just follow the leader. If you're on your own, you'll want to head for the Grand Socco to get oriented. You can either take a taxi (cheap) or walk (about 10 gently but potentially confusing uphill minutes through the colorful lanes of the medina). The entire port area is undergoing extensive reconstruction through at least 2018, so you may find some changes from the way things are described here.

Given the renovations at the port, and the hilly nature of the city, a small blue **Petit Taxi** is the best way to get into town (described later, under "Getting Around Tangier"). Because prices from the port are not regulated, confirm what you'll pay before you hop in. An honest cabbie will charge you 20-30 dh (about $3) for a ride from the ferry into town; less scrupulous drivers will try to charge closer to 100 dh.

If you're determined to **walk** into town, head out through the port entrance gate (by the mosque), cross the busy street to an open lot, and then follow the old city walls, with the landmark Hotel Continental on your right. After passing the Hotel Continental, look for a street ramp at the end of the lot. Go up this ramp onto Rue de Portugal, and follow it as it curves around the old city wall. At the corner of the wall, take the first right onto Rue de la Plage. This will lead you past the market and into the Grand Socco.

By Plane

The Tangier Airport (Aeroport Ibn Battouta, airport code: TNG) is small, new-feeling, slick, and well-organized, with ATMs, cafés, and other amenities. Air Arabia, Iberia, Royal Air Maroc, Ryanair, and Vueling fly from here to Madrid and other cities in Spain, as well as other major European destinations.

To get into downtown Tangier, taxis should run you about 150 dh and take 30 minutes. If spending the night, ask your hotel to arrange for a taxi and the fare in advance, which feels less intimidating—they generally charge the same as hiring a taxi on your own.

GETTING AROUND TANGIER

There are two types of taxis: avoid the big, beige Mercedes "Grand Taxis," which are the most aggressive and don't use their meters (they're designed for longer trips outside the city center, are OK for the airport, but have been known to take tourists for a ride in town...in more ways than one). Look instead for **Petit Taxis**—blue with a yellow stripe (they fit 2-3 people). These generally use their meters, are very cheap, and only circulate within the city. However, at the port, Petit Taxis are allowed to charge whatever you'll pay without using the meter, so it's essential to agree on a price up front.

Be aware that Tangier taxis sometimes "double up"—if you're headed somewhere, the driver may pick up someone else who's going in the same direction. However, you don't get to split the fare: Each of you pays full price (even though sometimes the other passenger's route takes you a bit out of your way).

When you get in a taxi, be prepared for a white-knuckle experience. Drivers, who treat lanes only as suggestions, prefer to straddle the white lines rather than stay inside them. Pedestrians add to the mayhem by fearlessly darting out every which way along the street. It's best to just close your eyes.

HELPFUL HINTS

Money: The exchange rate is 10 dh = about \$1; 11 dh = about €1.

If you're on a tour or only day-tripping, you can just stick with euros—most businesses happily take euros or even dollars. But for a longer stay, it's classier to use the local currency—and you'll save money. If you're on your own, it's fun to get a pocketful of dirhams.

An ATM is located at the port exchange desks in the parking lot of the port, and a few others are around the Grand Socco (look for one just to the left of the archway entrance into the medina); more are opposite the TI along Boulevard Pasteur. ATMs work as you expect them to, and are often less hassle than exchanging money. Banks and ATMs have uniform rates.

If you can't find an ATM, exchange desks are quick, easy, and fair. (Just understand the buy-and-sell rates—they should be within 10 percent of one another with no other fee.

If you change €50 into dirhams and immediately change the dirhams back, you should have about €45.) Look for the official *Bureaux de Change* offices, where you'll get better rates than at the banks. There are some on Boulevard Pasteur, and a handful between the Grand and Petit Soccos. The official change offices all offer the same rates, so there's no need to shop around.

Convert your dirhams back to euros before catching the ferry—it's cheap and easy to do here (change desks at the port keep long hours), but very difficult once you're back in Spain.

Phoning: To call Tangier from Spain, dial 00 (Europe's international access code), 212 (Morocco's country code), then the local number (dropping the initial zero). To dial Tangier from elsewhere in Morocco, dial the local number in full (keeping the initial zero). If roaming, one of the three Moroccan carriers will pick up your signal: Maroc Telecom, Orange, or Inwi.

Keeping Your Bearings: Tangier's maps and street signs are frustrating. I ask in French for the landmark: *Où est...?* ("Where is...?," pronounced oo ay, as in *"oo ay medina?"* or *"oo ay Kasbah?"*). It can be fun to meet people this way. However, most people who offer to help you (especially those who approach you) are angling for a tip—young and old, locals see dollar signs when a traveler approaches. To avoid getting unwanted company, ask for directions only from people who can't leave what they're doing (such as the only clerk in a shop) or from women who aren't near men. There are fewer hustlers in the new (but less interesting) part of town. Be aware that most people don't know the names of the smaller streets (which don't usually have signs), and tend to navigate by landmarks. In case you get the wrong directions, ask three times and go with the consensus. If there's no consensus, it's time to hop into a Petit Taxi.

Mosques: Tangier's mosques (and virtually all of Morocco's) are closed to non-Muslim visitors.

Tours in Tangier

LOCAL GUIDES

If you're on your own, you'll be to street guides what a horse's tail is to flies...all day long. Seriously—it can be exhausting to constantly deflect come-ons from anyone who sees you open a guidebook. If only to have your own translator, and a shield from less scrupulous touts who hit up tourists constantly throughout the old town, I recommend hiring a guide.

When you hire a guide, be very clear about your interests.

Guides, hoping to get a huge commission from your purchases, can cleverly turn your Tangier day into the Moroccan equivalent of the Shopping Channel. Truth be told, some of these guides would work for free, considering all the money they make on commissions when you buy stuff. State outright that you want to experience the place, its people, and the culture—not its shopping. Request an outline of what your tour will include, and once your tour is underway, if your guide deviates from your expectations, speak up.

The guides that I've worked with and recommend here speak great English, are easy to get along with, will meet you at the ferry dock, and charge fixed rates. Any of these guides will make your Tangier experience more enjoyable for a negligible cost. They can also book your ferry tickets for the same cost as booking directly: They'll give you a reference number to give at the ticket office in Tarifa, then you'll pay them for the tickets when you meet in Tangier. While each has their own specific itineraries, the two basic options are more or less the same: a half-day walking tour around the medina and Kasbah (generally 3-5 hours); or a full-day "grand tour" that includes the walk around town as well as a minibus ride to outlying viewpoints—the Caves of Hercules and Cape Spartel (7-8 hours, generally also includes lunch at your expense in a restaurant the guide suggests). Prices are fairly standard from guide to guide. If you're very pleased with your guide, he'll appreciate a tip. If you're displeased with your guide, please let me know at www.ricksteves.com.

Aziz ("Africa") Benami is energetic and fun to spend the day with. He seems to be on a first-name basis with everyone in town, and will happily tailor a tour to your interests (half-day walking tour-€15/person, full-day minibus and walking tour-€35/person, full-day tour including round-trip ferry to/from Tarifa-€79/person, traditional Moroccan lunch-€15/person, market visit and cooking class-€65/person or €55 if added to walking tour, also offers day and multiday trips to destinations across Morocco, mobile 06-6105-0537, from the US or Canada dial toll-free 1-888-745-7305, www.tangierprivateguide.com, info@tangierprivateguide.com).

Aziz Begdouri is an old Rick Steves friend who runs private tours of Tangier and the area. He also manages the recommended hotel La Maison Blanche. Contact him in advance to decide how he can create a tour for you (€45/person, mobile 06-6163-9332, Spanish mobile 600-625-655, aziztour@hotmail.com).

Ahmed Taoumi, who has been guiding for more than 30

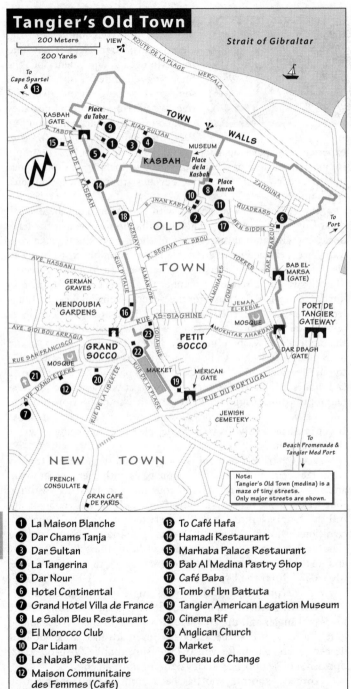

Tangier's Old Town

200 Meters

200 Yards

VIEW

Strait of Gibraltar

ROUTE DE LA PLAGE

MERCALA

TOWN

WALLS

To Cape Spartel & **13**

KASBAH GATE

R. TABOR

Place du Tabor

R. RIAD SULTAN

9

1   **3**   **4**

MUSEUM

15

5

KASBAH

Place de la Kasbah

14

Place Amrah

ZAITOUNA

8

10

QUADRASS

11

R. JNAN KABTAN

2

17

BEN SIDDIK

6

To Port

18

OLD

GZENAYA

ALMANZOR

RUE D'ITALIE

R. SEGAVA   R. SBOU

TOWN

TORRES

DAR EL BAROUD

BAB EL-MARSA (GATE)

AVE. HASSAN I

GERMAN GRAVES

MENDOUBIA GARDENS

ALMOHADES

CONM

JEMAA EL-KEBIR

PORT DE TANGIER GATEWAY

16

RUE AS-SIAGHINE

MOSQUE

AVE. SIDI BOU ARRAQIA

23

TOUAHINE

PETIT SOCCO

MOKHTAR AHARDAN

DAR DBAGH GATE

RUE SAN FRANCISCO

GRAND SOCCO

22

MARKET

MÉRICAN GATE

Mosque

21

AVE. D'ANGLETERRE

12

20

RUE DE LA LIBERTÉE

19

RUE DU PORTUGAL

7

RUE DE LA PLAGE

JEWISH CEMETERY

To Beach Promenade & Tangier Med Port

N E W   T O W N

FRENCH CONSULATE

GRAN CAFÉ DE PARIS

Note:
Tangier's Old Town (medina) is a maze of tiny streets.
Only major streets are shown.

1 La Maison Blanche
2 Dar Chams Tanja
3 Dar Sultan
4 La Tangerina
5 Dar Nour
6 Hotel Continental
7 Grand Hotel Villa de France
8 Le Salon Bleu Restaurant
9 El Morocco Club
10 Dar Lidam
11 Le Nabab Restaurant
12 Maison Communitaire des Femmes (Café)

13 To Café Hafa
14 Hamadi Restaurant
15 Marhaba Palace Restaurant
16 Bab Al Medina Pastry Shop
17 Café Baba
18 Tomb of Ibn Battuta
19 Tangier American Legation Museum
20 Cinema Rif
21 Anglican Church
22 Market
23 Bureau de Change

years, has a friendly and professorial style (half-day walking tour including short panoramic car ride up into town—€20/person, full-day grand tour with minibus—€35/person, also offers minibus side-trips to nearby destinations and discounted ferry tickets, mobile 06-6166-5429, from Spain dial 00-212-6-6166-5429, www. visitangier.com, taoumitour@hotmail.com).

Abdellatif ("Latif") Chebaa is personable and is dedicated to making visitors comfortable (half-day walking tour—€15/person, grand tour—€35/person, mobile 06-6107-2014, from Spain dial 00-212-6-6107-2014, visittangier@gmail.com).

Other Options: I've had good luck with the **private guides who meet the boat.** If you're a decent judge of character, try interviewing guides when you get off the ferry to find one you click with, then check for an official license and negotiate a good price. These hardworking, English-speaking guides offer their services for the day for €15.

Sights in Tangier

GRAND SOCCO AND NEARBY
▲▲Grand Socco

This big, bustling square is a transportation hub, market, popular meeting point, and the fulcrum between the new town and the old town (medina). A few years ago, it was a pedestrian nightmare and a perpetual traffic jam. But now, like much of Tangier, it's on the rise. Many of the sights mentioned in this spin-tour are described in more detail later in this chapter.

◆ **Self-Guided Spin-Tour:** The Grand Socco is a good place to get oriented to the heart of Tangier. Stand on the square between the fountain and the mosque (the long building with arches and the tall tower). We'll do a slow clockwise spin.

Start by facing the **mosque**—newly remodeled with a long arcade of keyhole arches, and with a colorfully tiled minaret. Morocco is a decidedly Muslim nation, though its take on Islam is

progressive, likely owing to the country's crossroads history. For example, women are relatively free to dress as they like. Five times a day, you'll hear the call to prayer echo across the rooftops of Tangier, from minarets like this one. Unlike many Muslim countries, Morocco doesn't allow

Women in Morocco

Some visitors to Tangier expect to see women completely covered head-to-toe by their kaftans. In fact, only about one-quarter of Moroccan women adhere strictly to this religious code. Some just cover their head (allowing their face to be seen), while others eliminate the head scarf altogether. Some women wear only Western-style clothing. This change in dress visibly reflects deeper shifts in Moroccan attitudes about women's rights.

Morocco is one of the more progressive Muslim countries. As in any border country, contact with other cultures fosters the growth of new ideas. Bombarded with Spanish television and visitors like you, change is inevitable. Another proponent of change is King Mohammed VI, who was only 35 years old when he rose to the throne in 1999. For the first time in the country's history, the king personally selected a female adviser to demonstrate his commitment to change. The king also married a commoner for...get this...*love*. And even more shocking, she's seen in public. (Sexual mores are traditional, however—sex outside of marriage is illegal in Morocco, as is homosexual behavior.)

But recent times have brought transformations to Moroccan society. Schools are now coed (something taken for granted in the West for decades), although many more boys than girls are enrolled in school, especially in rural areas. In 2004, the legal age for women to marry was raised to 18 instead of 15 (although arranged marriages are still commonplace). Other changes made it more difficult to have a second wife. Verbal divorce and abandonment are no longer legal—disgruntled husbands must now take their complaints to court. And for the first time, women can divorce their husbands. If children are involved, whoever takes care of the kids gets the house.

Morocco took another step forward with its 2011 constitutional reforms, which guarantee women "civic and social" equality. But it will take time for changes in the law to be thoroughly translated into practice.

non-Muslims to enter its mosques (with the exception of its biggest and most famous one, in Casablanca). This custom may have originated decades ago, when occupying French foreign legion troops spent the night in a mosque, entertaining themselves with wine and women. Following this embarrassing desecration, it was the French government—not the Moroccans—who instituted the ban that persists today.

Locals say that in this very cosmopolitan city, any time you see a mosque, you'll find a church nearby. Sure enough, peeking up behind the mosque, you can barely make out the white, crenellated top of the **Anglican Church**'s tower (or at least the English flag above it—a red cross on a white field). A fascinating architectural hybrid of Muslim and Christian architecture, this house of worship is well worth a visit.

Also behind the mosque, you can see parts of a sprawling **market.** (This features mostly modern goods; the far more colorful produce, meat, and fish market is across the square.) Those market stalls used to fill the square you're standing in; traditionally the Grand Socco was Tangier's hub for visiting merchants. The gates of town would be locked each evening, and vendors who did not arrive in time spent the night in this area. (Nearby were many cara-vanserai—old-fashioned inns.) But several years ago, this square was dramatically renovated by the visionary king, Mohammed VI, and given a new name: "April 9th 1947 Square," commemorating the date in 1947 when an earlier king, Mohammed V, appealed to his French overlords to grant his country its independence. (France eventually complied, peacefully, in 1956.) In just the last few years, Mohammed VI tamed the traffic, added the fountain you're stand-ing next to, and turned this into a delightfully people-friendly space.

Spin a few more degrees to the right, where you'll see the cren-ellated gateway marked *Tribunal de Commerce*—the entrance to the **Mendoubia Gardens,** a pleasant park with a gigantic tree and a quirky history that reflects the epic story of Tangier (particularly from the 1920s to the 1950s, when multiple foreign powers shared control of this city). At the top of the garden gateway, notice the Moroccan flag: a green five-pointed star on a red field. The five points of the star represent the five pillars of Islam; green is the color of peace, and red represents the struggles of hard-fought Mo-roccan history.

Spinning farther right, you'll see the **keyhole arch** marking the entrance to the medina. (If you need cash, notice the ATM and exchange booths just to the left of this gateway.) To reach the heart of the medina—the Petit Socco (the café-lined little brother of the square you're on now)—go through this arch and take the first right.

In front of the arch, you'll likely see **day laborers** looking for work. Each one rests next to a symbol of the kind of work he spe-cializes in: a bucket of paintbrushes for a painter, a coil of wiring for an electrician, and a loop of hose for a plumber.

Speaking of people looking for work, how many locals have of-fered to show you around ("Hey! What you looking for? I help you!") since you've been standing here, holding this guidebook? Get used to it. While irritating, it's understandable. To these very poor people, you're impossibly rich—your pocket change is at least a good day's wage. If someone pesters you, you can simply ignore them, or say *"Lah shokran"* (No, thank you). But be warned: The moment you engage them, you've just prolonged the sales pitch.

Back to our spin-tour: To the right of the main arch, and just before the row of green rooftops, is the low-profile entrance to the **market** *(souk)*. A barrage on all the senses, this is a fascinating place to explore. The row of green rooftops leads toward Rue de la Plage, with more market action.

Continue spinning another quarter-turn to the tall, white building at the top of the square labeled **Cinema Rif.** This historic movie house still plays films (in Arabic, French, and occasionally English). The street to the left of the cinema takes you to Rue de la Liberté, which eventually leads through the modern town to the TI (about a 15-minute walk). Just to the right of the cinema, notice the yellow terrace, which offers the best view over the Grand Socco (just go up the staircase). It's also part of a café, where you can order a Moroccan tea (green tea, fresh mint, and lots of sugar), enjoy the view over the square, and plot your next move.

▲St. Andrew's Church

St. Andrew's Anglican Church, tucked behind a showpiece mosque, embodies Tangier's mingling of Muslim and Christian tradition. The land on which the church sits was a gift from the

sultan to the British community in 1881, during Queen Victoria's era. Shortly thereafter, this church was built. Although fully Christian, the church is designed in the style of a Muslim mosque. The Lord's Prayer rings the arch in Arabic, as verses of the Quran would in a mosque. Knock on the door—Ali or his son Yassin will greet you and give you a "thank you very much" tour. The garden surrounding the church is a tranquil, parklike cemetery. On Sundays and Thursdays, an im-

TANGIER

promptu Berber **farmers market** occupies the sidewalk out front (about 9:00-13:00).

Cost and Hours: A tip of about 20 dh is appreciated; open daily 9:30-18:00 except closed during Sunday services.

Mendoubia Gardens

This pleasant park, accessed through the castle-like archway off of the Grand Socco, is a favorite place for locals to hang out, and also has a surprising history. Walk through the gateway to see the trunk of a gigantic banyan tree, which, according to local legend, dates from the 12th century. Notice how the extra supportive roots have grown from the branches down to the ground.

The large building to the left—today the business courthouse *(Tribunal de Commerce)*—was built to house the representative of the Moroccan king, back in the early 20th century when Tangier was ruled as a protectorate of various European powers and needed an ambassador of sorts to keep an eye out for Moroccan interests. The smaller house on the right (behind the giant tree) is currently the marriage courthouse (used exclusively for getting married or divorced), but it was once the headquarters of the German delegation in Tangier. France originally kept Germany out of the protectorate arrangement by giving them territory along the Congo River. But in 1941, when Germany was on the rise in Europe and allied with Spain's Franco, it joined the mix of ruling powers in Tangier. Although Germans were only here for a short time (until mid-1942), they have a small cemetery in what's now the big park in front of you. Go up the stairs and around the blocky Arabic monument. At the bases of the trees beyond it, you'll find headstones of German graves...an odd footnote in the very complex history of this intriguing city.

Boulevard Pasteur

In the oldest part of the new town, this street is the axis of cosmopolitan Tangier. The street is lined with legendary cafés, the most storied of which is the Gran Café de Paris, which has been doing business here since 1920 (daily early until late, at Place de France, just across from the French consulate). Moroccans call this the "tennis" street because while sitting at an al fresco café, your head will be constantly swiveling back and forth to watch the passing parade.

A block farther along is the beautiful Place de Faro terrace, with its cannons and views back to Spain. It's nicknamed "Terrace of the Lazy Ones": instead of making the trek down to the harbor, family members came here in the old days to see if they could spot ships returning with loved ones who'd been to Mecca.

MEDINA (OLD TOWN)

Tangier's medina is its convoluted old town—a twisty mess of narrow stepped lanes, dead-end alleys, and lots of local life spilling out into the streets. It's divided roughly into two parts: the lower medina, with the Petit Socco, market, American Legation, and bustling street life; and, at the top, the more tranquil Kasbah.

Lower Medina

A maze of winding lanes and tiny alleys weave through the old-town market area. Write down the name of the gate you came in, so you can enjoy being lost—temporarily. In an effort to help orient hopelessly turned-around tourists, Tangier has installed map signboards with suggested walking tours at the major medina gates.

Petit Socco

This little square, also called Souk Dahel ("Inner Market"), is the center of the lower medina. Lined with tea shops and cafés, it has a romantic quality that has long made it a people magnet. In the 1920s, it was the meeting point for Tangier's wealthy and influential elite; by the 1950s and '60s, it drew Jack Kerouac and his counterculture buddies. Nursing a coffee or a mint tea here, it's easy to pretend you're a Beat Generation rebel, dropping out from Western society and delving deeply into an exotic, faraway culture. More recently, filmmakers have been drawn here. Scenes from both *The Bourne Ultimatum* and *Inception* were filmed on the streets between the Grand and Petit Soccos.

The Petit Socco is ideal for some casual people-watching over a drink. You can go to one of the more traditional cafés, but **Café Central**—with the large awnings and look of a European café—is accessible, and therefore the most commercialized and touristy (coffees, fruit drinks, and meals; long hours daily).

▲▲Market (Souk)

The medina's market, just off the Grand Socco, is a highlight. Wander past piles of fruit, veggies, and olives, countless varieties of bread, and fresh goat cheese wrapped in palm leaves. Phew! You'll find everything but pork.

Entering the market through the door from the Grand Socco, turn right to find butchers, a cornucopia of produce (almost all of it from Morocco), more butchers, piles of olives, and yet more butchers. The chickens are plucked and hung to show they have been killed according to Islamic guidelines *(halal):* Animals are slaughtered with a sharp knife in the name of Allah, head toward Mecca, and drained of their blood. The far aisle (parallel and to the left of where you're walking) has more innards and is a little harder to stomach.

You'll see women vendors— often wearing straw hats decorated with ribbons or colorful striped skirts—scattered around the market; these are Berbers, who ride donkeys to the city from the nearby Rif Mountains, mostly on Tuesdays and Thursdays. (Before taking photos of these women, or any people you see here, it's polite to ask permission.)

Eventually you'll emerge into the large white market of fish-sellers; with the day's catch from both the Mediterranean and the Atlantic, this is like a textbook of marine life. The door at the far end of the fish market pops you out on the Rue Salah El-dine Al Ayoubi; a right turn takes you back to the Grand Socco, but a left turn leads to the (figurative and literal) low end of the market—a world of very rustic market stalls under a corrugated plastic roof. While just a block from the main market, this is a world apart, and not to everyone's taste. Here you'll find cheap produce, junk shops, electronics (such as recordable CDs and old remote controls), old ladies sorting bundles of herbs from crinkled plastic bags, and far less sanitary-looking butchers than the ones inside the main market hall (if that's possible). Peer down the alley filled with a twitching poultry market, which encourages vegetarianism.

The upper part of the market (toward the medina and Petit Socco) has a few food stands, but more nonperishable items, such as clothing, cleaning supplies, toiletries, and prepared foods. Scattered around this part of the market are spice-and-herb stalls (usually marked *hérboriste*), offering a fragrant antidote to the meat stalls. In addition to cooking spices, these sell homegrown Berber cures for ailments. Pots hold a dark-green gelatinous goo—a kind of natural soap.

If you're looking for souvenirs, you won't have to find them... they'll find you, in the form of aggressive salesmen who approach you on the street and push their conga drums, T-shirts, and other trinkets in your face. Most of the market itself is more focused on

Bargaining Basics

No matter what kind of merchandise you buy in Tangier, the shopping is...Moroccan. Bargain hard! The first price you're offered is simply a starting point, and it's expected that you'll try to talk the price way down. Bargaining can become an enjoyable game if you follow a few basic rules:

Determine what the item is worth to you. Before you even ask a price, decide what the item's value is to you. Consider the hassles involved in packing it or shipping it home.

Determine the merchant's lowest price. Many merchants will settle for a nickel profit rather than lose the sale entirely. Work the cost down to rock bottom, and when it seems to have fallen to a record low, walk away. That last price the seller hollers out as you turn the corner is often the best price you'll get. If the price is right, go back and buy.

Look indifferent. As soon as the merchant perceives the "I gotta have that!" in you, you'll never get the best price.

Employ a third person. Use your friend who is worried about the ever-dwindling budget or who doesn't like the price or who is bored and wants to return to the hotel. This can help to bring the price down faster.

Show the merchant your money. Physically hold out your money and offer him "all you have" to pay for whatever you are bickering over. He'll be tempted to just grab your money and say, "Oh, OK."

If the price is too much, leave. Never worry about having taken too much of the merchant's time. They are experts at making the tourist feel guilty for not buying. It's all part of the game.

locals, but the medina streets just above the market are loaded with souvenir shops. Aside from the predictable trinkets, the big-ticket items here are tilework (such as vases) and carpets. You'll notice many shops have tiles and other, smaller souvenirs on the ground floor, and carpet salesrooms upstairs.

▲▲▲Exploring the Medina

Appealing as the market is, one of the most magical Tangier experiences is to simply lose yourself in the lanes of the medina. A first-time visitor cannot stay oriented—so don't even try. I just wander, knowing that uphill will eventually get me to the Kasbah and downhill will eventually lead me to the port. Expect to get a little lost...going around in circles is part of the fun. Pop in

TANGIER

to see artisans working in their shops: mosaic tilemakers, thread spinners, tailors. While shops are on the ground level, the family usually lives upstairs. Doors indicate how many families live in the homes behind them: one row of decoration for one, another parallel row for two.

Many people can't afford private ovens, phones, or running water, so there are economical communal options: phone desks

(called *teleboutiques*), baths, and bakeries. If you smell the aroma of baking bread, look for a hole-in-the-wall bakery, where locals drop off their ready-to-cook dough (as well as meat, fish, or nuts to roast). You'll also stumble upon communal taps, with water provided by the government, where people come to wash. Cubby-hole rooms are filled with kids playing video games on old TVs—they can't afford their own at home, so they come here instead.

Go on a photo safari for ornate "key-hole" doors, many of which lead to neighborhood mosques (see photo). Green doors are the color of Islam and symbolize peace. The ring-shaped door knockers double as a place to hitch a donkey.

As you explore, notice that some parts of the medina seem starkly different, with fancy wrought-iron balconies. This is the

approximately 20 percent of the town that was built and controlled by the Spaniards and Portuguese living here (with the rest being Arabic and Berber). The two populations were separated by a wall, the remains of which you can still trace running through the medina. It may seem at first glance that these European zones are fancier and "nicer" compared to the poorer-seeming Arabic/Berber zones. But the Arabs and Berbers take more care with the insides of their homes—if you went behind these humble walls, you'd be surprised how pleasant the interiors are. While European cultures externalize resources, Arab and Berber cultures internalize them.

The medina is filled with surprises for which serendipity is your best or only guide. As you wander, keep an eye out for the legendary **Café Baba** (up a few stairs on Rue Doukkala—not far from Place Amrah, daily 10:00-24:00). Old, grimy, and smoky, it's been around since the late 1940s and was a hippie hangout in the 1960s and '70s—the Rolling Stones smoked hash here (on the wall there's still a battered picture of Keith Richards holding a pipe). Enjoy a mint tea here and take in the great view over the old quarter, including a lush mansion just across the way formerly owned by American heiress Barbara Hutton.

One of the few sights revered by Moroccans that can be entered by non-Muslim visitors is the **tomb of Ibn Battuta.** Hiding at the top of a narrow residential lane (Rue Ibn Battuta), this simple mausoleum venerates the man considered the Moroccan Marco Polo. What started as a six-month pilgrimage to Mecca in 1325 stretched out to some 30 years for Ibn Battuta, as he explored throughout the Islamic world and into India and China. (If you visit the tomb, remove your shoes before entering, and leave a small tip for the attendant.) No one really knows if it's actually Ibn Battuta interred here, but that doesn't deter locals from paying homage to him.

▲Tangier American Legation Museum

Located at the bottom end of the medina (just above the port), this unexpected museum is worth a visit. Morocco was one of the first countries to recognize the newly formed United States as an independent country (in 1777). The original building, given to the United States by the sultan of Morocco, became the fledgling government's first foreign acquisition. It was declared a US National Historic Landmark in 1983.

Cost and Hours: 20 dh, Mon-Fri 10:00-17:00, Sat 10:00-15:00; during Ramadan daily 10:00-15:00, otherwise closed Sun year-round; Rue d'Amérique 8, tel. 0539-935-317, www.legation.org.

Visiting the Museum: This was the US embassy (or consulate) in Morocco from 1821 to 1961, and it's still American property—our only National Historic Landmark overseas. Today this non-profit museum and research center, housed in a 19th-century mansion, is a strangely peaceful oasis within Tangier's intense old town. It offers a warm welcome and lots of interesting artifacts—all well described in English. The ground floor is filled with an art gallery. In the stairwell, you'll see photos of kings with presidents, and a letter with the news of Lincoln's assassination. Upstairs are more paintings, as well as model soldiers playing out two battle scenes from Moroccan history. These belonged to American industrialist Malcolm Forbes, who had a home in Tangier (his son donated these dioramas to the museum). Rounding out the upper floor are more paintings, and wonderful old maps of Tangier and Morocco. A visit here is a fun reminder of how long the US and Morocco have had good relations.

• *When you've soaked in enough old-town atmosphere, make your way to the Kasbah (see map on page 302). Within the medina, head uphill, or exit the medina gate and go right on Rue Kasbah, which follows the old wall uphill to Bab Kasbah (a.k.a. Porte de la Kasbah), a gateway into the Kasbah.*

Kasbah

Loosely translated as "fortress," a *kasbah* is an enclosed, protected residential area near a castle that you'll find in hundreds of Moroccan towns. Originally this was a place where a king or other leader could protect his tribe. Tangier's Kasbah comprises the upper quarter of the old town. A residential area with twisty lanes and some nice guesthouses, this area is a bit more sedate and less claustrophobic than parts of the medina near the market below.

Way-finding here has always been a challenge for visitors. You can look for tile signs with street names posted on many corners, and spray-painted blue numbers mark each intersection. Eventually, these numbers will be painted over...once, and if, a permanent system is decided on. Some tourist walking routes are marked by red-and-green arrows (an effort that's been largely unsuccessful).

▲Kasbah Museum

On Place de la Kasbah, you'll find the Dar el-Makhzen, a former sultan's palace that now houses a history museum with a few historical artifacts. While there's not a word of English, some of the exhibits are still easy to appreciate, and the building itself is beautiful.

Cost and Hours: 20 dh, Wed-Mon 10:00-18:00, closed for prayer Fri 12:00-13:30 and all day Tue, tel. 0539-932-097.

Visiting the Museum: Most of the exhibits surround the central, open-air courtyard; rooms proceed roughly chronologically

as you move counterclockwise, from early hunters and farmers to prehistoric civilizations, Roman times, the region's conversion to Islam, and the influence of European powers. The two-story space at the far end of the courtyard focuses on a second-century mosaic floor depicting the journey of Venus. The big 12th-century wall-size map (in Arabic) shows the Moorish view of the world: with Africa on top (Spain is at the far right). Nearby is an explanation of terra-cotta production (a local industry), and upstairs is an exhibit

TANGIER

on funerary rituals. Near the entrance, look for signs to *jardin* and climb the stairs to reach a chirpy (if slightly overgrown) garden courtyard. While the building features some striking tilework, you just can't shake the feeling that the best Moorish sights are back in Spain.

Place de la Kasbah

Because the Kasbah Museum (while modest) is the city's main museum, the square in front of the palace attracts more than its share

of tourists. That means it's also a vivid gauntlet of amusements waiting to ambush parading tour groups: snake charmers, squawky dance troupes, and colorful water vendors. These colorful Kodak-moment hustlers make their living off the many tour groups passing by daily. (As you're cajoled, remember that the daily minimum wage here for men as skilled as these beggars is $10. That's what the gardeners you'll pass in your walk earn each day. In other words, a €1 tip is an hour's wage for these people.) If you draft behind a tour group, you won't be the focus of the hustlers. But if you take a photo, you must pay.

Before descending out of the Kasbah, don't miss the ocean viewpoint—as you stand in the square and face the palace, look to the right to find the hole carved through the thick city wall (Bab Dhar, "Sea Gate"). This leads out to a large natural terrace with fine views over the port, the Mediterranean, and Spain.

The lower gate of the Kasbah (as you stand in Place de la Kasbah facing the palace, it's on your left) leads to a charming little alcove between the gates, where you can see a particularly fine tile fountain: The top part is carved cedarwood, below that is carved plaster, and the bottom half is hand-laid tiles. In this area, poke down the tiny lane to the left of the little shop—you'll find that it leads to a surprisingly large courtyard ringed by fine homes.

Matisse Route

The artist Henri Matisse traveled to Tangier in 1912-13. The culture, patterns, and colors that he encountered here had a lifelong effect on the themes in much of his subsequent art. The diamond-shaped stones embedded in the street (you'll have to look hard to

TANGIER

find them; they're on the narrow lane leading up along the left side of the palace) mark a "Matisse Route" through the Kasbah, from the lower gate to the upper; those who know his works will spot several familiar scenes along this stretch. Just off the Grand Socco, on Rue de la Liberté, is the instantly recognizable Grand Hotel Villa de France, where Matisse lived and painted while in Tangier.

TANGIER BEACH

Lined with lots of fishy eateries and entertaining nightclubs, this fine, wide, white-sand crescent beach (Plage de Corniche) stretch-

es eastward from the port. The locals call it by the Spanish word *playa*. It's packed with locals doing what people around the world do at the beach—with a few variations. Traditionally clad moms let their kids run wild. You'll see people—young and old—covered in hot sand to combat rheumatism. Early, late, and off-season, the beach becomes a popular venue for soccer teams. The palm-lined pedestrian street along the waterfront was renamed for King Mohammed VI, in appreciation for recent restorations. While the beach is cleaner than it once was, it still has more than its share of litter—great for a stroll, but maybe not for sunbathing or swimming. If you have a beach break in mind, do it on Spain's Costa del Sol.

Nightlife in Tangier

Nighttime is great in Tangier. If you're staying overnight, don't relax in a fancy hotel restaurant. Get out and about in the old town after dark. In the cool of the evening, the atmospheric squares and lanes become even more alluring. It's an entirely different experience and a highlight of any visit. The Malataba area in the new town (along Avenue Mohammed VI) is an easy cab ride away and filled with modern nightclubs. (But remember, this isn't night-owl Spain—things die down by around 22:00.)

El Minzah Hotel hosts traditional music most nights for those having dinner there (see "Eating in Tangier," later; 85 Rue de la Liberté, tel. 0539-935-885). The **El Morocco Club** has a sophisticated piano bar.

The **Cinema Rif,** the landmark theater at the top of the Grand Socco, shows movies in French—which the younger generation is required to learn—Arabic, and occasionally English. The cinema is worth popping into, if only to see the Art Deco interior. As movies cost only 25 dh, consider dropping by to see a bit of whatever's on (closed Mon, tel. 0539-934-683).

Sleeping in Tangier

I've recommended two vastly different types of accommodations in Tangier: cozy Moroccan-style (but mostly French-run) guesthouses in the maze of lanes of the Kasbah neighborhood, at the top of the medina (old town); and modern international-style hotels, most of which are in the urban-feeling new town, a 10-to-20-minute walk from the central sights.

Remember, if you want to call Tangier from Europe, dial 00 (Europe's international access code), 212 (Morocco's country code), then the local number (dropping the initial zero). June through mid-September is high season, when rooms may be a bit more expensive and reservations are wise.

GUESTHOUSES AND A HOTEL IN THE KASBAH

In Arabic, *riad* means "guesthouse." You'll find these in the atmospheric old quarter known as the medina. While the lower part of the medina is dominated by market stalls and tourist traps—and can feel a bit seedy after dark—the upper part (called the Kasbah, for the castle that dominates this area) is more tranquil and feels very residential. All of my recommendations are buried in a labyrinth of lanes that can be very difficult to navigate; a map gives you a vague sense of where to go, but it's essential to ask for very clear directions when you reserve. If you're hiring a guide in Tangier, ask him to help you find your *riad*. (If you're on your own, you can try asking directions when you arrive—but many local residents take that as an invitation to tag along and hound you for tips.) The communal nature of *riad*s means that occasional noise from other guests can be an issue; bring your earplugs.

When you arrive at your *riad*, don't look for a doorbell—the tradition is to use a doorknocker. All of the guesthouses listed here are in traditional old houses, with rooms surrounding a courtyard atrium, and all have rooftop terraces where you can relax and enjoy sweeping views over Tangier. All include breakfast; many also serve good Moroccan dinners, which cost extra and should be arranged beforehand, typically that morning. Some also offer hammams (Turkish-style baths) with massages and spa treatments. Some lack stand-alone showers; instead, in Moroccan style, you'll find a handheld shower in a corner of the bathroom.

$$$$ La Maison Blanche ("The White House"), run by Aziz Begdouri, one of my recommended guides, has nine rooms in a restored traditional Moroccan house. Modern and attractively decorated, each room is dedicated to a personality who's spent time in Tangier—including a travel writer I know well. With its friendly vibe, great view terrace, and lavish setting, this is a great splurge (all with bathtubs, air-con, just inside the upper Kasbah gate at Rue Ahmed Ben Ajiba 2, tel. 0539-375-188, www. lamaisonblanchetanger.com, info@lamaisonblanchetanger.com).

$$$$ Dar Chams Tanja, just below the lower Kasbah gate, has seven elegant, new-feeling rooms with all the comforts surrounding a clean-white inner courtyard with lots of keyhole windows. While pricey, it's impeccably decorated, has a proper French-expat ambience, and boasts incredible views from its rooftop terrace (air-con, hammam, massage service, Rue Jnan Kabtan 2, tel. 0539-332-323, www.darchamstanja.com, darchamstanja@gmail.com).

$$$$ Dar Sultan rents six romantically decorated rooms on a pleasant street in the heart of the Kasbah with a small rooftop terrace (some rooms with balconies, Rue Touila 49, tel. 0539-336-061, www.darsultan.com, dar-sultan@menara.ma).

$$$ La Tangerina, run by Jürgen (who's German) and his Moroccan wife, Farida, has 10 comfortable rooms that look down into a shared atrium. At the top is a gorgeous rooftop seaview balcony (cash only, wood-fired hammam, turn left as you enter the upper Kasbah gate and hug the town wall around to Riad Sultan 19, tel. 0539-947-731, www.latangerina.com, info@latangerina.com).

$$$ Dar Nour, run with funky French style by Philippe, Jean-Olivier, and Catherine, has an "Escher-esque" floor plan that sprawls through five interconnected houses (it's "labyrinthine like the medina," says Philippe). The 10 homey rooms feel very traditional, with lots of books and lounging areas spread throughout, and a fantastic view terrace on the roof (cash only, Wi-Fi in lobby only, Rue Gourna 20, mobile 06-6211-2724, www.darnour.com, contactdarnour@yahoo.fr).

$$ Hotel Continental—at the bottom of the old town, facing the port—is the Humphrey Bogart option, a grand old place sprawling along the old town. It has lavish, atmospheric, and recently renovated public spaces, a chandeliered breakfast room, and 53 spacious bedrooms with rough hardwood floors and new bathrooms. Jimmy, who's always around and runs the shop adjacent to the lobby, says he offers everything but Viagra. When I said, "I'm from Seattle," he said, "206." Test him—he knows your area code (family rooms, Dar Baroud 36; follow my directions for walking into town from the port, but take a right through the yellow gateway—Bab Dar Dbagh—marked *1339* and then take a right and follow the signs, tel. 0539-931-024, hcontinental@iam.net.ma). This hotel's terrace aches with nostalgia. Back during the city's glory days, a ferry connected Tangier and New York. American novelists would sit out on the terrace of Hotel Continental, never quite sure when their friends' boat would arrive from across the sea.

MODERN HOTELS IN THE MODERN CITY

These hotels are centrally located, near the TI, and within walking distance of the Grand Socco, medina, and market.

$$$$ Grand Hotel Villa de France, perched high above the Grand Socco, has been around since the 19th century, when Eugène Delacroix stayed here and started a craze for "Orientalism" in European art. Henri Matisse was a guest in 1912-13, painting what he saw through his window. After sitting empty for years, the hotel was restored and reopened. Lavish public spaces, including a restaurant and view terrace, have more charm than most of the 58 modern, updated rooms, but a Matisse-inspired leaf design echoes throughout and adds a bit of character to an otherwise business-like hotel. Suites have a more Moroccan vibe but are not quite worth the splurge (intersection of Rue Angleterre and Rue Hollande, tel. 0539-333-111, www.leroyal.com/ghvdf, reservation@ghvdf.com).

$$$$ Atlas Rif & Spa Hotel, recently restored to its 1970s glamour, is a worthy splurge. Offering 127 plush, modern rooms, sprawling public spaces, a garden, pool, and grand views, it feels like an oversized boutique hotel. Overlooking the harbor, the great Arabic lounge—named for Winston Churchill—compels you to relax (some view rooms, air-con, elevator, 3 restaurants, spa and sauna, Avenue Mohammed VI 152, tel. 0539-349-300, www.hotelsatlas.com, atlastanger@menara.ma).

$$ Hotel Rembrandt feels just like the 1940s, with a restaurant, a bar, and a swimming pool surrounded by a great grassy garden. Its 70 rooms are outdated and simple, but clean and comfortable, and some come with views (air-con, elevator, a 5-minute walk above the beach in a busy urban zone at Boulevard Mohammed VI 1, tel. 0539-333-314, reservation@hotelrembrandt.ma).

Eating in Tangier

Moroccan food is a joy to sample. First priority is a glass of the refreshing "Moroccan tea"—green tea that's boiled and steeped once, then combined with fresh mint leaves to boil and steep some more, before being loaded up with sugar. Tourist-oriented restaurants have a predictable menu. For starters, you'll find a Moroccan tomato-based vegetable soup *(harira)* or Moroccan salad (a combination of fresh and stewed vegetables). Main dishes include couscous (usually with chicken, potatoes, carrots, and other vegetables and spices); *tagine* (stewed meat served in a fancy dish with a cone-shaped top); and *briouates* (small savory pies). Everything comes with Morocco's distinctive round, flat bread. For dessert, it's pastries—typically, almond cookies.

I've mostly listed places in or near the medina. (If you'd prefer the local equivalent of a yacht-club restaurant, survey the places along the beach.) Moroccan waiters expect about a 10 percent tip.

$$$ Le Saveur du Poisson is an excellent bet for the more adventurous, featuring one room cluttered with paintings adjoining a busy kitchen. There are no choices here. Just sit down and let owner Muhammad or his son, Hassan, take care of the rest. You get a rough hand-carved spoon and fork. Surrounded by lots of locals and unforgettable food, you'll be treated to a multicourse menu. Savor the delicious fish dishes—Tangier is one of the few spots in Morocco where seafood is a major part of the diet. The fruit punch—a mix of seasonal fruits brewed overnight in a vat—simmers in the back room. Ask for an explanation, or even a look. The desserts are full of nuts and honey. The big sink in the room is for locals who prefer to eat with their fingers (Sat-Thu 12:00-16:00 & 19:00-22:00, closed Fri and during Ramadan; walk down Rue de la Liberté roughly a block toward the Grand Socco from El Minzah Hotel, look for the stairs leading down to the market stalls and go down until you see fish on the grill; Escalier Waller 2, tel. 0539-336-326).

$$$ El Minzah Hotel offers a fancier yet still-authentic experience. The atmosphere is classy but low-stress. It's where unadventurous tourists and local elites dine. Dress up and choose between two dining zones: The white-tablecloth continental (French) dining area, called El Erz, is stuffy; while in the Moroccan lounge, El Korsan, you'll be serenaded by live traditional music (music nightly 20:00-23:00, belly-dance show at 20:30 and 21:30, no extra charge for music). There's also a cozy wine bar here—a rarity in a Muslim country—decorated with photos of visiting celebrities. At lunch, light meals and salads are served poolside (all dining areas open daily 13:00-16:00 & 20:00-22:30, Rue de la Liberté 85, tel. 0539-333-444).

$$ Le Salon Bleu has decent Moroccan food and some of the most spectacular seating in town: perched on a whitewashed terrace overlooking the square in front of the Kasbah Museum, with 360-degree views over the rooftops. Hike up the very tight spiral staircase to the top level, with the best views and lounge-a-while sofa seating. French-run (by the owners of the recommended Dar Nour guesthouse), it offers a simple menu of Moroccan fare—the appetizer plate is a good sampler for lunch or to share for an afternoon snack. While there is some indoor seating, I'd skip this place if the weather's not ideal for lingering on the terrace (daily 10:00-22:00, Place de la Kasbah, mobile 06-6211-2724). You'll see it from

TANGIER

the square in front of the Kasbah; to reach it, go through the gate to the left (as you face it), then look right for the stairs up.

El Morocco Club has three distinct zones. Outside, it's a **$** terrace café, serving a light menu of sandwiches, quiches, and salads in the shade of a rubber tree. At night a bouncer lets you into a **$$$** fine restaurant with a Med-Moroccan menu of grilled fish, roasted lamb, and creamy risottos. Guests at the restaurant have entrée to the wonderfully grown-up piano bar: a sophisticated lounge with vintage Tangier photos and zebra-print couches (café daily from 9:00; restaurant and piano bar Tue-Sun from 20:00, closed Mon; Place du Tabor, just inside the Kasbah gate, tel. 0539-948-139).

$$$ Le Fabrique has nothing to do with old Morocco. But if you want a break from couscous and keyhole arches, this industrial-mod brasserie with concrete floors and exposed brick has a menu of purely French classics—a good reminder that in the 20th century, Tangier was nearly as much a French city as a Moroccan one (Mon-Sat 20:00-23:00, closed Sun; Rue d'Angleterre 7, tel. 0539-374-057). It's a steep 10-minute walk up from the Grand Socco: Head up Rue d'Angleterre (left of Cinema Rif) and hike up the hill until the road levels out—it's on your left.

$$ Dar Lidam has two floors of spacious dining areas and an outdoor terrace with views. If you're looking for a low-stress restaurant in the heart of the Kasbah, you'll find it here, just behind the recommended hotel Dar Chams Tanja. They serve traditional Moroccan fare such as *pastella*—a savory-sweet chicken pastry, *harira*, couscous, and *tagines* (generally daily 12:00-21:00, sometimes closed Sat 18:00-19:00, Rue Dakakine 6, tel. 0539-332-386).

$$ Le Nabab is geared for tourists, but offers more style and less crass commercialism than the tourist traps listed next. Squirreled away in a mostly residential neighborhood just below the lower Kasbah gate (near the top of the medina), Le Nabab offers a menu of predictable Moroccan favorites in a sleek concrete-and-white-tablecloths dining room with a few echoes of traditional Moroccan decor. The 199-dh three-course meal is a good deal to sample several items (Mon-Sat 12:00-15:00 & 19:00 until late, closed Sun; below the lower Kasbah gate—bear left down the stairs, then right, and look for signs; Rue Al Kadiria 4, mobile 06-6144-2220).

$ Maison Communitaire des Femmes, a community center for women, hides an inexpensive, hearty lunch spot that's open to everyone and offers a tasty 60-dh two-course lunch. Profits support the work of the center (daily 12:00-16:00, last order at 15:30, also open 9:00-11:00 & 15:30-18:00 for cakes and tea, pleasant terrace out back, near slipper market just outside Grand Socco, Place du 9 Avril, tel. 0539-947-065).

$ Café Hafa, a basic outdoor café cascading down a series of cliff-hugging terraces, is a longtime Tangier landmark. Find your way here with a taxi or your guide, but don't rush—you'll want to settle in to sip your tea and enjoy the fantastic views. Tangier's most famous expat, the writer Paul Bowles, used to hang out here (simple pizzas and brochettes, daily 8:30 until late, in the Marshan neighborhood west of the medina on Avenue Hadi Mohammed Tazi).

PASTRIES

Both French and Moroccan pastries are available throughout the city. Moroccan pastries and cookies are often offered with mint tea in cafés or hotels and are served for dessert after meals. But for those with a serious sweet tooth, this won't cut it. Instead, step into a *pâtisserie* to choose from the variety of local sweets made with almonds, pistachios, cashews, pine nuts, peanuts, dates, honey, and sugar. Go to the counter and ask for *"une boîte petite"* (a little box). Point to what you want to fill it with—you'll pay by the weight. One easy and delicious spot is **$ Bab Al Medina,** just off the Grand Socco (daily 6:00-22:00, Rue d'Italie 28, tel. 06-6715-1779). It has two sections: a café with pizzas and shawarma, and a bakery that offers Moroccan and French pastries, bread, and Moroccan *crêpes* (called *baghrir*, these have nooks and crannies similar to a crumpet). Eat at the café's tables or on your hotel terrace for a sweet sunset.

TOURIST TRAPS

Tangier seems to specialize in very touristy Moroccan restaurants designed to feed and entertain dozens or even hundreds of tour-group members with overpriced and predictable menus of Moroccan classics, and often live music and belly dancing. The only locals you'll see here are the waiters. For day-trippers who just want a safe, comfortable break in the heart of town, these restaurants' predictability and Moroccan clichés are just perfect. For other travelers, these places are tour-group hell and make you thankful to be free. Each local guide has their own favorite, but these are the best-known.

$$ Hamadi is as luxurious a restaurant as a tourist can find in Morocco, with good food at reasonable prices (long hours daily, Rue Kasbah 2, tel. 0539-934-514).

$$$$ Marhaba Palace has the most impressive interior, with huge keyhole arches ringing a grand upstairs hall slathered in colorful tilework. It also has the highest prices—hardly a good value. It's near the upper gate to the Kasbah, so it's convenient for a meal just before heading downhill through town to the medina and market (daily 10:00-23:00, Rue Kasbah, tel. 0539-937-927).

Tangier Connections

By Train: In Tangier, all train traffic normally comes and goes from the Gare Tanger Ville station, one mile from the city center and a short Petit Taxi ride away. Train info: www.oncf.ma.

From Tangier by Train to: Rabat (7/day, 3.5-4 hours), **Casablanca** (station also called **Casa Voyageurs,** 7/day, 5 hours), **Marrakech** (7/day, 8.5-9 hours, transfer in Casablanca or Sidi Kacem; 1 direct overnight train, 10.5 hours), **Fès** (4/day, 4.5 hours).

By Bus: Bus information is available at the TI or by calling the CTM bus company (tel. 0522-541-010; schedules may also be online at www.ctm.ma).

From Tangier by Bus to: Ceuta and **Tétouan** (hourly, 1 hour).

From Fès by Bus to: Casablanca (10/day, 5.5 hours), **Marrakech** (4/day, 8 hours), **Rabat** (8/day, 3.5 hours), **Meknès** (10/day, 45 minutes), **Tangier** (6/day, 7 hours).

From Rabat by Bus to: Casablanca (2/hour, 45 minutes), **Fès** (5/day, 3 hours), **Tétouan** (5/day, 4.5-6 hours, 4 trains/day, 6 hours).

From Casablanca by Bus to: Marrakech (9/day, 3.5 hours).

From Marrakech by Bus to: Meknès (2/day, 7 hours), **Ouarzazate** (6/day, 4 hours).

By Plane: Flights within Morocco are convenient and reasonable (about $130 one-way from Tangier to Casablanca).

Morocco Beyond Tangier

Morocco gets much better as you go deeper into the interior. The country is incredibly rich in cultural thrills, though you'll pay a price in hassles and headaches—it's a package deal. But if adventure is your business, Morocco is a great option. Moroccan trains are quite good. Second class is cheap and comfortable. Buses connect all smaller towns very well. By car, Morocco is easy. Invest in a good Morocco guidebook to make this trip: Consider titles from

Lonely Planet and Rough Guide. Here are a few tips and insights to get you started.

If you're relying on public transportation for your extended tour, sail to Tangier, blast your way through customs, ignore any hustler who tells you there's no way out until tomorrow, and hop in a Petit Taxi for the train station. From there, set your sights on Rabat, a dignified European-type town with fewer hustlers, and make it your get-acquainted stop in Morocco. Trains go farther south from Rabat.

If you're driving a car, crossing the border can be a bit unnerving, since you'll be forced to jump through several bureaucratic hoops. You'll go through customs at both borders, buy Moroccan insurance for your car (cheap and easy), and feel at the mercy of a bristly bunch of shady-looking people you'd rather not be at the mercy of. Don't pay anyone on the Spanish side. Consider tipping a guy on the Moroccan side if you feel he'll shepherd you through. Relax and let him grease those customs wheels. He's worth it. As soon as possible, hit the road and drive to Chefchaouen, the best first stop for those with their own wheels. Drive defensively and never rely on the oncoming driver's skill. Night driving is dangerous. Pay a guard to watch your car overnight.

Moroccan Towns

Chefchaouen
Just two hours by bus or car from Tétouan, this is the first pleasant town beyond the north coast. Monday and Thursday are colorful market days. Wander deep into the whitewashed old town from the main square.

Rabat
Morocco's capital and most European city, Rabat is the most comfortable and least stressful place to start your North African trip. You'll find a colorful market (in the old neighboring town of Salé), bits of Islamic architecture (Mausoleum of Mohammed V), the king's palace, mellow hustlers, and fine hotels.

Fès
More than just a funny hat that tipsy Shriners wear, Fès is Morocco's religious and artistic center, bustling with craftspeople,

pilgrims, shoppers, and shops. Like most large Moroccan cities, it has a distinct new town from the French colonial period, as well as an exotic (and stressful) old walled Arabic town (the medina), where you'll find the market.

For 12 centuries, traders have gathered in Fès, founded on a river at the crossroads of two trade routes. Soon there was an irrigation system; a university; resident craftsmen from Spain; and a diverse population of Muslims, Christians, and Jews. When France claimed Morocco in 1912, they made their capital in Rabat, and Fès fizzled. But the Fès marketplace is still Morocco's best.

TANGIER

Marrakech

Morocco's gateway to the south, Marrakech is where the desert, mountain, and coastal regions merge. This market city is a constant folk festival, bustling with Berber tribespeople and a colorful center. The new city has the train station, and the main boulevard (Mohammed V) is lined with banks, airline offices, a post office, a tourist office, and comfortable hotels. The old city features the maze-like market and the huge Djemaa el-Fna, a square seething with people—a 43-ring Moroccan circus.

Over the Atlas Mountains

Extend your Moroccan trip several days by heading south over the Atlas Mountains. Take a bus from Marrakech to Ouarzazate (short stop), and then to Tinerhir (great oasis town, comfy hotel, overnight stop). The next day, go to Er Rachidia and take the overnight bus to Fès.

By car, drive from Fès south, staying in the small mountain town of Ifrane, and then continue deep into the desert country past Er Rachidia, and on to Rissani (market days: Sun, Tue, and Thu). Explore nearby mud-brick towns still living in the Middle Ages. Hire a guide to drive you past where the road stops, and head cross-country to an oasis village (Merzouga), where you can climb a sand dune and watch the sun rise over the vastness of Africa. Only a sea of sand separates you from Timbuktu.

PRACTICALITIES

This section covers just the basics on traveling in Spain (for much more information, see *Rick Steves Spain*). You'll find free advice on specific topics at www.ricksteves.com/tips.

Money

Spain uses the euro currency: 1 euro (€) = about $1.10. To convert prices in euros to dollars, add about 10 percent: €20 = about $22, €50 = about $55. (Check www.oanda.com for the latest exchange rates.)

The standard way for travelers to get euros is to withdraw money from an ATM (known as a *cajero automático*) using a debit or credit card, ideally with a Visa or MasterCard logo. To keep your cash, cards, and valuables safe, wear a money belt.

Before departing, call your bank or credit-card company: Confirm that your card(s) will work overseas, ask about international transaction fees, and alert them that you'll be making withdrawals in Europe. Also ask for the PIN number for your credit card—you may need it for Europe's "chip-and-PIN" payment machines (allow time for your bank to mail your PIN to you).

Dealing with "Chip and PIN": Most credit and debit cards now have chips that authenticate and secure transactions. European cardholders insert their chip card into the payment slot, then enter a PIN. (For most US cards, you provide a signature.) Any American card, whether with a chip or an old-fashioned magnetic stripe, will work at Europe's hotels, restaurants, and shops. But some self-service chip-and-PIN payment machines—such as those at train stations, toll roads, or unattended gas pumps—may not accept your card, even if you know the PIN. If your card won't work, look for a cashier who can process the transaction manually—or pay in cash.

Dynamic Currency Conversion: If merchants or hoteliers offer to convert your purchase price into dollars (called dynamic currency conversion, or DCC), refuse this "service." You'll pay extra in fees for the expensive convenience of seeing your charge in dollars. If an ATM offers to "lock in" or "guarantee" your conversion rate, choose "proceed without conversion." Other prompts might state, "You can be charged in dollars: Press YES for dollars, NO for euros." Always choose the local currency.

Staying Connected

The simplest solution is to bring your own device—mobile phone, tablet, or laptop—and use it just as you would at home (following the tips below, such as connecting to free Wi-Fi whenever possible).

To call Spain from a US or Canadian number: Whether you're phoning from a landline, your own mobile phone, or a Skype account, you're making an international call. Dial 011-34 and then the nine-digit number. (The 011 is our international access code, and 34 is Spain's country code.) If dialing from a mobile phone, you can enter + in place of the international access code—press and hold the 0 key.

To call Spain from a European country: Dial 00-34 followed by the nine-digit number. (The 00 is Europe's international access code.)

To call within Spain: Just dial the local nine-digit number.

To call from Spain to another country: Dial 00 followed by the country code (for example, 1 for the US or Canada), then the area code and number. If calling European countries whose phone numbers begin with 0, you'll usually have to omit that 0 when you dial.

Tips: If you bring your own mobile phone, consider getting an international plan; most providers offer a global calling plan that cuts the per-minute cost of phone calls and texts, and a flat-fee data plan.

Use Wi-Fi whenever possible. Most hotels and many cafés offer free Wi-Fi, and you'll likely also find it at tourist information offices, major museums, and public-transit hubs. With Wi-Fi you can use your phone or tablet to make free or inexpensive domestic and international calls via a calling app such as Skype, Face-Time, or Google+ Hangouts. When you can't find Wi-Fi, you can use your cellular network to connect to the Internet, send texts, or make voice calls. When you're done, avoid further charges by manually switching off "data roaming" or "cellular data."

It's possible to stay connected without a mobile phone. To make cheap international calls from any phone (even your hotel-room phone), you can buy a prepaid international phone card in Spain (called a *tarjeta telefónica con código).* Dial the toll-free access number, enter the card's PIN code, then dial the number. Calling from your hotel-room phone without using an international phone card is usually expensive. Though they are disappearing in Spain, you may still find public pay phones in post offices and train sta-

Sleep Code

Hotels are classified based on the average price of a standard double room without breakfast in high season.

$$$$	**Splurge:** Most rooms over €170
$$$	**Pricier:** €130-170
$$	**Moderate:** €90-130
$	**Budget:** €50-90
¢	**Backpacker:** Under €50
RS%	**Rick Steves discount**

Unless otherwise noted, credit cards are accepted, hotel staff speak basic English, and free Wi-Fi is available. Comparison-shop by checking prices at several hotels (on each hotel's own website, on a booking site, or by email). For the best deal, *book directly with the hotel.* Ask for a discount if paying in cash; if the listing includes RS%, request a Rick Steves discount.

tions. For more on phoning, see www.ricksteves.com/phoning. For a one-hour talk on "Traveling with a Mobile Device," see www.ricksteves.com/travel-talks.

Sleeping

I've categorized my recommended accommodations based on price, indicated with a dollar-sign rating (see sidebar). I recommend reserving rooms in advance, particularly during peak season. Once your dates are set, check the specific price for your preferred stay at several hotels. You can do this either by comparing prices on Hotels.com or Booking.com, or by checking the hotels' own websites. To get the best deal, contact my family-run hotels directly by phone or email. When you go direct, the owner avoids the 20 percent commission, giving them wiggle room to offer you a discount, a nicer room, or free breakfast. If you prefer to book online or are considering a hotel chain, it's in your advantage to use the hotel's website.

For complicated requests, send an email with the following information: number and type of rooms; number of nights; arrival date; departure date; and any special needs. Use the European style for writing dates: day/month/year. Hoteliers typically ask for your credit-card number as a deposit.

Some hotels are willing to make a deal to attract guests: Try emailing several to ask their best price. In general, hotel prices can soften if you do any of the following: offer to pay cash, stay at least three nights, or travel off-season.

Some hotels include Spain's 10 percent IVA tax in the room price; others tack it onto your bill. When asking about prices, it's smart to check about the room tax.

Restaurant Price Code

I've assigned each eatery a price category, based on the average cost of a typical main course (or 2-3 tapas). Drinks, desserts, and splurge items (steak and seafood) can raise the price considerably.

$$$$	**Splurge:** Most main courses over €20
$$$	**Pricier:** €15-20
$$	**Moderate:** €10-15
$	**Budget:** Under €10

In Spain, takeout food is **$**; a basic tapas bar or no-frills sit-down eatery is **$$**; a casual but more upscale tapas bar or restaurant is **$$$**; and a swanky splurge is **$$$$**.

Eating

I've categorized my recommended eateries based on price, indicated with a dollar-sign rating (see sidebar). By our standards, Spaniards eat late, having lunch—their biggest meal of the day—around 13:00-16:00, and dinner starting about 21:00. At restaurants, you can dine with tourists at 20:00, or with Spaniards if you wait until later.

For a fun early dinner at a bar, build a light meal out of tapas—small appetizer-sized portions of seafood, salads, meat-filled pastries, deep-fried tasties, and so on. Many of these are displayed behind glass, and you can point to what you want. Tapas typically cost about €5-10 a plate. While the smaller "tapa" size (which comes on a saucer-size plate) is handiest for maximum tasting opportunities, many bars sell only larger sizes: the *ración* (full portion, on a dinner plate) and *media-ración* (half-size portion). *Jamón* (hah-MOHN), an air-dried ham similar to prosciutto, is a Spanish staple. Other key terms include *bocadillo* (baguette sandwich), *frito* (fried), *a la plancha* (grilled), *queso* (cheese), *tortilla* (omelet), and *surtido* (assortment).

Many bars have three price tiers, which should be clearly posted: It's cheapest to eat or drink while standing at the bar *(barra),* slightly more to sit at a table inside *(mesa* or *salón),* and most expensive to sit outside *(terraza).* Wherever you are, be assertive or you'll never be served. *Por favor* (please) grabs the attention of the server or bartender. If you're having tapas, don't worry about paying as you go (the bartender keeps track). When you're ready to leave, ask for the bill: *"¿La cuenta?"*

Tipping: To tip for a few tapas, round up to the nearest euro. At restaurants with table service, if a service charge is included in the bill, add about 5 percent; if it's not, leave 10 percent.

Transportation

By Train and Bus: For train schedules, visit Germany's excellent all-Europe website (www.bahn.com) or Spain's RENFE (www.

renfe.com). Since trains can sell out, it's smart to buy your tickets in advance at a travel agency (easiest), at the train station (can be crowded, be sure you're in the right line; you'll pay a five percent service fee at the ticket window), or online (at www.renfe.com). Be aware that the website rejects nearly every attempt to use a US credit card—use PayPal; or from the US try www.ricksteves.com/rail. Futuristic, high-speed trains (such as AVE) can be priced differently according to their time of departure. To see if a rail pass could save you money, check www.ricksteves.com/rail.

Buses pick up where the trains don't go, reaching even small villages. But because routes are operated by various competing companies, it can be tricky to pin down schedules (check with local bus stations, tourist info offices, or www.movelia.es). For dirt-cheap long-distance bus fares, check out www.flixbus.co.uk.

By Plane: Consider covering long distances on a budget flight, which can be cheaper than a train or bus ride. For flights within Spain, check out www.vueling.com, www.iberia.com, or www.aireuropa.com; to other European cites, try www.easyjet.com and www.ryanair.com. To compare several budget airlines, see www.skyscanner.com.

By Car: It's cheaper to arrange most car rentals from the US. If you're planning a multicountry itinerary by car, be aware of often-astronomical international drop-off fees. For tips on your insurance options, see www.ricksteves.com/cdw, and for route planning, consult www.viamichelin.com. It's also required that you carry an International Driving Permit (IDP), available at your local AAA office ($20 plus two passport-type photos, www.aaa.com).

Superhighways come with tolls, but save lots of time. Each toll road *(autopista de peaje)* has its own pricing structure, so tolls vary. Payment can be made in cash or by credit or debit card (credit-card-only lanes are labeled *"vias automáticas";* cash lanes are *"vias manuales").* Spaniards love to tailgate; otherwise, local road etiquette is similar to that in the US. Ask your car-rental company for details, or check the US State Department website (www.travel.state.gov, search for Spain in the "Learn about your destination" box, then click on "Travel and Transportation").

A car is a worthless headache in cities—park it safely (get tips from your hotelier). As break-ins are common, be sure all of your valuables are out of sight and locked in the trunk, or even better, with you or in your hotel room.

Helpful Hints

Emergency Help: For **police** help, dial 091. To summon an **ambulance**, call 112. For passport problems, call the **US Embassy** (in Madrid, tel. 915-872-200) or the **Canadian Embassy** (in Madrid, tel. 913-828-400). If you have a minor illness, do as the locals do and go to a pharmacist for advice. Or ask at your hotel for help—they'll know of the nearest medical and emergency services. For other concerns, get advice from your hotelier.

Theft or Loss: Spain has particularly hardworking pickpockets—wear a money belt. Assume beggars are pickpockets and any scuffle is simply a distraction by a team of thieves. If you stop for any commotion or show, put your hands in your pockets before someone else does.

To replace a passport, you'll need to go in person to an embassy (see above). Cancel and replace your credit and debit cards by calling these 24-hour US numbers collect: Visa—tel. 303/967-1096, MasterCard—tel. 636/722-7111, American Express—tel. 336/393-1111. In Spain, to make a collect call to the US, dial 900-99-0011; press zero or stay on the line for an operator. File a police report either on the spot or within a day or two; you'll need it to submit an insurance claim for lost or stolen rail passes or travel gear, and it can help with replacing your passport or credit and debit cards. For more information, see www.ricksteves.com/help.

Time: Spain uses the 24-hour clock. It's the same through 12:00 noon, then keep going: 13:00, 14:00, and so on. Spain, like most of continental Europe, is six/nine hours ahead of the East/West Coasts of the US.

Siesta and Paseo: Many Spaniards (especially in rural areas) still follow the traditional siesta schedule: From around 14:00 to 17:00, many businesses close as people go home for a big lunch with their family. Then they head back to work (and shops reopen) from about 17:00 to 21:00. (Many bigger stores stay open all day long, especially in cities.) Then, after a late dinner, whole families pour out of their apartments to enjoy the cool of the evening, stroll through the streets, and greet their neighbors—a custom called the paseo.

Sights: Major attractions can be swamped with visitors; carefully read and follow this book's crowd-beating tips (visit at quieter times of day, or—where possible—reserve ahead). Opening and closing hours of sights can change unexpectedly; confirm the latest times on their websites or at the local tourist information office. At many churches, a modest dress code is encouraged and sometimes required (no bare shoulders or shorts).

Holidays and Festivals: Spain celebrates many holidays, which can close sights and attract crowds (book hotel rooms ahead). For more on holidays and festivals, check Spain's website: www.spain.info. For a simple list showing major—though not all—events, see www.ricksteves.com/festivals.

Numbers and Stumblers: What Americans call the second floor of a building is the first floor in Europe. Europeans write dates as day/month/year, so Christmas 2019 is 25/12/19. Commas are decimal points and vice versa—a dollar and a half is 1,50, and there are 5.280 feet in a mile. Spain uses the metric system: A kilogram is 2.2 pounds; a liter is about a quart; and a kilometer is six-tenths of a mile.

Resources from Rick Steves

This Snapshot guide is excerpted from my latest edition of *Rick Steves Spain,* is one of many titles in my ever-expanding series of guidebooks on European travel. I also produce a public television series, *Rick Steves' Europe,* and a public radio show, *Travel with Rick Steves.* My website, www.ricksteves.com, offers free travel information, a forum for travelers' comments, guidebook updates, my travel blog, an online travel store, and information on European rail passes and our tours of Europe. If you're bringing a mobile device, my free Rick Steves Audio Europe app features dozens of free, self-guided audio tours of the top sights in Europe, plus radio shows and travel interviews about Spain. You can get Rick Steves Audio Europe via Apple's App Store, Google Play, or the Amazon App-store. For more information, see www.ricksteves.com/audioeurope.

Additional Resources

Tourist Information: www.spain.info
Passports and Red Tape: www.travel.state.gov
Packing List: www.ricksteves.com/packing
Travel Insurance: www.ricksteves.com/insurance
Cheap Flights: www.kayak.com or www.google.com/flights
Airplane Carry-on Restrictions: www.tsa.gov/travelers
Updates for This Book: www.ricksteves.com/update

How Was Your Trip?

To share your tips, concerns, and discoveries after using this book, please fill out the survey at www.ricksteves.com/feedback. Thanks in advance.

Spanish Survival Phrases

Spanish has a guttural sound similar to the J in Baja California. In the phonetics, the symbol for this clearing-your-throat sound is the italicized *h*.

English	Spanish	Pronunciation
Good day.	*Buenos días.*	bway-nohs dee-ahs
Do you speak English?	*¿Habla Usted inglés?*	ah-blah oo-stehd een-glays
Yes. / No.	*Sí. / No.*	see / noh
I (don't) understand.	*(No) comprendo.*	(noh) kohm-prehn-doh
Please.	*Por favor.*	por fah-bor
Thank you.	*Gracias.*	grah-thee-ahs
I'm sorry.	*Lo siento.*	loh see-ehn-toh
Excuse me.	*Perdóneme.*	pehr-doh-nay-may
(No) problem.	*(No) problema.*	(noh) proh-blay-mah
Good.	*Bueno.*	bway-noh
Goodbye.	*Adiós.*	ah-dee-ohs
one / two	*uno / dos*	oo-noh / dohs
three / four	*tres / cuatro*	trays / kwah-troh
five / six	*cinco / seis*	theen-koh / says
seven / eight	*siete / ocho*	see-eh-tay / oh-choh
nine / ten	*nueve / diez*	nway-bay / dee-ayth
How much is it?	*¿Cuánto cuesta?*	kwahn-toh kway-stah
Write it?	*¿Me lo escribe?*	may loh ay-skree-bay
Is it free?	*¿Es gratis?*	ays grah-tees
Is it included?	*¿Está incluido?*	ay-stah een-kloo-ee-doh
Where can I buy / find...?	*¿Dónde puedo comprar / encontrar...?*	dohn-day pway-doh kohm-prar / ayn-kohn-trar
I'd like / We'd like...	*Quiero / Queremos...*	kee-ehr-oh / kehr-ay-mohs
...a room.	*...una habitación.*	oo-nah ah-bee-tah-thee-ohn
...a ticket to ___.	*...un billete para ___.*	oon bee-yeh-tay pah-rah ___
Is it possible?	*¿Es posible?*	ays poh-see-blay
Where is...?	*¿Dónde está...?*	dohn-day ay-stah
...the train station	*...la estación de trenes*	lah ay-stah-thee-ohn day tray-nays
...the bus station	*...la estación de autobuses*	lah ay-stah-thee-ohn day ow-toh-boo-says
...the tourist information office	*...la oficina de turismo*	lah oh-fee-thee-nah day too-rees-moh
Where are the toilets?	*¿Dónde están los servicios?*	dohn-day ay-stahn lohs sehr-bee-thee-ohs
men	*hombres, caballeros*	ohm-brays, kah-bah-yay-rohs
women	*mujeres, damas*	moo-heh-rays, dah-mahs
left / right	*izquierda / derecha*	eeth-kee-ehr-dah / day-ray-chah
straight	*derecho*	day-ray-choh
When do you open / close?	*¿A qué hora abren / cierran?*	ah kay oh-rah ah-brehn / thee-ay-rahn
At what time?	*¿A qué hora?*	ah kay oh-rah
Just a moment.	*Un momento.*	oon moh-mehn-toh
now / soon / later	*ahora / pronto / más tarde*	ah-oh-rah / prohn-toh / mahs tar-day
today / tomorrow	*hoy / mañana*	oy / mahn-yah-nah

In a Spanish Restaurant

English	Spanish	Pronunciation
I'd like / We'd like...	Quiero / Queremos...	kee-**ehr**-oh / kehr-**ay**-mohs
...to reserve...	...reservar...	ray-sehr-**bar**
...a table for one / two.	...una mesa para uno / dos.	oo-nah may-sah pah-rah oo-noh / dohs
Non-smoking.	No fumador.	noh foo-mah-**dohr**
Is this table free?	¿Está esta mesa libre?	ay-**stah** ay-stah may-sah lee-bray
The menu (in English), please.	La carta (en inglés), por favor.	lah **kar**-tah (ayn een-**glays**) por fah-**bor**
service (not) included	servicio (no) incluido	sehr-**bee**-thee-oh (noh) een-kloo-**ee**-doh
cover charge	precio de entrada	**pray**-thee-oh day ayn-**trah**-dah
to go	para llevar	**pah**-rah yay-**bar**
with / without	con / sin	kohn / seen
and / or	y / o	ee / oh
menu (of the day)	menú (del día)	may-**noo** (dayl **dee**-ah)
specialty of the house	especialidad de la casa	ay-spay-thee-ah-lee-**dahd** day lah **kah**-sah
tourist menu	menú turístico	meh-**noo** too-**ree**-stee-koh
combination plate	plato combinado	**plah**-toh kohm-bee-**nah**-doh
appetizers	tapas	**tah**-pahs
bread	pan	pahn
cheese	queso	**kay**-soh
sandwich	bocadillo	boh-kah-**dee**-yoh
soup	sopa	**soh**-pah
salad	ensalada	ayn-sah-**lah**-dah
meat	carne	**kar**-nay
poultry	aves	**ah**-bays
fish	pescado	pay-**skah**-doh
seafood	marisco	mah-**ree**-skoh
fruit	fruta	**froo**-tah
vegetables	verduras	behr-**doo**-rahs
dessert	postres	**poh**-strays
tap water	agua del grifo	**ah**-gwah dayl **gree**-foh
mineral water	agua mineral	**ah**-gwah mee-nay-**rahl**
milk	leche	**lay**-chay
(orange) juice	zumo (de naranja)	**thoo**-moh (day nah-**rahn**-hah)
coffee	café	kah-**feh**
tea	té	tay
wine	vino	**bee**-noh
red / white	tinto / blanco	**teen**-toh / **blahn**-koh
glass / bottle	vaso / botella	**bah**-soh / boh-**tay**-yah
beer	cerveza	thehr-**bay**-thah
Cheers!	¡Salud!	sah-**lood**
More. / Another.	Más. / Otro.	mahs / **oh**-troh
The same.	El mismo.	ehl **mees**-moh
The bill, please.	La cuenta, por favor.	lah **kwayn**-tah por fah-**bor**
tip	propina	proh-**pee**-nah
Delicious!	¡Delicioso!	day-lee-thee-**oh**-soh

For hundreds more pages of survival phrases for your trip to Spain, check out *Rick Steves' Spanish Phrase Book*.

INDEX

INDEX

INDEX

INDEX

Explore Europe

At ricksteves.com you can browse through thousands of articles, videos, photos and radio interviews, plus find a wealth of money-saving travel tips for planning your dream trip. And with our mobile-friendly website, you can easily access all this great travel information anywhere you go.

TV Shows

Preview the places you'll visit by watching entire half-hour episodes of Rick Steves' Europe (choose from all 100 shows) on-demand, for free.

your travel dreams into affordable reality

Radio Interviews

Enjoy ready access to Rick's vast library of radio interviews covering travel

tips and cultural insights that relate specifically to your Europe travel plans.

Travel Forums

Learn, ask, share! Our online community of savvy travelers is a great resource

for first-time travelers to Europe, as well as seasoned pros. You'll find forums on each country, plus travel tips and restaurant/hotel reviews. You can even ask one of our well-traveled staff to chime in with an opinion.

Travel News

Subscribe to our free Travel News e-newsletter, and get monthly updates from Rick on what's happening in Europe.

Rick's Free Travel App

Get your FREE **Rick Steves Audio Europe**™ app to enjoy...

- Dozens of self-guided tours of Europe's top museums, sights and historic walks
- Hundreds of tracks filled with cultural insights and sightseeing tips from Rick's radio interviews
- All organized into handy geographic playlists
- For Apple and Android

With Rick whispering in your ear, Europe gets even better.

Find out more at ricksteves.com

Gear up for your next adventure at ricksteves.com

Light Luggage

Pack light and right with Rick Steves' affordable, custom-designed rolling carry-on bags, backpacks, day packs and shoulder bags.

Accessories

From packing cubes to moneybelts and beyond, Rick has personally selected the travel goodies that will help your trip go smoother.

Experience maximum Europe

Save time and energy

This guidebook is your independent-travel toolkit. But for all it delivers, it's still up to you to devote the time and energy it takes to manage the preparation and logistics that are essential for a happy trip. If that's a hassle, there's a solution.

Rick Steves Tours

A Rick Steves tour takes you to Europe's most interesting places with great

great tours, too!

with minimum stress

guides and small groups of 28 or less. We follow Rick's favorite itineraries, ride in comfy buses, stay in family-run hotels, and bring you intimately close to the Europe you've traveled so far to see. Most importantly, we take away the logistical headaches so you can focus on the fun.

travelers—nearly half of them repeat customers—along with us on four dozen different itineraries, from Ireland to Italy to Athens. Is a Rick Steves tour the right fit for your travel dreams? Find out at ricksteves.com, where you can also request Rick's latest tour catalog.

Join the fun

This year we'll take thousands of free-spirited

Europe is best experienced with happy travel partners. We hope you can join us.

A Guide for Every Trip

BEST OF GUIDES

Full color easy-to-scan format, focusing on Europe's most popular destinations and sights.

Best of France
Best of Germany
Best of England
Best of Europe
Best of Ireland
Best of Italy
Best of Spain

COMPREHENSIVE GUIDES

City, country, and regional guides with detailed coverage for a multi-week trip exploring the most iconic sights and venturing off the beaten track.

Amsterdam & the Netherlands
Barcelona
Belgium: Bruges, Brussels, Antwerp & Ghent
Berlin
Budapest
Croatia & Slovenia
Eastern Europe
England
Florence & Tuscany
France
Germany
Great Britain
Greece: Athens & the Peloponnese
Iceland
Ireland
Istanbul
Italy
London
Paris
Portugal
Prague & the Czech Republic
Provence & the French Riviera
Rome
Scandinavia
Scotland
Spain
Switzerland
Venice
Vienna, Salzburg & Tirol

THE BEST OF ROME

ome, Italy's capital, is studded with
man remnants and floodlit-fountain
ares. From the Vatican to the Colos-
m, with crazy traffic in between, Rome
onderful, huge, and exhausting. The
ds, the heat, and the weighty history

of the Eternal City where Caesars walked
can make tourists wilt. Recharge by taking siestas, gelato breaks, and after-dark
walks, strolling from one atmospheric
square to another in the refreshing evening air.

Rick Steves guidebooks are published by Avalon Travel, an imprint of Perseus Books, a Hachette Book Group company.

POCKET GUIDES

Compact, full color city guides with the essentials for shorter trips.

Amsterdam
Athens
Barcelona
Florence
Italy's Cinque Terre
London
Munich & Salzburg

Paris
Prague
Rome
Venice
Vienna

SNAPSHOT GUIDES

Focused single-destination coverage.

Basque Country: Spain & France
Copenhagen & the Best of Denmark
Dublin
Dubrovnik
Edinburgh
Hill Towns of Central Italy
Krakow, Warsaw & Gdansk
Lisbon
Loire Valley
Madrid & Toledo
Milan & the Italian Lakes District
Naples & the Amalfi Coast
Northern Ireland
Normandy
Norway
Reykjavik
Sevilla, Granada & Southern Spain
St. Petersburg, Helsinki & Tallinn
Stockholm

CRUISE PORTS GUIDES

Reference for cruise ports of call.

Mediterranean Cruise Ports
Northern European Cruise Ports

Complete your library with...

TRAVEL SKILLS & CULTURE

Study up on travel skills and gain insight on history and culture.

Europe 101
European Christmas
European Easter
European Festivals
Europe Through the Back Door
Postcards from Europe
Travel as a Political Act

PHRASE BOOKS & DICTIONARIES

French
French, Italian & German
German
Italian
Portuguese
Spanish

PLANNING MAPS

Britain, Ireland & London
Europe
France & Paris
Germany, Austria & Switzerland
Ireland
Italy
Spain & Portugal

Avalon Travel
Hachette Book Group
1700 Fourth Street
Berkeley, CA 94710

Text © 2017 by Rick Steves' Europe, Inc. All rights reserved.
Maps © 2017 by Rick Steves' Europe, Inc. All rights reserved.
Portions of this book originally appeared in *Rick Steves Spain 2018*

Printed in Canada by Friesens
Fifth Edition. First printing November 2017.
ISBN 978-1-63121-681-7

For the latest on Rick's lectures, guidebooks, tours, public radio show, and public television
series, contact Rick Steves' Europe, 130 Fourth Avenue North, Edmonds, WA 98020, tel.
425/771-8303, www.ricksteves.com, rick@ricksteves.com.

Rick Steves' Europe
Managing Editor: Jennifer Madison Davis
Special Publications Manager: Risa Laib
Assistant Managing Editor: Cathy Lu
Editors: Glenn Eriksen, Tom Griffin, Katherine Gustafson, Mary Keils, Suzanne Kotz,
  John Pierce, Carrie Shepherd
Editorial & Production Assistant: Jessica Shaw
Editorial Intern: Alexandra Ivy
Researchers: Amanda Buttinger, Robert Wright
Contributor: Gene Openshaw
Graphic Content Director: Sandra Hundacker
Maps & Graphics: David C. Hoerlein, Lauren Mills, Mary Rostad

Avalon Travel
Senior Editor and Series Manager: Madhu Prasher
Editor: Jamie Andrade
Associate Editor: Sierra Machado
Editorial Intern: Rachael Sablik
Copy Editor: Maggie Ryan
Proofreader: Suzie Nasol
Indexer: Stephen Callahan
Production & Typesetting: Christine DeLorenzo, Rue Flaherty, Sarah Wildfang
Cover Design: Kimberly Glyder Design
Maps & Graphics: Kat Bennett, Mike Morgenfeld

Photo Credits
Front Cover: The Plaza de España, Sevilla © Hoang Bao Nguyen | Dreamstime
Title Page Photo: Cathedral of Seville and La Giralda © kasto/123rf.com
Page 141: Court of the Lions, Alhambra, Granada © Pavel Dospiva | Dreamstime
Additional Photography: Dominic Arizona Bonuccelli, Rich Earl, Cameron Hewitt, David
C. Hoerlein, Suzanne Kotz, Pat O'Connor, Gene Openshaw, Jessica Shaw, Robyn Stencil,
Rick Steves, Robert Wright, Wikimedia Commons—PD-Art/PD-US. Photos are used by
permission and are the property of the original copyright owners.

ABOUT THE AUTHOR

RICK STEVES

 Since 1973, Rick has spent about four months a year exploring Europe. His mission: to empower Americans to have European trips that are fun, affordable, and culturally broadening. Rick produces a best-selling guidebook series, a public television series, and a public radio show, and organizes small-group tours that take over 20,000 travelers to Europe annually. He does all of this with the help of a hardworking, well-traveled staff of 100 at Rick Steves' Europe in Edmonds, Washington, near Seattle. When not on the road, Rick is active in his church and with advocacy groups focused on economic justice, drug policy reform, and ending hunger. To recharge, Rick plays piano, relaxes at his family cabin in the Cascade Mountains, and spends time with his partner Trish, son Andy, and daughter Jackie. Find out more about Rick at www.ricksteves.com and on Facebook.

More for your trip!
Maximize the experience with Rick Steves as your guide

Guidebooks
Barcelona and Portugal guides make side-trips smooth and affordable

Phrase Books
Rely on Rick's Spanish Phrase Book & Dictionary

Rick's TV Shows
Preview your destinations with 8 shows on Spain

Free! Rick's Audio Europe™ App
Hear Spain travel tips from Rick's radio shows

Small Group Tours
Take a lively Rick Steves tour through Spain

For all the details, visit ricksteves.com